Gareth Gaskell

Phonetics and Phonology in Language Comprehension and Production

Phonology and Phonetics 6

Editor

Aditi Lahiri

Mouton de Gruyter
Berlin · New York

Phonetics and Phonology in Language Comprehension and Production

Differences and Similarities

Edited by

Niels O. Schiller
Antje S. Meyer

Mouton de Gruyter
Berlin · New York   2003

Mouton de Gruyter (formerly Mouton, The Hague)
is a Division of Walter de Gruyter GmbH & Co. KG, Berlin.

ISBN 3 11 017872 9

Bibliographic information published by Die Deutsche Bibliothek

Die Deutsche Bibliothek lists this publication in the Deutsche Nationalbibliografie;
detailed bibliographic data is available in the Internet at <http://dnb.ddb.de>.

For Pim

Table of Contents

List of authors

Anne Cutler

Max Planck Institute for Psycholinguistics, Nijmegen, The Netherlands

Delphine Dahan

Max Planck Institute for Psycholinguistics, Nijmegen, The Netherlands

Gary S. Dell

University of Illinois and Beckman Institute, Urbana-Champaign, Illinois, USA

James Emil Flege

University of Alabama, Birmingham, Alabama, USA

Carol A. Fowler

Yale University and Haskins Laboratories, New Haven, Connecticut, USA

Louis Goldstein

Yale University and Haskins Laboratories, New Haven, Connecticut, USA

Jean K. Gordon

University of Iowa, Iowa City, Iowa, USA

Frank Guenther

Boston University, Boston, Massachusetts, USA

Peter Hagoort

F. C. Donders Centre for Neuroimaging and Max Planck Institute for Psycholinguistics, Nijmegen, The Netherlands

Judith F. Kroll

Pennsylvania State University, University Park, Pennsylvania, USA

James M McQueen

Max Planck Institute for Psycholinguistics, Nijmegen, The Netherlands

Antje S. Meyer

University of Birmingham, England

Ardi Roelofs

Max Planck Institute for Psycholinguistics and F. C. Donders Centre for Neuroimaging, Nijmegen, The Netherlands

Niels O. Schiller

University of Maastricht and Max Planck Institute for Psycholinguistics, Nijmegen, The Netherlands

Bernadette Schmitt

University of Maastricht, The Netherlands

Núria Sebastián-Gallés

University of Barcelona, Spain

Miranda van Turennout

F. C. Donders Centre for Neuroimaging and Max Planck Institute for Psycholinguistics, Nijmegen, The Netherlands

Pienie Zwitserlood

University of Münster, Germany

Introduction to the relation between speech comprehension and production

Niels O. Schiller and Antje S. Meyer

The present book explores how phonological and phonetic knowledge is represented and used in speech comprehension and production. These processes are obviously quite different: In one case a person hears and understands an acoustic input, whereas in the other case, the person produces an acoustic signal expressing a message to be conveyed. Therefore it is not surprising that many researchers have studied phonological and phonetic processing in either speech production or comprehension without considering the other process too much. This "divide-and-conquer" strategy has been very successful and has led to a wealth of empirical data and detailed production and comprehension models.

However, in addition to the obvious differences there are equally obvious similarities between speech production and comprehension: They both involve the use of linguistic knowledge; when a person learns a first or second language, productive and receptive skills develop hand-in-hand, and when language is impaired after brain damage, the loss is rarely confined to production or comprehension. When language is used in natural contexts, speaker and listener collaborate, as the speaker is the person creating the input for the listener and each speaker is also a listener of his or her own speech and, a moment earlier or later, the speech of the other person.

Given these obvious similarities and differences between speech production and comprehension, it seems worthwhile to ask how *exactly* they are related or different from each other. A number of specific research questions suggest themselves. For instance, is there one mental lexicon that holds all information required for production and comprehension and is accessed in both processes, or are there separate dedicated lexica for each function? If there are separate lexica,

are they organized according to similar or entirely different principles? How are the processes underlying speech planning and comprehension related? Are some processes involved both in production
and comprehension? Are there processes that run in opposite directions in planning and comprehension? Which brain areas are involved in speech production and comprehension? Which are engaged
in both and which in only one of these functions? These questions
seem interesting and important to us in their own right. Providing
answers to some of them should help us understand the overall architecture of the cognitive system involved in the use of language. In
addition, evidence and theories concerning the relationship between
production and comprehension should have implications for theories
primarily concerned with production or with comprehension. Evidently, a theory of speech production should explain what is known
about speaking, but it should be compatible with theories and evidence concerning speech comprehension. Likewise, a theory of comprehension should explain how people understand speech, but it
should not clash with what is known about speech production.

In preparation of this book, we invited experts from different areas
of psycholinguistics to discuss phonological and phonetic processing
in speech production and comprehension. Unsurprisingly, the authors
filled in this general brief in different ways.

Dell and Gordon discuss the effects of neighborhood density (the
number words that are phonologically similar to a given word) in
speech production and comprehension. Many properties of words
have similar effects in production and comprehension tasks. However, neighborhood density is an interesting exception. High
neighborhood density has detrimental effects in comprehension tasks,
but facilitatory effects in speech production tasks. Dell and Gordon
account for these results within an interactive activation model of
speech processing. The opposing effects of neighborhood density
arise because production and comprehension tasks create different
competitive environments. Phonological neighbors are potent competitors to the targets to be selected in speech comprehension but not
in production tasks, where the set of competitors is defined on semantic grounds.

McQueen, Dahan, and Cutler focus on the mapping of the speech signal onto stored representations in speech recognition and compare it to the analogical mapping of stored representations onto articulatory commands in speech production. They draw attention to striking differences between current comprehension and production models: All comprehension models assume that lexical access involves the parallel evaluation of several lexical hypotheses. This process is continuous, i.e. it does not involve discrete processing stages, and it is graded, i.e. lexical candidates may be more or less strongly activated depending on the amount of support they receive by the acoustic input. As the authors demonstrate there is strong empirical support for this view. By contrast, the evidence for continuous processing in speech production is far less convincing. Therefore, serial stage models of production co-exist with continuous models, which assume a limited degree of cascading of information. However, no production model posits the widespread cascading generally assumed in models of comprehension. In addition, the information passed on through the processing steps of production models appears to be rather more categorical than the fine-grained phonetic information used at all levels of the comprehension process. As McQueen and colleagues explain, these differences may be linked to differences in the tasks faced by language users during speech production and comprehension: A system continuously processing fine grained phonetic detail is ideally suited to the purposes of speech comprehension, but such a system may not be perfect for production.

Zwitserlood discusses the representation and processing of morphological information. Drawing on evidence from studies of speech production and comprehension she presents a strong case for a separate level of morphological representation, distinct from syntactic, semantic, and phonological levels. Like Roelofs (though for different reasons) she argues that there must be separate phonological and phonetic components for production and comprehension, while the other levels, possibly including the morphological level, are likely to be shared.

Roelofs reviews several computationally implemented models of spoken word recognition and production and discusses whether a single shared system can support word form access in production and comprehension. As he points out, such a system must have bi-directional links between sublexical and lexical units. This would imply feedback from the sublexical to the lexical level in production, and from the lexical to the sublexical level in comprehension. Roelofs reviews findings from a variety of sources and concludes that there is no evidence that would force us to assume such bi-directional links. He therefore proposes an architecture with separate but closely linked feed-forward systems for production and comprehension. This view is compatible with recent neuro-imaging studies suggesting that phonological processing in production and comprehension of speech engages separate subregions within Wernicke's area.

Goldstein and Fowler discuss the relation between speech production and perception from the point of view of Articulatory Phonology. In Articulatory Phonology, vocal tract activity is analyzed into constriction actions (gestures) of distinct vocal organs (e.g., lip closure). These gestures are seen as atoms of a combinatorial system and are organized into temporally overlapping structures. The authors argue for the need of a "common currency" between production and perception and propose that gestures may serve as the common phonological currency. Gestures are preserved from language planning, via production to perception, and directly structure the acoustic signal. Listeners perceive gestures, not acoustic cues.

Guenther addresses the control of speech movements. In his view, speech motor planning and auditory speech processing are closely linked as, for instance, the targets for speech movements are defined in auditory and orosensory terms. Guenther proposes a neural network model of speech production and speech motor acquisition (DIVA), which captures speech-planning processes from the syllabic level to the level of muscle commands. (By contrast, Roelofs' WEAVER++ model specifies speech-planning process up to the syllabic level). DIVA accounts for a wide range of behavioral data, including results of studies of articulatory kinematics and the development of speech motor skill development. It is also a model of the neural representations underlying speech production. Speech perception and production are supported by separate, but closely linked cortical areas.

Van Turennout, Schmitt, and Hagoort describe how event-related brain potentials (ERPs), such as the N200 component, and lateralized readiness potentials (LRPs) can be used to determine the relative order in which speakers, listeners, and readers retrieve semantic, syntactic, and word form information and the time required for each of these processing steps. The elegance of this approach lies in the fact that very similar experimental paradigms and tasks can be used to study word production and comprehension. Van Turennout and colleagues review ERP studies showing that in picture naming, conceptual information is retrieved first, followed by the retrieval of syntactic information and, finally, the retrieval of the phonological form of the picture name. These results offer strong support for the WEAVER++ model of speech production (see the chapter by Roelofs), which predicts exactly this ordering of the retrieval processes. The model predicts that in word comprehension, the ordering of the retrieval processes should be reversed. The results of ERP studies (as well as other evidence) support the assumption that word form information is indeed accessed before syntactic and conceptual information (see also the chapter by McQueen et al.). However, the available data do not strongly constrain assumptions about the relative ordering of access to semantic and syntactic information.

Sebastián-Gallés and Kroll discuss the acquisition and organization of sound systems in bilingual infants and adults. An important theoretical issue they take up is whether the sound systems of the two languages of a bilingual speaker are strictly separated, or whether during the use of one language the sound system of the other language also becomes activated. They review the evidence from a large number of production and comprehension studies and conclude that lexical access is nonselective with regard to language. Interestingly, the task defines which part of the lexicon of the non-target language becomes activated. In production tasks, the activated names are those of translation equivalents of the targets, whereas in comprehension tasks, the activated words are words that sound similar to the targets.

Flege discusses the acquisition and representation of phonetic categories by second language (L2) learners and monolingual native speakers of the same language. His Speech Learning Model (SLM) assumes that the cognitive capacities underlying speech acquisition remain intact in adults, i.e. even beyond a *critical period* for language acquisition postulated in some models. Adults retain the ability to form new phonetic categories for speech sounds encountered in a second language. However, native-like phonetic category formation becomes less likely with increasing age because the phonetic systems of the two languages are not completely separate. In the course of L1 phonetic category development (the end-point of which has not yet been determined) L2 speech sounds become more likely to be perceptually assimilated to existing L1 categories, blocking the formation of new L2 categories. Less accurate perception of L2 phonetic segments may lead to less accurate production of L2 speech sounds. Flege provides empirical evidence from production and perception studies demonstrating that (late) L2 learners indeed often do not distinguish to the standards of L1 speakers between different L2 segments.

As the reader will discover, the chapters of the book do not offer simple answers to the questions about the relationship between speech comprehension and production formulated above. Nor can they be joined together to form a unified theory accounting for speech production and comprehension. In fact, determining which production and comprehension architectures would be compatible is itself quite a complex issue. However, the reader will also discover that there is good agreement across authors on a number of important basic points: First, concerning the representation of phonological and phonetic knowledge, there is wide agreement that language users either have one shared store of knowledge which they access in different ways in speech production and comprehension, or separate, but closely linked stores. Nobody assumes that there are entirely independent representations used exclusively in production and comprehension. As pointed out by Roelofs, a shared system must be one with feedback between levels. This demonstrates that one's view of the relationship between production and comprehension can have important implications for the design of the individual systems. A second point of consensus, highlighted in several chapters (Dell and Gordon, McQueen et al., and Zwitserlood) is that seemingly discrepant findings from production and comprehension research can often be reconciled by carefully considering the task demands faced by listeners and speakers. Third, several chapters illustrate that similar experimental methods can be used for studying both domains, which is of utmost importance for systematic investigations of differences and similarities between speech production and comprehension. Similarly, computational models can be designed that can be used to simulate both production and comprehension processes. Finally, it is evident that cognitive models of speech processing should be developed in tandem with models of the neurological basis of these processes. We hope that these communalities represent a solid foundation for further research into the relation between speech production and comprehension.

We would like to end on a couple of personal notes. First, we wish to express our gratitude to the colleagues who reviewed chapters of the book for us. These are Dani Byrd, Albert Costa, Markus Damian, Laurie Feldman, Gareth Gaskell, Ray Kent, Tom Münte, Pascal Perrier, Rob Schreuder, Roel Smit, Marianne Starren, Patricia Tabossi, and Michael Vitevitch. Their contribution was greatly appreciated by the authors and the editors alike. Second, we wish to point out that this book is the result of a conspiracy by authors, reviewers and editors to create kind-of-a-Festschrift (only better) for a person who hates Festschriften but deserves one more than anyone else: Pim Levelt. Thank you, Pim, for everything!

Niels Schiller and Antje Meyer
Maastricht and Birmingham, March 2003

Neighbors in the lexicon: Friends or foes?

Gary S. Dell and Jean K. Gordon

1. Introduction

What makes a word easy to say? For the most part, the same things that make a word easy to understand make that word easy to say. Consider word frequency. Common words can be both produced (e.g. Caramazza et al. 2001; Dell 1990; Jescheniak and Levelt 1994) and recognized (e.g. Luce and Pisoni 1998; Oldfield and Wingfield 1965; Soloman and Postman 1952) with greater facility than rare words. One would be quite surprised to learn otherwise, because both production and recognition are adaptive systems designed to process the most likely events with the greatest ease.

Other lexical variables also affect production and recognition similarly. Concrete words are favored over abstract words in both production (e.g. Martin, Saffran, and Dell 1996) and recognition (Strain, Patterson, and Seidenberg 1995). Predictable words can be recognized (Morton and Long 1976) and produced (Griffin and Bock 1998) more quickly than those that are less congruent with their contexts. Even the speed associated with the perception of shorter words has its counterpart in production. The articulation of single-syllable words can begin more quickly than that of two-syllable words (Meyer, Roelofs, and Levelt 2003). None of these results are surprising. Our intuitions as well as our psychological theories are built around assumptions that lead to efficient processing for simple or familiar mental entities, regardless of whether those entities are incoming stimuli or outgoing responses.

This chapter focuses on a lexical property that appears to have opposite effects on receptive and expressive processes. That property is the number of words that are phonologically similar to the targeted word, called *phonological neighborhood density*. A word that is highly similar in sound to many other words is said to come from a *dense* neighborhood; a word with few similar-sounding words inhabits a *sparse* neighborhood. By the most popular current estimation procedure (Luce et al. 1990), two words are considered to be "neighbors" if they differ by only one phoneme, either substituted, added, or omitted. Thus, *cat* has *cast*, *rat*, and *at* among its 35 neighbors and, by most criteria, would be considered to come from a dense neighborhood. In contrast, *dog* has only 8 neighbors. Many long words (e.g. *elephant*) and the occasional short word (e.g. *again*) have no neighbors at all. (Neighborhood densities were determined from the Hoosier Mental Lexicon, an on-line lexicon of almost 20,000 English words, Luce et al. 1990.)

Neighborhood density has been established, then, as another dimension along which words may differ. But what is the implication of this? Does having many neighbors make it easier or harder to process a word? Neighborhood density was originally proposed to be one of the variables underlying the ubiquitous facilitative effects of frequency and familiarity (Eukel 1980; Nusbaum, Pisoni and Davis 1984). Nusbaum and colleagues collected familiarity ratings for the words in the Hoosier Mental Lexicon, and compared these to frequencies gathered from written corpora of text (Kucera and Francis 1967). The weak relationship found between these two measures ($r = 0.43$) led them to propose that impressions of word familiarity may be more strongly related to "the lexical density of the phonotactic spaces in which the words occur in the lexicon" (Nusbaum et al. 1984). If this were the case, having many neighbors would make it easier to process a word, just as greater familiarity does. However, subsequent word recognition studies demonstrated the opposite result, that words from dense neighborhoods are recognized more slowly and less accurately than those from sparse neighborhoods (e.g. Goldinger, Luce, and Pisoni 1989; Luce 1986; Luce and Pisoni 1998; Vitevitch and Luce 1998, 1999). But this finding also has a logical explanation. When one is attempting to determine what word best matches an incoming auditory string, the target word's neighbors are competitors. They may be mistaken for the target or, at minimum, create a temporary distraction. Thus, neighbors are a negative influence.

During expressive processes, then, what would be the predicted effect of neighborhood density? Do phonologically similar words compete with the target for production as they do for recognition? Or do they act to support the retrieval of the target? Are neighbors friends or foes? Although there have been few studies to date, results quite consistently show that neighborhood density has an effect on speech production opposite to its effect on speech recognition (Gordon 2000, 2002; Harley and Bown 1998; Vitevitch 1997, 2002). Having many neighbors makes the production of a word *more* accurate, and possibly faster as well. Somehow, competitive neighbors have become cooperative neighbors.

In this chapter we review studies that have examined the effects of neighborhood density on spoken word processing, concentrating on the findings showing that density promotes accuracy in production. We seek to explain those findings in terms of the two-step interactive-activation model of lexical access (Dell et al. 1997), a model that has been designed to account for speech errors in normal and aphasic individuals. Ultimately, we argue that the interactive property of the model – that activation feeds back from phonological units to lexical units during production – allows for a target word's neighbors to increase the probability with which that word is selected and to promote its accurate encoding at the phonological level.

2. Phonological Neighborhoods in Auditory Word Recognition

All major theories of word recognition propose that representations of structurally similar neighbors of a target word are activated when the target is presented. The activated neighbors may delay or, in extreme circumstances, derail the recognition of the target. This is true for theories concerned with printed words (e.g. Grainger and Jacobs 1996) as well as theories of spoken-word perception (e.g. McClelland and Elman 1986; Norris 1994). Some spoken-word theories propose that interference comes primarily from those neighbors that are similar to the target at the word's beginning, as in the Cohort Model (Marslen-Wilson and Welsh 1978). That is, the neighborhood consists of the "cohort" of words consistent with the incoming auditory stimulus; this cohort shrinks as more and more of the input is perceived, and the target word is distinguished from its competitors. Other theories suggest that words overlapping with the target at any position may be neighbors, as in the Neighborhood Activation Model (NAM; Luce 1986; Luce and Pisoni 1998).

However the neighborhood is defined, studies of spoken-word recognition clearly show the competitive effect of neighbors. In auditory naming (i.e. word repetition) tasks, words with more neighbors are named more slowly than words with fewer neighbors, using either a straightforward density count (Luce and Pisoni 1998) or a frequency-weighted measure of density (Vitevitch and Luce 1998).[1] Dense neighborhoods also slow responses to words in auditory lexical decision (Luce and Pisoni 1998; Vitevitch and Luce 1999) and same-different judgment tasks (Vitevitch and Luce 1999), as well as decreasing the accuracy of word identification when targets are presented under noisy conditions (Goldinger, Luce, and Pisoni 1989; Luce and Pisoni 1998).

The hypothesized mechanism for competition between a target and its neighbors varies. There may be lateral inhibition between units representing similar words (e.g. McClelland and Elman 1986). Alternatively, the competition may be expressed indirectly through either the mathematics of the recognition decision rule (e.g. Luce and Pisoni 1998), or the dynamics of learned connection weights that map between distributed representations of word forms and word meanings (e.g. Gaskell and Marslen-Wilson 1997; Plaut and Shallice 1993). Regardless of the mechanism, though, neighbors detract from recognizing a target word. Word recognition is inherently a process of discriminating the target from other similar words; the fewer similar words there are, the easier the discrimination.

3. Phonological Neighborhoods in Spoken Word Production

Studies of word production tell a very different story. In a series of error studies, Vitevitch (1997, 2002) has shown that, in fact, a dense phonological neighborhood appears to facilitate accurate speech production. In the first of these studies, Vitevitch (1997) compared a corpus of spontaneously occurring form-related word substitutions (collected by Fay and Cutler 1977) to a control corpus randomly selected from a large database of words matched to the error-target corpus on length and grammatical class. He found the error-target corpus to be lower in frequency, and to have lower neighborhood density and neighborhood frequency values than the control corpus. In order to examine these findings in more controlled tasks, Vitevitch (2002) elicited phonological speech errors using two different techniques. In the first, sound exchanges, or spoonerisms, were induced using the SLIPs technique devised by Baars, Motley, and MacKay (1975). The second experiment made use of a tongue-twister task (after Shattuck-Hufnagel 1992) in which strings of similar-sounding words were repeatedly read aloud as quickly as possible. In both of these tasks, significantly fewer errors were made on the stimuli coming from high-density neighborhoods than those from low-density neighborhoods. Furthermore, in the second task, the density effect was maintained when the stimuli in high- and low-density conditions were equated on dimensions of word frequency, neighborhood frequency, word familiarity rating, and the distribution of initial phonemes.

In addition to facilitating the *accuracy* of word production, a dense neighborhood also appears to facilitate the *efficiency* of word production (Vitevitch 2002). In a picture-naming study, Vitevitch found that pictures from high-density neighborhoods were named more quickly (but no less accurately) than those from low-density neighborhoods. As in the tongue-twister task, the two sets of stimuli were equated for word frequency and familiarity, as well as neighborhood frequency. These results were then replicated with stimuli that were also equated on positional segment and biphone probabilities, illustrating that the density effect cannot be attributed solely to sublexical effects of phonotactic probability.[2] In a final ex-

perimental manipulation, Vitevitch factored out any potential con-
founding effects of articulatory ease, by changing the response requirement to a button press indicating retrieval of the name of the
picture.

The facilitative effect of density on speech errors has also been
supported by studies of the tip-of-the-tongue (ToT) phenomenon
(Harley and Bown 1998; see also Vitevitch and Sommers in prep.).
Contrary to the *interference hypothesis* (e.g. Jones 1989), which proposes that activated neighbors (or "interlopers") actually block successful access to the target, both Harley and Bown as well as Vitevitch and Sommers found that more ToTs were produced on words
from low- than high-density neighborhoods. Together, these results
suggest that, in production, lexical items benefit from an accumula-
tion of activation spreading from phonologically related items, which
makes them easier to retrieve and less susceptible to error. Furthermore, this facilitation appears to extend beyond sublexical frequency
effects.

In studies of aphasic errors, neighborhood variables are also beginning to be considered. The finding of a reverse length effect in the
naming responses of one aphasic subject (Best 1995) was hypothesized to be due to the fact that longer words have fewer neighbors, so
there is less competition for their access. However, a *post-hoc* analysis assessing the effect of density (dubbed *nness* by Best) unexpect-
edly showed *greater* accuracy for items with more neighbors. Thus,
even for a subject who showed an atypical effect of length on naming
performance, a facilitative effect of density was indicated once length
was controlled. But does this effect extend beyond this single case? A
study by Gordon (2002) suggests that the facilitative effect of
neighborhood density in speech production applies more generally to
the aphasic population.

Gordon (2002) conducted two different speech production tasks –
picture naming and picture description – with a large, unselected
group (n = 36) of aphasic subjects, and analyzed the speech errors
which were made during the tasks. In the picture-description task, the
set of incorrectly produced targets (error-targets) was compared to a
similar set of correctly produced targets (correct-targets) gathered

from the same speech samples. That is, each target that was produced in error by a given subject was paired with a target of the same length and grammatical class that was produced accurately by that subject. Results showed that the error-targets were less frequent, and came from less dense neighborhoods than the correct-targets.

In the picture-naming task, the accuracy of responses in the Philadelphia Naming Test (Roach et al. 1996) was correlated with characteristics of the stimulus items. Measured across subjects, accuracy showed a moderate positive correlation with frequency ($r = 0.44$) and neighborhood density ($r = 0.41$), and a moderate negative correlation with number of syllables ($r = -0.40$). Because length is highly confounded with neighborhood density ($r = -0.76$), the density correlations were recalculated for items of each syllable length. Although the correlation between accuracy and density for the one-syllable targets was close to zero ($r = 0.08$, n = 100), a significant correlation was found between accuracy and density for the two-syllable targets ($r = 0.28$, n = 53). (There were not enough three- and four-syllable targets to provide a reliable indication of the relationship for those items.) Both tasks, then, showed a facilitative effect of density.

To summarize the experimental results to date, the density of the phonological neighborhood in which words reside affects the accuracy of speech production in both non-brain-damaged and aphasic speakers. Moreover, the effect of neighborhood density on production is consistently facilitative, in apparent contradiction to the competitive density effect observed in word recognition studies. How can these results be reconciled within a theoretically motivated model of lexical access?

4. Phonological-Lexical Interaction during Production

There are two challenges that confront modelers seeking to explain the beneficial effect of neighborhood density on speech production. The first is to specify how a target's phonological neighbors can exert an influence in a semantically driven task like production. The second is to explain why that influence has the opposite effect to that demonstrated in recognition studies.

Word recognition is a form-driven process; the phonological representation of the target is activated directly by the incoming auditory stimulus. Because neighbors share part of the target's phonology, they too will become partially activated during the recognition process. In contrast, word production is driven by the meaning to be expressed. It is not immediately apparent how this process leads to the activation of formally similar neighbors. Nonetheless, speech production errors suggest that such activation does occur. Form-related word substitutions, such as saying *present* instead of *pressure*, or *button* for *butter,* are a relatively common type of slip in normal speech (Fromkin 1971; Fay and Cutler 1977). These errors, sometimes called *malapropisms,* can also be prevalent in the speech of certain aphasic individuals (e.g. Martin and Saffran 1992; Goldrick and Rapp 2001). The occurrence of malapropisms suggests that neighbors are activated during speech production, at least some of the time.

The question of how the neighbors of a production target can become active requires us to consider, more generally, the nature of lexical access in production. Lexical access is assumed to occur through spreading activation in a network of units representing words, their meanings, and their component sounds. The input to lexical access is an activated representation of the meaning of the word being sought. This might be a single conceptual unit (e.g. Roelofs 1992) or several units corresponding to conceptual or semantic features (e.g. Dell et al. 1997; Rapp and Goldrick 2000). The output of lexical access is an ordered set of units representing the target word's phonological or phonetic segments, or features, along with its nonsegmental properties such as stress (e.g. Roelofs 1997; Levelt, Roelofs, and Meyer 1999). This process of translating the input into the output requires two distinct steps – retrieval of the word representation from semantics (or *lemma access*), and retrieval of the phonological units corresponding to the selected lemma (or *phonological access*) (Fromkin 1971; Garrett 1975; Levelt, Roelofs, and Meyer 1999). The lemma is a lexical representation, typically a single unit, associated with the word's grammatical properties, which mediates between the semantic input and the phonological output.

Although it is agreed that phonological access follows lemma access, there is controversy regarding the extent to which the two steps are truly separate. According to *discrete-stage* theories (Levelt, Roelofs, and Meyer 1999), lemma access must be completed before phonological access begins. As a result, only the selected lemma undergoes phonological access. *Cascaded* theories (Caramazza 1997; Humphreys et al. 1988), however, relax this constraint. During lemma access, it is generally assumed that both the target lemma and competing semantically related lemmas are activated. A cascaded theory, unlike a discrete theory, would propose that the phonological units of these competing lemmas become active before the lemma access stage settles on the target. *Interactive* theories (Dell et al. 1997; Harley 1993; Stemberger 1985) blur the two stages even more. Like the cascaded theories, interactive theories allow for all activated lemmas, whether targeted or not, to activate their phonological representations. Furthermore, interactive theories allow for active phono logical units to feed activation back to the lemma level. Thus, lemma and phonological units continually send activation to one another.

Interactive theories offer a simple mechanism for the activation of a target's neighbors during production. Here we illustrate this mechanism using the two-step interactive-activation model of Dell and colleagues (1997). However, any theory allowing for phonological-lexical interaction would suffice. Figure 1 illustrates the model's lexical network. The network contains separate layers for semantic features, words (lemmas), and phonemes. The connections are excitatory and bi-directional. Top-down connections link semantic features to words, and words to their component phonemes. Bottom-up connections do the reverse, thus providing interactive feedback.

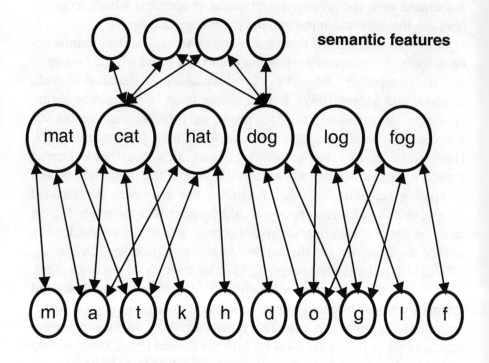

Figure 1. The Architecture of the Two-Step Interactive-Activation Model

Lemma access in the model begins with a jolt of activation to the semantic features of the target, here assumed to be CAT. Activation spreads throughout the network for a fixed number of time steps, according to a noisy linear activation rule:

$$(1) \quad A(j,t) = A(j,t-1)(1-q) + \sum w(i,j)A(i,t-1) + noise$$

$A(j,t)$ is the activation of unit j at time step t, q is the rate with which activation decays, and $w(i,j)$ is the connection weight between unit i and unit j. During each time step, each unit's activation level is perturbed by normally distributed noise with a mean of zero and a standard deviation proportional to the unit's activation.

While lemma access is proceeding, the target word unit, in this case CAT, will normally obtain the most activation. However, the network as a matter of course activates several other word units. Semantically related words such as DOG obtain some activation from shared semantic units. Most importantly for our purposes, formally related neighbors become activated. This is because activation spreads from the target word to its phonemes (/k/, /æ/, /t/) during lemma access – the cascading property of the model – and from those phonemes back to all words that contain them (e.g. MAT) – the interactive property of the model. Word units for neighbors will, naturally, become more active than words that are not related in form to the target.

Lemma access is concluded by a selection process. At a specified time step, the most activated word unit of the appropriate syntactic category is chosen. So, in the case in which the noun CAT is the target, the most activated noun is selected. Most likely, this will be CAT. However, due to the contribution of noise, a semantically related word (DOG), a formally related word or malapropism (MAT), or a mixed semantic-formal word (RAT) could be incorrectly selected instead, provided that it is a noun. If the noise is extreme, an unrelated noun such as LOG might be chosen. Selection is followed by a jolt of activation to the selected word unit. The jolt is controlled by grammatical processes, ensuring that the selected word belongs to the correct syntactic category, and, if a sentence is being produced, that the word is produced at the appropriate time during production of the sentence.

This jolt of activation also marks the beginning of the stage of phonological access. Activation again spreads throughout the network, feeding forward and backward. After a given period of time, the most activated phonemes are, in turn, selected and linked to their respective positions in a phonological frame, a structure that represents the metrical and syllabic properties of the target. Normally, the target phonemes, /k/, /æ/, and /t/, will be most active, but because of the interaction between the phoneme and word layers, the target's neighbors are also activated during phonological access, just as they were during lemma access. Under noisy conditions, this may result in a phonologically similar word being selected instead of the target

(MAT) or, with more extreme disruption, an unrelated word (LOG) or a non-word (DAT).

In contrast to interactive models, discrete-stage and cascaded models of lexical access do not naturally allow for the activation of neighbors. In these models, the phonological properties of the target do eventually become activated – this occurs after lemma access for discrete-stage models, and both during and after lemma access for cascaded models – but lexical units that share these phonological properties are not routinely activated by the production process. How, then, do these models account for the production of phonologically related errors?

If non-interactive models are augmented with an internal monitoring mechanism, a target's neighbors will become active during production (Levelt, Roelofs, and Meyer 1999). Internal monitoring is the checking of planned speech for errors before it is spoken. In the discrete-stage WEAVER++ model of lexical access, this monitoring is assumed to occur through the comprehension system, a system that converges with the production system at the lemma level (Roelofs in press). A phonological representation of the planned utterance is transmitted to the comprehension system, with the result that similar words are activated through normal word-recognition mechanisms. For example, if CAT is the target word for production, the monitoring of its phonological representation results in a reactivation of the lemma for CAT, along with some activation of neighboring lemmas such as CAP or CAN. The activation of neighbors by monitoring gives non-interactive models a mechanism for malapropism errors to occur (Levelt, Roelofs, and Meyer 1999). If phonological access is incomplete (for example, only the first two sounds of CAT are retrieved), monitoring this incomplete representation will lead to neighboring lemmas that may be as active as the targeted lemma. If one of them is in the target grammatical category (e.g. the noun CAP), it may be selected, leading to a malapropism.[3]

Thus far, we have considered how neighbors could become activated during production. Phonological-lexical feedback in interactive models directly leads to the activation of neighbors during both lemma and phonological access. In discrete-stage models, internal monitoring through the comprehension system allows for the activation of neighbors after the creation of a target's phonological representation. The next issue that must be considered is that of how the activation of neighbors could benefit production. In the following section, we use the two-step interactive-activation model to explore the consequences of neighborhood structure in an interactive model. We will show that, although there are some competitive effects from activated neighbors, this model predicts that denser neighborhoods are associated with greater accuracy in both lemma and phonological access.

5. Effects of Neighborhood Density in an Interactive Model

The effects of neighborhood density on speech production were examined by manipulating the characteristics of the lexicon in the two-step interactive-activation model (Gordon and Dell 2001). This model employs very simple lexicons of single-syllable, consonant-vowel-consonant (CVC) words and was originally constructed to simulate error patterns shown by normal speakers. Dell and colleagues (1997) set up the model by selecting parameters so that the model's behavior matched the pattern of errors produced by normal speakers during a picture-naming test, the Philadelphia Naming Test (Roach et al. 1996). The critical error categories in this test were: correct responses (CAT), semantic errors (e.g. DOG), formal errors or malapropisms (e.g. MAT), mixed semantic-formal errors (e.g. RAT), unrelated word errors (e.g. LOG), and non-words (e.g. DAT). Most of the model's responses (97%) were correct, the remaining responses consisting primarily of semantic errors (2%) and mixed errors (1%).

By altering two of the model's parameters, Dell et al. (1997) were also able to simulate patterns of errors made by aphasic subjects on the same test. In the normal model, all of the weights (w(i,j)), had been set to the same value, 0.1, and the decay rate was 0.5 per time step. To produce aphasic deficits, the model was "lesioned" by either reducing the connection weights or increasing the decay rate. Both forms of lesioning increased error rates by reducing the activation of network units, which caused the noise to have more of an impact. However, the two types of lesions resulted in different error patterns. Weight lesions increased the chance of non-word and unrelated-word errors because these errors reflect circumstances in which activation at one processing level is inconsistent with other levels. If weights are low, information about what is activated at one level cannot be effectively sent to other network levels. Decay lesions, in contrast, increased the occurrence of related word errors, either semantic, mixed, or formal errors. In this case, the connection weights are still strong, so activation still spreads effectively between layers. Thus, errors tend to be more closely related to the target, either in form, meaning, or both. By varying these two parameters, Dell and colleagues found that they could set up the model to mimic the picture-naming error patterns of each of 21 aphasic patients with a fair degree of success. In essence, each patient could be characterized by the model in terms of his/her lesioned weight and decay values. These values, in turn, were used to predict other aspects of the patients' speaking behavior (see Dell et al. 1997 for details).

The same principles were applied here. We examined the effect of neighborhood density on the model's accuracy using both a normal version of the model, and versions designed to reflect aphasic lesions (Gordon and Dell 2001). We started with a simple lexicon consisting of a target, CAT, two phonological neighbors, HAT and MAT, one semantically related word, DOG, and two unrelated words, LOG and FOG (refer back to Figure 1). This was designated the *dense* neighborhood. A *sparse* neighborhood was created by eliminating one of the target's neighbors (HAT), and an *empty* neighborhood was created by removing both of them.[4]

5.1. Simulation using normal parameters

To explore the effect of neighborhoods, we first examined the model's performance with the dense, sparse, and empty neighborhoods using normal weight (0.1) and decay (0.5) parameters[5]. The model attempted to produce the target 100,000 times. Accuracy and error rates are shown in Table 1. Although the accuracy was generally very high, more errors were produced as the neighborhood became sparser, in keeping with the facilitative effects of density shown for normal speakers. The facilitative effect is apparent not only in the overall accuracy rates (the proportion of cases in which the model's final output is correct), but also in the rates of lemma and phonological accuracy (see Table 1). Lemma accuracy is the proportion of cases in which the target lemma was selected, regardless of whether it was then encoded correctly. Phonological accuracy is the proportion of correct lemmas that were also phonologically encoded correctly, in essence, factoring the effects of lemma accuracy out of the overall accuracy rate.

Table 1. Effects of Neighborhood Density on the Normal Model.

Neighborhood			
Measure	Dense	Sparse	Empty
Overall Accuracy (%)	97.8	97.6	96.9
Lemma Accuracy (%)	97.9	97.8	97.6
Phonological Accuracy (%)	99.9	99.8	99.3
Correct (out of 100,000)	97,799	97,607	96,932
Semantic Errors	2113	2215	2415
Formal Errors	3	0	0
Unrelated Errors	0	0	0
Non-word Errors	85	178	653

The bottom part of Table 1 presents the raw frequencies of each error type as a function of neighborhood density. The facilitative effect of density is clearly seen in the lower numbers of both semantic and non-word errors, as neighborhood density increases. The only error type that increases with increasing density is formal errors, although these are extremely rare with normal parameters in the model (and in normal speakers performing a picture-naming task).

5.2. Simulations using lesioned parameters

If the facilitative effect of neighborhood density depends on the interactive nature of the model, then alterations to the model that disrupt the flow of activation should reduce the role of density. Two types of lesions, previously found to accurately represent a majority of lexical access deficits in fluent aphasia (Dell et al. 1997), were also implemented in this study. Reducing the strength of connection weights, which disrupts the ability of the model to spread activation from one layer of nodes to the next, was predicted to result in a diminished density effect. On the other hand, increasing the rate of decay of activation, although expected to increase error rates overall, should not affect the facilitative effect of density.

Each type of lesion was simulated at three different levels of severity, but for the sake of simplicity, only one is reproduced here (for more details, see Gordon and Dell 2001). The decay lesion was implemented by increasing the decay rate parameter from $q = 0.5$ to $q = 0.9$; the weight lesion was implemented by decreasing the connection weight parameter from $p = 0.1$ to $p = 0.0033$. The overall accuracy of production was approximately equivalent for each lesion type, representing a moderate-to-severe lexical access deficit.

Results for the decay-lesioned model are shown in Table 2. As predicted, a clear effect of neighborhood density is evident in the rates of overall accuracy, as well as lemma and phonological accuracy; all three rates are reduced as neighborhood density is decreased. The raw frequencies of each error type, provided in the lower half of the graph, show that, as density decreases, all error types increase except formal errors, which decrease because there are fewer opportunities for such errors.

Table 3 illustrates the results for the weight-lesioned model. Here, the effect of neighborhood density is obviously reduced, as predicted. In fact, overall accuracy and lemma accuracy rates *rise* slightly as density is decreased, suggesting a slight competitive effect. The raw frequency counts for each error type show that, as in the normal and decay-lesioned models, the numbers of semantic and non-word errors increase with decreasing density and, as in the decay-lesioned model, the number of unrelated errors increases as well. However, the differences are not as great here as in the other two models, and are therefore overwhelmed by the reduction in formal errors that necessarily occurs with fewer neighbors. Thus, when target activation is low enough, and the spread of activation between levels is disrupted, the increased opportunity for error provided by a larger neighborhood creates a competitive environment.

Table 2. Effects of Neighborhood Density on the Decay-Lesioned Model.

Neighborhood			
Measure	Dense	Sparse	Empty
Overall Accuracy (%)	47.8	40.2	25.4
Lemma Accuracy (%)	66.6	66.0	65.0
Phonological Accuracy (%)	71.7	60.9	39.1
Correct (out of 10,000)	4779	4019	2542
Semantic Errors	1553	1956	2426
Formal Errors	1654	599	0
Unrelated Errors	457	677	865
Non-word Errors	1557	2749	4167

5.3. The role of neighbors in production and comprehension

Why do additional neighbors increase the accuracy of the model? We know that phonological-lexical feedback leads to the activation of neighboring words. By itself, though, that does not explain the greater accuracy. Neighbors are activated during word recognition, and one would not expect them to contribute to more accurate recognition, but rather the contrary.

Table 3. Effects of Neighborhood Density on the Weight-Lesioned Model.

Neighborhood

Measure	Dense	Sparse	Empty
Overall Accuracy (%)	33.7	35.1	36.4
Lemma Accuracy (%)	62.5	65.6	68.7
Phonological Accuracy (%)	54.0	53.4	52.9
Correct (out of 10,000)	3373	3507	3636
Semantic Errors	816	886	980
Formal Errors	1267	649	0
Unrelated Errors	828	905	1004
Non-word Errors	3716	4053	4380

To show this, we did a simple simulation of word recognition using the same interactive activation model. We made only two changes, reflecting the change from production to a word recognition task: (1) Instead of semantic input, the input was phonological. Each of the target phonemes, /k/, /æ/, and /t/, received a jolt of activation analogous to the jolts given to semantic units during production. (2) The most activated word node after the given number of time steps was chosen as the recognized word. Everything else – connection weights, decay rate, noise parameters, number of time steps allowed for spreading activation – was the same as in the production simulations. Again, the correct target was CAT. Testing the same three neighborhood densities, we found, as expected, that neighbors are highly detrimental to recognition. Accuracy was 100%, 82%, and 58% for the empty, sparse, and dense neighborhoods, respectively. All errors consisted of selecting a phonological neighbor instead of the target.

The recognition simulation demonstrates that the interactive spread of activation is not, by itself, responsible for the production model's facilitative effects of density. Exactly the same interactive model, when used for recognition, creates an inhibitory effect of density. Clearly, it is the combination of interaction and the *task* of production that leads to the beneficial influence of neighbors.

Neighbors promote accurate production in the model because they enhance the activation of the target word, but do not enhance the activation of its principal semantic competitors. Because production is a semantically driven task, semantic features are activated first, and semantically related words therefore receive more spreading activation throughout the entire process of lexical access than do other nontarget words in the lexicon. Thus, a production target's main competitors are semantically related rather than phonologically related words. This explains the prevalence of semantically related errors in normal speakers. The primary challenge of the production task, then, is to ensure that the target's activation (CAT) exceeds the activation of competing semantic neighbors (DOG).

When the target has phonological neighbors (MAT and HAT), these become activated and, in turn, send activation back to the target, *via* their shared phoneme units (/æ/ and /t/). Thus, in a dense neighborhood, the target and its neighbors all have higher activations than they would in a sparse neighborhood. Consequently, the greater activation of CAT caused by MAT and HAT promotes the selection of CAT over DOG, which does not benefit from the activation of MAT and HAT. It is true that MAT and HAT also receive more activation, but these phonological neighbors are not serious contenders in the contest. (Note that when the facilitation provided by neighbors is reduced, as in the weight-lesioned model, the formal neighbors *do* become serious contenders.) In this way, the phonological neighbors reinforce the activation of the target relative to its semantic competition.

The benefit to the model's production from neighbors occurs both during lemma and phonological access. Both CAT and its phonemes benefit from interaction with neighbors. During lemma access, neighbors keep CAT's lemma activation above that of DOG. As a result, semantic errors are less likely in dense neighborhoods. For example, in Table 1, there were 302 fewer semantic errors in the dense neighborhood than in the empty one. During phonological access, the neighbors contribute directly to the activation of the target's phonemes. This contribution primarily prevents non-word errors, as these are the most common errors of phonological access. Compare the 653 non-word errors produced in the empty neighborhood to only 85 in the dense neighborhood.

In summary, production and comprehension differ in their response to neighborhood density in the model because production and comprehension tasks create different competitive environments. When the task dictates that phonological neighbors are serious competitors, a densely populated phonological neighborhood is detrimental to fast and accurate retrieval. When the task dictates that other words are the main competitors, neighborhood density promotes accurate retrieval of the target.

5.4. Predictions for aphasic error patterns

Our analysis of the model makes specific predictions regarding the effects of neighborhood density on speech production in aphasia. If the mechanism by which density exerts a facilitative influence is accurately represented, then the effect of neighborhood density on aphasic error patterns will differ depending on the underlying lexical access impairment. Specifically, aphasic subjects with decay-rate lesions should show density effects similar to those shown by normal subjects, whereas aphasic subjects with connection-weight lesions should show attenuated, if not absent, neighborhood effects. Moreover, neighbors should generally help prevent aphasic errors that occur at lemma access such as semantic errors, as well as phonological errors such as non-words.

As a preliminary investigation of these hypotheses, the aphasic subjects examined by Gordon (2002) were classified as either "decay-lesioned" or "weight-lesioned" (for details of the classification procedure, see Dell et al. 1997). Item-level correlations between neighborhood density and the picture-naming response proportions were calculated for each subject group separately (see Table 4). Contrary to predictions, both weight-lesioned and decay-lesioned subjects showed significant positive correlations between overall accuracy and density (using 2-, 3-, and 4-syllable items, the items most sensitive to density effects in Gordon's study). However, the expected reduction of the neighborhood effect for weight-lesioned subjects *was* observed in the correlations of density with semantic errors and non-word errors. The incidence of semantic errors was significantly negatively correlated with neighborhood density for the decay-lesioned subjects, but not the weight-lesioned subjects. Similarly, the incidence of non-word errors, representing phonological encoding accuracy, was significantly negatively correlated with density only for the decay-lesioned subjects. Admittedly, the correlations and the differences between them were small. Nevertheless, the results are suggestive of a difference between aphasic subjects that accords with predictions of the model. Most importantly, the correlations show that larger neighborhoods are associated with fewer semantic (lemma access) errors as well as fewer errors of phonological encoding.

Table 4. Correlations of Neighborhood Density with Incidence of Correct Responses, Semantic Errors, and Non-word Errors.

Subject Group		
Response	Decay-Lesioned	Weight-Lesioned
Correct Responses	0.30*	0.27*
Semantic and Mixed Errors	- 0.27*	- 0.09
Non-word Errors	- 0.29*	- 0.22

* indicates significantly different from 0

6. Conclusions and Caveats

We have argued that lexical-phonological interaction can explain the beneficial effects of neighbors on production, and investigated the properties of a particular interactive model. Insofar as this kind of interaction has independent motivation from other production facts, it is a viable explanation for the neighborhood effect. Indeed, lexical-phonological feedback has been implicated in speech-error phenomena such as the existence of a syntactic category constraint on malapropisms (e.g. Harley and MacAndrew 2001) and the tendency for semantic errors to exhibit formal relations (the *mixed error effect*, Martin et al. 1996). Recently, interactive models have been offered to explain how these phenomena are disrupted or preserved in aphasia (Dell et al. 1997; Gordon 2002; Rapp and Goldrick 2000). Moreover, interaction provides a mechanism for the tendency for phonological errors to create words over non-words (the *lexical-bias effect*, Baars, Motley, and MacKay 1975; Dell 1986, 1990; Nooteboom in press). This evidence has not been viewed as providing a definitive case for interaction, however. These error effects could arise, instead, from a suitably configured internal monitoring system (e.g. Levelt, Roelofs, and Meyer 1999; Roelofs in press). The existence of these non-interactive accounts for error effects leads to the final issue that we confront in this chapter. Is there truly a need to posit interaction to account for neighborhood effects?

Our claim is that interaction leads to the activation of a target's phonological neighbors and offers a mechanism to explain why this interaction is beneficial in production. In a discrete model such as that of Levelt and colleagues (1999), the assumption that planned speech is monitored by the comprehension system also provides for the activation of the target's neighbors. It is unclear, though, how this process could increase the speed or accuracy of either lemma or phonological access in this model. The activation of neighbors makes them available as possible errors if they are selected instead of the target. However, their activation would not contribute to the activation of the target without adding assumptions to the model. Thus, the comprehension monitor, which offers a discrete model a way to deal with interactive error effects, does not explain the neighborhood density effect.

There is, however, another way that neighbors could contribute positively to production in a discrete model. A word with many neighbors will tend to have sublexical units that are frequent. In the model of Levelt et al. (1999), for example, the phonetic syllable units are assumed to be sensitive to their frequency of usage. To the extent that words from dense neighborhoods tend to have frequent syllables, words with those syllables would be encoded faster in the model. At this point in time, the available data cannot definitively rule out the alternative sublexical frequency explanation. However, two sources of evidence are potentially problematic for this alternative.

First, there is the finding by Vitevitch (2002) that the neighborhood density facilitation of picture-naming latencies was preserved even when positional phoneme frequencies and biphone frequencies were equated between sparse and dense targets. The suggestion is that what matters is the lexical representations of neighbors themselves rather than the consequences of density for sublexical frequency. However, it still could be the case that the frequency of larger sublexical units, such as phonetic syllables, is confounded with density in the study.

The other relevant finding is Gordon and Dell's (2001) report that the rate of aphasic semantic errors was negatively associated with neighborhood density. So, neighbors were protective against semantic errors as well as phonological errors, a result that was predicted by the simulations using the interactive model (Tables 1 to 3). The alternative explanation based on sublexical frequency could explain faster or more accurate word-form encoding, but not more accurate discrimination at the lemma level between a target and its semantic competitors. Again, though, there is good reason to withhold judgment. The relevant correlations were weak and the study has yet to be replicated.

In summary, a word's phonological neighbors have complex influences on the processing of that word. Whether neighbors are competitive or cooperative depends on the task: Neighbors are costly in recognition but beneficial in production. Lexical-phonological interaction provides a simple and motivated explanation for the benefits of neighbors in production and the evidence, although preliminary, is consistent with that explanation.

Acknowledgements

This research was supported by NSF SBR 98-73450, NIH DC-00191, and the Natural Sciences and Engineering Research Council of Canada. The authors thank Judy Allen for contributions to the manuscript, and the editors and one anonymous reviewer for helpful comments.

Notes

1. Frequency-weighted neighborhood densities were calculated by summing the log frequencies of all of the neighbors of a given target word.
2. Phonotactic probability was calculated by two measures: the sum of the positional segment probabilities of the phonemes in a word (i.e. how frequently each phoneme occurs in that word position), and the sum of the probabilities of each sequential pair of phonemes.
3. Although internal monitoring provides a mechanism for discrete-stage models to produce malapropisms, such a mechanism is not incompatible with other models. In fact, the evidence that internal monitoring occurs is quite strong (see Levelt, Roelofs, and Meyer 1999 for review) and hence any complete account of production would include this kind of monitoring.
4. The model's neighbors differed from the target at the initial position. This is arbitrary. The same results would occur if they differed at other positions because the implemented model encodes the phonemes of a single-syllable word in parallel.
5. Other parameters were the same as in Dell et al. 1997: Intrinsic noise SD = .01; Noise slope parameter = 0.16; n = 8 time steps for lemma access, and n = 8 for phonological access; semantic jolt = 100, divided over 10 feature units; word jolt = 100 to selected word.

References

Baars, Bernard, Michael Motley and Donald G. MacKay
    1975   Output editing for lexical status in artificially elicited slips of the tongue. *Journal of Verbal Learning and Verbal Behavior* 14: 382-391.
Best, Wendy M.
    1995   A reverse length effect in dysphasic naming: When elephant is easier than ant. *Cortex* 31: 637-652.
Caramazza, Alfonso
    1997   How many levels of processing are there in lexical access? *Cognitive Neuropsychology* 14: 177-208.
Caramazza, Alfonso, Albert Costa, Michele Miozzo and Yanchao Bi
    2001   The specific-word frequency effect: Implications for the representation of homophones n speech production. *Journal of Experimental Psychology: Learning, Memory, and Cognition* 27: 1430-1450.
Dell, Gary S.
    1986   A spreading activation theory of retrieval in language production. *Psychological Review* 93: 283-321.
Dell, Gary S.
    1990   Effects of frequency and vocabulary type on phonological speech errors. *Language and Cognitive Processes* 5: 313-349.
Dell, Gary S., Myrna F. Schwartz, Nadine Martin, Eleanor M. Saffran and Debra A. Gagnon
    1997   Lexical access in aphasic and nonaphasic speakers. *Psychological Review* 104: 801-838.
Eukel, Brian
    1980   Phonotactic basis for work frequency effects: Implications for lexical distance metrics. *Journal of the Acoustical Society of America* 68 (Supplement 1): S33.
Fay, David and Anne Cutler
    1977   Malapropisms and the structure of the mental lexicon. *Linguistic Inquiry* 8: 505-520.
Fromkin, Victoria A.
    1971   The non-anomalous nature of anomalous utterances. *Language* 47: 27-52.
Garrett, Merrill F.
    1975   The analysis of sentence production. In: G. H. Bower (ed.), *The psychology of learning and motivation*, 133-175. San Diego, CA: Academic Press.

Gaskell, M. Gareth and William D. Marslen-Wilson
   1997   Integrating form and meaning: A distributed model of speech
                 perception. *Language and Cognitive Processes* 12: 613-656.
Goldinger, Stephen D., Paul A. Luce and David B. Pisoni
   1989   Priming lexical neighbors of spoken words: Effects of competi-
                 tion and inhibition. *Journal of Memory and Language* 28: 501-
                 518.
Goldrick, Matthew and Brenda Rapp
   2001   What makes a good neighbor? Evidence from malapropisms.
                 Brain and Language 79: 141-143
Gordon, Jean K.
   2000   *Aphasic Speech Errors: Spontaneous and Elicited Contexts.*
                 McGill University, Montreal, Quebec.
Gordon, Jean K.
   2002   Phonological neighborhood effects in aphasic speech errors:
                 Spontaneous and structured contexts. *Brain and Language* 82:
                 113-145.
Gordon, Jean K. and Gary S. Dell
   2001   Phonological neighborhood effects: Evidence from aphasia and
                 connectionist modeling. *Brain and Language* 79: 21-23.
Grainger, Jonathan and Arthur M. Jacobs
   1996   Orthographic processing in visual word recognition: A multiple
                 read-out model. *Psychological Review* 103: 518-565.
Griffin, Zenzi M. and J. Kathryn Bock
   1998   Constraint, word frequency, and the relationship between lexical
                 processing levels in spoken word production. *Journal of Memory
                 and Language* 38: 313-338.
Harley, Trevor A.
   1993   Connectionist approaches to language disorders. *Aphasiology* 7:
                 221-249.
Harley, Trevor A. and Helen E. Bown
   1998   What causes a tip-of-the-tongue state? Evidence for lexical
                 neighbourhood effects in speech production. *British Journal of
                 Psychology* 89: 151-174.
Harley, Trevor A. and Siobhan B.G. MacAndrew
   2001   Constraints upon word substitution speech errors. *Journal of Psy-
                 cholinguistic Research* 30: 395-418.
Humphreys, Glyn W., Jane M. Riddoch and Philip T. Quinlan
   1988   Cascade processes in picture identification. *Cognitive Neuropsy-
                 chology* 5: 67-104.

Jescheniak, Jörg D. and Willem J. M. Levelt
   1994   Word frequency effects in speech production: Retrieval of
                 syntactic information and of phonological form. *Journal of
                 Experimental Psychology: Learning, Memory, and Cognition* 20:
                 824-843.
Jones, Gregory V.
   1989   Back to Woodworth: Role of interlopers in the tip-of-the-tongue
                 phenomenon. *Memory & Cognition* 17: 69-76.
Kucera Henry and Winthrop Francis
   1967   *Computational analysis of present-day American English*. Provi-
                 dence, R.I.: Brown University Press.
Levelt, Willem J. M., Ardi Roelofs and Antje S. Meyer
   1999   A theory of lexical access in speech production. *Behavioral and
                 Brain Sciences* 22: 1-75.
Luce, Paul A.
   1986   Neighborhoods of words in the mental lexicon. Research on
                 Speech Perception, Technical Report No. 6. Speech Research
                 Laboratory, Indiana University, Bloomington, IN.
Luce, Paul A. and David B. Pisoni
   1998   Recognizing spoken words: The Neighborhood Activation
                 Model. *Ear and Hearing* XX: 19-36.
Luce, Paul A., David B. Pisoni and Stephen D. Goldinger
   1990   Similarity neighborhoods of spoken words. In: G. T. M. Altmann
                 (ed.), *Cognitive Models of Speech Processing*, 122-147. Cam-
                 bridge, MA: MIT Press.
Marslen-Wilson, William and Alan Welsh
   1978   Processing interactions and lexical access during word recogni-
                 tion in continuous speech. *Cognitive Psychology* 10: 29-63.
Martin, Nadine and Eleanor M. Saffran
   1992   A computational account of deep dysphasia: Evidence from a
                 single case study. *Brain and Language* 43: 240-274.
Martin, Nadine, Eleanor M. Saffran and Gary S. Dell
   1996   Recovery in deep dysphasia: Evidence for a relationship between
                 auditory-verbal STM capacity and lexical errors in repetition.
                 Brain and Language 52: 83-113.
McClelland, James L. and Jeffrey L. Elman
   1986   The TRACE model of speech perception. *Cognitive Psychology*
                 18: 1-86.
Meyer, Antje S., Ardi Roelofs and Willem J. M. Levelt
   2003   Word length effects in picture naming: The role of a response
                 criterion. *Journal of Memory and Language* 48: 131-147.

Morton, John and John Long
  1976   Effect of word transition probability on phoneme identification. *Journal of Verbal Learning and Verbal Behavior* 15: 43-52.
Nooteboom, Sieb G.
  In press   Listening to one's self: Monitoring speech production. In: R. J. Hartsuiker et al. (eds.), *Phonological encoding in normal and pathological speech.*
Norris, Dennis
  1994   Shortlist: A connectionist model of continuous speech recognition. *Cognition* 52: 189-234.
Nusbaum, Howard C., David B. Pisoni and Christopher K. Davis
  1984   *Sizing up the Hoosier Mental Lexicon: Measuring the familiarity of 20,000 words:* Progress Report No. 10, Indiana University.
Oldfield, Richard C. and Arthur Wingfield
  1965   Response latencies in naming objects. *Quarterly Journal of Experimental Psychology* 17: 273-281.
Plaut, David C. and Tim Shallice
  1993   Deep dyslexia: A case study of connectionist neuropsychology. *Cognitive Neuropsychology* 10: 377-500.
Rapp, Brenda and Matthew Goldrick
  2000   Discreteness and interactivity in spoken word production. *Psychological Review* 107: 460-499.
Roach, April, Myrna F. Schwartz, Nadine Martin, Rita A. Grewal and Adelyn Brecher
  1996   The Philadelphia Naming Test: Scoring and rationale. *Clinical Aphasiology* 24: 121-133.
Roelofs, Ardi
  1992   A spreading-activation theory of lemma retrieval in speaking. *Cognition* 42: 107-142.
Roelofs, Ardi
  1997   The WEAVER model of word-form encoding in speech production. *Cognition,* 64, 249-284.
Roelofs, Ardi
  In press   Errors biases in word planning and monitoring by aphasic and nonaphasic speakers: Comment on Rapp and Goldrick (2000). *Psychological Review.*
Shattuck-Hufnagel, Stephanie
  1992   The role of word structure in segmental serial ordering. *Cognition* 42: 213-259.
Soloman, Richard L. and Leo Postman
  1952   Frequency of usage as a determinant of recognition thresholds for words. *Journal of Experimental Psychology* 43: 195-201.

Stemberger, Joseph P.
1985   An interactive activation model of language production. In: A.
            W. Ellis (ed.), *Progress in the psychology of language* (Vol. 1),
            143-186. Hillsdale, NJ: Erlbaum.
Strain, Eamon, Karalyn Patterson and Mark S. Seidenberg
1995   Semantic effects in single-word naming. *Journal of Experimental
            Psychology: Learning, Memory and Cognition* 21: 1140-1154.
Vitevitch, Michael S.
1997   The neighborhood characteristics of malapropisms. *Language
            and Speech* 40: 211-288.
Vitevitch, Michael S. and Paul A. Luce
1998   When words compete: Levels of processing in perception of spo-
            ken words. *Psychological Science* 9: 325-329.
Vitevitch, Michael S.
2002   The influence of phonological similarity neighborhoods on
            speech production. *Journal of Experimental Psychology: Learn-
            ing, Memory, and Cognition* 28: 735-747.
Vitevitch, Michael S. and Paul A. Luce
1999   Probabilistic phonotactics and neighborhood activation in spoken
            word recognition. *Journal of Memory and Language* 40: 374-
            408.
Vitevitch, Michael S. and Mitchell S. Sommers
In prep.   The role of neighbors in the tip-of-the-tongue state.

Continuity and gradedness in speech processing

James M. McQueen, Delphine Dahan, and
Anne Cutler

1. Introduction

Spoken language comprehension is a decoding process. The talker's
message is encoded in the physical speech signal in complex patterns
of acoustic energy, in the three dimensions of amplitude, frequency
and time. The listener's task is to extract the underlying message
from this code. The key to cracking the code is the listener's prior
knowledge about the phonological form of words. This phonological
information, however it may be stored in lexical memory, is the only
means by which listeners can extract a message from the hissing,
humming, chirping stream of sounds that impinges on their ears
when someone speaks.

In this chapter, we review what is currently known about the way
in which listeners map the speech signal onto stored lexical knowledge. We argue that the lexical access process involves the parallel
evaluation of multiple lexical hypotheses. We also argue that lexical
access is continuous: There are no discrete component stages in the
process; instead, information flows in cascade through the recognition system. We then describe evidence which suggests that this
evaluation process is graded: Not only are there no discrete processing stages, but also the information that is passed through the system
is graded rather than categorical. For example, a word is not simply
either in the lexical competitor set or out of it; each word has its own
variable degree of support. Recent results suggest that the scale
against which the support for different words is measured has a resolution that is more fine-grained than could be captured by a purely

phonemic analysis of the speech signal. That is, subphonemic differences in the signal appear to influence lexical access.

We then discuss speech production in the light of these findings about speech comprehension. While the assumptions of continuity and gradedness in lexical access are widely held in accounts of speech decoding, both of these assumptions are questioned in some accounts of speech encoding. In a leading theory of lexical access in speech production, for example, there are discrete processing stages, and word-form representations contain only phonemic information (Levelt, Roelofs, and Meyer 1999). We discuss why the processing of phonetic and phonological information may be so different in speech encoding and in speech decoding, and suggest that the evidence on the fine-grained detail in the speech signal challenges an aspect of the Levelt et al. model.

2. Continuous multiple evaluation in speech decoding

2.1. Activation

The recognition of a word involves the parallel evaluation of many other candidate words. As speech unfolds over time, the words that are consistent with the current input are considered in parallel. The "multiple activation" metaphor is often used to describe this process: Each candidate word is considered to have a continuously varying activation value associated with it. A candidate's activation represents the amount of support from the speech signal that that word has at that time. The activation metaphor captures the idea that multiple competitor words are evaluated at the same time, and that the evaluation is incremental.

This view of speech decoding is very plausible given the nature of the task with which the listener is faced. Speech is very complex and changes rapidly over time. Processing speech incrementally can therefore reduce the memory load of storing all the acoustic details of the current signal. It also reduces delay in the recognition process: Incremental processing allows a word to be recognized as soon as it can be (when sufficient information has accumulated to distinguish it from its competitors), rather than after the delays which could arise as different serial processing stages reach completion in a non-incremental model.

Processing speech incrementally, however, implies processing it on the basis of partial and very often ambiguous information. There are an infinite number of possible utterances that a talker might say, but a very limited inventory of sounds with which a talker can encode any one utterance. One can estimate that there are likely to be more than 1000 times as many words in any given language as there are phonemes. Phoneme inventories generally lie nearer the lower end of the range 10-100 sounds (Maddieson 1984), while a lexicon is likely to be in the range 10,000-100,000 words (depending on how one defines what a word is). The lexical-phonological space is thus very dense, with many words sharing the same sound sequences (e.g., words which begin in the same way, words which rhyme, and words which have shorter words embedded entirely within them).

The ambiguity of speech is amplified by the variability of the speech signal (even the same talker will never pronounce the same word in exactly the same way twice), and by the fact that speech is often uttered in a noisy environment. Finally, the lack of fully reliable cues to word boundaries in continuous speech (as reliable as the white spaces between written words in an English text such as this) adds to the complexity of the word-recognition problem. Not only is a given stretch of speech likely to offer support for many different words; it is also unclear a priori how many words that stretch of speech might contain, and where they might begin and end.

The price that has to be paid for the benefits of incremental processing, therefore, is that it entails the analysis of a multiply-ambiguous signal. One way to deal with this ambiguity but still achieve optimal incremental recognition consists of considering all lexical candidates compatible with the current, yet incomplete, input, and settling on one interpretation when support for this interpretation safely outweighs support for the others. Later arriving information can then help to confirm or disconfirm earlier interpretations of the input. This processing is embodied in the assumptions of multiple activation and competition, shared by all current models of spoken-word recognition.

It is important to point out, however, that the activation of a word can mean different things to different theorists. Some theories assume that a word corresponds to an abstract representation of the form of a word, itself associated with a representation or representations corresponding to that word's meaning. This form representation is a category that abstracts from all variations in the acoustic realization of a word. Other theories assume that no such abstract form representation exists. All instances or episodes of that word are stored with all their acoustic details (so called traces). On such accounts, a word is a category at the meaning level that is abstracted from all its form-based instances.

There is considerable empirical support for the assumptions of multiple activation and relative evaluation of lexical candidates. Evidence for the activation of multiple candidate words as the form of a spoken word unfolds over time comes from cross-modal semantic priming experiments. These studies show that partial information in the speech signal can trigger the activation of the meaning of multiple matching candidate words. Competitors beginning at the same time are activated (e.g., in Dutch, faster responses to associates of both *kapitein*, captain, and *kapitaal*, capital, were found when listeners heard [kɑpɪt] than when they heard the beginning of an unrelated word; Zwitserlood 1989; see also Moss, McCormick, and Tyler 1997; Zwitserlood and Schriefers 1995). Words embedded in longer words can also be activated (e.g., in English, listeners responded more rapidly to an associate of *bone* when they heard *trombone* than when they heard an unrelated word; Shillcock 1990, but see also Luce and Lyons 1999, Swinney 1981, and Vroomen and de Gelder 1997). Furthermore, words straddling word boundaries in the input are also activated. In English, faster responses to associates of both *lips* and *tulips*, for example, were found when listeners heard *two lips* than in a control condition (Gow and Gordon 1995). Likewise, in Italian, responses to an associate of *visite*, visits, for example, were faster when listeners heard *visi tediati*, bored faces, than in a control condition (Tabossi, Burani, and Scott 1995).

In recognition memory experiments, false positive errors have been found on words which had not been presented earlier in the experiment but which began in the same way as words which had been presented earlier (Wallace, Stewart, and Malone 1995; Wallace et al. 1995, 1998). These errors suggest that the non-studied words were indeed activated when the studied words were heard.

Eye-tracking experiments, where participants' fixations to pictures on a computer screen are collected while they are auditorily instructed to click on one of the pictures, have also provided evidence for multiple-candidate activation. As the name of the target picture unfolds over time, participants make more fixations to pictures with names compatible with the available spoken information (e.g., looks to picture of a beetle when the initial sounds of *beaker* are heard) than to unrelated pictures (Allopenna, Magnuson, and Tanenhaus 1998; see also Tanenhaus et al. 2000).

The meanings of word candidates are thus available before the word that was actually heard can be unambiguously identified. This fact has important consequences for theories of spoken-word recognition. It demonstrates that semantic representations of words can be activated when their corresponding form representations have been activated but before the support for one particular form has outweighed the support for other forms. The activation process is thus continuous, rather than staged, between form- and meaning-representation levels.

2.2. Competition

As multiple candidates are activated by partial spoken input, the degree of evidence for each of them is evaluated with respect to the other words, and this relative evaluation affects the recognition of the target word. This lexical competition process has considerable empirical support. Multiple lexical activation and evaluation can be inferred from the effects of manipulating the lexical neighborhood density of target words (the number and frequency of similar sounding words). It is harder to recognize a word in a dense neighborhood than in a sparse neighborhood because of stronger inter-word competition in the denser neighborhood (Cluff and Luce 1990; Luce 1986; Luce and Large 2001; Vitevitch and Luce 1998, 1999).

The number of competitors beginning at a different point in the input than the target word also influences ease of target recognition. For example, recognizing a word embedded in a longer nonsense word tends to be harder when the nonsense word contains a sequence consistent with many other words than when that sequence is consistent with fewer words (Norris, McQueen, and Cutler 1995; Vroomen and de Gelder 1995).

Competition between specific candidate words has also been observed. Listeners find it harder to spot words embedded in the onsets of longer words (like *sack* in [sækrəf], the beginning of *sacrifice*) than in matched sequences which are not word onsets (like [sækrək]; McQueen, Norris, and Cutler 1994). This kind of competition also occurs when the target and competitor begin at different points in the signal (e.g., spotting *mess* in [dəmɛs], the beginning of *domestic*, is harder than in the nonword onset [nəmɛs]; McQueen et al. 1994).

The effects of the competition process extend over time. In priming paradigms, responses to target words tend to be slower when they are preceded by phonologically related prime words than when they are preceded by unrelated words. This suggests not only that target words are activated when related primes are heard, and that they lose the competition process, but also that this has negative consequences for the subsequent processing of those targets. Inhibitory effects have been found in phonetic priming experiments (in which target words are preceded by primes which share phonetic features but no phonemes with the targets; Goldinger et al. 1992; Luce et al. 2000) and in phonological priming experiments (where primes and targets share onset phonemes; Monsell and Hirsh 1998; Slowiaczek and Hamburger 1992). Note, however, that inhibitory effects in phonological priming are sometimes weak or absent (see, e.g., Praamstra, Meyer, and Levelt 1994, and Radeau, Morais, and Segui 1995). This may be because the inhibitory effects are concealed by strategic factors (see, e.g., Monsell and Hirsh 1998, for discussion).

Models of spoken word recognition like the Cohort model (Marslen-Wilson 1987, 1993), TRACE (McClelland and Elman 1986),

1986), Shortlist (Norris 1994), the Distributed Cohort Model (DCM; Gaskell and Marslen-Wilson 1997), the Neighborhood Activation Model (NAM; Luce and Pisoni 1998) and PARSYN (Luce et al. 2000) differ in very many respects. They all have one thing in common, however. They all share the assumption that, as a listener hears a section of speech, the words that are consistent with that input are considered in parallel, with the respective evidence for each word evaluated relative to the other words.

This relative-evaluation algorithm is implemented in different ways in these models. One way to implement the relative evaluation algorithm is to allow lexical representations to compete directly and actively with one another (as in TRACE, Shortlist and PARSYN). Two other implementations have been proposed. First, as in the NAM and the Cohort model, relative evaluation can occur at a decision stage, where differential degrees of support for candidates are passively compared (i.e., unlike in active competition models, the evaluation has no influence on the activation of competitors). Second, relative evaluation can be achieved via the indirect form of competition or interference that occurs as a connectionist model with highly distributed lexical representations generates a particular activation pattern (as in the DCM).

Although each of these implementations can account for many effects, the available data impose some constraints on the choice between them. A recent eye-tracking study (Dahan et al. 2001b) found effects of a competitor's interference on the target's activation before the complete name of the target had been heard and processed. These data suggest that the evaluation of a candidate's activation proportional to its competitors' activation must take place in a continuous manner. These results thus challenge competition implementations in which relative evaluation only occurs at a discrete stage of processing.

Experiments showing that competition can take place between words beginning at different points in the speech stream (e.g., McQueen et al. 1994) support the implementation of competition via direct links between candidates, and call the plausibility of models with decision-stage competition into question. Direct competition provides a more efficient means than decision-stage competition by which words that do not all start at the same point in the input can be evaluated relative to one another (see McQueen et al. 1995, for further discussion).

2.3. Summary

Speech decoding thus appears to involve the parallel activation of multiple lexical hypotheses, and the relative evaluation of those hypotheses. This process is incremental and continuous. Words are activated even when they match the signal only partially (e.g., when a given stretch of speech can be continued in different ways, a number of different lexical paths will be considered). Furthermore, activation does not stop at the level of word-form representations; it continues through to the semantic level, such that the meanings of competitors can be activated before the word that was actually present in the input can be fully identified. Information thus flows in cascade through the recognition system, with no serial sub-stages in the process.

3. Gradedness in speech decoding

How is lexical activation modulated during the comprehension process? There are two inter-related aspects to this question. The first concerns the parameters which determine whether a given word should enter or leave the competitor set. The second concerns the metric which is used to compute the goodness of fit of any given word to the input. We will argue that words are not activated in an all-or-none fashion. Instead, lexical representations are activated in a graded way. Activation levels reflect the degree of support the speech signal provides for particular words; they change continuously over time as the information in the signal changes. We will also argue that a phoneme-based evaluation metric in the computation of lexical goodness of fit is insufficient. Finer-grained information than can be captured by a phonemic transcription modulates lexical activation.

3.1. The determinants of lexical activation

Our review of the evidence for multiple activation of candidate words and for competition between those candidates suggests that all words that are consistent with the information in the speech signal are considered, and that partial information is sufficient for lexical activation. What are the constraints on this process, however? How much matching material does there have to be in the signal to cause activation? The evidence suggests that the position of the matching information in the word, the length of that word, and the number of lexical competitors it has are all determinants of its activation. The frequency of occurrence of words also plays a role in lexical activation (see, e.g., Dahan, Magnuson, and Tanenhaus 2001a; Luce and Pisoni 1998).

The recognition system appears to be quite intolerant of mismatching information in word-initial position. Marslen-Wilson and Zwitserlood (1989) found, in a Dutch cross-modal priming experiment, that responses for example to *bij*, bee, an associate of *honing*, honey, were faster after listeners had heard the prime *honing* than after they had heard an unrelated prime word. But there was no overall priming effect when the prime rhymed with the base word and indeed shared all segments with the base word except for its initial phoneme, neither when it was another word (*woning*, dwelling) nor when it was a nonword (*foning*). This result suggests that a very strict criterion may be used to determine whether a word is considered as a candidate: Mismatch of one phoneme in word-initial position may be sufficient to block lexical access.

The nature of the difference between the prime words and the base words seems to be critical, however (Connine, Blasko, and Titone 1993). Connine et al. observed cross-modal associative priming for base word primes (e.g., *service* as prime, *tennis* as target) and a weaker priming effect for nonword primes differing from the base words in only one or two features (*zervice-tennis*), but no reliable effect for nonword primes differing from the base words on more than two features (*gervice-tennis*). These featural distances were computed from the number of articulatory features that the two phonemes share (Jakobson, Fant, and Halle 1952). Marslen-Wilson,

Moss, and van Halen (1996) observed a similar pattern of results, using intra-modal (auditory-auditory) priming in Dutch: facilitation was strongest for target words preceded by associates (e.g., *tomaat-rood*, tomato-red, and *tabak-pijp*, tobacco-pipe), weaker when the prime was a nonword which differed by only one feature on its initial segment from the base word (*pomaat-rood*), and weaker still when the difference involved two or more features (*nabak-pijp*). In contrast to the Connine et al. study, however, the difference between the two mismatch conditions was not significant.

Featural distance manipulations have also been carried out using the phoneme monitoring task. The logic here is that phoneme monitoring response latencies reflect degree of lexical activation. Lexical influences on phonemic decision-making have been modeled either as the consequence of top-down feedback from the lexicon on pre-lexical phoneme representations (as in TRACE), or as a consequence of a feedforward process from the lexicon to a level of processing where explicit phoneme decisions are made (as in the Merge model, Norris, McQueen, and Cutler 2000). On either the feedback or feedforward account, if a word is more strongly activated, it will facilitate phonemic decision-making more strongly. Connine et al. (1997) asked listeners to detect the final /t/, for example, in the base word *cabinet*, a minimal mismatch nonword *gabinet* (one feature change on the initial phoneme), a maximal mismatch nonword *mabinet* (many features changed) and a control nonword *shuffinet*. Phoneme monitoring latencies were fastest for targets in base words, slower for targets in minimal mismatch nonwords, slower still for targets in maximal mismatch nonwords, and slowest of all for targets in control nonwords. These results are thus consistent with the claim that lexical activation does not depend on a perfect phonemic match in word-initial position.

Evidence of activation of rhyming words with initial mismatch has also been observed using the eye-tracking paradigm (e.g., listeners look at a picture of a speaker when they hear *beaker*; Allopenna et al. 1998). The tendency to look at pictures of rhyming competitors is, however, weaker than the tendency to look at pictures of competitors which begin in the same way as the spoken word (e.g., looks at a beetle given *beaker*; Allopenna et al. 1998). This finding reflects a general tendency that competitors which begin in the same way as target words are more strongly activated (in spite of perhaps greater mismatch) than rhyme competitors (compare, for example, the results of Zwitserlood, 1989, which gave evidence of activation of *kapitaal* when the initial sounds of *kapitein* were heard, with those of Zwitserlood and Marslen-Wilson, 1989, where there was apparently no activation of *honing* by *woning*). This tendency is likely to be due to the relative position of the mismatching information, to the temporal properties of speech, and to lexical competition. In the Allopenna et al. example, *beetle* may be just as plausible a candidate as *beaker* early in the *beaker* sequence, so for at least some time they are likely to be equally strong competitors. But *speaker* will always be at a disadvantage because of its initial mismatch; it can therefore never become as strong a competitor as the target *beaker*.

Recent support for this view of the dynamics of lexical activation comes from a phoneme monitoring study. Frauenfelder, Scholten, and Content (2001) found evidence of lexical activation of long French words when the words were distorted by a single feature change on their initial phoneme (e.g., *vocabulaire*, vocabulary, produced as *focabulaire*). Responses to target phonemes were faster in these distorted words than in control nonwords, but only when the target phoneme was word-final (i.e., according to Frauenfelder et al., only when enough time had elapsed for the positive evidence later in the word to override the negative effects of the early mismatch).

Frauenfelder et al. (2001) also examined the impact of mismatch occurring later in the input. There was no evidence of activation of *vocabulaire* given *vocabunaire*, for example (i.e., responses to target phonemes in these distorted words, e.g., the final /r/ of *vocabunaire*, were no faster than in control nonwords). This result suggests that the activation of words which have already been activated (given their initial perfect match) is strongly reduced when mismatching material is heard. Soto-Faraco, Sebastián-Gallés, and Cutler (2001) reached a similar conclusion on the basis of a series of cross-modal fragment-priming experiments. Spanish listeners' responses to *abandono*, abandonment, for example, were faster, relative to a control condition, if they had just heard the matching fragment *aban*, and slower if they had just heard the mismatching fragment *abun*, the onset of *abundancia*, abundance. Soto-Faraco et al. argue that this inhibitory effect reflects the joint influence of the mismatching information and lexical competition (e.g., inhibition of *abandono* by *abundancia*).

It appears, therefore, that polysyllabic words which begin in a different way from what was actually heard can be activated in spite of the initial mismatch, and that long words, once activated, are penalized when a later-occurring mismatch occurs. Shorter (i.e., monosyllabic) words, however, appear to be less strongly activated when they mismatch with the input. Research on the effects of initial mismatch with monosyllabic words has suggested that robust activation of any particular monosyllabic candidate depends on how many words are close matches to the signal. Milberg, Blumstein, and Dworetzky (1988) observed intra-modal priming on lexical decisions to targets preceded by nonwords differing from associates of those targets by one or more features on the initial phoneme (e.g., responses to *dog* were faster after the prime *gat* than after an unrelated prime, presumably due to the activation of *cat*). But this effect may depend on the fact that *gat* is itself not a word, leaving *cat* as the best match to the signal. When there is a strong alternative candidate word, however, there may be no activation of mismatching words. Gow (2001), for example, found no evidence of activation (in a cross-modal form-priming experiment) of monosyllabic words like *guns* when listeners heard close lexical competitors like *buns*.

Connine, Blasko, and Wang (1994), also using a cross-modal priming task, presented listeners with auditory stimuli in which the initial sound was ambiguous between two different phonemes, such as a sound half way between /b/ and /p/, and in which both interpretations of the sequence was a word (e.g., [?ɪg], consistent with both *big* and *pig*). Facilitative priming was observed on responses to visually presented associates of both these words (e.g., *little* and *hog*). This suggests that the lexical access process is more tolerant of mismatch when the input differs from a word by less than one phoneme. But this effect was not replicated by Marslen-Wilson et al. (1996): There was no facilitation of responses to *wood*, for example, after hearing [?læŋk], which is consistent with both *plank* and *blank*. Mar-

Marslen-Wilson et al. found a priming effect, however, when only one of the endpoints was a word: Responses to *job*, for example, an associate of *task*, were facilitated when [?ɑsk] was heard, where [?] was ambiguous between /t/ and /d/ and *dask* is a nonword. It therefore again appears to be the case that degree of lexical activation of mismatching words depends on the lexical competitor environment.

Finally, it is important to note that tolerance to mismatching information is modulated by the phonological context. A body of research has examined how the recognition system deals with the variation in the signal caused by phonological processes such as assimilation (see, e.g., Coenen, Zwitserlood, and Boelte 2001; Gaskell and Marslen-Wilson 1996, 1998, 2001; Gow 2001; Marslen-Wilson, Nix, and Gaskell 1995). These studies have shown that words can be recognized in spite of the phonemic changes caused by assimilation, but only when those changes are contextually appropriate. Thus, for example, the word *night* is activated given the input [naɪp], but only if it appears in a context which licenses the assimilation of place of articulation of the final coronal consonant /t/ to bilabial [p], as in *night bus*.

The evidence on the effect of mismatch on lexical activation thus suggests that the lexical access process is not highly tolerant of mismatching information. Words that mismatch with the signal by more than a phoneme are unlikely to be considered as serious candidates if the mismatching information is at or near the beginning of the word, or rapidly rejected as plausible candidates if the mismatch occurs later in the word. The position of the mismatch, the length of the word, the number of lexical competitors, and the phonological context all appear to influence the tolerance of the system. The pattern of results on this issue is complex, however, and further work will be required to establish how these different factors interact in determining lexical activation. Nevertheless, it seems clear that, as speech unfolds over time, candidate words become, remain or cease to be active depending both on the amount of bottom-up support they have and on the amount of support other words have. When the available evidence does not clearly favor one word, all plausible candidates remain activated, but as soon as disambiguating information is available, the system appears to settle rapidly on the winning candidate and to reject the losers (McQueen, Norris, and Cutler 1999; Norris et al. 2000).

3.2. Graded goodness of fit

This view of the dynamics of the lexical access process suggests that each word's activation reflects its moment-by-moment goodness of fit with the available input. What metric is used in this computation? One possibility is that the degree of activation of a word reflects the activation of its components. The simplest metric that could be used to compute a word's activation would be to count the number of components of that word which are consistent with the signal. Word activation could then vary as a function of the number of matching components. This metric would of course depend on a level of processing, prior to lexical access, at which those components would be recognized, and on specification of what those components are.

Theories of speech decoding which assume abstract lexical form representations often also assume prelexical abstract representations. The minimal difference between one word and any other word in the listener's language must be a phonemic difference (a word's nearest lexical neighbor cannot differ from that word by less than one phoneme). One obvious candidate for the abstract representations that exist at the prelexical level is therefore the phoneme, as indeed is instantiated in Shortlist and TRACE. Other theories have questioned the benefits of an intermediate analysis of the signal, since this may discard useful acoustic information. For these models, the degree of activation of a word reflects the similarity between the signal and its non-decomposable form representation (Klatt 1979, 1989), or all stored traces (Goldinger 1998). Nevertheless, the assumption of an abstract prelexical level in many models has led to a focus on the effects of abstract differences (such as phonemic differences) on lexical activation.

Could lexical activation thus depend simply on the number of matching phonemes each word has with a given input? The results of the studies on mismatch in lexical access described above suggest that lexical activation levels cannot be based on this simple metric. Several of those studies have shown that subphonemic differences influence lexical activation. Connine et al. (1993, 1997) showed that the number of features with which a phoneme mismatches a lexically specified phoneme influences the degree of activation of that word.

Further evidence that lexical activation varies as a function of subcategorical differences comes from an auditory-auditory associative priming study by Andruski, Blumstein and Burton (1994). Lexical decision responses to *fruit*, for example, were faster when *fruit* was preceded by *pear* than when it was preceded by an unrelated word (*jet*). This priming effect was modulated, however, by the Voice Onset Time (VOT) of the initial unvoiced stop consonants of the related primes (e.g., of the [p] of *pear*). The [p] was presented in its normal form, with the VOT reduced by one-third, and with the VOT reduced by two-thirds. The reductions made the VOT less like that of a prototypical [p] and more like that of the voiced counterpart [b], but both types of reduction produced tokens which were still heard as [p]. Although all three forms of the word *pear* primed *fruit*, responses were significantly slower after the more extremely edited prime had been heard than after the less extremely edited prime or the natural prime. These results suggest again that lexical activation is graded: words beginning with unvoiced stops appear to have been more weakly activated when their stops were shorter than normal than when their stops were of normal duration. Similar effects have also been observed using the identity priming task, where target words were preceded either by the same natural tokens of those words, or by tokens with shortened VOTs (Utman, Blumstein, and Burton 2000).

Yet another demonstration that lexical activation is modulated by fine-grained information in the speech signal has arisen from research on assimilation. As mentioned above, this research has shown that listeners can recognize the word *night* given the input [naɪp] but only if it appears in an appropriate context, such as *night bus*. Recent data suggests that the recognition system is sensitive to subphonemic cues to assimilation (Gow 2002): The [raɪp] in *right berry* is not the same as the [raɪp] in *ripe berry*, and this allows listeners to resolve potential lexical ambiguities caused by assimilation.

The influence of subphonemic variation on lexical activation has also been observed in studies examining the perception of words and nonwords containing mismatching acoustic-phonetic information (Dahan et al. 2001b; Marslen-Wilson and Warren 1994; McQueen et al. 1999; Streeter and Nigro 1979; Whalen 1984, 1991). Such items are created by cross-splicing sequences that originate from different words and nonwords. For example, a cross-spliced version of a non-word like *smob* can be constructed by concatenating the initial portion (up to the vowel) of the word *smog* or the nonword *smod* with the final consonant of a token of the nonword *smob* (i.e., smo[g/d] + [smo]b). Although these cross-spliced versions would both consist of the phonemic sequence /smɒb/, the vocalic portion would contain formant-transition information consistent with a velar [g] or a dental [d], which would mismatch with the final bilabial stop release burst [b]. A variety of lexical and phonetic tasks have shown that the lexical status of the cross-spliced portions of such stimuli (e.g., /smɒ/ from the word *smog* or the nonword *smod*) influences how much effect the mismatching coarticulatory information has (see Dahan et al. 2001b; Marslen-Wilson and Warren 1994; and McQueen et al. 1999 for further details). The interaction of the effects of subphonemic information and lexical information in tasks which probe lexical activation shows that subcategorical information influences processes at the lexical level.

All of these subphonemic effects contradict the suggestion that word activation is computed on the basis of the number of matching phonemes. More generally, they challenge the view that the prelexical stage is phonemic and discrete. If a categorical phonemic representation of the speech signal were computed at the prelexical level, and this were to occur in a serial fashion, such that a phonemic parse of the input was completed prior to lexical access, the lexical level would not be sensitive to featural differences among phonemes. One phoneme would be like any other, and lexical goodness of fit would have to be based on some measure of the number of matching phonemes. Such models can therefore be rejected.

These results, however, are consistent with models in which pre-lexical representations are activated in proportion to their acoustic match with the input and in which a word's activation in turn reflects the prelexical activation pattern. Although the manipulations in the above studies have all been subcategorical, the effects can still be described phonemically. Number of mismatching features, for example, can be represented in terms of degree of support for particular phonemes. Likewise, subcategorical variation in VOT can be represented by the relative activation of voiced versus unvoiced stops, and subcategorical mismatch in cross-spliced words can modulate the amount of support for each of the phonemes involved in the splice.

These results are thus consistent with models like TRACE and Shortlist in which the prelexical representations are phonemic. In these models, information spreads continuously up to the lexical level. There is no serial stage at which an absolute phonemic categorization of the input is made prior to lexical access. TRACE is an interactive-activation model in which activation cascades continuously between representations (McClelland and Elman 1986). Although in the implemented version of Shortlist there is categorical phonemic input to the lexicon, this implementation is considered to be a mere approximation of a more continuous process (Norris 1994; Norris et al. 2000). If the degree of activation of prelexical phoneme representations can vary continuously, and this activation can spread to lexical representations, then subphonemic effects on lexical activation can be explained. The present results would of course also be consistent with models in which the prelexical representations are larger or smaller than the phoneme, so long as those representations have graded activation values and pass activation continuously up to the lexicon.

3.3. *Phonemic decoding is not sufficient*

Results from several recent experiments, however, impose stronger constraints on the granularity of the lexical activation process. In these new experiments, the relative activation of different words sharing the same phonemic sequences was measured. In contrast to the studies described above, therefore, the information that was varied in these new studies did not offer differential support for alternative phonemes. Instead, it provided support for one or another lexical interpretation of the same phonemic sequence. As we describe in more detail below, there is no straightforward way to represent this kind of information in terms only of the relative degree of activation of different phonemes.

Tabossi et al. (2000) have shown in Italian that the phonetic consequences of syllabic structure on the realization of phoneme sequences affect the activation of words that match those sequences. A word that mismatched the syllabic structure of the input (e.g., *si.lenzio*, silence, when the input consisted of the syllable fragment [sil]) received less support from the input than a word that matched this structure (e.g., *sil.vestre*, silvan). The reverse was true when the input was the fragment [si.l], taken from *si.lenzio*. On a purely phonemic analysis, the fragments were identical. Nevertheless, the subphonemic difference between the two types of fragment (cued at least in part by a small but robust durational difference in the vowels) seems to have been fed forward to the lexicon, influencing word activation. It might appear that the results could be modeled in terms of the degree of activation of prelexical phonemic representations (the amount of activation of /s/, /i/ and /l/, for example). But, because the evidence does not at the same time favor alternative phonemes and thus alternative words with different phonemic transcriptions, there is no way in such an account for the lexical level to distinguish between the different types of input. Additional, non-phonemic information must therefore influence lexical activation.

Spinelli, McQueen, and Cutler (2003), in a study of liaison in French, examined the activation of vowel- and consonant-initial words (e.g., *oignon*, onion, and *rognon*, kidney) in phrases like *C'est le dernier oignon* (It's the last onion). In this context, the final [ʁ] of *dernier* is produced and resyllabified with the following syllable, making the phrase phonemically identical to *C'est le dernier rognon*. Acoustic analyses revealed however that there were reliable durational differences in the pivotal consonants depending on the speaker's intentions (e.g., the medial [ʁ] was longer in *dernier rog-*

non than in *dernier oignon*). In cross-modal identity priming experiments, only responses to the words that the speaker intended to utter were facilitated reliably. Although in both cases the information was consistent with an [ʁ], the durational distinction appears to have influenced the lexical level, helping listeners to retrieve the speaker's intended message.

One way of accommodating these results on syllabification and liaison is to assume that prelexical representations are allophonic variations of phonemes, rather than context-independent phonemes (as in the PARSYN model, Luce et al. 2000). Allophones are variants of phonemes that are conditioned by the context in which they occur. This context can be the position of the phoneme within a syllable (such as syllable onset or coda), or whether the syllable in which the phoneme occurs is stressed or unstressed.

Allophonic analysis of the speech signal could account for Tabossi et al.'s (2000) results (e.g., the [l] in [si.l] could be a different allophone from that in [sil], leading to differential activation of *silenzio* and *silvestre*). Likewise, the results of Spinelli et al. (2003) could be explained if liaison consonants (like the [ʁ] *in dernier oignon*) provided more support for a syllable-final allophone while word-initial consonants (like the [ʁ] in *dernier rognon*) provided more support for a syllable-initial allophone (note that on this account, resyllabification in liaison contexts is incomplete).

An allophonic model could also account for the effects on word activation of lexical stress or pitch-accent patterns in languages that use these prosodic factors. Lexical stress information appears to influence the degree of activation of words in languages like Spanish (Soto-Faraco et al. 2001) and Dutch (Cutler and Donselaar 2001), that is, in languages where this information is important for lexical disambiguation (see Cutler, Dahan, and Donselaar 1997, for a review). Soto-Faraco et al., for example, found an inhibitory stress mismatch effect in cross-modal fragment priming (e.g., the fragment *prinCI-*, the beginning of *prinCIpio*, which is stressed on the second syllable, produced slower responses to the visual target *principe*, which is stressed on the first syllable, *PRINcipe*, than did an unrelated fragment).

It has been suggested that lexical stress information is not used in the initial lexical access process in English because it is not useful for lexical disambiguation (Cutler 1986). More recent research, however, has shown that lexical activation is modulated by stress information in English, but less so for native speakers than for Dutch-English bilinguals (Cooper, Cutler, and Wales 2002). Stress information may modify word activation more strongly in the bilinguals because they have had more opportunity to learn the value of this information (i.e., in processing the native language, Dutch). These results therefore support the suggestion that suprasegmental information is used to the extent that it is useful. In fixed-stress languages like French, therefore, where lexical stress information is not contrastive, this information does not appear to modulate lexical activation (Dupoux et al. 1997; Peperkamp and Dupoux 2002). A different kind of suprasegmental information, that for pitch-accent patterns in Japanese words, also appears to be used in lexical access (Cutler and Otake 1999). Again, pitch-accent information can be used for lexical disambiguation in Japanese.

Suprasegmental influences on lexical activation could be captured by models with prelexical allophonic representations. Allophonic as well as phonemic models, however, are challenged by experiments which have examined the recognition of sequences which, on either a phonemic or allophonic transcription, would be lexically ambiguous. Gow and Gordon (1995) compared the lexical activation generated by ambiguous sequences that consist of one or two words (such as *two lips* or *tulips*). Their results suggest that word activation can be modulated by the presence of acoustic cues marking word onsets in the signal. Evidence for the activation of a word embedded in the sequence (e.g., *lips*) was found in two-word sequences (e.g., *two lips*), that is, when word-onset cues may be available, but not in matched one-word sequences (e.g., *tulips*).

Recent research on the activation of words embedded in the onsets of longer words also challenges models which only encode purely segmental information (even allophonic models with context-sensitive segments). Davis, Marslen-Wilson, and Gaskell (2002) and Salverda, Dahan, and McQueen (submitted) have shown that subtle durational differences between productions of an ambiguous sequence (e.g., /pɑn/ in Dutch), as either a monosyllabic word (*pan*, id.) or as the onset of a longer word (*panda*, id.), bias listeners' interpretation of the sequence in favor of the speaker's intentions. For example, Salverda et al. demonstrated that the temporary activation of the embedded word *pan*, upon hearing the carrier word *panda*, was larger when the syllable *pan* was of a longer duration. This bias in word activation may arise from the tendency (in the sample Salverda et al. recorded, and presumably in the Dutch language in general) for monosyllabic words to be longer than equivalent sequences which form the initial portion of polysyllabic words. Salverda et al. suggest that this may be the result of segmental lengthening at the edge of prosodic domains.

3.4. Summary

There is a growing body of evidence demonstrating fine-grained modulation of the amount of support for particular words during lexical access. A model in which the number of matching phonemes between each candidate word and the input are counted is therefore not realistic. Nor are models in which there is a discrete and categorical stage of processing prior to lexical access: Just as word-form activation appears to spread continuously to word meanings, so too does the activation of prelexical representations spread to word forms.

Some results on the spread of fine-grained information to the lexicon are consistent with a variety of prelexical representational options: These are experiments in which the information could be used to evaluate the relative support in the input for different phonemic sequences. But other results do impose constraints on the nature of prelexical processing: These are experiments which have shown that there is variation in lexical activation even when only one phonemic sequence is strongly supported by the signal (i.e., where two signals with the same phonemic transcription have differential effects on the activation of words). A purely phonemic analysis would not capture allophonic variation in the speech signal (e.g., that due to syllable structure or lexical stress patterns); nevertheless, such variation does appear to influence lexical activation. Allophonic representations (i.e., one for each contextually-constrained variant of each phoneme) may therefore be preferred. But there is now evidence that lexical activation is also sensitive to differences that cannot be captured by allophonic representations.

It is not yet clear how best to model the latest data on lexical activation. One can consider two possible approaches. One is to maintain prelexical segmental representations (e.g., in terms of phonemes), but to add a parallel level of suprasegmental representations (i.e., representation of syllabic structures, lexical stress patterns, prosodic-domain boundaries, etc.). It is interesting to note here that the fine-grained information which appears to modulate lexical activation, while it can be described as subphonemic, or even suballophonic, can also be viewed as suprasegmental, in that it involves prosodic structures which are larger than the segment. On this account, word activation would be modulated by the match with both segmental and suprasegmental representations. An attractive feature of this approach is that it provides a unified account of, on the one hand, the data that could perhaps be explained by a model with prelexical allophonic representations (e.g., Spinelli et al. 2003; Soto-Faraco et al. 2001; Tabossi et al. 2000) and, on the other hand, the data which challenge allophonic models (Davis et al. 2002; Gow and Gordon 1995; Salverda et al. submitted).

The other possibility is to reject a prelexical level of processing and to assume instead that the signal is directly mapped onto lexical representations. These representations could consist of prototypes of the form of each word (as in the model proposed by Klatt 1979, 1989) or of the combination of all the traces associated with each word (as in the episodic view of Goldinger 1998). In both of these types of direct-mapping model, considerable detail about the acoustic-phonetic form of words can be stored at the lexical level. Either class of direct-mapping model could thus account for the sensitivity of the lexical access process to all the fine-grained aspects of the input, as long as those cues are word specific.

Speech decoding therefore involves the parallel graded activation of multiple candidate words. This process is continuous: There are no discrete sub-stages of processing – information flows in cascade from the prelexical to the lexical level, and from representations of word form to representations of word meaning. This process is also graded: The activation of representations at each of these levels changes continuously over time, as information from the speech signal accrues, and as different candidate words compete with each other. Differences in degree of lexical activation appear to reflect aspects of the speech signal which cannot be captured by a purely segmental description of that signal.

4. Speech production

The view that the processing of phonological information in spoken word comprehension is continuous and graded stands in stark contrast to the view that lexical access in speech production is staged and categorical (Levelt et al. 1999). Why might the flow of information through the speech encoding process, and the nature of that information, be different from that in speech decoding? In this section, we will examine the arguments concerning these two issues in speech production, in the light of the comprehension evidence.

4.1. Flow of information in production and perception

We have argued that, in perception, activation spreads continuously from the prelexical level to the word-form level, and on up to the meaning level. But in WEAVER++ (Levelt et al. 1999; see also Roelofs, this volume), word-form production consists of two discrete stages of processing (Levelt et al. refer to a rift between the conceptual/syntactic domain and the phonological/articulatory domain). There is spread of activation involving multiple words between the conceptual and lemma levels (lemmas are syntactic representations of words which code grammatical properties like gender). There is also spread of activation among multiple representations at the word-form and phonological encoding levels. But there is a discrete step between the lemma and word-form representations: Only the form of the selected lemma is activated.

Levelt et al. motivate this assumption of seriality in two ways: first, on the theoretical grounds that it would be counterproductive to activate unnecessary phonology; and second, on empirical grounds (see, e.g., Levelt et al. 1991). More recent experiments, however, have shown that the strongest version of this seriality hypothesis is not tenable (e.g., Peterson and Savoy [1998] presented evidence for parallel activation of the phonological forms of both members of synonym pairs like *couch-sofa*). Levelt et al. (1999) therefore suggest that multiple activation of word forms may be limited to cases where more than one lemma is selected, as when a near-synonym has to be produced under time pressure. The assumption of seriality in WEAVER++ can thus be preserved: Only word-forms for selected lemmas are activated, but there are some circumstances where more than one lemma can be selected.

In addition to the findings of Peterson and Savoy (1998), Jescheniak and Schriefers (1998) and Cutting and Ferreira (1999) have provided evidence suggesting that, at least under some circumstances, activation does flow continuously from semantics to phonology during speech production. Such results, while they can be explained by the WEAVER++ model (see Levelt et al. 1999 for discussion), also support the assumptions of continuous spreading activation in the DSMSG model (Dell 1986; Dell et al. 1997; Dell and Gordon, this volume). The DSMSG model is an interactive two-step account of lexical access in production. The first step is lemma access, the second is phonological access. During lemma access, activation spreads from semantic units to lemma units but also cascades down to phonological units. In addition to this feedforward activation, there is positive feedback from lemmas to semantic representations and from phonological representations to lemmas. The most activated lemma nodes are therefore the target and its semantically and formally related neighbors: The most highly activated lemma node is selected. The second step begins when the selected lemma node is given a large jolt of activation. Activation then spreads to the phonological units associated with the selected word, and, via the feedback connections, back to lemma and semantic representations. In contrast to WEAVER++, the DSMSG model therefore embodies an interactive rather than modular theory. But, because activation from the serially

ordered jolts dominates the activation pattern, the model is only locally interactive. Activation at the semantic level has only mild effects at the phonological level and vice-versa. Nevertheless, the
model correctly predicts that there are situations where there is
(weak) activation of phonological representations that are not required for the utterance that is actually produced.

In the production literature, therefore, there is no consensus on
whether information flow is staged or cascaded. This contrasts with
the agreement that has been reached that processing operates in cascade in speech comprehension. We suggest that there are two reasons
for this difference. The first is the evidence. Our review of the comprehension literature makes clear that there is overwhelming empirical support for continuous flow of information up to the meaning
level. The data on cascaded processing in production are scarcer, and
what results there are can be explained by a staged model (Levelt et
al. 1999).

The second reason is based on arguments about the nature of
speech encoding and decoding. Levelt et al. (1999) have argued that
activating the phonology of an unintended word during speech production is unlikely to assist phonological encoding, and thus that it is
inefficient to activate unnecessary phonology. This is a key motivation for the assumption of staged processing in WEAVER++. This is
also a motivation for the activation jolts in the DSMSG model, which
act to bias phonological encoding strongly in favor of the intended
word. Limited cascade (i.e., only enough to activate the phonology of
the intended word before lemma selection is completed) could be of
some benefit, however. As Dell et al. (1997) point out, it might be
helpful to have access to the phonological form of a candidate lemma
to ensure that its form is available before that lemma is selected. It is
to the speaker's advantage if (s)he chooses a lemma whose form will
later be easy to find. Dell et al. claim that this would reduce the incidence of tip-of-the-tongue (TOT) states, where the speaker makes a
commitment to a word for which the phonological form is not acces-
sible (or only partially available).

Note, however, that this motivation for limited cascade of information in production is dependent on the assumption of feedback: for
a benefit to accrue, the phonological level must be able to impact on

processing at the lemma level. It is therefore not clear whether even limited cascade would be beneficial to speech production. Only models with feedback could use cascaded processing to reduce the number of TOT states. In a model without feedback, continuous flow from the lemma level to the wordform level would not help to reduce TOT states. This potential benefit of cascaded processing thus depends on the additional assumption of feedback in the production system. There is no evidence which makes it necessary to make this assumption (Levelt et al. 1999; see Dell and Gordon, this volume, and Roelofs, this volume, for further discussion of the evidence for and against feedback in the production system). In the absence of good evidence in support of feedback, no strong argument can be made for the benefits of even limited cascaded processing in speech encoding. It may therefore be better to interpret the results which can be taken as evidence for cascade in production (Cutting and Ferreira 1999; Jescheniak and Schriefers 1998; Peterson and Savoy 1998) in ways which are consistent with a feedforward staged model (i.e., as Levelt et al. 1999 do). It is clear, however, that, irrespective of whether or not there is feedback in phonological encoding, widespread cascade of information right through the production system would be counterproductive because it would make speaking harder.

One might want to argue that cascaded processing in perception is also counterproductive. It might be unproductive to activate unnecessary meanings during comprehension, that is, the meanings of the candidate words which lose the lexical competition process. Would it not be efficient to restrict meaning activation to that of the winning word form? One could imagine a two-stage process: The first stage would be to select one word form on the basis of its fit with the signal; the second stage would be to access its meaning and integrate it into the context.

The listener's task, however, is to derive the message the talker intended from an infinite range of possible utterances. Furthermore, the input to phonological processing in perception is more likely to be impoverished than the input to phonological processing in production. As we have argued earlier, cascaded processing from the acoustic signal to the lexical-form level assists in the decoding process when information is missing from or not yet available in the input.

Likewise, it is also useful for information to cascade from the word-form level to the meaning level in perception. Some ambiguities may be impossible to resolve on the basis of form-based information alone (e.g., those due to polysemous words). Since meaning constraints are thus sometimes essential for comprehension, it makes sense to use them as soon as possible. Higher-level information may then also help to resolve temporary ambiguities in the signal (i.e., before disambiguating form information has been heard). Activating the candidates' meanings incrementally allows some candidates to be disfavored on the basis of the integration of their meaning within the context.

A number of studies have indeed demonstrated very early effects of context on spoken word recognition. In these studies, listeners heard spoken sentences while event-related brain potentials were recorded. As the initial sounds of a word that matched or mismatched the context were heard, but before the acoustic information allowed listeners to distinguish the word from its competitors, brain responses were shown to vary as a function of the semantic congruency of the word (Van Berkum et al. in press; Van den Brink, Brown, and Hagoort 2001; Van Petten et al. 1999). Contextual influences occurring before sufficient acoustic information has accrued for listeners to be able to identify a word uniquely show not only that listeners have rapid access to word meanings, but also that they use this information in their evaluation of the incoming speech signal as soon as that information is available. Since the meaning level can therefore assist in the comprehension process, it is highly beneficial to pass information continuously up to that level.

This comparison of speech production with speech comprehension thus suggests that the two systems may differ with respect to how information flows during talking versus listening. There is more evidence in favor of continuous flow of information in comprehension than in production, and that which is available on production can be explained by a staged model. Even in production models with cascaded processing there are limits on the extent to which information flows between the different stages of lexical encoding. Furthermore, there are good design reasons why there may be cascaded processing in perception and staged processing in production. The nature of the task faced by the listener makes fully cascaded processing valuable in comprehension, while the nature of the task faced by the talker makes fully cascaded flow of information in production detrimental.

4.2. Granularity in production

We argued above that the lexical level of the comprehension system is sensitive to fine-grained (i.e., subphonemic) differences in the speech signal. This means that those differences must be a systematic part of the signal (i.e., they are not just noise). It therefore follows that the speech production system must produce those differences in a systematic fashion. In WEAVER++ (see Levelt et al. 1999 for details), however, a word form in production is a "bare-bones" representation, consisting of a sequence of phonemes that is unsyllabified and has no stress pattern (unless the word has an irregular stress pattern). Syllables and regular stress patterns are built on the fly during "prosodification" – a post-lexical stage of phonological encoding which computes, among other things, the syllabification of phoneme strings within phonological phrases.

One of the reasons which Levelt et al. use to motivate this assumption is that syllabification depends on surrounding context (e.g., the final /v/ of *save* is syllable final, but, at least on some accounts, will be syllable initial in the cliticized phrase *save it*). That is, the syllabification of a word is not fixed and immutable (see Levelt et al. 1999 for further discussion). In WEAVER++, therefore, there is no lexical representation of, for example, the duration of the first syllable of *panda* or of the first and only syllable of *pan*: Both syllables are simply the string of phonemes /p/, /ɑ/, /n/. But listeners are sensitive to the durational differences between tokens of syllables like /pɑn/ coming from these different contexts, and talkers tend to produce such syllables in a systematic way (Davis et al. 2002; Salverda et al. submitted). Similarly, listeners are sensitive to other fine-grained details in the speech signal (e.g., that due to syllabification, liaison or assimilation; see above), and talkers produce those details. How then might a model like WEAVER++ account for this production behavior?

One possibility is that, in the context of WEAVER++, the post-lexical prosodification procedure could be enriched with more prosodic knowledge (e.g., in the embedded word case, knowledge that results in segmental lengthening at the edge of prosodic domains). Specification of this prosodic hierarchy would run in parallel with the lexical-segmental encoding process, and these prosodic specifications could then be added to the phonological words generated during prosodification (i.e., the same process as in the existing model, but with a richer prosodic component). During production, therefore, there would be no lexical specification of segmental duration (or any other subphonemic detail) in particular words: Durational differences would emerge as a result of the specifications provided by the prosodic hierarchy.

In perception, however, as the evidence we have summarized shows, the recognition system uses subphonemic details to modulate the activation of lexical representations. Perceptual word-form representations must therefore be sensitive in some way to these subphonemic differences. Note that this does not mean that each individual lexical representation in the perceptual system must include detailed acoustic information (e.g., durational specifications). As we suggested earlier, subphonemic acoustic information could influence the activation of prelexical suprasegmental representations, which in turn would modulate word-form representations. A word's activation would thus change as a function of a match to an abstract specification, rather than as the result of a direct match with subphonemic information. For example, the activation of *pan* could be boosted if the duration of the syllable [pan] indicated that the word *pan* was aligned with the edge of a prosodic domain. Irrespective of how exactly subphonemic information exerts its effect on lexical activation in perception, though, it is clear that this information can arise from a production system in which that information is not coded lexically.

The proposal that fine-grained information modulates lexical activation in perception but is specified post-lexically in production is consistent with our claim that the two processing systems are fine-tuned to the different task demands of speech decoding and encoding. The listener needs to be able to recognize that a word in an utterance is a token of a particular word, and knowledge that goes beyond that word's segmental make-up can assist in that process (and indeed appears to do so). Phonetic detail assists comprehension because the more information there is for listeners to use, the easier it will be for them to distinguish one word from another.

The talker, on the other hand, needs to build an utterance given a conceptual message. While the segmental material for a given word must be stored lexically and retrieved when that word is to be spoken, it could be much more efficient to complete the phonological encoding of that word in its utterance context using post-lexical rules. There is certainly no need for phonetic detail at the stage of lemma selection, where the choice between words is semantic. There might also be no need for phonetic or phonological details, beyond the bare segmental information, at the word-form stage, since words are selected on the basis of semantic specifications (i.e., spread of activation from lemmas). There may therefore be an interesting asymmetry between the lexical selection process in perception, where phonetic/phonological information is primary and semantic information is secondary, and the lexical selection process in production, where semantic information is primary and phonetic/phonological information is secondary.

The evidence on subphonemic detail in the speech signal is thus consistent with the assumptions of "bare-bones" word-form representations and post-lexical prosodification in WEAVER++. But this evidence challenges another assumption of this model: the mental syllabary (Levelt et al. 1999; Levelt and Wheeldon 1994). The output of the phonological encoding (prosodification) stage in WEAVER++ forms the input to the phonetic encoding stage, where gestural programs for articulation are generated. According to the theory, gestural programs for high-frequency syllables are stored, in precompiled form, in a syllabary (there is also a second mechanism for the phonetic encoding of infrequent or novel syllables). Talkers tend to use only a relatively small inventory of common syllables for most of their speech output (one can estimate that 500 syllables are enough to cover 80% of all English speech, Levelt et al. 1999, and 85% of all Dutch speech, Schiller et al. 1996). The syllabary is thus motivated by the idea that it would be efficient to store precompiled motor programs for a set of frequently recurring syllabic patterns.

The production data associated with the study of subphonemic effects in perception suggest, however, that each token of a syllable that a talker produces is not always the same. The [ʁ] in the third syllable of *dernier rognon* will tend to be longer than the [ʁ] in the third syllable of *dernier oignon* (Spinelli et al. 2003), the [l] in the second syllable of *two lips* will tend to be longer than the [l] in *tulips* (Gow and Gordon 1995), the syllable [pɑn] will tend to be longer when the talker intends the word *pan* than when the talker wants to say *panda* (Salverda et al. submitted), and so on. These findings call into question the motivation for the syllabary that speech consists by and large of a relatively small number of recurring patterns, and, more generally, cast doubt on the notion of the syllabary.

Levelt et al. (1999) point out that the fine detail of syllables can change as a consequence of coarticulation (where motor instructions for successive syllables overlap in time). But this suggestion concerns a process which occurs after the syllabary has been accessed and is therefore consistent with the syllabary hypothesis. In the cases of subphonemic differences which disambiguate words or sequences of words which would otherwise be identical, however, these differences need to be specified before phonetic encoding. That is, the phonetic encoder needs, as part of its input, a specification of the difference between the two readings of a phonemically ambiguous sequence. If the fine detail were to arise at the prosodification stage (as we have suggested it might in order to generate the segmental duration differences between *dernier rognon* and *dernier rognon*, between *two lips* and *tulips*, between *pan* and *panda,* etc.), then it would be specified before the syllabary was accessed. The same would be true if the details were coded at the lexical level in the model. But if there is only one gestural program for each syllable, syllabary access would obliterate these prespecified distinctions.

It seems clear that, in any account of speech production, there must be a means by which speakers can generate very fine-grained, but nonetheless systematic phonetic details. In WEAVER++, it appears that lexical or prosodic specifications would have to be able to modify motor programs after they have been accessed from the syllabary. This, however, seems to undermine any benefit that could be had from the storage of only a limited number of precompiled syllabic motor programs.

5. Conclusions

We have argued that speech decoding is continuous and graded. Information flows through the recognition system in cascade all the way up to the meaning level, with no discrete processing stages. In this system, multiple words are evaluated in parallel; these candidate words compete with each other, and their activation is modulated by subphonemic detail in the speech signal. We have suggested that such a system is well suited to the demands of listening to speech.

The way that phonetic and phonological information is processed in speech encoding appears to be very different. Lexical access is a two-stage process, with, on some accounts, strict seriality, and, on other accounts, limited cascade between levels. In no current production model is there massive parallel activation of word forms. Furthermore, it appears that subphonemic detail need not be specified at the lexical level in production. Instead, this type of detail could be filled in by post-lexical rules. Again, this view appears well suited to the task demands of speaking. The evidence on subphonemic detail in the speech signal, however, calls into question the hypothesis that the phonetic encoding of speech involves a mental syllabary. This evidence therefore demands not only the development of speech decoding models which can accommodate subphonemic effects but also an account of the genesis of these effects within models of how talkers encode speech.

References

Allopenna, Paul D., James S. Magnuson and Michael K. Tanenhaus
    1998   Tracking the time course of spoken word recognition using eye movements: Evidence for continuous mapping models. *Journal of Memory and Language* 38: 419-439.
Andruski, Jean E., Sheila E. Blumstein and Martha W. Burton
    1994   The effect of subphonetic differences on lexical access. *Cognition* 52: 163-187.

Cluff, Michael S. and Paul A. Luce
1990   Similarity neighborhoods of spoken two-syllable words: Retroactive effects on multiple activation. *Journal of Experimental Psychology: Human Perception and Performance* 16: 551-563.
Coenen, Else, Pienie Zwitserlood and Jens Bölte
2001   Variation and assimilation in German: Consequences for lexical access and representation. *Language and Cognitive Processes* 16: 535-564.
Connine, Cynthia M., Dawn G. Blasko and Debra Titone
1993   Do the beginnings of spoken words have a special status in auditory word recognition? *Journal of Memory and Language* 32: 193-210.
Connine, Cynthia M., Dawn G. Blasko and Jian Wang
1994   Vertical similarity in spoken word recognition: Multiple lexical activation, individual differences, and the role of sentence context. *Perception & Psychophysics* 56: 624-636.
Connine, Cynthia M., Debra Titone, Thomas Deelman and Dawn G. Blasko
1997   Similarity mapping in spoken word recognition. *Journal of Memory and Language* 37: 463-480.
Cooper, Nicole, Anne Cutler and Roger Wales
2002   Constraints of lexical stress on lexical access in English: Evidence from native and nonnative listeners. *Language and Speech* 45: 207-228.
Cutler, Anne
1986   *Forbear* is a homophone: Lexical prosody does not constrain lexical access. *Language and Speech* 29: 201-220.
Cutler, Anne, Delphine Dahan and Wilma van Donselaar
1997   Prosody in the comprehension of spoken language: A literature review. *Language and Speech* 40: 141-201.
Cutler, Anne and Wilma van Donselaar
2001   *Voornaam* is not a homophone: Lexical prosody and lexical access in Dutch. *Language and Speech* 44: 171-195.
Cutler, Anne and Takashi Otake
1999   Pitch accent in spoken-word recognition in Japanese. *Journal of the Acoustical Society of America* 105: 1877-1888.
Cutting, J. Cooper and Victor S. Ferreira
1999   Semantic and phonological information flow in the production lexicon. *Journal of Experimental Psychology: Learning, Memory, and Cognition* 25: 318-344.
Dahan, Delphine, James S. Magnuson and Michael K. Tanenhaus
2001a   Time course of frequency effects in spoken-word recognition: Evidence from eye movements. *Cognitive Psychology* 42: 317-367.

Dahan, Delphine, James S. Magnuson, Michael K. Tanenhaus and Ellen M. Hogan
2001b   Subcategorical mismatches and the time course of lexical access: Evidence for lexical competition. *Language and Cognitive Processes* 16: 507-534.

Davis, Matt H., William D. Marslen-Wilson and M. Gareth Gaskell
2002   Leading up the lexical garden-path: Segmentation and ambiguity in spoken word recognition. *Journal of Experimental Psychology: Human Perception and Performance* 28: 218-244.

Dell, Gary S.
1986   A spreading-activation theory of retrieval in sentence production. *Psychological Review* 93: 283-321.

Dell, Gary S., Myrna F. Schwartz, Nadine Martin, Eleanor M. Saffran and Deborah A. Gagnon
1997   Lexical access in aphasic and nonaphasic speakers. *Psychological Review* 104: 801-838.

Dupoux, Emmanuel, Christophe Pallier, Núria Sebastián-Gallés and Jacques Mehler
1997   A destressing deafness in French. *Journal of Memory and Language* 36: 399-421.

Frauenfelder, Uli H., Mark Scholten and Alain Content
2001   Bottom-up inhibition in lexical selection: Phonological mismatch effects in spoken word recognition. *Language and Cognitive Processes* 16: 583-607.

Gaskell, M. Gareth and William D. Marslen-Wilson
1996   Phonological variation and inference in lexical access. *Journal of Experimental Psychology: Human Perception and Performance* 22: 144-158.

Gaskell, M. Gareth and William D. Marslen-Wilson
1997   Integrating form and meaning: A distributed model of speech perception. *Language and Cognitive Processes* 12: 613-656.

Gaskell, M. Gareth and William D. Marslen-Wilson
1998   Mechanisms of phonological inference in speech perception. *Journal of Experimental Psychology: Human Perception and Performance* 24: 380-396.

Gaskell, M. Gareth and William D. Marslen-Wilson
2001   Lexical ambiguity resolution and spoken word recognition: Bridging the gap. *Journal of Memory and Language* 44: 325-349.

Goldinger, Stephen D.
1998   Echoes of echoes?: An episodic theory of lexical access. *Psychological Review* 105: 251-279.

Goldinger, Stephen D., Paul A. Luce, David B. Pisoni and Joanne K. Marcario
1992   Form-based priming in spoken word recognition: The roles of competition and bias. *Journal of Experimental Psychology: Learning, Memory, and Cognition* 18: 1211-1238.

Gow, David W.
2001   Assimilation and anticipation in continuous spoken word recognition. *Journal of Memory and Language* 45: 133-159.
Gow, David W.
2002   Does English coronal place assimilation create lexical ambiguity? *Journal of Experimental Psychology: Human Perception and Performance* 28: 163-179.
Gow, David W. and Peter C. Gordon
1995   Lexical and prelexical influences on word segmentation: evidence from priming. *Journal of Experimental Psychology: Human Perception and Performance* 21: 344-359.
Jakobson, Roman, C. Gunnar M. Fant and Morris Halle
1952   *Preliminaries to Speech Analysis: The Distinctive Features and their Correlates.* Cambridge, MA: Massachusetts Institute of Technology Press.
Jescheniak, Jörg D. and Herbert Schriefers
1998   Discrete serial versus cascaded processing in lexical access in speech production: Further evidence from the co-activation of near-synonyms. *Journal of Experimental Psychology: Learning, Memory, and Cognition* 24: 1256-1274.
Klatt, Dennis H
1979   Speech perception: A model of acoustic-phonetic analysis and lexical access. *Journal of Phonetics* 7: 279-312.
Klatt, Dennis H.
1989   Review of selected models of speech perception. In: William D. Marslen-Wilson (ed.), *Lexical Representation and Process*, 169-226. Cambridge, MA: Massachusetts Institute of Technology Press.
Levelt, Willem J. M., Ardi Roelofs and Antje S. Meyer
1999   A theory of lexical access in speech production. *Behavioral and Brain Sciences* 22: 1-75.
Levelt, Willem J. M., Herbert Schriefers, Dirk Vorberg, Antje S. Meyer, Thomas Pechmann and Jaap Havinga
1991   The time course of lexical access in speech production: A study of picture naming. *Psychological Review* 98: 122-142.
Levelt, Willem J. M. and Linda R. Wheeldon
1994   Do speakers have access to a mental syllabary? *Cognition* 50: 239-269.
Luce, Paul A.
1986   Neighborhoods of Words in the Mental Lexicon (Ph.D. dissertation, Indiana University). In: *Research on Speech Perception*, Technical Report No. 6, Speech Research Laboratory, Department of Psychology, Indiana University.

Luce, Paul A., Stephen D. Goldinger, Edward T. Auer and Michael S. Vitevitch
   2000   Phonetic priming, neighborhood activation, and PARSYN. *Perception & Psychophysics* 62: 615-625.
Luce, Paul A. and Nathan R. Large
   2001   Phonotactics, density, and entropy in spoken word recognition. *Language and Cognitive Processes* 16: 565-581.
Luce, Paul A. and Emily A. Lyons
   1999   Processing lexically embedded spoken words. *Journal of Experimental Psychology: Human Perception and Performance* 25: 174-183.
Luce, Paul A. and David B. Pisoni
   1998   Recognizing spoken words: The Neighborhood Activation Model. *Ear and Hearing* 19: 1-36.
Maddieson, Ian
   1984   *Patterns of Sounds*. Cambridge: Cambridge University Press.
Marslen-Wilson, William D.
   1987   Functional parallelism in spoken word-recognition. *Cognition* 25: 71-102.
Marslen-Wilson, William D.
   1993   Issues of process and representation in lexical access. In: Gerry T. M. Altmann and Richard Shillcock (eds.), *Cognitive Models of Speech Processing: The Second Sperlonga Meeting*, 187-210. Hillsdale, NJ: Erlbaum.
Marslen-Wilson, William D., Helen E. Moss and Stef van Halen
   1996   Perceptual distance and competition in lexical access. *Journal of Experimental Psychology: Human Perception and Performance* 22: 1376-1392.
Marslen-Wilson, William D., Andy Nix and M. Gareth Gaskell
   1995   Phonological variation in lexical access: Abstractness, inference and English place assimilation. *Language and Cognitive Processes* 10: 285-308.
Marslen-Wilson, William D. and Paul Warren
   1994   Levels of perceptual representation and process in lexical access: Words, phonemes, and features. *Psychological Review* 101: 653-675.
Marslen-Wilson, William D. and Pienie Zwitserlood
   1989   Accessing spoken words: the importance of word onsets. *Journal of Experimental Psychology: Human Perception and Performance* 15: 576-585.
McClelland, James L. and Jeffrey L. Elman
   1986   The TRACE model of speech perception. *Cognitive Psychology* 10: 1-86.
McQueen, James M., Anne Cutler, Ted Briscoe and Dennis Norris
   1995   Models of continuous speech recognition and the contents of the vocabulary. *Language and Cognitive Processes* 10: 309-331.

McQueen, James M., Dennis Norris and Anne Cutler
1994   Competition in spoken word recognition: Spotting words in other words. *Journal of Experimental Psychology: Learning, Memory, and Cognition* 20: 621-638.
McQueen, James M., Dennis Norris and Anne Cutler
1999   Lexical influence in phonetic decision making: Evidence from subcategorical mismatches. *Journal of Experimental Psychology: Human Perception and Performance* 25: 1363-1389.
Milberg, William, Sheila E. Blumstein and Barbara Dworetzky
1988   Phonological factors in lexical access: Evidence from an auditory lexical decision task. *Bulletin of the Psychonomic Society* 26: 305-308.
Monsell, Stephen and Katherine W. Hirsh
1998   Competitor priming in spoken word recognition. *Journal of Experimental Psychology: Learning, Memory, and Cognition* 24: 1495-1520.
Moss, Helen E., Samantha F. McCormick and Lorraine K. Tyler
1997   The time course of activation of semantic information during spoken word recognition. *Language and Cognitive Processes* 10: 121-136.
Norris, Dennis
1994   Shortlist: A connectionist model of continuous speech recognition. *Cognition* 52: 189-234.
Norris, Dennis, James M. McQueen and Anne Cutler
1995   Competition and segmentation in spoken-word recognition. *Journal of Experimental Psychology: Learning, Memory, and Cognition* 21: 1209-1228.
Norris, Dennis, James M. McQueen and Anne Cutler
2000   Merging information in speech recognition: Feedback is never necessary. *Behavioral and Brain Sciences* 23: 299-325.
Peperkamp, Sharon and Emmanuel Dupoux
2002   A typological study of stress 'deafness'. In: Carlos Gussenhoven and Natasha Warner (eds.), *Papers in Laboratory Phonology 7*, 203-240. Berlin: Mouton de Gruyter.
Peterson, Robert R. and Pamela Savoy
1998   Lexical selection and phonological coding during language production: Evidence for cascaded processing. *Journal of Experimental Psychology: Learning, Memory, and Cognition* 24: 539-557.
Praamstra, Peter, Antje S. Meyer and Willem J. M. Levelt
1994   Neurophysiological manifestations of phonological processing: Latency variation of a negative ERP component time-locked to phonological mismatch. *Journal of Cognitive Neuroscience* 6: 204-219.

Radeau, Monique, José Morais and Juan Segui
    1995   Phonological priming between monosyllabic spoken words. *Journal of Experimental Psychology: Human Perception and Performance* 21: 1297-1311.
Salverda, Anne Pier, Delphine Dahan and James M. McQueen
    submitted The role of prosodic boundaries in the resolution of lexical embedding in speech comprehension.
Schiller, Niels O., Antje S. Meyer, R. Harald Baayen and Willem J. M. Levelt
    1996   A comparison of lexeme and speech syllables in Dutch. *Journal of Quantitative Linguistics* 3: 8-28.
Shillcock, Richard C.
    1990   Lexical hypotheses in continuous speech. In: Gerry T. M. Altmann (ed.), *Cognitive Models of Speech Processing: Psycholinguistic and Computational Perspectives*, 24-49. Cambridge, MA: Massachusetts Institute of Technology Press.
Slowiaczek, Louisa M. and Mary B. Hamburger
    1992   Prelexical facilitation and lexical interference in auditory word recognition. *Journal of Experimental Psychology: Learning, Memory, and Cognition* 18: 1239-1250.
Soto-Faraco, Salvador, Núria Sebastián-Gallés and Anne Cutler
    2001   Segmental and suprasegmental mismatch in lexical access. *Journal of Memory and Language* 45: 412-432.
Spinelli, Elsa, James M. McQueen and Anne Cutler
    2003   Processing resyllabified words in French. *Journal of Memory and Language* 48: 233-254.
Streeter, Lynn A. and Georgia N. Nigro
    1979   The role of medial consonant transitions in word perception. *Journal of the Acoustical Society of America* 65: 1533-1541.
Swinney, David A.
    1981   Lexical processing during sentence comprehension: Effects of higher order constraints and implications for representation. In: Terry Myers, John Laver and John Anderson (eds.), *The Cognitive Representation of Speech*, 201-209. Amsterdam: North-Holland.
Tabossi, Patrizia, Cristina Burani and Donia Scott
    1995   Word identification in fluent speech. *Journal of Memory and Language* 34: 440-467.
Tabossi, Patrizia, Simona Collina, Michela Mazzetti and Marina Zoppello
    2000   Syllables in the processing of spoken Italian. *Journal of Experimental Psychology: Human Perception and Performance* 26: 758-775.
Tanenhaus, Michael K., James S. Magnuson, Delphine Dahan and Craig Chambers
    2000   Eye movements and lexical access in spoken language comprehension: Evaluating a linking hypothesis between fixations and linguistic processing. *Journal of Psycholinguistic Research* 29: 557-580.

Utman, Jennifer A., Sheila E. Blumstein and Martha W. Burton
    2000   Effects of subphonetic and syllable structure variation on word recognition. *Perception & Psychophysics* 62: 1297-1311.
Van Berkum, Jos J. A., Pienie Zwitserlood, Peter Hagoort and Colin Brown
    in press   When and how do listeners relate a sentence to the wider discourse? Evidence from the N400 effect. *Cognitive Brain Research*.
Van den Brink, Dannie, Colin Brown and Peter Hagoort
    2001   Electrophysiological evidence for early contextual influences during spoken-word recognition: N200 versus N400 effects. *Journal of Cognitive Neuroscience* 13: 967-985.
Van Petten, Cyma, Seana Coulson, Susan Rubin, Elena Plante and Marjorie Parks
    1999   Time course of word identification and semantic integration in spoken language. *Journal of Experimental Psychology: Learning, Memory, and Cognition* 25: 394-417.
Vitevitch, Michael S. and Paul A. Luce
    1998   When words compete: Levels of processing in spoken word recognition. *Psychological Science* 9: 325-329.
Vitevitch, Michael S. and Paul A. Luce
    1999   Probabilistic phonotactics and neighborhood activation in spoken word recognition. *Journal of Memory and Language* 40: 374-408.
Vroomen, Jean and Beatrice de Gelder
    1995   Metrical segmentation and lexical inhibition in spoken word recognition. *Journal of Experimental Psychology: Human Perception and Performance* 21: 98-108.
Vroomen, Jean and Beatrice de Gelder
    1997   Activation of embedded words in spoken word recognition. *Journal of Experimental Psychology: Human Perception and Performance* 23: 710-720.
Wallace, William P., Mark T. Stewart and Christine P. Malone
    1995   Recognition memory errors produced by implicit activation of word candidates during the processing of spoken words. *Journal of Memory and Language* 34: 417-439.
Wallace, William P., Mark T. Stewart, Thomas R. Shaffer and John A. Wilson
    1998   Are false recognitions influenced by prerecognition processing? *Journal of Experimental Psychology: Learning, Memory, and Cognition* 24: 299-315.
Wallace, William P., Mark T. Stewart, Heather L. Sherman and Michael Mellor
    1995   False positives in recognition memory produced by cohort activation. *Cognition* 55: 85-113.
Whalen, Doug H.
    1984   Subcategorical phonetic mismatches slow phonetic judgments. *Perception & Psychophysics* 35: 49-64.

Whalen, Doug H.
  1991   Subcategorical phonetic mismatches and lexical access. *Perception & Psychophysics* 50: 351-360.
Zwitserlood, Pienie
  1989   The locus of the effects of sentential-semantic context in spoken-word processing. *Cognition* 32: 25-64.
Zwitserlood, Pienie and Herbert Schriefers
  1995   Effects of sensory information and processing time in spoken-word recognition. *Language and Cognitive Processes* 10: 121-136.

The internal structure of words: Consequences for listening and speaking

Pienie Zwitserlood

1. Introduction

All domains of linguistics and psycholinguistics in one way or another deal with words. Words usually correspond to conceptual units, and they are the building blocks of syntactic phrases. Indeed, the whole concept of a mental lexicon hinges on the notion *word*, and phonology deals with the stuff that (phonological) words are made of. But what is a word? The views of laypersons, when confronted with this question, are revealing: Words are seen as sequences of letters, separated by spaces (cf. Miller 1991). Clearly, literacy has a strong impact on such insights. As an answer to the question "Name a difficult word" one usually gets conceptually difficult or rare words (e.g., *gauge*, *serendipity*) rather than words with complex and unusual sound combinations (e.g., *strength*, *grudge*). Also rare are answers such as the German word *Abfallbereinigung* (waste disposal), consisting of six morphemes. Apparently, morphologically complex words, which consist of other words or word parts, are not considered to be difficult.[1]

What a word is, is as difficult to define in psycholinguistics as in linguistics. According to Di Sciullo and Williams (1987), one can view words either as morphological or syntactic objects, which constitute the atoms for rule-governed combination, or as mere things stored in a mental lexicon. Psycholinguists are often undeservedly accused of adhering to the latter view. In what follows, different ideas of what might count as words, in a more psychological sense of atoms of language processing will be considered. The focus will be on morphemes. One important question is whether morphemes are represented as independent elements in lexical memory. If so, the next issue is how morphemes are connected with other types of information belonging to words – phonological or semantic, for instance. Considering that speakers often create new words by concatenating existing morphemes, the answer to the first question might seem obvious. But there is more than one theoretical solution to verbal creativity, and the implication that morphemes are separately represented in the mental lexicon is not mandatory. A final important question is whether units corresponding to morphemes are shared between language comprehension and production.

To decide on such questions is by no means an easy endeavor. On the one hand, there is an extensive body of psycholinguistic literature on the role of morphology in word recognition, be it mainly in the visual domain. Models of morphological processing and representation in language comprehension are quite refined, debates are raging concerning the extent to which morphological processing is rule-governed, and an abundance of new data become available on a regular basis (Feldman 1995a; Frost and Katz 1992; Frost and Grainger, 2000, for overviews). In contrast, the empirical harvest from the field of language production is rather meager. This is compensated by clear and outspoken theoretical positions as to the role of morphemes in speaking (see Levelt 1989; Levelt, Roelofs and Meyer 1999). Moreover, linguistic theories take a clear production perspective on morphology, and assume an interdependence of morphology and phonology (cf. Katamba 1993; Spencer and Zwicky 1998). Whether this has a processing correlate in the language user remains to be seen.

To facilitate an evaluation of the psychological status of morphemes, I provide some background into the relevant units and the flow of information processing in listening and speaking (section 2). Section 3 aims at a conceptual clarification of different types of morphological complexity. This is followed by a review of the relationship between morphology and meaning in section 4. Here, I argue for independence between the two domains, and present data in support of separate morphological representations in the lexicon. In section 5, I address the interface between the phonological make up and prosodic structure of words, and their morphological structure. Old and new data are recruited to strengthen the case for the representational and computational independence of morphemes from units of phonological processing. Finally, in section 6, I evaluate the issue of shared or separate representations, in particular morphemes, in speaking and language understanding in the light of the available evidence. Throughout, I will concentrate on models for and data from spoken in- and output, and revert to the vast literature on visual language processing only where relevant.

2. Processes and types of information in language comprehension and production

Speaking and language understanding are highly complex cognitive functions, with many sub-processes operating on many different types of stored linguistic information. In the course of the last thirty years, separate models have been developed for speaking and listening, though both skills are united in every normal language user. It is thus not surprising that models of language production (Dell 1986; Garrett 1988; Levelt 1989) and comprehension (Forster 1978; Marslen-Wilson 1987; McClelland and Elman 1986) reveal a substantial overlap concerning the types of information involved in producing and understanding language. Most models incorporate conceptual/semantic, syntactic, morphological, and form (phonological and orthographic) information. Obviously, by the very nature of speaking and understanding language, models differ with respect to the directionality and timing with which these information sources come into play.

The information that impinges on the listener is the acoustic speech input, which has to be mapped onto information stored in lexical and semantic/conceptual memory. Information present in the speech input is used to access word forms (also known as phonological representations, or lexemes) in the mental lexicon. Word forms specify what sounds words are made of. There is evidence that more than one word form temporarily becomes activated by the speech input (Marslen-Wilson 1987, 1993; Zwitserlood 1989; Zwitserlood and Schriefers 1995; see also Cutler and Clifton 1999; Cutler and

McQueen 1995). For instance, the word forms of *robe, rope, road, rose, role, roast, roam, rogue* all are briefly active when listening to the first part of /rob/. Consequently, a process of selection is needed to decide which of these forms best matches the input. Even before this selection takes place, additional information besides sound structure becomes available, such as syntactic properties of words and conceptual information (Zwitserlood 1989). Syntactic properties of words are necessary for the parser, the component of the comprehension system responsible for the analysis of the syntactic structure of utterances. Finally, of course, semantic concepts associated with words constitute the building blocks for an integrated representation of the meaning of the speaker's utterance.

It is apparent that the flow of information in language comprehension is from sound to meaning and obviously, this is different in speaking. A speaker first has to decide what to say before actually saying it, and concepts in semantic memory are the constructs of his preverbal message. The speaker thus starts where a listener ends up, and the directionality of processing in speaking is from concepts to articulation. Speech production models (cf. Levelt 1989; Levelt et al. 1999) assume that multiple concepts and lexical representations become active on the basis of (parts of) the message a speaker wishes to convey. The picture of a rose, for example, can activate the concept and lexical information belonging to *rose*, but to some extent also information pertinent to *scent, red, plant, bush, tulip, daffodil, lily,* and *geranium*. The lexical representations that are activated when a concept is on its way of being expressed correspond to what Kempen and Huijbers (1983) have coined *lemma*, specifying a word's syntactic properties such as word class and gender information. Access to multiple lemmas necessitates selection: The singling out of the one lemma whose word form will eventually be pronounced. In the above example, the lemma for *rose* has to win the competition with simultaneously activated lemmas of related concepts.

The phonological make-up of a word is represented at the wordform (or lexeme) level. Some models assume that, with very few exceptions, activation of word forms is not possible until one lemma has been selected (Levelt et al. 1999; Roelofs 1992). In the above example, the word form /roz/ becomes available as soon as the lemma for *rose* has won over its competitors. Others allow for the simultaneous activation of multiple lemmas and multiple word forms (Dell 1988, Jescheniak and Schriefers 1998, Starreveld and La Heij 1995), and some even dispute the necessity of distinguishing between lemmas and word forms (Caramazza 1997).

Word forms make available the speech segments of words, and these segments are the building blocks for the next step in production: the process of phonological encoding. Many researchers believe that word forms are not translated into articulatory gestures as a whole, but that there is a process by which the segments of the word form are associated to the word's metrical structure, which entails the specification of its syllable structure and stress pattern (Dell 1988; Meyer 1991; Shattuck-Hufnagel 1979). Word forms can also be combined into larger units (phonological words) by such a process, accounting for cliticization and syllabification across word boundaries (e.g., he had it → /hi.hæ.dɪt/).[2] After phonological encoding, a phonetic code can be generated. This code subsequently specifics the input to the articulators, leading to the actual pronunciation of what the speaker intended to say.

Where do morphemes come into play during speaking and listening? Models of language comprehension can be positioned along a continuum, with "no explicit role for morphology" at the left end, and "only morphemes in the lexicon" at the right (no pun intended). Models in a connectionist tradition find themselves close to the left end (Plaut and Gonnermann 2000; Plaut et al. 1996; Rueckl et al. 1997; see also Butterworth 1983), older proposals such as the one by Taft and Forster (1975), which have only morphemes in the lexicon, are examples of the other pole. Many models are in between and allow for access to complex words as well as to constituent morphemes (Burani and Caramazza 1987; Caramazza, Laudanna and Romani 1988; Frauenfelder and Schreuder 1992; Schreuder and Baayen 1995; Schriefers 1999, for an overview). In addition, models are differentially sensitive to distinctions between inflectional and derivational morphology (see below).

The speech production model by Levelt et al. (1999) is quite detailed as to the role of morphology. First, lexemes are of the size of morphemes, not of complex words. Words such as *replicate*, whose one-time morphological make up is lost to the contemporary language user, are considered to be monomorphemic. Second, the model assumes one concept, and one lemma, for derived words and compounds that the speaker is familiar with. So, a word such as *restless* corresponds to one concept, and its one lemma specifies that it is an adjective. It is only at the word form level that the word is connected to two morphemes: *rest* and *less*. Third, the situation is different for novel combinations (*mobielloos*, without a cellular phone) and infrequent existing ones. These are supposed to be built on the fly, by combining multiple concepts (*mobiel* and *loos*), addressing corresponding lemmas, and morphemes at the form stratum. The availability of conceptual and lemma units, even for bound derivational morphemes (e.g., *-less*, *-ness*, *-ful*), clearly is a prerequisite for morphological creativity (cf. Baayen 1994).

In sum, comprehension and production models assume many information sources pertaining to words: phonological, morphological, syntactic, and conceptual information, stored at different levels in lexical and semantic memory. Given intrinsic differences between production and comprehension with respect to the directionality of information processing, the selection – and thus decision – as to which word is going to be uttered or which word is actually heard is made at different levels in the two language processing modes. Whereas lemmas are selected in production, word forms are selected in comprehension.

3. Types of morphological complexity

Words can be morphologically simple (*fog, house, laugh*) or complex (*befogged, housing, laughed*), but what exactly is subsumed under this type of complexity? A first distinction that is important in morphology is between roots and affixes. Roots are the irreducible cores of words, to which morphological processes apply: *Root* is the root of *roots, rootless, rootlet,* and *rootstock*. Affixes are bound morphemes that cannot occur on their own, such as *-s, -ed, -ment, re-, un-* or *-ity*. Another concept is labeled "base", defined as any unit onto which affixes can be added. So, *rooted* is the base of *rootedness*, if such word exists. A subclass of bases is called stems, onto which inflectional processes can apply (Katamba 1993).

Three types of morphological complexity are traditionally distinguished in linguistic theory on word structure: Inflection, derivation, and compounding, and hefty volumes are filled with theoretical work on any of these (cf. Anderson 1992; Spencer and Zwicky 1998). Inflection refers to morphological processes that do not change word class nor produce variation in the meaning of the root morpheme (snore – snored; night – nights). Examples of what can be inflectionally signaled are number and gender for nouns and adjectives, degree forms *(bigger, biggest)* for adjectives, person, number, tense and aspect for verbs.

In contrast, derivation may change word class (*man – manly*), gender (*Mensch*, man, masc., *Menschheit*, manhood, neuter) and does change meaning *(loved – unloved)*. Compounds at least contain two bases or roots: *bedpan, headscarf,* or *Datenverarbeitungsweiterbildungsangebot*, meaning something like "offer for further instruction in the domain of information technology".[3] Although the distinction between inflection and derivation seems to be a sharp one, this has been criticized by a number of linguists (cf. Bybee 1985; Dressler 1989). Booij (2002) evaluates the criteria that are supposed to differentiate between inflection and derivation, and cites exceptions to almost every criterion. For example, not only derivation may change syntactic class: Participles, which are inflected verb forms, can be used as adjectives. Also, inflection might be semantically more transparent than derivation, but opaque participle forms exist (*verkikkerd*, in love with, lit. befrogged). Still, Booij maintains that the distinction between inflection and derivation is important, since the basis for derivation normally corresponds to the stem form, without inflectional affixes.

How do linguistically motivated distinctions of morphological classes translate to language processing? An issue that has incited a lively debate in the community concerns inflection, in particular, the distinction between regular and irregular inflection. Regular inflection is what applies as a rule: Add an *–s* to make something plural in English, add *–ed* if past tense is needed. Obviously then, forms such as *mice, oxen, went,* or *slept* are irregular. There is a host of research in language comprehension that is congruent with this view, but the distinction becomes far less clear-cut, when languages with a more complex plural system than English are considered (cf. Clahsen 1999; Pinker 1999). Evidence for the psychological reality of the distinction between inflection and derivation is not abundant. The claim that inflected words are semantically more closely related to their base than derived words is supported by differences in the amount of facilitation that is obtained in experiments on morphology (cf. Feldman 1995b).

Exceptions aside, morphologically complex words are similar in meaning to their roots, and this holds even for derived words and compounds. Moreover, complex words share segments with their roots (e.g., *create – creativity*). This suggests that what linguists and psycholinguists consider to be morphological relatedness might in fact be a mere combination of two other types of similarity: Of meaning and of form. To decide whether the morphological make up of words is represented as a separate type of information, the two domains with which morphology interfaces will be considered next.

4. The morphology – meaning interface

Before turning to the relationship between morphology and meaning, it is important to at least briefly discuss the interplay between morphology and syntax. As argued in section 2, the mental lexicon stores syntactic properties of words, which specify a word's gender, grammatical class, and argument structure. Syntactic properties serve similar functions in language production and comprehension. In production, they are indispensable for the construction and eventual production of grammatically structured sentences. Likewise, syntactic features are used by the parsing system during comprehension, for the analysis of the syntactic structure of the utterance.

Theories of language production often represent syntactic properties of words at a level that is separate from the morphological and
phonological level (Garrett 1988; Levelt et al. 1999). Comprehension
models also dissociate syntactic and phonological information. In
some views, syntactic properties and morphological make-up of
words are both specified in connection to a central lexical representation or entry, but each in a different format (Marslen-Wilson 1989,
1993; Schreuder and Baayen 1995). But although syntactic and morphological information is separated in production and comprehension
models, there could well be a busy interface between the two components. Derivational affixes, for example, frequently specify syntactic
properties. Words ending in *–ness*, *-ment* or *-ity* are nouns, words
ending in *–ful*, *-less* or *–al* are adjectives. The language system, in
particular the parser, could exploit these regularities, which are carried by morphemes and relevant to syntax (cf. Bergman, Hudson and
Eling, 1988).[4]

In understanding language, the most important information belonging to words is not what morphemes, speech segments or phonological features they are made of, but what they mean. It might thus
come as a surprise that the representation of meaning is often considered to be outside the direct scope of psycholinguistics, with the exception of research on semantic ambiguity (e.g., the multiple meanings of *bank*; cf. Simpson 1994). Meaning, or, more accurately,
knowledge about persons, objects, events, states, actions, etc. is the
domain of psychologists who are concerned with knowledge structures in long-term memory. A distinction should be made between
procedural (how to tie a shoelace, to drive a car) and declarative or
semantic knowledge. Semantic memory can be viewed as a network
of concepts, interconnected by means of labeled arcs, which specify
the relations between concepts (Collins and Quillian 1969; Roelofs
1992, for an overview). Concepts thus are non-linguistic entities.
They are used in thinking and problem solving; they can be addressed
by information from the sensory systems without any language involvement. People without language have concepts; other species
have concepts as well (Schaller 1992; Wasserman, Kiedinger, and
Bhatt 1988).

In Levelt et al.'s (1999) model of speaking, concepts are connected to lemmas, the first linguistic level which is accessed after preverbal processing. Similarly, the highest language-level representations in comprehension models, the lexical representations or entries, are linked to conceptual memory. But a one-to-one relationship between concepts and lexical entries is not warranted. Cross-linguistic examples are abundant: Where sentences are necessary to specify a concept in one language, one word suffices in another. Consider also the case of synonymy. It might well be that *die* and *kick the bucket* are connected to one and the same concept, as might be the case for *sterben* and *abkratzen* (to die). Moreover, since the latter verb is polysemous (meaning both *die* and *scrape off*), it has to be connected to minimally two concepts.

There is an increasing body of evidence as to the independence of morphology and meaning in language processing. The studies mainly use priming techniques, in which target words (e.g., *red*) are preceded by related prime words (*redness*) or unrelated control primes (*wasteful*). The following picture emerges. No facilitation (in some studies, even interference) is observed when primes and targets merely share speech segments or graphemes (e.g., *silly* and *sill*; *kerst* (christmas) and *kers* (cherry)). But effects are different for morphologically related primes and targets, even in the absence of semantic similarity. Many studies show clear facilitation, even when there is no obvious semantic relationship between two morphologically related words: *umbringen* (kill) primes *bringen* (bring), *drankorgel* (drunkard) primes *orgel* (organ), and – in some studies - *apartment* primes *apart* (Drews, Zwitserlood, Bolwiender, and Heuer 1994; Grainger, Colé, and Segui 1991; Laudanna, Badecker, and Caramazza 1989; Stolz and Feldman 1995; Zwitserlood 1994; but see Marslen-Wilson et al. 1994). In addition, it was shown that the contribution of semantics to morphological processing is both time and task dependent (Feldman, Barac-Cikoja and Kostiç 2002; Feldman and Prostko 2002).

The few studies on speech production show similar results: Roelofs and Baayen (2002) showed positive preparation effects in a task called implicit priming for words that share the first morpheme, independent of semantic transparency. Similarly, we found no impact of semantic transparency with the classic picture-word interference paradigm. We investigated the impact of morphologically complex distractor words (compounds in this case) on the latencies to name pictures with names that were identical with one constituent of the distractor. The conditions, examples, and results are summarized in Table 1.

In Experiment 1, we investigated the first constituent of compound words. We used compounds such as *Ziegenkäse* (goat cheese) and *Ziegenpeter* (mumps) as distractors with pictures of simple objects, such as a goat (*Ziege*). We found a very sound effect of morphological relatedness, but only a minimal impact (7 ms) of semantic transparency (Dohmes, Zwitserlood, and Bölte, 2001 in preparation).

Table 1. Conditions and results from two picture-word interference studies with morphologically complex distractors

	distractor	target picture	mean latency in ms
Experiment 1			
transparent	Ziegenkäse (goats cheese)		666
opaque	Ziegenpeter (mumps)		673
unrelated	Damenuhr (ladies watch)		788
Experiment 2			
transparent	Korbstuhl (wicker chair)		686
opaque	Dachstuhl (roof truss)		688
unrelated	Bierglas (beer glass)		796

Clearly, the size of the morphological effect is quite impressive, when compared to facilitation obtained in priming studies with word targets and word primes. Elsewhere, we argue that two types of information positively contribute in picture naming: (1) maximal over-lap at the level of segments, given that all speech segments needed to produce the picture name are specified by the distractor, and (2) the sharing of a morpheme between distractor and picture name – here even in the absence of a semantic relationship (see Zwitserlood, Bölte and Dohmes 2000).

In the second experiment, we tried to increase the likelihood of a semantic effect, by using picture names that were identical to the second constituent of the distractor (e.g., *Korbstuhl*, wicker chair, and *Dachstuhl,* roof truss, with a picture of a chair). Given that the second constituent is the compound's head, we believed that the transparent compound might serve as a competitor for the picture's lemma, similar to distractors such as *collie* or *cat* to the picture of a dog. Under those conditions, the distractor interferes with picture naming (Schriefers, Meyer, and Levelt 1990; Starreveld and La Heij 1995; Zwitserlood et al. 2000). The standard interpretation is that the distractor serves as a competitor, at the lemma level, to the lemma of the picture, which has to be named. Distractors such as *Korbstuhl* are as related to their picture as cats are to dogs. Hence, we expected in-terference, or at least a modulation of the facilitation due to morpho-logical relatedness. The opaque compound is semantically unrelated to the picture, so there should be no interference. What we found is easily summarized: A large facilitation effect, but not a hint of a dif-ference as a function of semantic transparency (Dohmes et al. 2001).

In sum, the empirical evidence from both production and compre-hension clearly favors an independence of morphological and seman-tic processing and representation. This is suggestive of an independ-ent level of morphological representation in the lexicon, but we still have to disentangle morphological information and word-form in-formation. This will be done by evaluating the interface between morphological and phonological processing.

5. The phonology – morphology interface

As argued in section 2, what words sound or look like, must in some way be stored in a mental lexicon. Word forms, specifying this type of information, are necessary for language production and comprehension, for speech as well as for reading and writing. In alphabetic writing systems, words are almost always neatly separated by spaces. Clearly, connected speech does not have the equivalent of such spaces. It is still somewhat of a mystery how our speech processing system manages to map information extracted from the speech input onto lexical representations, and what type of information (features, segments, syllables?) this might be (cf. Cutler 1998; Nygaard and Pisoni 1995, and below). Besides the problem of speech segmentation, a number of questions should be asked concerning word forms: What are the units represented at the form level, and what is the nature of their specification? Are morphemes potential units of lexical form? Moreover, are the same word forms used in producing and understanding language?

5.1. Phonological and morphological representations in speaking and listening

The model by Levelt et al. (1999) is quite precise as to where morphemes reside. In the default case of known words, a selected lemma activates its morphological structure (e.g., clear + ing), and word forms are of the size of morphemes (e.g., *clear, -ing*), which specify their constituent speech segments ([klir], [ɪŋ]). These segments are subsequently combined with the word's metrical frame (specifying syllable structure and stress) into the syllables of phonological words: /kli.rɪŋ/ (Levelt et al. 1999; Roelofs 1995, 1996, 1997). Interactive models such as the one by Dell and colleagues (Dell 1988, Dell and Juliano 1996) also assume morpheme-sized word forms.

In contrast, researchers in speech comprehension argue that form representations, which are accessed on the basis of the speech input, might be larger than morphemes. Motivation for this comes from two interdependent sources. First, speech information reaches the listener in an intrinsic left-to-right manner: The beginning of a word reaches the ears before its end. This has consequences for the mapping of incoming speech onto word form representations. Of course, the system could parse a word such as *intake* by first mapping /ɪn/ onto the morpheme *in*, before proceeding with /teɪk/ (see Taft 1985, Taft and Forster 1975). However, there is experimental evidence that spoken inputs such as *intake* initially also activate word forms such as *India*, which does not possess the morpheme *in*. These data suggest – at least for spoken word processing – that the access units at the form level in language comprehension are larger than individual morphemes (Schriefers, Zwitserlood, and Roelofs 1991; Tyler et al. 1988).

But even if access units are larger than morphemes, there is by now ample evidence from comprehension studies that the morphological structure of surface strings such as *unlucky* is indeed represented in the mental lexicon. Many researchers believe that morphological complexity is coded at a lexical level that is subsequent to access representations. In this view, a single word form exists for every real word, monomorphemic and complex ones alike. These word forms are connected to lexical entries, which specify constituent morphemes of words. Lexical entries are more abstract than access representations; they are supposed to be shared by visual and spoken input. Morphological relatedness between words can be implemented in terms of entries sharing morphemes, or of morphological families (Drews and Zwitserlood 1995; Feldman and Fowler 1987; Marslen-Wilson et al. 1994; Schreuder and Baayen 1995).

There is one potential problem for this type of view: The fact that the word forms of morphologically related words do not seem to compete with each other during word recognition. Perhaps paradoxically, this finding comes from priming studies that at the same time provide evidence for a dissociation of morphological and word form information. Results from these studies show that targets (e.g., *luck*) are reacted to faster when preceded by a morphologically (and semantically) related prime (*lucky*) than by unrelated primes (*ready*).[5] Crucially, this does not hold when primes and targets are merely related in form: *sill* is not facilitated by *silly*. In such cases, interference instead of facilitation is often observed. This interference is taken as evidence for selection at the level of word forms that was argued for earlier (Drews and Zwitserlood 1995; Grainger et al. 1991; Laudanna et al. 1989; Marslen-Wilson et al. 1994). But if word forms do not code morphological structure, why do morphologically related word forms not seem to compete with each other? There is more than one possible answer to this still unresolved question. One option is that there is indeed competition between morphologically related word forms. However, negative effects of competition are masked in the data by large facilitatory effects due to morphological relatedness, coded at a consecutive level (Drews and Zwitserlood 1995; see also Allen and Badecker 2002).

In sum, morphemes clearly seem to play a role in language processing. They are evidently incorporated in production models. In comprehension, word forms at the phonological level are connected to lexical entries, which code morphological information. Interestingly, there seem to be differences between language production and comprehension with respect to what the units of representation at the word-form or lexeme level might be. This does not come as a surprise, considering differences in the flow of information described in section 2. It was argued there that speech production does not involve the direct output of (morpheme-sized) word forms to the articulators. Additional processes intervene, creating syllabic, phonetic strings and articulatory motor programs. Even for languages that are rife with monosyllabic morphemes, the syllabification of such morphemes often depends of preceding or following material (e.g., clearing → /kli.rɪŋ/; see section 5.2.). So, the input to the comprehension system is clearly not in terms of the morphemes from production. In what follows, data from an experiment will be presented that addressed the interplay between two potential sources of information that the speech input makes available to the listener: Syllables and morphemes. I test the assumption that during early phases of processing speech input, syllabic information takes precedence over morphological information. More precisely, I will argue that cues signaling syllable boundaries become available to the listener earlier than morphological information – for which the lexicon needs to be contacted. This assumption is a logical consequence of what was argued above for language production: In speaking, morphemes precede syllables.

5.2.   Syllables and morphemes: A monitoring study

As argued above, it is still an unresolved issue how exactly contact is established between the continuous speech stream and representations of word form in the mental lexicon. Some models posit solutions for this problem, by continuously propagating small pieces of information present in the speech input – features, for example - onto lexical representations (e.g., Lahiri and Marslen-Wilson 1991; McClelland and Elman 1986). Others have sought to determine by what means the continuous input is segmented into units, which can be used as intermediary between input and word forms in the lexicon. One of the hotly debated units was and is the syllable. In a seminal study, Mehler, Dommergues, Frauenfelder, and Segui (1981) investigated the role of syllables in speech segmentation in French. They used a monitoring paradigm, in which participants had to decide whether a target, specifying a sequence of speech sounds (e.g., BAL, or BA), was present in a sequence of words, which were presented auditorily (e.g., *garotte, montaigne, balance*). The data from this study showed that reaction times to correctly detect such targets were faster when they exactly corresponded to the first syllable of the word that contained them. Thus, participants were faster to detect BA in *ba.lance* than in *bal.con*. For BAL, the pattern was reversed.

For a while, syllables ranked highly on everyone's agenda. Other Romance languages showed similar results (Bradley, Sanchez-Casas and Garcia-Albea 1993; Morais et al. 1989; Sebastián-Gallés, Dupoux and Segui 1992), but syllabic units seemed to fare less well in Germanic languages, most prominently in English (Cutler et al. 1986; Cutler and Norris 1988). We replicated the "Romance" syllable effect for Dutch (Zwitserlood et al. 1993), be it that we also found evidence for ambisyllabicity in Dutch: The sharing of intervocalic consonants by two syllables (e.g., the /l/ the English word *balance*, /bæləns/, constitutes both the coda of the first and the onset of the second syllable). The picture became even more clouded when others failed to replicate, in French, the original results obtained by Mehler et al. (Frauenfelder and Content 1999). The trend of the time was to turn away from syllables. But times change, and interesting insights can still be gained from experiments on syllables. I will report one of my own below, and will come back to the conflicting patterns of result summarized here.

In the two experiments with Dutch materials that are reported here, I used the monitoring task to look at potential interactions between syllabic structure and morphological complexity. The conditions and the type of materials used are illustrated in Table 2.

Two sets of materials were used: derived words and compounds. There were 24 pairs of words in each material set, and all words had main stress on the first syllable. The shared the first morpheme, *help*, in both *helper* (male helper) and *helpster* (female helper); *-er* and *-ster* are derivational suffixes denoting agentivity. The words of each pair were combined with two targets (e.g., /hɛl/ and /hɛlp/), which were auditorily presented before the spoken word that carried the target. Participants in the experiments had to decide whether the target was present in the carrier word that followed. The carrier words differed with respect to their syllable structure. In the derived set, the first syllable of the second word of each pair corresponded to the complete morpheme (e.g., help in *help.ster*); this was not the case for the first word.

Table 2. Conditions and examples of the monitoring study.

derived words			target	
syllable structure	examples		CVV or CVC	CVVC or CVCC
CVV word	dra.ger	/draχər/	/dra/	/draχ/
CVC word	hel.per	/hɛlpər/	/hɛl/	/hɛlp/
CVVC word	draag.baar	/draχbar/	/dra/	/draχ/
CVCC word	help.ster	/hɛlpstər/	/hɛl/	/hɛlp/
compounds			target	
syllable structure	examples		CVV or CVC	CVVC or CVCC
CVV word ? *	koopavond	/kopavɔnt/	/ko/	/kop/
CVC word ? *	melkemmer	/mɛlkɛmər/	/mɛl/	/mɛlk/
CVVC word	koop.flat	/kopflɛt/	/ko/	/kop/
CVCC word	melk.fles	/mɛlkflɛs/	/mɛl/	/mɛlk/

Note: * only if onset maximization applies for compounds

Due to the principle of onset maximization, consonants in the coda position of the first morpheme (e.g., /l/ and /p/ in *help*) move to the onset of following syllable, unless the first or the second syllable becomes an illegal one in the language. Given that syllables ending in short vowels are not allowed in Dutch (and that /lp/ is not a legal syllable onset), only the /p/ moves in the example. As a result, the first morpheme straddles the syllable boundary: *hel.per.* This is coded as a CVC.C type of syllabification in Table 2. The first morpheme of half of the word pairs had long vowels (e.g., /draχər/, *drager*, carrier). Given that syllables can end in long vowels in Dutch, the coda consonant of the first morpheme moves to the onset of the second syllable (CVV.C).

For compounds, syllable structure is less clear. If onset maximization also applies for compounds, the resulting syllabic structure of a compound such as *koopavond* (lit: purchase evening; evening at which shops close later than usual) should be /ko.pa.vɔnt/. There is linguistic evidence that onset maximization does not apply in compounds. The idea is that each constituent of a compound is a phonological word, and that syllabification takes place within and not across phonological words (cf. Booij 1995; Wiese 2000). As a phonetic correlate of a syllable boundary, in German – somewhat less so in Dutch – there is a glottal stop in compounds before morphemes starting with a vowel: /aufʔɛsən/ (*aufessen*, to eat up), or /gɔltʔadər/ (*Goldader*, vein of gold; cf. Wiese, 2000). Note that there are exceptions to the blocking of the principle of onset maximization in compounds: *aardappel* (potato, lit. earth apple) is syllabified as /ar.dapəl/, not /art.apəl/. These exceptions, however, are not common and often concern semantically opaque compounds.

In a first experiment, both targets were combined with each word of a pair, as in the study by Mehler et al. (1981). The procedure was different: Both carriers and targets were presented auditorily. Each trial had the spoken target followed by an acoustic distractor (always the word *klaar*, ready), again followed by the carrier word, for example: *hel – klaar – helpster.* For the monitoring task, participants had to press a button if a target was completely contained in the carrier word. Therefore, the target string was part of the carrier word on only half of the trials. There was some overlap between targets and carrier words for some of the fillers, which thus served as catch trails (e.g., *raak – klaar – raadsel*).

The mean monitoring latencies of this experiment, presented in Figure 1, showed the following. For derived words, reactions are clearly faster when the target coincided with the first syllable of the carrier word. This shows up as a crossover interaction between target (CVV/CVC vs. CVVC/CVCC) and syllabic structure of the carrier words. The pattern replicates what was found by Mehler et al. (1981) for French, and in our earlier study on Dutch (Zwitserlood et al. 1993). Of interest for the present purposes, there is an additional advantage for targets that correspond to the first morpheme of the spoken carrier word. Monitoring latencies are faster for targets that coincide with the first syllable as well as the first morpheme of the word (CVVC/CVCC targets in CVVC/CVCC words: mean RT 622 ms.), as compared to the situation where there is mere syllabic match (CVV/CVC targets in CVV/CVC words: Mean RT 641 ms.). Note that this only holds if the morpheme-sized target complies with the syllabic structure of the word!

The data for the compounds unequivocally support the hypothesis that onset maximization is blocked in compounds. Monitoring latencies are faster for targets corresponding to the first morpheme (CVVC/CVCC) than for CVV/CVC targets. This holds for both types of carrier word. Apparently, consonants in the coda position of the first syllable (the /k/ in *melkemmer*, milk bucket) do not move to the onset of the second syllable, even if this syllable is onsetless. This confirms what was predicted from phonological theory (Booij 1995; Wiese 2000). The rule of onset maximization does not apply at constituent boundaries in compounds – at least for the materials used here.

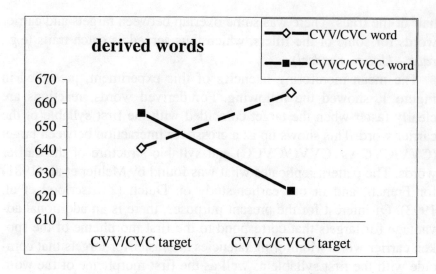

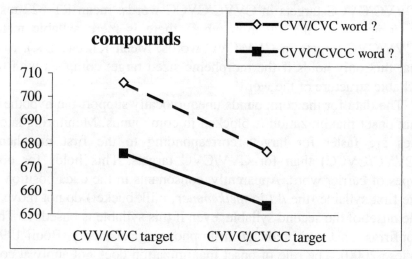

Figure 1. Mean monitoring latencies for derived and compounded carrier words; data from the first monitoring experiment.

Overall, the data indicate that from a speaking perspective, syllabification is controlled by morphology, given the blocking of a phonological rule for one particular type of morphologically complex word. One explanation could be that the syllabic structure of (complex) words is coded with the word forms in the mental lexicon. This option is not really considered in speech perception, and clearly not favored by production theories. Levelt et al. (1999) assume (1) morpheme-sized word forms in the lexicon, which cannot contain the types of syllable boundary at issue, (2) that the domain of phonological encoding is larger than lexical words (and morphemes). If this holds, an alternative interpretation goes as follows. Due to phonological encoding or subsequent processing stages, speakers leave cues as to where syllable boundaries are. If this is so, the participants in the monitoring study seem to pick up on such cues, which must be rather strong and compelling, given that monitoring latencies crucially depend on syllabic rather than morphological match between targets and carrier words.

To check the presence of cues to syllabic boundaries in the speech signal, a second experiment was carried out with the same material, but one major change. The carrier words of each pair were cross-spliced, that is, the part corresponding to the first morpheme was carefully cut off from one word and changed place with the same part in the other word. Thus, the /hɛl.p/ part of *helper* was added to the /stər/ of its partner word, to create a new stimulus /hɛl.pstər/, with a syllabic cue that does not correspond to the natural syllable boundary of that word. Similarly, /hɛlp./ from *helpster* was added to /ər/ from *helper*, creating /hɛlp.ər/. The same was done to the compounds, for which the cross-splicing should not matter. If the relevant information to syllabic boundaries indeed resides in the speech signal (and not in the word forms in the lexicon), the pattern of effects should correspond to the syllabic boundaries of the words from which the parts are excised.

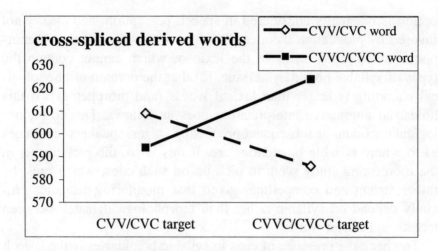

Figure 2a.   Mean monitoring latencies for cross-spliced derived carrier words from the second monitoring experiment

These data, shown in Figure 2a and 2b, provide a very strong demonstration of the listeners' reliance on cues in the speech input that signal syllable boundaries. What the participants heard were clearly words such as *helpster, helper, zorgelijk* or *zorgzaam*, be it with syllabic boundary cues in wrong places. But their monitoring latencies are clearly not based on the theoretically correct syllable structure of such words. Instead, latencies depend on the syllabic boundary information of the word from which the parts of speech corresponding to the targets were excised.

In sum, the results from both experiments together provide compelling evidence for a dissociation of early processes that operate on the speech input, and processes that take the morphological structure of words into account. The early processes are driven by the input, not by lexical information: They operate on cues present in the speech signal. Evidence for sensitivity to morphology was also present in the data (as was the case in Zwitserlood et al. 1993), but only in the presence of a syllabic match. The monitoring task apparently is also sensitive to lexical effects.

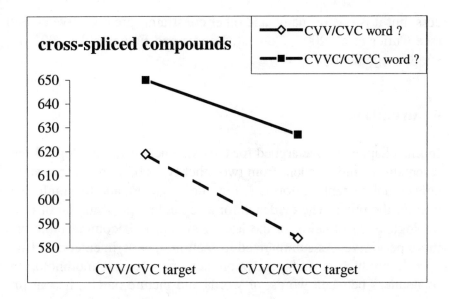

Figure 2b. Mean monitoring latencies for cross-spliced compounded carrier words; second monitoring experiment

Some 10 years ago, these results might have been interpreted as evidence for syllables as pre-lexical units in speech perception. Already in our earlier work on syllables in Dutch, we argued against this view and took the position that syllabic information aids the process of parsing the speech input for lexical access (Zwitserlood et al. 1993). This interpretation is fully compatible with the pattern of data reported here: Syllable boundary cues assist speech segmentation and lexical access. When a boundary cue is present (together with all kinds of other information), access to lexical word forms is initiated. If the boundary leaves the morpheme intact (as with *help.ster*, female helper, or *draag.baar*, carryable), access to word forms containing that morpheme is fast and efficient. Interestingly, after years of debate about the status of syllables in lexical access and word recognition, many authors reach similar conclusions. If one abandons the idea that syllables are pre-lexical units, many of the conflicting results summarized above can be reconciled. A cue to a syllable boundary is one type of information that can aid lexical access, but it is one of many, and other constraints are operative as well (see Cutler et al. 2002; Content, Kearns and Frauenfelder 2001, for similar arguments).

6. An outlook

In this chapter, I have argued for the existence of morphological representations, independent from two other types of stored information: conceptual-semantic information on the one hand, and form information on the other. The evidence for a separate representation of morphological information in the lexical system is becoming more and more pervasive. As summarized in section 4, experimental data from speech production and perception demonstrate that morphological relatedness between words, or words and picture names, has an impact even in the absence of semantic overlap. The data from section 5 clearly argue for an independence of morphological effects from those due to form similarity. Comprehension studies show that form overlap often produces negative effects, whereas morphological similarity leads to facilitation. Production studies reveal positive effects due to shared segments between distractor words and picture names (e.g., *grave* as distractor to the picture of grapes). But we showed that these effects are much smaller than those of combined morphological and form overlap (e.g., with distractors such as *grapevine*; Zwitserlood et al. 2000).

In section 2, I discussed which types of information about words are crucial for both speaking and listening: Conceptual and syntactic information, morphological make up, speech segments and so on.

Which of these units could be shared between speaking and listening? It would clearly go against everything that Occam's razor stands for to assume separate conceptual representations. There is no need to assume reduplication, and no evidence pointing in that direction. What about syntactic features? As far as I know, there are no arguments in favor of separate representations of lexico-syntactic information for speaking and listening. But the situation is less clear for morphemes and word forms.

On the basis of the evidence cited in section 5, I argued that separate word forms might well be involved in language comprehension and production. The main reasons for this is not the one made by Levelt and colleagues, who are unhappy with forward and backward connections within this part of the lexical network (Levelt et al. 1999; Roelofs, Meyer, and Levelt 1996; Roelofs this volume). It is my belief that word forms used in understanding speech are intrinsically different from those used in speaking, and that this is dictated by the left-to-right temporal availability of information. At least for the auditory domain, our own data (Schriefers et al. 1991; Zwitserlood 1989; Zwitserlood et al. 1993), those by Tyler et al. (1988) and the results from the monitoring studies reported here all point in the same direction: The word forms of speech perception are larger than individual morphemes. They are activated on the basis of information that can be extracted from the speech input (such as syllabic boundary cues), and they are robust with respect to lawful phonological variation (Coenen, Zwitserlood, and Bölte 2001; Gaskell and Marslen-Wilson 1998). All this makes sense, given that what reaches the listener is the output of the final processing stages during speaking. These packages of articulatory gestures – possibly syllable-sized – are a far way off from the lexeme representations that give rise to them during earlier phases of speech production.

There is one question that remains. Is it possible that the same morphological representations are used in comprehension and production? Even if I just argued that word forms are different, morphemes could be still shared. Clearly, this is difficult if morphological structure is coded at the level of the word forms of perception, but I just argued against this, and there are interesting alternative proposals. Let us consider production models first. The model of Levelt et al. (1999) incorporates lemma nodes, which specify syntactic features and are hooked up to their constituent morphemes. This has a remarkable resemblance to what is proposed for comprehension: lexical entries and their connected types of information. Lexical entries are essentially "empty" nodes for words, they are associated with concepts in semantic memory and provide a connection to the syntactic features of the units they represent. Crucially, they also are linked to the morphological make up of words (Marslen-Wilson et al. 1994). But the morphemes in the speech production model are part of the form stratum. In Levelt et al. (1999) and Roelofs (this volume), the morphemes actually constitute the word forms of speech production. Does this pose insoluble problems for the issue of shared morphemes in production and comprehension? I think not. If the perceptual word forms I just argued for were integrated as a separate tier of comprehension-specific access representations, these could be linked to a morphemic level of representation that is shared between speaking and language understanding. Thus, if the proposals, for production and for comprehension were in some way integrated, the same representations could be used at almost every level of processing – save the lower input and output levels. Despite the fact that the brain has other options, parsimony of cognitive function and storage is as attractive as ever.

Acknowledgements

I am very grateful to Agnes Bolwiender, who prepared the stimuli for the monitoring studies and ran the subjects, to the MPI for Psycholinguistics, where the experiments were carried out, to Else Coenen for all her help with this chapter. Special thanks to the reviewers for their valuable comments, to Niels Schiller for his unbelievable patience, and to Jens Bölte, Christian Dobel and Dirk Vorberg, for their concrete and moral support.

Notes

1. These observations are based on an informal questionnaire among psychology students. Actually, one student gave "Abfallbereinigung" as an answer, with the comment that she/he knew these were the words I liked best.
2. The dot is used throughout to indicate syllabic boundaries.
3. Such words are created by civil servants who do not partake enough in these offers.

4. Note that there is no possibility to exploit these regularities in the speech production model by Levelt and colleagues. Word class is coded at the lemma level, which is blind to the morphological complexity of normal, frequent words. So, the process of grammatical encoding, which operates on the syntactically relevant information carried by lemmas, has no way of knowing the difference between a morphologically simple noun such as *captain* and a complex one such as *brightness*.
5. As argued in section 4, this also holds in the absence of a semantic relation between the two morphologically related words.

References

Allen, Mark and William Badecker
  2002   Inflectional regularity: Probing the nature of lexical representation in a cross-modal priming task. *Journal of Memory and Language* 46: 705-722.
Anderson, Stephen R.
  1992   *A Morphous Morphology.* Cambridge, UK: Cambridge University Press.
Baayen, R. Harald
  1994   Productivity in production. *Language and Cognitive Processes* 9: 447-469.
Bergman, Marijke W., Patrick T. Hudson and Paul A. Eling
  1988   How simple complex words can be: Morphological processing and word representations. *Quarterly Journal of Experimental Psychology: Human Experimental Psychology* 40A: 41-72.
Booij, Geert
  1995   *The phonology of Dutch.* Oxford: Clarendon Press.
Booij, Geert
  2002   *The morphology of Dutch.* Oxford: Oxford University Press.
Bradley, Dianne C., Rosa M. Sanchez-Casas and Jose E. Garcia-Albea
  1993   The status of the syllable in the perception of Spanish and English. *Language and Cognitive Processes* 8: 197-233.
Burani, Christina and Alfonso Caramazza
  1987   Representation and processing of derived words. *Language and Cognitive Processes* 2: 217-227.

Butterworth, Brian
  1983   Lexical representation. In: Brian Butterworth (ed.), *Language
              Production: Vol. 2. Development, writing and other language
              processes*, 257-294. London: Academic Press.
Bybee, Joan
  1985   *Morphology: A study of the relation between meaning and form.*
              Amsterdam: Benjamins.
Caramazza, Alfonso
  1997   How many levels of processing are there in lexical access? *Cog-
              nitive Neuropsychology* 14: 177-208.
Caramazza, Alfonso, Alessandro Laudanna and Cristina Romani
  1988   Lexical access and inflectional morphology. *Cognition* 28: 297-
              332.
Clahsen, Harald
  1999   Lexical entries and rules of language: A multidisciplinary study
              of German reflection. *Behavioral and Brain Sciences* 22: 991-
              1060.
Coenen, Else, Pienie Zwitserlood and Jens Bölte
  2001   Variation and assimilation in German: Consequences for lexical
              access and representation. *Language and Cognitive Processes* 16:
              535-564.
Collins, Allan M. and M. Ross Quillian
  1969   Retrieval time from semantic memory. *Journal of Verbal Learn-
              ing and Verbal Behavior* 8: 240-247.
Content, Alain, Ruth K. Kearns and Uli H. Frauenfelder
  2001   Boundaries versus onsets in syllabic segmentation. *Journal of
              Memory and Language* 45: 177-199.
Cutler, Anne
  1998   Prosodic structure and word recognition. In Angela D. Friederici
              (ed.), *Language comprehension: A biological perspective*, 41-70.
              Berlin: Springer.
Cutler, Anne and Charles Clifton Jr.
  1999   Comprehending spoken language: A blueprint of the listener. In:
              Colin M. Brown and Peter Hagoort (eds.), *The neurocognition of
              language*, 123-166. Oxford: Oxford University Press.

Cutler, Anne and James M. McQueen
  1995   The recognition of lexical units in speech. In: Beatrice de Gelder
                and Jose Morais (eds.), *Speech and Reading: A comparative Ap-
                proach*, 33-47. Hove: Lawrence Erlbaum.
Cutler, Anne, James McQueen, Dennis Norris and Somejean, A.
  2002   The role of the silly ball. In: Emmanuel Dupoux (ed.), *Language,
                brain and cognitive development. Essays in honor of Jacques
                Mehler*, 181-194. Cambridge, MA: MIT Press.
Cutler, Anne, Jacques Mehler, Dennis Norris and Juan Segui
  1986   The syllable's differing role in the segmentation of French and
                English. *Journal of Memory and Language* 25: 385-400.
Cutler, Anne and Dennis Norris
  1988   The Role of Strong Syllables in Segmentation for Lexical Access.
                *Journal of Experimental Psychology: Human Perception and
                Performance* 14: 113-121.
Dell, Gary S.
  1986   A spreading activation theory of retrieval in language production.
                Psychological Review 93: 283-321.
Dell, Gary S.
  1988   The retrieval of phonological forms in production. Tests of pre-
                dictions from a connectionist model. *Journal of Memory and
                Language* 27: 124-142.
Dell, Gary S. and Cornell Juliano
  1996   Computational models of phonological encoding. In: Ton
                Dijkstra and Koenraad de Smedt (eds.), *Computational psycho-
                linguistics: AI and connectionist models of human language
                processing*, 328-359. Philadelphia, PA: Taylor and Francis.
Di Sciullo, Anna-Maria and Edward Willliams
  1987   *On the definition of word.* Cambridge, MA: MIT Press.
Dohmes, Petra, Pienie Zwitserlood and Jens Bölte
  2001   Wenn   Gürtelrose   Rose   bahnt   -   Morphologie   und
                Bedeutungstransparenz beim Sprechen. In: Alf Zimmer, Klaus
                Lange,   and   Karl-Heinz   Bäuml   (eds.),   *Experimentelle
                Psychologie. 43. Tagung experimentell arbeitender Psychologen*,
                29. Lengerich: Pabst.

Dohmes, Petra, Pienie Zwitserlood and Jens Bölte
in preparation The impact of morphological complexity and semantic transparency on picture naming.

Dressler, Wolfgang U.
1989   Prototypical differences between inflection and derivation. *Zeitschrift für Phonetik, Sprachwissenschaft und Kommunikations-forschung* 43: 3-10.

Drews, Etta and Pienie Zwitserlood
1995   Morphological and orthographic similarity in visual word recognition. *Journal of Experimental Psychology: Human Perception and Performance* 21: 1098-1116.

Drews Etta, Pienie Zwitserlood, Agnes Bolwiender and Uwe Heuer
1994   Lexikalische Repräsentation morphologischer Strukturen. In S. Felix, C. Habel and G. Rickheit (eds.), *Kognitive Linguistik: Repräsentation und Prozesse*, 273-298. Opladen: Westdeutscher Verlag.

Feldman, Laurie B.
1995a   *Morphological aspects of language processing.* Hillsdale, NJ: Lawrence Erlbaum.

Feldman, Laurie B.
1995b   Beyond orthography and phonology: Differences between inflections and derivations. *Journal of Memory and Language* 33: 442-470.

Feldman, Laurie B., Dragana Barac-Cikoja and Aleksandar Kostiç
2002   Semantic aspects of morphological processing: Transparency effects in Serbian. *Memory & Cognition* 30: 629-636.

Feldman, Laurie B. and Carol A. Fowler
1987   The inflected noun system in Serbo-Croatian: Lexical representation of morphological structure. *Memory & Cognition* 15: 1-12.

Feldman, Laurie Beth and Brendon Prostko
2002   Graded aspects of morphological processing: Task and processing time. *Brain and Language*, 8: 12-27.

Forster, Kenneth I.
1978   Accessing the Mental Lexicon. In: Edward C. T. Walker (ed.), *Explorations in the Biology of Language*, 257-297. Hassocks, Sussex: Harvester Press.

Frauenfelder, Uli and Alain Content
1999   The role of the syllable in spoken word recognition: Access or segmentation? In: *Proceedings of Deuxièmes Journées d'Études Linguistiques*, 1-8. Nantes, France: Université de Nantes.

Frauenfelder, Uli and Robert Schreuder
1992   Constraining psycholinguistic models of morphological processing and representation: The role of productivity. In: Geert Booij and Jaap van Marle (eds.), *Yearbook of Morphology 1991*, 165-183. Dordrecht: Kluwer.

Frost, Ram and Leonard Katz
1992   *Orthography, Phonology, Morphology, and Meaning*. Oxford: North-Holland.

Frost, Ram and Jonathan Grainger
2000   *Crosslinguistic perspectives on morphological processing*. Hove, UK: Psychology Press.

Garrett, Merrill F.
1988   Processes in language production. In: F. J. Newmeyer (ed.), *Linguistics: The Cambridge survey*. Vol. III. *Biological and psychological aspects of language*, 69-96. Cambridge, MA: Harvard University Press.

Gaskell, Gareth and William Marslen-Wilson
1998   Mechanisms of phonological inference in speech perception. *Journal of Experimental Psychology: Human Perception and Performance* 24: 380-396.

Grainger, Jonathan, Pascale Colé and Juan Segui
1991   Masked morphological priming in visual word recognition. *Journal of Memory and Language* 30:370-384.

Jescheniak, Jörg D. and Herbert Schriefers
1998   Discrete serial versus cascaded processing in lexical access in speech production: Further evidence from the coactivation of near synonyms. *Journal of Experimental Psychology: Learning, Memory, and Cognition* 24: 1256-1274.

Katamba, Francis
1993   *Morphology*. Houndmills, Basingstoke: MacMillan Press.

110 *Pienie Zwitserlood*

Kempen, Gerard and Peter Huijbers
    1983   The lexicalization process in sentence production and naming:
                Indirect election of words. *Cognition* 14: 185-209.
Lahiri, Aditi and William Marslen-Wilson
    1991   The mental representation of lexical form: A phonological ap-
                proach to the recognition lexicon. *Cognition* 38: 245-294.
Laudanna, Alessandro, William Badecker and Alfonso Caramazza
    1989   Priming homographic stems. *Journal of Memory and Language*
                28: 531-546.
Levelt, Willem J. M.
    1989   *Speaking. From intention to articulation.* Cambridge, MA: MIT
                Press.
Levelt, Willem J. M., Ardi Roelofs and Antje S. Meyer
    1999   A theory of lexical access in speech production. *Behavioral and
                Brain Sciences* 22: 1-75.
Marslen-Wilson, William
    1987   Functional parallelism in spoken word recognition. *Cognition* 25,
                71-102.
Marslen-Wilson, William
    1989   Access and Integration: Projecting Sound onto Meaning. In: Wil-
                liam Marslen-Wilson (ed.), *Lexical Representation and Process*,
                3-24. Cambridge, MA: MIT Press.
Marslen-Wilson, William
    1993   Issues of Process and Representation in Lexical Access. In: Gerry
                Altmann and Richard Shillcock (eds.), *Cognitive Models of
                Speech Processing: The Second Sperlonga Meeting*, 187-210.
                Hove, East Sussex: Lawrence Erlbaum.
Marslen-Wilson, William, Lorraine K. Tyler, Rachelle Waksler and Lianne Older
    1994   Morphology and meaning in the English mental lexicon. *Psycho-
                logical Review*, 101: 3-33.
McClelland, James L. and Jeffrey L. Elman
    1986   The TRACE model of speech perception. *Cognitive Psychology*
                18: 1-86.
Mehler, Jaques, Jean Y. Dommergues, Uli Frauenfelder and Juan Segui
    1981   The syllable's role in speech segmentation. *Journal of Verbal
                Learning and Verbal Behavior* 20: 298-305.

Meyer, Antje S.

1991   The time course of phonological encoding in language production: Phonological encoding inside the syllable. *Journal of Memory and Language* 30: 69-89.

Miller, George A.

1991   *The Science of Words*. New York: Scientific American Library.

Morais, José, Alain Content, Luz Cary, Jacques Mehler and Juan Segui

1989   Syllabic segmentation and literacy. *Language and Cognitive
Processes* 4: 57-67.

Nygaard, Lynne C. and David B. Pisoni

1995   Speech Perception: New Directions in Research and Theory. In:
Joanne L. Miller and Peter D. Eimas (eds), *Speech, Language,
and Communication,* 63-96. San Diego, CA: Academic Press.

Pinker, Steven

1999   *Words and Rules: The Ingredients of Language*. New York: Basic Books.

Plaut, David C. and Laura M. Gonnermann

2000   Are non-semantic morphological effects incompatible with a distributed connectionist approach to lexical processing? *Language
and Cognitive Processes* 15: 445-485.

Plaut, David C., James L. McClelland, Mark S. Seidenberg and Karalyn Patterson

1996   Understanding normal and impaired word reading: Computational
principles in quasi regular domains. *Psychological Review* 103:
56-115.

Roelofs, Ardi

1992   A spreading-activation theory of lemma retrieval in speaking.
Cognition 42: 107-142.

Roelofs, Ardi

1995   The WEAVER model of word- form encoding in speech production. *Cognition* 64: 249-284.

Roelofs, Ardi

1996   Serial order in planning the production of successive morphemes
of a word. *Journal of Memory and Language* 35: 854-876.

Roelofs, Ardi

1997   Syllabification in speech production: Evaluation of WEAVER.
Language and Cognitive Processes 12: 657-693.

Roelofs, Ardi, Antje S. Meyer and Willem J. M. Levelt
1996   Interaction between semantic and orthographic factors in concep-
          tually driven naming: Comment on Starreveld and La Heij. *Jour-
          nal of Experimental Psychology: Learning, Memory, and Cogni-
          tion* 22: 246-251.
Roelofs, Ardi and R. Harald Baayen
2002   Morphology by itself in planning the production of spoken words.
          Psychonomic Bulletin and Review 9: 132-138.
Rueckl, Jay G., Michelle Mikolinski, Michal Raveh, Caroline S. Miner and F. Mars
1997   Morphological priming, fragment completion, and connectionist
          networks. *Journal of Memory and Language* 36: 382-405.
Schaller, Susan
1992   *A Man without Words.* New York, NY: Summit Books.
Schreuder, Robert and R. Harald Baayen
1994   Prefix stripping re-revisited. *Journal of Memory and Language*
          33: 357-375.
Schreuder, Robert and R. Harald Baayen
1995   Modeling morphological processing. In: Laurie B. Feldman (ed.),
          Morphological aspects of language processing, 131-154. Hills-
          dale, NJ: Lawrence Erlbaum.
Schriefers, Herbert
1999   Morphology and word recognition. In: Angela D. Friederici (ed.),
          Language comprehension: A biological perspective, 101-132.
          Berlin: Springer.
Schriefers, Herbert, Pienie Zwitserlood and Ardi Roelofs
1991   The identification of morphologically complex spoken words.
          Continuous processing or decomposition? *Journal of Memory
          and Language* 30: 26-47.
Schriefers, Herbert, Antje S. Meyer and Willem J. M. Levelt
1990   Exploring the time course of lexical access in production: Pic-
          ture-word interference studies. *Journal of Memory and Language*
          29: 86-102.
Sebastián-Gallés, Núria, Emmanuel Dupoux and Juan Segui
1992   Contrasting syllabic effects in Catalan and Spanish. *Journal of
          Memory and Language* 31: 18-32.

Shattuck-Hufnagel, Stephanie
    1979   Speech errors as evidence for a serial order mechanism in sen-
                tence production. In: William E. Cooper and Edwin. C. T.
                Walker (eds.), *Sentence processing: Psycholinguistic studies pre-
                sented to Merrill Garrett*, 295-342. Hillsdale, NJ: Lawrence Erl-
                baum.
Simpson, Greg
    1994   Context and the processing of ambiguous words. In: Morton Ann
                Gernsbacher (ed.), *Handbook of Psycholinguistics*, 359-374. San
                Diego: Academic Press.
Spencer, Andrew and Zwicky, Arnold
    1998   *Handbook of Morphology*. Oxford: Blackwell.
Starreveld, Peter A. and Wido La Heij
    1995   Semantic interference, orthographic facilitation, and their interac-
                tion in naming tasks. *Journal of Experimental Psychology:
                Learning, Memory and Cognition*, 21: 686-698.
Stolz Jennifer A. and Laurie B. Feldman
    1995   The role of orthographic and semantic transparency of base mor-
                pheme morphological processing. In: Laurie B. Feldman (ed.),
                Morphological aspects of language processing, 109-129. Hills-
                dale, NJ: Lawrence Erlbaum.
Taft, Marcus
    1985   The decoding of words in lexical access: A review of the
                morphographic approach. In: Derek Besner, T. Waller and G.
                Mackinnon (eds.), *Reading research: Advances in theory and
                practice* (Vol.5), 83-123. New York: Academic Press.
Taft, Marcus and Kenneth I. Forster
    1975   Lexical storage and retrieval of prefixed words. *Journal of Verbal
                Learning and Verbal Behavior* 14: 638-647.
Tyler Lorraine K., William Marslen-Wilson, J. Rentoul, and P. Hanney
    1988   Continuous and discontinuous access in spoken word-recognition:
                The role of derivational prefixes. *Journal of Memory and Lan-
                guage* 27: 368-381.

Wasserman, E. A., R. E. Kiedinger and R. S. Bhatt
1988   Conceptual behavior in pigeons: Categories, subcategories, and pseudocategories. *Journal of Experimental Psychology: Animal Behavior Processes* 14: 235-246.

Wiese, Richard
2000   *The Phonology of German*. Oxford: Oxford University Press.

Zwitserlood, Pienie
1989   The effects of sentential-semantic context in spoken-word processing. *Cognition* 32: 25-64.

Zwitserlood, Pienie
1994   The role of semantic transparency in the processing and representation of Dutch compounds. *Language and Cognitive Processes* 9: 341-368.

Zwitserlood, Pienie and Herbert Schriefers
1995   Effects of sensory information and processing time in spoken-word recognition. *Language and Cognitive Processes* 10: 121-136.

Zwitserlood Pienie, Herbert Schriefers, Aditi Lahiri and Wilma van Donselaar
1993   The role of syllables in the perception of spoken Dutch. *Journal of Experimental Psychology: Learning, Memory and Cognition* 19: 260-271.

Zwitserlood, Pienie, Jens Bölte and Petra Dohmes
2000   Morphological effects on speech production: Evidence from picture naming. *Language and Cognitive Processes* 15: 563-591.

Modeling the relation between the production and recognition of spoken word forms

Ardi Roelofs

In de spraak vinden het gemoeds- en het verstandsleven, beide, den klaar-
sten vorm van uitdrukking, die wederkeerig op de ontwikkeling van beide
krachtig terugwerkt [In speech, our emotional and intellectual lives find
their clearest form of expression, which in turn forcefully feeds back on the
development of both] (Donders 1870: 10)

1. Introduction

The production of spoken words and their recognition have been in-
tensively investigated in psycholinguistics during the past several
decades. On the one hand, spoken word recognition has been investigated using tasks such as cross-modal semantic priming (e.g., Swinney et al. 1979; Warren 1972), auditory lexical decision (e.g.,
McCusker, Hillinger, and Bias 1981), speech shadowing (e.g., Cherry
1957; Marslen-Wilson 1973), phoneme monitoring (e.g., Foss 1969;
Frauenfelder and Segui 1989), gating (e.g., Grosjean 1980), and word
spotting (e.g., Cutler and Norris 1988). Furthermore, research has
used eye-tracking techniques to monitor participants' eye-movements
as they follow spoken instructions to manipulate real objects (e.g.,
Tanenhaus et al. 1995). Spoken word recognition has also been studied using neuroimaging techniques (see Price, Indefrey, and Van
Turennout 1999, and Hickok and Poeppel 2000, for reviews).

On the other hand, spoken word production has been investigated
mainly through the analyses of corpora of naturally occurring speech
errors (e.g., Dell and Reich 1981; Fromkin 1971; Garrett 1975; Shattuck-Hufnagel 1979; Stemberger 1985) and, more recently, in experiments using the picture naming task and Stroop-like paradigms
such as picture-word interference (e.g., Glaser and Düngelhoff 1984;

Jescheniak and Levelt 1994; Lupker 1979; Roelofs 1992; Schriefers, Meyer, and Levelt 1990; Stroop 1935; see Levelt 1989, and MacLeod 1991, for reviews). The measurement of interest is usually the time it takes to name the pictures, although studies have also examined the naming errors that are occasionally made (e.g., Martin et al. 1996), the eye-gaze durations using a head-mounted eye-camera (e.g., Griffin and Bock 2000; Meyer et al. 1998; Meyer and Van der Meulen 2000), and the brain areas involved (e.g., Levelt et al. 1998; see Indefrey and Levelt 2000, for a meta-analysis of 58 neuroimaging studies of word production).

The empirical investigations have lead to the development of detailed computationally implemented models of spoken word recognition (see Norris, McQueen, and Cutler 2000a, 2000b for discussion), and spoken word production (see Levelt 1989, 1999 for reviews). However, the relationship between production and recognition has received surprisingly little attention (see Monsell 1987, for a review). Yet, an examination of the literature in the recognition and production domains reveals that both lines of research distinguish between levels of phonological features, phonemes, and words in form-based processing. Furthermore, the cognitive neuroscience literature, focussing independently either on speech recognition or production, has identified a brain area, the left posterior superior temporal lobe, that participates in the phonemic level of processing in both speech perception and production (see Buchsbaum, Hickok, and Humphries 2001, for a review). This raises the question whether a single system participates in phonetic and phonological processing during both production and recognition (e.g., Allport 1984; MacKay 1987) or whether there are separate phonetic and phonological systems for production and recognition (e.g., Dell et al. 1997; Levelt, Roelofs, and Meyer 1999a). This issue is addressed in the current chapter.

Although the computational models independently developed for speech production and recognition have addressed several types of data sets, most models (with as only exception the error-based models of spoken word production) have attempted to account for chronometric findings, such as speech production and recognition latencies, eye-gaze durations and the distribution of eye-fixation probabilities over time, and the time course of brain activation. Interestingly, the first person to measure speech recognition and production latencies, Donders (1868), also developed a model for eye movements and examined cerebral blood flow, which, together with a subtractive method he designed, underlies two of the most widely used modern functional neuroimaging techniques in speech recognition and production research, PET (positron emission tomography) and fMRI (functional magnetic resonance imaging). Donders was also interested in the mechanisms underlying speech. In his monograph "De physiologie der spraakklanken, in het bijzonder van die der Nederlandsche taal" [The physiology of speech sounds, in particular those of the Dutch language] (Donders 1870), he gave a detailed account of the acoustic and phonetic properties of (Dutch) speech sounds and how they are articulated. In his chronometric work, Donders held that mentally progressing from hearing speech to producing speech involves a *translation* process, that is, the mental processes dealing with speech input and output are different. Donders lacked, however, the theoretical apparatus to precisely specify and develop his ideas about mental processes — the basics of the computational theory of mind (and its modeling tools) he would have needed took the full first half of the twentieth century to develop.

At the time Donders conducted his revolutionary chronometric studies, Wernicke (1874) made the seminal observation that brain-damaged patients with speech recognition deficits (today called Wernicke's aphasics) often have fluent but phonemically disordered speech production. Based on a post-mortem examination of one of his patient's lesion site, Wernicke proposed that the left posterior superior temporal lobe of the human brain stores "auditory word images" that are activated in both speech recognition and production, and that these auditory images are translated into "motor word images" (presumed to be stored in frontal areas) during speech production. The activation of the auditory word images during speech production was supposed to assist the selection of the appropriate motor word images. Consequently, when the auditory word images are lesioned (as in Wernicke's aphasia), or when the anatomical pathways connecting auditory and motor systems are disrupted (as Wernicke assumed in the case of conduction aphasia), the selection of motor images was assumed to be no longer appropriately constrained, explaining the phonemic paraphasias.

Almost a century later, at the end of the 1960s, Liberman et al. (1967) proposed a motor theory of speech perception, which holds that the target representations of speech perception are the very same articulatory motor programs that are used for speech production. No translation is necessary to go from perception to production. And two decades later, MacKay (1987) developed a general theory in which spoken language comprehension and language production are accomplished in their entirety by one and the same system.

In this chapter, I address the issue of shared versus separate systems for speech recognition and production within the context of computationally implemented models of spoken word recognition and production, specifically TRACE (McClelland and Elman 1986), Shortlist (Norris 1994), the DSMSG model (Dell 1986; Dell et al. 1997), and WEAVER++ (Levelt et al. 1999a; Roelofs 1992, 1997a). Due to space limitations, other models such as the unimplemented model of Caramazza (1997) are not discussed. A problem with Mac-Kay's (1987) theory for present purposes is that it is rather speculative and that it has not been specified computationally, which makes it difficult to evaluate the implications. The claims of Liberman et al. (1967) mainly concerned early aspects of speech perception, whereas I focus on spoken word recognition and production in this chapter. In particular, I concentrate on the representation and processing of word forms. Issues concerning word forms are to a certain extent independent of higher-order aspects of speech. For example, Levelt et al. (1999a) argued for separate form-based systems for speech recognition and production, but for shared syntactic and semantic systems.

In what follows, I make a case for a modern version of Donders' original position of closely linked but distinct mental systems for speech recognition and production as far as word forms is concerned. After a short excursion to Donders' pioneering work measuring the latencies of speech production and recognition, I discuss some of the most important computationally implemented models of spoken word recognition and production, with an eye on their time course characteristics and the relation between recognition and production, along with some key empirical findings supporting the models. In particular, I briefly discuss the most prominent recognition model that assumes feedback (TRACE) and the model that does not (Shortlist), and the most prominent production model that assumes feedback (DSMSG) and a model that does not (WEAVER++). All four models achieve form processing through activation networks.

For spoken word recognition and production to be subserved by the same system of representations and processes, the presence of bottom-up phoneme-to-word links (for recognition) and top-down word-to-phoneme links (for production) in the system is a necessary condition. The existence of top-down links in a spreading activation network for production implies activation feedback in the same network during recognition, and the existence of bottom-up links for recognition implies feedback during production. If there is no good evidence for feedback in both recognition and production, then it is unlikely that recognition and production are achieved by the very same system.

Feedback is not a sufficient condition for a shared system, however. Form recognition and production may be achieved by separate systems, each including feedback (cf. DSMSG). Furthermore, although in interactive models like TRACE and DSMSG, feedback occurs mandatorily, there is the logical possibility that in a shared recognition/production system, the bottom-up links may be operative only during actual word recognition and the top-down links only during actual word production (cf. Norris et al. 2000b). To evaluate this latter possibility, evidence from combined recognition/production tasks rather than from pure recognition or pure production tasks is critical. Three such tasks are auditory picture-word interference, auditory lexical decision during object naming, and auditory priming during speech preparation. Evidence from these tasks is discussed. Finally, I discuss evidence from recent functional neuroimaging studies examining Wernicke's claim that exactly the same brain area, the posterior superior temporal lobe, participates in both speech recognition and production. Alternatively, different subregions of this broad area could be involved. I conclude that the available evidence supports the idea of separate but closely linked feedforward-only systems for word-form production and recognition.

2. Donders' ground-breaking work

Donders' work in the nineteenth century has in many respects antici-pated the modern experimental study of speech production and rec-ognition. His techniques and views are strikingly modern. Donders took great interest in eye movements, for which he developed a me-chanical model. Furthermore, he investigated cerebral circulation (e.g., Donders 1849) and highly valued the discovery of the metabo-lism of the brain suggesting its action. "As in all organs, the blood undergoes a change as a consequence of the nourishment of the brain". One "discovers in comparing the incoming and outflowing blood that oxygen has been consumed" (Donders [1868] 1969: 412). This latter insight, together with a task-subtractive method designed by Donders, underlies the two most widely used functional imaging techniques, PET and fMRI. Donders published on natural selection in 1848, some ten years before Darwin's "The origin of species" ap-peared in print. Donders realized that the mind is not the brain, but is what the brain does: "A complete knowledge of the functioning of the brain, with which each mental process is connected, does not carry us a step further in the understanding of the nature of their rela-tion" (Donders [1868] 1969: 412). He lacked the formal language to specify mental processes precisely, but discovered another handle on them: response time. Until then, the received view held that the men-tal operations involved in responding to a stimulus occur instantane-ously. "But will all quantitative treatment of mental processes be out of the question then? By no means! An important factor seemed to be susceptible to measurement: I refer to the time required for simple mental processes" (Donders [1868] 1969: 413-414).

Donders attempted to describe the processes going on in the mind by analyzing cognitive activity into separate, discrete stages that the brain goes through when faced with different tasks. To this end, he measured, among other things, speech production latencies and had participants respond to spoken stimuli by manual key-press responses.

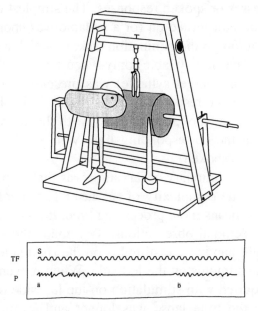

Figure 1. The "noematachograph and phonautograph" designed by Donders to measure speech recognition and production latencies. See the text for an explanation of their working.

Figure 1 provides a sketch of the "noematachograph and phonautograph" designed by Donders to measure speech recognition and production latencies. An experimental trial proceeded as follows. Two participants A and B were seated before the mouth of the phonautograph. While the cylinder was rotated, A uttered a syllable and B had to repeat it as quickly as possible without making mistakes (cf. Cherry 1957; Marslen-Wilson 1973). The beginning of the oscillations caused by each of the two sounds was marked on paper by points *a* and *b* on line P. The time interval between the two points was deduced from the oscillation (261 Hz) of a tuning-fork (TF) recorded simultaneously. The latency of the response (in milliseconds) was found by counting the number of oscillations recorded between *a* and *b*, irrespective of their length; a constant speed of rotation of the cylinder was not required.

Donders used a large variety of tasks. The stimuli could be lights, colors, written syllables, or spoken syllables, and the responses could be manual key presses or spoken responses. The simplest task was to press a key when a light turned on (or a syllable was spoken). More complex was the go/no-go discrimination task, in which a participant had to press a key (speak a syllable) only when a prespecified target (one of two lights, or a target syllable) was presented. And finally, the most complex, choice response task had lights (syllables) associated with different keys (spoken responses), with the appropriate key to be pressed when the corresponding light went on (or the corresponding syllable was spoken).

Donders' basic, revolutionary observation was that response latencies increased with the complexity of the task: The involvement of more mental stages means more processing time. In passing, he made a number of other seminal observations. "We made the subjects respond with the right hand to the stimulus on the right side, and with the left hand to the stimulus on the left side. When movement of the right hand was required with stimulation on the left side or the other way around, then the time lapse was longer and errors common" (Donders [1868] 1969: 421). This S-R compatibility phenomenon was rediscovered a century later, and came to be called the "Simon effect" (Simon 1967). Furthermore, at the end of his classic article on the measurement of mental processing times, Donders reports that "distraction during the appearance of the stimulus is always punished with prolongation of the process" (Donders [1868] 1969: 428). This observation is interesting in the light of the later research exploiting distraction, such as color-word Stroop (Stroop 1935) and picture-word interference (Lupker 1979).

3. Modeling spoken word recognition

Exactly a century after Donders' seminal article, Morton (1969) published the first modern, discrete two-stage model of word recognition and production, the Logogen model. According to this model, each word is represented by a "logogen", which is a counter collecting perceptual evidence (during recognition) or conceptual evidence (during production) for the word. When the tally exceeds threshold, the logogen fires, and the syntactic and semantic make-up (during recognition) or articulatory program (during production) of the word is made available. In its original form, assuming a discrete step from word forms to meanings in perceptual processing, the Logogen model no longer gives a correct account of spoken word recognition (although its discreteness assumption may be correct for spoken word production, as I argue later): One of the key observations from modern research of spoken word recognition is that as speech unfolds, multiple word candidates become partially activated and compete for selection (see McQueen, Dahan, and Cutler this volume). The multiple activation concerns not only the forms but also the syntactic properties and meanings of the words. In contrast, the Logogen model holds that only the meaning of the recognized word becomes available.

To account for the activation of multiple lexical candidates, models of spoken word recognition such as the seminal, verbally specified Cohort model of Marslen-Wilson and colleagues (e.g., Marslen-Wilson and Welsh 1978) claim that, on the basis of the first few hundred milliseconds of the speech stream, all words that are compatible with this spoken fragment are activated in parallel in the mental lexicon. For example, when a listener hears the fragment CA, a cohort of words including *cat*, *camel*, *captain* and *captive* becomes activated. Computationally implemented models of spoken word recognition, such as TRACE (McClelland and Elman 1986) and Shortlist (Norris 1994), all instantiate this insight in one form or another.

Evidence for the multiple activation of lexical candidates during word recognition comes from cross-modal semantic priming experiments (e.g., Moss, McCormick, and Tyler 1997; Zwitserlood 1989). For example, Zwitserlood (1989) asked participants to listen to spoken words (e.g., CAPTAIN) or fragments of these words (e.g., CAPT). The participants had to take lexical decisions by means of a key press to written probes that were presented at the offset of the spoken primes. The decision time was measured. The spoken fragments reduced the lexical decision latency for target words that were semantically related to the complete word as well as to cohort competitors. For example, spoken CAPT facilitated the response to the visual probe SHIP (semantically related to *captain*) and also to the probe GUARD (semantically related to *captive*). When the spoken prime was the complete word (CAPTAIN), the lexical decision to SHIP was facilitated but the response to GUARD was not. The activation of multiple meanings was detected as early as 130 milliseconds from the onset of the spoken prime (i.e., during hearing CA), even when the prime was heard in a sentential context that made one of the cohort competitors more plausible than the others.

In activating multiple lexical candidates, the beginning of words plays an important role. Several studies (e.g., Connine, Blasko, and Titone 1993; Marslen-Wilson and Zwitserlood 1989) have shown that when the first phonemes of a spoken non-word prime and the source word from which it is derived differ in more than two phonological features (such as place, voicing, and manner features, e.g., the prime ZANNER derived from MANNER), no cross-modal semantic priming is observed on the lexical decision to a visually presented probe (e.g., STYLE). Marslen-Wilson, Moss, and Van Halen (1996) observed that a difference of one phonological feature between the first phoneme of a *word* prime and its source word leads to no cross-modal semantic priming effect. Using a head-mounted eye-camera to monitor listeners' eye fixations, Allopenna, Magnuson, and Tanenhaus (1998) observed that, for example, hearing the word COLLAR (a rhyme competitor of *dollar*) had less effect than hearing DOLPHIN (a cohort competitor of *dollar*) on the probability of fixating a visually presented target dollar. The reason why Allopenna et al. observed some activation of rhyme competitors while the cross-modal semantic priming studies detected no activation may not only be the use of a different technique (eye tracking vs. cross-modal semantic priming of lexical decision), but also a difference in what was measured. Whereas Allopenna et al. measured the activation of the rhyme competitor directly (i.e., the effect of auditorily presenting COLLAR on the activation of *dollar*), the cross-modal studies measured rhyme activation indirectly (via the semantic relationship of the rhyme competitor to a test probe). Taken together, the evidence suggests that in spoken word recognition, cohort competitors are more strongly activated than rhyme competitors, even when the rhyme competitors differ only in the initial phoneme from the actually presented spoken word or non-word.

3.1. The TRACE model

How do computational models account for the time course findings, and is there evidence for top-down feedback during spoken word recognition? For many years, the most prominent implemented model of spoken word recognition has been the TRACE model (e.g., McClelland and Elman 1986). TRACE I was built to model findings on phoneme perception and TRACE II (hereafter TRACE) was developed to specifically address issues in spoken word recognition. TRACE falls into the class of interactive-activation models, with activation feedback from later (i.e., lexical) to earlier (i.e., sublexical) levels in spoken word recognition.

Figure 2 illustrates the architecture of TRACE. There are three layers of nodes in TRACE, which represent word forms: a phonological feature level, a phoneme level, and a word level. Syntactic and semantic levels are not included in the model, and, unlike the Logogen model, the relation to speech production is not specified. TRACE represents time by repeating each node at each level for a great number of time slices. As time progresses, feature nodes are activated in successive time slices. Feature nodes activate phoneme nodes, which in turn activate word nodes. Activation flows upwards as well as downwards, so nodes at previous and upcoming time slices can be activated because of the overlap between features and phonemes and between phonemes and words. In TRACE simulations, feature nodes are activated by mimicking acoustic information at 5-msec intervals, with each phoneme node receiving activation from a span of 11 feature nodes. Each phoneme node activates word nodes and features nodes that are consistent with the phoneme, and each phoneme node inhibits all other phoneme nodes at the same temporal position. Finally, each word node inhibits all other word nodes at the

same temporal position and each word nodes activates all of its constituent phonemes.

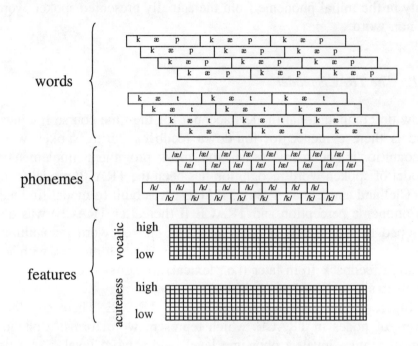

Figure 2. Architecture of the TRACE model of spoken word recognition.

With regard to the time course of word recognition, TRACE
largely follows the early Cohort model. Word nodes make up a candidate set (the cohort) as their onset specifications match the acoustic
input. When mismatch occurs, word nodes become deactivated, until
a single candidate stands out from the rest and is thereby recognized.
Words that are activated by their initial phonemes contribute to the
activation of their other phonemes by providing top-down feedback,
whereas word nodes whose initial phonemes are not matched are
suppressed by lateral inhibition and therefore become less activated.
Allopenna et al. (1998) showed by TRACE simulations that the
model could provide an excellent fit to their findings concerning cohort and rhyme activation using the eye-tracking paradigm.

Logically, spoken word recognition requires bottom-up but not
top-down links. Indeed, Frauenfelder and Peeters (1998) ran TRACE

simulations showing that the performance of the model does not worsen when its top-down links are removed. As concerns the empirical side of feedback, TRACE predicts mandatory lexical effects on phoneme processing, which has been challenged by the results of phoneme monitoring experiments. Marslen-Wilson and Warren (1994) examined the effect of lexical status on subphonemic mismatch (i.e., conflicting featural cues as to the identity of a phoneme) by cross-splicing words and non-words. They observed that the lexical status of the source of the cross-spliced material had little effect for words, whereas it had a large effect for non-words. However, in TRACE simulations run by Marslen-Wilson and Warren (1994), the lexical status of the source yielded an effect in the model both for non-words and words, contrary to the real data.

Moreover, in a replication and extension of the study by Marslen-Wilson and Warren (1994), McQueen, Norris, and Cutler (1999) observed that the effect for non-words on phoneme monitoring was dependent on the exact experimental situation. When a wide range of to-be-monitored phonemes was used and the assignment of responses to the left and right hand was varied from trial to trial, as in the study of Marslen-Wilson and Warren (1994), lexical effects in cross-spliced non-words were obtained. However, when the task was made simpler, by using a smaller range of phonemes and keeping the response hand assignment constant, no effect was obtained. Similarly, Cutler et al. (1987) observed that lexical effects in monitoring for word-initial phonemes in monosyllabic targets depended on list composition. In particular, lexical effects were present only when the filler items in the lists varied in the number of syllables. When only monosyllabic fillers were used, no lexical effect was obtained. Moreover, Eimas et al. (1990) observed that lexical effects in phoneme monitoring turned up only when a secondary task directed attention to the lexical level. Lexical effects emerged with noun/verb classification and lexical decision but not with word-length judgment as secondary task, again in contrast to what TRACE predicts.

To conclude, TRACE does a good job in capturing the overall time course of word recognition. However, there is little supporting evidence for the mandatory top-down feedback implemented in

TRACE. Given the success of the model in capturing the time course findings, it is important to know whether similar modeling approaches without feedback can be more successful. Norris (1994) and Norris et al. (2000a) claim that Shortlist presents such an approach.

3.2. The Shortlist model

Shortlist, developed by Norris (1994), combines a recurrent phoneme recognition network and a lexical competition network, in which words detected in the input speech stream are entered as candidates (the shortlist) and compete with each other for recognition (see Figure 3). Syntactic and semantic levels are not included in the model, and the relation to speech production is not specified. The lexical competition network of Shortlist is roughly equivalent to the word level of TRACE but with words included only once and all sub-threshold-activated words and their connections removed. Between-word inhibition in Shortlist's competition network is proportional to the phonological overlap between the words. The competition network is wired on the fly on the basis of the phonemes detected by the phoneme recognition network. In the actual simulations, phoneme strings are looked up serially in an electronic dictionary to make simulations with a realistic vocabulary feasible. The words in the competition network inhibit each other for a fixed number of processing cycles, after which their activations are recorded. This whole process of looking up words and dynamically wiring them in the competition network is repeated for each subsequent phoneme in the speech signal. The word that stands out from the competition and that best covers all input phonemes is the recognized word.

Shortlist successfully captures the basic findings about the time course of word recognition. Words join the competition network as their onset phonemes match the acoustic input. When mismatch occurs, word nodes become deactivated, until a single candidate stands out from the rest and is thereby recognized. Words whose initial phonemes are not matched are suppressed by lateral inhibition and therefore become less activated. This explains the finding that cohort competitors are more activated than rhyme competitors. Furthermore, Norris et al. (2000a) showed that a variant of Shortlist that was designed to perform phoneme monitoring, Merge, could handle all extant findings that seemingly suggested top-down feedback, leading them to conclude that "feedback is never necessary" (Norris et al. 2000a: 299). Merge's architecture connects input phoneme nodes to lexical nodes, and both types of nodes are connected to phoneme decision nodes. These connections are feedforward-only. Inhibitory competition operates at the lexical level (corresponding to the competition network of Shortlist) and the phoneme decision level.

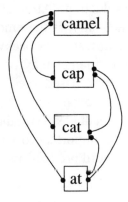

Figure 3. The pattern of inhibitory connections between candidates in a Shortlist competitive lexical network created by presenting as input CA. The figure shows only a subset of candidates matching the input.

Norris et al. (2000a, 2000b) assumed that the connections from the lexical nodes to the phoneme decision nodes in Merge are dynamically built when a listener is asked to perform a phoneme monitoring task (likewise, Shortlist's competition network is built as required). This explains the observations of Cutler et al. (1987), Eimas et al. (1990), and McQueen et al. (1999) that lexical effects in phoneme monitoring are dependent on the exact experimental situation. If the task encourages the use of lexical information, connections are built from both the input phoneme nodes and the lexical nodes to the phoneme decision nodes, which leads to lexical effects on phoneme monitoring. If the use of lexical knowledge is not encouraged, only the input and phoneme decision nodes are connected, leading to an absence of lexical effects on phoneme monitoring.

In summary, if the speech recognition system also serves speech production, top-down connections should be present and their influence should be detectable. However, to date, there is no convincing positive evidence for top-down feedback in spoken word recognition. Evidence that, on first sight, would seem to suggest top-down influences from the lexical to the sublexical levels, can be explained by a model without feedback (i.e., Shortlist/Merge).

It may be argued that spoken word recognition is a more highly practiced skill than their production: After all, speech recognition precedes production ontogenetically. If the amount of practice is reflected in the strengths of the upward and backward links in a shared recognition/production system, then it may be possible to find evidence for bottom-up, recognition-based feedback (via the stronger recognition links) in production even when there is no evidence for top-down, production-based feedback (via the weaker production links) in recognition. Thus, it is important to see whether there is evidence for feedback in spoken word production, to which I turn now.

4. Modeling spoken word production

We saw that the Logogen model (Morton, 1969) no longer provides a tenable account of spoken word recognition (which involves the activation of multiple meanings rather than a single one, as implied by the Logogen model). However, the model's account of speech production seems to do better: One of the key observations from modern research on speech production is that words are planned in two major steps. In a first, conceptually driven phase, multiple lexical candidates become partially activated and compete for selection. In a second phase, an articulatory program for the highest activated and selected lexical candidate is constructed. There appears to be no form activation for semantic alternatives except for synonyms (Levelt et al. 1991a, 1999a). The two-step assumption is supported by evidence from both speech errors and chronometric studies (e.g., Levelt et al. 1999a; Roelofs 2003), although it is a hotly debated issue whether the absence of word-form activation for semantic alternatives is due to architectural discreteness (Levelt et al. 1999a 1999b) or to mere functional discreteness (Dell and O'Seaghdha 1991).

Another question that has received much attention is whether there is feedback from phonemes to lexical forms in speech production. One of the classic arguments for feedback is that there are lexical influences on phoneme errors in speech production, the so-called lexical bias. Lexical bias is the finding that form errors create real words rather than non-words with a frequency that is higher than would be expected by chance (e.g., Dell and Reich 1981). Most form errors are non-word errors, but word outcomes tend to be statistically overrepresented. For example, in planning to say "cat", the error "hat" (a word in English) is more likely than the error "zat" (not a word in English). A lexical bias in speech errors is not always observed. While Dell and Reich (1981) found a strong lexical bias in their corpus of errors in spontaneous speech, Garrett (1976) found no such effect and Stemberger (1985) found only a weak effect. In an analysis of the errors in picture naming of fifteen aphasic speakers, Nickels and Howard (1995) found no evidence for lexical bias. A feedback account of the lexical error bias is provided by the DSMSG model.

4.1. The DSMSG model

The DSMSG model (Dell 1986; Dell and O'Seaghdha 1991; Dell et al. 1997) assumes that the mental lexicon is a network that is accessed by spreading activation (the acronym DSMSG was proposed by Dell et al. 1997, and stands for the initials of the authors). Figure 4 illustrates a fragment of the network.

The nodes in the network are linked by equally weighed bidirectional connections. Unlike TRACE and Shortlist, all connections are excitatory; there are no inhibitory links. The network contains nodes for conceptual features (e.g., ANIMATE, FURRY, etc.), words (e.g., *cat*, *cap*), and phonemes (marked for syllable position, e.g., /onset k/ and

/coda t/). The more extensive version of the model proposed by Dell (1986) also contains a level of phonological feature nodes, which are connected to the phoneme nodes. Lexical access starts by supplying a jolt of activation to the set of conceptual features making up the intended thought. Activation then spreads through the network following a linear activation function with a decay factor. Lexical selection is accomplished by selecting the most highly activated word node after a fixed, predetermined number of time steps following the activation of the conceptual feature nodes. Next, the selected word node is given a jolt of activation, and the highest activated onset, nucleus, and coda phonemes are selected after a fixed number of time steps.

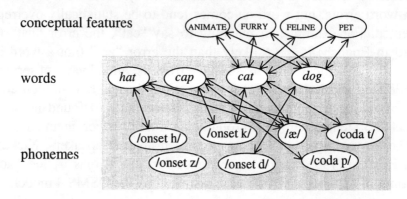

Figure 4. Fragment of the lexical network of the DSMSG model of spoken word production. The shaded area highlights the form level of planning.

The DSMSG model has been specifically designed to account for facts about speech errors of both normal and aphasic speakers: the kind of errors that occur and the constraints on their form and occurrence. According to the model, errors occur when, due to noise in the system, another node than the target one is the most highly activated node and gets erroneously selected. In spite of the presence of backward links in the production network, which might have served speech recognition, Dell et al. (1997) argue for a distinction between form networks for production and recognition. Under the assumption that word production and recognition are accomplished via one and the same form network, one expects a strong correlation between production and recognition accuracy in aphasia, as verified for the DSMSG model through computer simulations by Dell et al. (1997) and Nickels and Howard (1995). However, such correlations are empirically not observed for form errors by aphasic speakers (e.g., Dell et al. 1997; Nickels and Howard 1995). A distinction between input-form and output-form networks would explain the dissociations between production and recognition capabilities observed in aphasia.

Due to the DSMSG model's interactive nature, semantic and form activation closely follow each other and overlap in time. The model accounts for the finding that semantic activation *precedes* form activation by assuming that the semantic and form effects reflect the timing of the jolts of activation given to the network (with the jolt to the conceptual features preceding the jolt for word-form encoding) rather than activation spreading within the network itself (Dell and O'Seaghdha 1991). The lexical error bias is explained as due to backward spreading of activation from shared phoneme nodes to word nodes (e.g., from the /æ/ node activated by the target *cat* back to *cat* and the competitors *cap* and *hat*) and from these word nodes to other phoneme nodes (i.e., from *hat* to /onset h/). This does not happen for non-words, because there are no word nodes for such items in the network (i.e., there is no node *zat* to activate /onset z/). Thus, it is more likely that in planning to say "cat", /onset h/ is erroneously selected (yielding the error "hat") than that /onset z/ is selected (yielding the error "zat"). In the DSMSG model, activation spreads back automatically from phoneme nodes to word nodes. Thus, as in TRACE, lexical influences on phoneme processing in the DSMSG model are mandatory.

Similar to the lexical effects on phoneme processing in spoken word recognition, and contrary to what the interactive account of the DSMSG model implies, however, the lexical error bias is not a mandatory effect, as already suggested by the seminal study of Baars, Motley, and MacKay (1975). That the lexical error bias is not an inevitable effect is also suggested by the absence of the bias in a number of error corpora. Baars et al. observed that when all the target and filler items in an error-elicitation experiment are non-words, word slips do not exceed chance. Only when some words are included in the experiment as filler items does the lexical error bias appear. This effect of the filler context should not occur with automatic backward spreading of activation. Therefore, Levelt (1989) and Levelt et al. (1999a), among others, have argued that lexical bias is not due to production-internal activation feedback but that the error bias is at least partly due to self-monitoring of speech planning by speakers. When an experimental task exclusively deals with non-words, speakers do not bother to attend to the lexical status of their speech plan (as they normally often do, apparently), and lexical bias does not arise. Levelt (1989) proposed that self-monitoring of speech planning and production is achieved through the speaker's speech comprehension system, and this assumption has also been adopted for WEAVER++ (Levelt et al. 1999a).

4.2.   *The WEAVER++ model*

WEAVER++ (Levelt et al. 1999a; Roelofs 1992, 1996, 1997a, 1997b, 1998, 1999, 2003; Roelofs and Meyer 1998) assumes that word planning is a staged process, moving from conceptual preparation (including the conceptual identification of a pictured object in picture naming), via lemma retrieval (recovering the word as syntactic entity, including its syntactic properties, crucial for the use of the word in phrases and sentences) to word-form encoding, as illustrated in Figure 5.

Unlike the DSMSG model, WEAVER++ assumes two different lexical levels, namely levels of lemmas and morphemes (the latter representations are involved in word-form encoding), but this is not important for present purposes (see Levelt et al. 1999a, and Roelofs, Meyer, and Levelt 1998, for a theoretical and empirical motivation of the distinction). Comprehending spoken words traverses from word-form perception to lemma retrieval and conceptual identification. In the model, concepts and lemmas are shared between production and comprehension, whereas there are separate input and output representations of word forms. Consequently, the flow of information between the conceptual and the lemma stratum is bidirectional (Roelofs

1992), whereas it is unidirectional between lemmas and forms as well as within the form strata themselves (top-down for production and bottom-up for comprehension, like in Shortlist). After lemma retrieval in production, spoken word planning is a strictly feedforward process (Roelofs 1997a). Similar to what is assumed in the Logogen model, the transition from lexical selection to word-form encoding in WEAVER++ is a discrete step in that only the form corresponding to a selected lemma becomes activated.

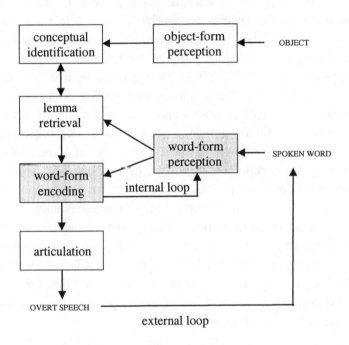

Figure 5. Flow of information in the WEAVER++ model during object naming and spoken word recognition. The shaded boxes indicate the form levels of recognition and production.

Following Levelt (1989), the WEAVER++ model incorporates two self-monitoring loops, an internal and an external one, both operating via the speech comprehension system. Functional brain imaging studies also have suggested that self-monitoring and speech recognition are served by the same neural structures (e.g., McGuire, Silbersweig, and Frith 1996; Paus et al. 1996). The external loop involves listening to self-produced overt speech, whereas the internal loop (which is assumed to be partly responsible for error biases) includes monitoring the speech plan by feeding a rightward incrementally generated phonological word back into the speech comprehension system (Levelt et al. 1999a). A phonological word representation specifies the syllables and, for polysyllabic words, the stress pattern across syllables. Thus, in WEAVER++ there exists feedback of activation from phonemes to lexical forms (see Levelt et al. 1999a, 1999b, for an extensive discussion of this point), except that the feedback engages the speech comprehension system rather than the production system itself. Form production and recognition are achieved by separate but closely linked feedforward systems.

Word planning in WEAVER++ is supported by a lexical network. There are three network strata, shown in Figure 6. A conceptual stratum represents concepts as nodes and links in a semantic network. A syntactic stratum contains lemma nodes, such as *cat*, which are connected to nodes for their syntactic class (e.g., *cat* is a noun, N). And a word-form stratum represents morphemes, phonemes, and syllable programs. The form of monosyllables such as *cat* establishes the simplest case with one morpheme <cat>, phonemes such as /k/, /æ/, and /t/, and one syllable program [kæt], specifying the articulatory gestures. Polysyllabic words such as *tiger* have their phonemes connected to more than one syllable program; for *tiger*, these program nodes are [taɪ] and [gər]. Polymorphemic words such as *catwalk* have one lemma connected to more than one morpheme; for *catwalk* these morphemes are <cat> and <walk>.

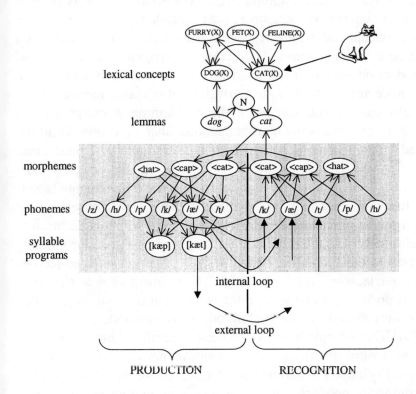

Figure 6. Fragment of the word production and comprehension networks of the WEAVER++ model. The shaded area highlights the form levels of recognition and production.

Information needed for word production planning is retrieved from the network by spreading activation. For example, a perceived object (e.g., cat) activates the corresponding concept node (i.e., CAT(X)). Activation then spreads through the network following a linear activation rule with a decay factor (cf. DSMSG). Each node sends a proportion of its activation to the nodes it is connected to. As in the DSMSG model, there are no inhibitory links. For example, CAT(X) sends activation to other concepts such as DOG(X) and to its lemma node *cat*. Selection of nodes is accomplished by production rules. A production rule specifies a condition to be satisfied and an action to be taken when the condition is met. A lemma retrieval production rule selects a lemma if the connected concept is flagged as the goal concept. For example, *cat* is selected for CAT(X) if it is the goal concept and *cat* has reached a critical difference in activation compared to other lemmas. The actual moment in time of firing of the production rule is determined by the ratio of activation of the lemma node and the sum of the activations of the other lemma nodes.

A selected lemma is flagged as the goal lemma. A morphological production rule selects the morpheme nodes that are connected to the selected lemma (<cat> is selected for *cat*). Phonological production rules select the phonemes that are connected to the selected morphemes (/k/, /æ/, and /t/ for <cat>) and rightward incrementally syllabify the phonemes (e.g., /k/ is made syllable onset: onset(/k/)) to create a phonological word representation. Finally, phonetic production rules select syllable-based motor programs that are appropriately connected to the syllabified phonemes (i.e., [kæt] is selected for onset(/k/), nucleus(/æ/), and coda(/t/)). The moment of selection of a program node is given by the ratio of activation of the target node and the sum of the activations of all other program nodes.

WEAVER++ implements a number of specific claims about how the spoken word production and recognition networks are related, as shown in Figure 6. To account for interference and facilitation effects from auditorily presented distractor words on picture naming latencies, Roelofs (1992, 1997a; Roelofs, Meyer, and Levelt 1996) assumed that form information activated in a speech recognition network activates compatible phoneme, morpheme, and lemma representations in the production network (see also Levelt et al. 1999a). For convenience, Figure 6 shows phoneme and lexical form nodes in the comprehension network (following McClelland and Elman 1986; Norris 1994), but this is not critical for present purposes (see Lahiri and Marslen-Wilson 1991, for a model of speech recognition that has no such phonemes). Covert self-monitoring involves feeding the rightward incrementally constructed phonological word representation from speech production into the speech comprehension system (Levelt et al. 1999a).

A lexical error bias arises within WEAVER++ in at least three ways (for discussion, see Roelofs in press). First, the bias occurs when speakers employ lexicality as an explicit monitoring criterion, as suggested by Levelt and colleagues (1989; Levelt et al. 1999a). Second, lexical bias arises as some form-related errors are due to lemma or morpheme selection failures (i.e., if they are "malapropisms") rather than phoneme selection failures. On the classic feedback account (e.g., Dell and Reich 1981), lexical bias arises in phoneme selection, but this does not need to be the case. Some errors may be lexical errors, perfectly in line with a theory that assumes a feedforward-only relation between lexical forms and their phonemes. A malapropism may occur when a speaker can generate only an incomplete form representation of the intended word, as in a tip-of-the-tongue state. This incomplete form is fed back to the conceptual system via the comprehension system, which leads to the activation of the lemmas of words that are phonologically related to the target. These lemmas typically will be semantically unrelated to the target. If one of these lemmas of the appropriate grammatical category is selected, a malapropism will occur. Third, lexical bias occurs in accessing motor programs for syllables (i.e., syllable program nodes in the network). Because the feedback loop through the speech comprehension system activates compatible morpheme representations in the production network, which activate corresponding syllable program nodes, the loop favors the selection of syllable programs that correspond to words. Note that in a context that de-emphasizes self-monitoring and a lexical involvement, such as the all-nonwords condition of Baars et al. (1975), a lexical-error bias should not occur, in agreement with the empirical findings. To conclude, in a model without production-internal backward links from phonemes to lexical forms such as WEAVER++, there are several factors that give rise to a tendency to produce word over non-word errors at a higher rate than chance.

The WEAVER++ model accounts for the finding that semantic effects precede form effects in time in terms of network activation patterns during the successive planning stages of lemma retrieval and word-form encoding. The assignment of the semantic and form effects of spoken distractors in object naming to different planning levels is independently supported by the finding that spoken cohort and rhyme distractors yield facilitation effects of similar size in picture naming (Collins and Ellis 1992; Meyer and Schriefers 1991; Meyer and Van der Meulen 2000), whereas they yield differential effects in spoken word recognition tasks. Cohort competitors are more strongly activated in spoken word comprehension than rhyme competitors, even when the first phoneme of the rhyme competitor deviates by only two phonological features from the actually presented spoken word (e.g., Allopenna et al. 1998; Connine et al. 1993; Marslen-Wilson and Zwitserlood 1989). In the next section, I argue that the dissociation of cohort and rhyme effects between production and recognition supports the assignment of semantic and form effects of spoken distractors to different planning levels in production (contrary to Starreveld and La Heij 1996) and that the dissociation challenges a shared production/recognition system.

5. Cohort versus rhyme effects

Meyer and Schriefers (1991) observed that when spoken cohort or rhyme distractors are presented over headphones during the planning of monosyllabic picture names (e.g., the spoken distractors CAP or HAT during planning to say the target word "cat"), both distractors yield faster latencies compared to unrelated distractors. When cohort or rhyme distractors (e.g., METAL or VILLAIN) are auditorily presented during the planning of disyllabic picture names (e.g., *melon*), both distractors yield faster latencies too. When the difference in time between distractor and target presentation is manipulated (e.g., SOA = -300, -150, 0, 150 ms), the SOA at which the faster latencies are first detected differs between cohort and rhyme distractors. In particular, faster latencies occur at an earlier SOA for cohort than for rhyme distractors (i.e., respectively, SOA = -150 ms and SOA = 0 ms). At SOAs where both effects are present (i.e., 0 and 150 ms), the magnitude of the facilitation effect from cohort and rhyme distractors was the same in the study of Meyer and Schriefers (1991). Collins and Ellis (1992) and Meyer and Van der Meulen (2000) made similar observations. Moreover, Meyer and Van der Meulen (2000) observed analogous effects of cohort and rhyme distractors on speakers' eye-gaze durations. Earlier studies by Meyer and colleagues using an eye-tracker to measure gaze durations during the naming of objects (e.g., Meyer et al. 1998) showed that a speaker keeps fixating a to-be-named perceived object until the phonological form of the object name has been prepared. Meyer and Van der Meulen (2000) observed that the eye-gaze durations were shortened to an equal extent with cohort and rhyme distractors as compared to unrelated distractor words. In contrast, in spoken word recognition, cohort competitors are more strongly activated than rhyme competitors.

The difference between the findings from cross-modal studies in the spoken word recognition literature and the findings from spoken distractors in picture naming is readily explained if one assumes that spoken distractor words do not activate rhyme competitors at the lemma level, but that rhyme relatedness effects result from activation of the corresponding phonemes in the production lexicon. Roelofs (1997a) provides such an account, implemented in WEAVER++, and reports computer simulations of the effects. On this account, METAL and VILLAIN activate the production phonemes that are shared with *melon* to the same extent (respectively, the phonemes of the first and second syllable), which explains the findings on picture naming of Meyer and Schriefers (1991). At the same time, METAL activates the lemma of *melon* whereas VILLAIN does not, which explains the findings on spoken word recognition. WEAVER++ simulations have shown that cohort activation does not result in facilitation of lemma retrieval in the model, unless there is also a semantic relationship involved (cf. Levelt et al. 1999b), as with *cat* and *camel*.

The finding that spoken cohort and rhyme distractors yield facilitation effects of similar size in picture naming, whereas they yield differential effects in spoken word recognition tasks challenges a shared production/recognition system. If the system is shared, it seems difficult to explain why priming the second syllable of a picture name by a spoken rhyme distractor leads to the same amount of facilitation as priming the name's first syllable by a spoken cohort distractor, while cohort competitors are more strongly activated than rhyme competitors in spoken word recognition. In contrast, if form recognition and production are achieved by separate feedforward systems (as in WEAVER++), then activation of forms in the recognition system may yield differential activation of cohort and rhyme competitors at the lexical level, while the corresponding cohort and rhyme phonemes may be equally activated in the production lexicon. If there is no feedback in the production lexicon, equal activation of cohort and rhyme phonemes does not lead to differential activation of cohort and rhyme competitors at the lemma level in production. This explains the differential influence of serial order on lexical and sublexical levels in production and recognition. The account requires separate form production and recognition networks without feedback.

6. Speaking while hearing words

Although in interactive models like TRACE and DSMSG feedback occurs automatically, there is the logical possibility that in a single recognition/production system, the bottom-up links may be operative only during actual word recognition and the top-down links only during actual word production. To evaluate this possibility, evidence from combined recognition/production tasks rather than from pure recognition or pure production tasks is critical. In the previous section, I discussed evidence from one task that meets the production/recognition simultaneity condition, namely auditory picture-word interference, which did not support feedback. In this section, evidence from two other tasks is discussed, namely auditory lexical decision during object naming and combined auditory priming/speech preparation.

6.1. Auditory lexical decision during object naming

Levelt et al. (1991a) combined picture naming with auditory lexical decision. Participants were asked to name pictured objects and, on some critical trials, they had to interrupt the preparation of the picture name and to make a lexical decision by means of a key press to an auditory probe presented after picture onset (i.e., with SOAs of 73, 373, or 673 ms). Thus, the speakers had to monitor for the lexical status of spoken probes while preparing to say the name of the object. The auditory lexical decision latency was the dependent variable. In this double-task situation, both forward and backward links should be operative, to meet the recognition (auditory lexical decision) and production (object naming) requirements of the double task. Thus, the double task meets the simultaneity condition for obtaining evidence for feedback, if it exists.

In one experiment, Levelt et al. looked at the time course of semantic and phonological effects. At the early SOA (73 ms), the lexical decision latencies were slowed down for spoken probes semantically related to the picture name as compared with unrelated probes. For example, in planning the production of "cat", lexical decisions were slower for the spoken probe DOG than for the probe CHAIR. In contrast, at all SOAs interference was obtained for phonologically related probes compared with unrelated ones. For example, decision latencies were longer for CAP than for CHAIR in planning the production of "cat" at all SOAs. The finding that the semantic effect was confined to the early SOA suggests that there is no feedback from phonemes to words in the speech production system, contrary to what is held by the DSMSG model. As we saw, the DSMSG model accounts for the timing of latency effects by assuming that the effects reflect the timing of jolts of activation to the conceptual and lexical representations rather than the activation within the network itself. However, although this may explain the early semantic effect, it fails to explain why phonological effects occur both early and late in time (whereas the jolt for word-form encoding is given only once, after lexical selection).

Another experiment conducted by Levelt et al. tested for phonological activation of semantic alternatives to the target. According to the DSMSG model, the phonemes of semantic competitors of the target (e.g., *dog* as a competitor of *cat*) should become active, whereas according to WEAVER++, they should not. Levelt et al. obtained no effect on the lexical decision latencies for spoken probes that were phonologically related to semantic competitors (LOG), whereas they did obtain semantic interference for such semantic competitors (DOG) themselves. This result supports the discrete view.

However, in a reply to Levelt et al., Dell and O'Seaghdha (1991) presented the results of computer simulations with the DSMSG model that suggested that phoneme activation does not necessarily happen for words that are phonologically related to semantic competitors (LOG). Because the phonemes are only indirectly activated (through the conceptual features shared between *cat* and *dog* and the phonemes shared between *dog* and *log*), they are not much activated at all in the DSMSG model, in agreement with the empirical findings. Thus, even though the DSMSG model is not architecturally discrete (as WEAVER++), it behaves in a functionally discrete manner. A problem with this counter-argument by Dell and O'Seaghdha is that it is based on activation patterns in the DSMSG network occurring *without* auditorily presented probes (see Levelt et al. 1991b, for discussion), which is not the situation tested by Levelt et al. As mentioned earlier, the influence of feedback is presumably best felt in combined production/recognition tasks. However, Dell and O'Seaghdha did not put the DSMSG model to such a test, thereby reducing the effect of the feedback links present in the model.

Another argument against the conclusions of Levelt et al. (1991a) came from Harley (1993), who presented the results from simulations using a very different network model, which, similar to TRACE, contained inhibitory links between nodes representing incompatible information (e.g., word nodes inhibited each other). In this model, the phonemes of phonological relatives of semantic alternatives did not become much activated, again, in simulations without auditory distractors. Furthermore, despite the backward spreading of activation in the network, there was no late semantic rebound (i.e., the model exhibited only an early semantic effect). Relevant for the issue of shared versus separate recognition/production systems, however, the semantic effect occurred early in Harley's model because there are no backward links from words to their meanings. Thus, the simulations cannot be taken as evidence for a single system achieving both production and recognition (word comprehension requires links from word forms to meanings).

To conclude, there is no positive evidence for feedback from a double auditory lexical decision/picture naming task. Of course, one may argue that the critical task was a perceptual one (i.e., auditory lexical decision), so the feedback effect should have come from the supposedly weaker speech production links. An experiment that engages the supposedly stronger recognition-based feedback links in a production task may provide a stronger test, which I discuss next.

6.2. Combined auditory priming/speech preparation

In Roelofs (2002), I report a study that tested for the combined effect of preparing the early parts of a to-be-produced word and auditory priming of later parts of that word. Participants produced disyllabic words out of small response sets in reaction to prompts. The words were unrelated or shared the first syllable (e.g., the syllable *me* in the responses *melon*, *metal*, and *merit*), which allowed for preparation of that syllable. At prompt onset, auditory syllable primes were presented that matched the second syllable of the response or not (e.g., LON or TAL for *melon*). Note that in this task situation, again, both forward and backward links should be operative, because production and recognition are involved. Thus, the combined auditory priming/speech preparation task meets the production/recognition simultaneity condition for obtaining evidence for feedback, if it exists.

Because preparation and priming aimed at different serial loci (i.e., in the example, the first and second syllable of the target), their combined effect should be additive or interactive depending on the theoretical position. Under the assumption of feedback from phonemes to lexical forms in production, the auditory second-syllable prime LON should facilitate the production of "melon" both directly and indirectly. The auditory prime LON activates the phonemes /l/, /ə/, and /n/ in the network (direct priming of the second syllable), which may spread activation back to the word node *melon*, which in turn may forwardly activate /m/ and /e/ (indirect priming of the first syllable). Such indirect priming is not possible when the first syllable is already prepared. Thus, the feedback view predicts an interaction between priming and preparation: The size of the effect of second syllable priming should depend on whether or not the first syllable is already prepared. However, the experiment yielded effects of both priming and preparation, but there was not even a hint of an interaction, challenging the assumption of feedback links in the production form network. In contrast, WEAVER++ simulations showed that this model could account for the observed, perfectly additive effects.

To conclude, there is no positive evidence for feedback from chronometric tasks that involve both spoken word production and recognition. Of course, although most computationally implemented models of production and recognition have addressed latency findings, other evidence cannot be ignored. In the introduction section, I mentioned that at the time Donders conducted his chronometric studies, Wernicke (1874) proposed that the left posterior superior temporal lobe is involved in both speech recognition and production. However, this brain area is broad and it is typically not uniformly affected by damage. Therefore, an important issue is whether exactly the same area is involved in recognition and production, as Wernicke claimed, or whether recognition and production are supported by distinct subregions of the left posterior superior temporal area.

7. Co-activation in functional neuroimaging studies

Neuroimaging studies have confirmed, independently for production and recognition, Wernicke's observation that the posterior superior temporal lobe is involved in production and recognition. In particular, studies suggest that this area in both hemispheres is involved in speech recognition and that the area in the left hemisphere is involved in speech production (see Buchsbaum et al. 2001, and Hickok and Poeppel 2000, for reviews).

It has been observed that transcranial magnetic stimulation of the posterior superior temporal lobe in either hemisphere disrupts speech perception. Furthermore, single unit recordings during brain surgery have revealed cells in the posterior superior temporal area in both hemispheres that respond selectively to speech input. Moreover, pure word deafness is commonly associated with bilateral lesions involving the area. Although there is bilateral involvement of the posterior superior temporal lobe in speech recognition, the speech stream seems to be asymmetrically analyzed in the time domain, with the right hemisphere analyzing phonetic information over a longer time window (i.e., 150-250 ms) than the left hemisphere (25-50 ms). Furthermore, several studies (see Buchsbaum et al. 2001, for a review) have suggested an involvement of the *left* posterior superior temporal lobe in speech production. For example, picture naming is facilitated by transcranial magnetic stimulation of the area in the left but not in the right hemisphere. Furthermore, a meta-analysis of 58 functional imaging studies by Indefrey and Levelt (2000) revealed activation of the left posterior superior temporal area in object naming, word generation, and syllable rehearsal.

Recently, Buchsbaum et al. (2001) conducted an event-related fMRI study to determine to what extent the posterior superior temporal lobe is involved in both speech recognition and production using a task that had both production and recognition components. While undergoing fMRI, participants listened to three non-words presented at a rate of one per second, which then had to be silently rehearsed for 27 seconds.

In relation to the perceptual phase of a trial, Buchsbaum et al. observed bilateral activation of the primary auditory cortex (i.e., Heschl's gyrus) and adjacent areas, and also activation of some frontal and parietal areas. Related to the motor phase of a trial, they observed, predominantly for the left hemisphere, activation of the lateral premotor and inferior frontal cortex, and also activation of some temporal areas. Most importantly, activation related to both the perceptual and motor phases of a trial was observed for two posterior superior temporal regions. One region concerned the superior temporal sulcus and lateral posterior superior temporal gyrus (pSTG), henceforth the ventral site. The other region concerned the posterior superior temporal planum (pSTP) and parietal operculum (PO), henceforth the dorsal site. Some participants showed activation of the ventral site in the right hemisphere, but no participant showed activation of the dorsal site in the right hemisphere. Less relevant for now, activation related to both the perceptual and motor phases of a trial was also observed for lateral premotor and inferior frontal regions, roughly corresponding to Broca's area (Brodmann's areas 44 and 45). Figure 7 illustrates the relevant perisylvian areas by means of a lateral view of the left hemisphere with the areas inside the Sylvian fissure exposed.

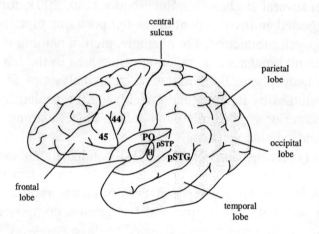

Figure 7. Lateral view of the left hemisphere of the human brain with the areas inside the Sylvian fissure exposed: pSTG = posterior superior temporal gyrus; pSTP = posterior superior temporal planum; PO = parietal operculum; H = Heschl's gyrus, which contains the primary auditory cortex; 44 and 45 refer to Brodmann's designations and make up Broca's area.

There were, however, differences in the time course of activation of the two posterior superior temporal sites. The ventral site showed more robust perception-related activation than did the dorsal site. Conversely, the dorsal site showed more robust motor-related activation than did the ventral site. The top panel of Figure 8 shows the observed blood flow responses in the ventral and dorsal subregions of Wernicke's area.

On the basis of these results, Buchsbaum et al. (2001) argued that there is overlap in the neural systems that participate in phonological aspects of speech recognition and production, supporting models (like Wernicke's) that posit overlap in the phonological input and output systems. However, on the basis of the results, it seems difficult to distinguish between overlapping systems and closely linked ones. Because the form input and output networks in WEAVER++ are tightly connected, and activation of one form network automatically leads to the activation of the other, the type of co-activation observed by Buchsbaum et al. (2001) is entailed. This claim was supported by WEAVER++ simulations, assuming that cerebral blood flow is a gamma function of network activation (cf. Roelofs and Hagoort 2002) and that the form-perception network is associated with ventral Wernicke and the form-production network with dorsal Wernicke. The latter is supported by anatomical evidence showing

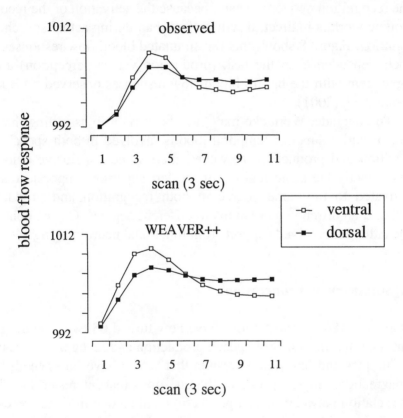

Figure 8. Blood flow responses in the ventral and dorsal subregions of Wernicke's area observed in the fMRI study by Buchsbaum et al. (2001) and in WEAVER++ simulations.

that Heschl's gyrus (primary auditory cortex) is connected via mono-synaptic pathways with ventral Wernicke, but there are no direct connections with dorsal Wernicke (Wise et al. 2001).

The bottom panel of Figure 8 shows the simulated blood flow responses in WEAVER++. During speech recognition, form activation in the recognition network automatically activates the corresponding forms in the production network. Because the activation of the production network is indirect, it will be less than during actual speech production. Similarly, during production, form activation in the production network automatically activates the corresponding forms in the recognition network. Again, because the activation of the recognition network is indirect, it will be less than during actual speech recognition. Figure 8 shows that the simulated blood flow responses and their dependence on the task (production versus perception) are in agreement with the brain's blood flow responses observed by Buchsbaum et al. (2001).

To conclude, Wernicke may have been right in assuming that the left posterior superior temporal lobe is involved in both speech recognition and production. However, there is no conclusive evidence that exactly the same regions of the left superior temporal area are activated to the same degree in both recognition and production rather than different subregions to different degrees. On the contrary, the latter has received support from functional neuroimaging.

8. Summary and conclusions

Donders' (1868) contributions have now turned 65 twice. During the past century, the study of speech production and recognition has used techniques and has yielded results that would have far exceeded his imagination. However, one of the questions that interested Donders, the relation between speech production and recognition, has received surprisingly little attention. In this chapter, I have made a case for a modern version of Donders' claim that mentally progressing from speech input to output involves a translation process. The case was made primarily on the basis of chronometric findings and their modeling within the recognition and production research traditions.

First, I have argued that there is no conclusive evidence in favor of production-internal or recognition-internal feedback, neither from recognition tasks nor from production tasks, and not even from tasks that combine both recognition and production. Furthermore, cohorts and rhymes play a different role in production and recognition, which challenges the view of a shared system. Second, although recent functional imaging studies have confirmed the observation of Donders' contemporary Wernicke that there exists a brain area, the posterior superior temporal lobe, which critically participates in both speech recognition and production, there is also evidence that suggests that different subregions of this broad area are differently involved in the two tasks. To conclude, the available evidence supports the idea of separate but closely linked feedforward systems for word-form recognition and production.

References

Allopenna, Paul D., James S. Magnuson and Michael K. Tanenhaus
   1998   Tracking the time course of spoken word recognition using eye movements: Evidence for continuous mapping models. *Journal of Memory and Language* 38: 419-439.

Allport, D. Alan
   1984   Speech production and comprehension: One lexicon or two? In: Wolfgang Prinz and Andries F. Sanders (eds.), *Cognition and motor processes*, 209-228. Berlin: Springer-Verlag.

Baars, Bernard J., Michael T. Motley and Donald G. MacKay
   1975   Output editing for lexical status from artificially elicited slips of the tongue. *Journal of Verbal Learning and Verbal Behavior* 14: 382-39.

Buchsbaum, Bradley R., Gregory Hickok and Colin Humphries
   2001   Role of the left posterior superior temporal gyrus in phonological processing for speech perception and production. *Cognitive Science* 25: 663-678.

Cherry, Colin
   1957   *On human communication.* New York: John Wiley.

Caramazza, Alfonso
   1997   How many levels of processing are there in lexical access? *Cognitive Neuropsychology* 14: 177-208.

Collins, Alan F. and Andrew Ellis
  1992   Phonological priming of lexical retrieval in speech production. *British Journal of Psychology* 83: 375-388.
Connine, Cynthia M., Dawn G. Blasko and Debra Titone
  1993   Do the beginnings of spoken words have a special status in auditory word recognition? *Journal of Memory and Language* 32: 193-210.
Cutler, Anne, Jacques Mehler, Dennis Norris and Juan Segui
  1987   Phoneme identification and the lexicon. *Cognitive Psychology* 19: 141-177.
Cutler, Anne and Dennis Norris
  1988   The role of strong syllables in segmentation for lexical access. *Journal of Experimental Psychology: Human Perception and Performance* 14: 113-121.
Dell, Gary S.
  1986   A spreading-activation theory of retrieval in sentence production. *Psychological Review* 93: 283-321.
Dell, Gary S. and Padraig O'Seaghdha
  1991   Mediated and convergent lexical priming in language production: A comment on Levelt et al. (1991). *Psychological Review* 98: 604-614.
Dell, Gary S. and Peter A. Reich
  1981   Stages in sentence production: An analysis of speech error data. *Journal of Verbal Learning and Verbal Behavior* 20: 611-629.
Dell, Gary S., Myrna F. Schwartz, Nadine Martin, Eleanor M. Saffran and Deborah A. Gagnon
  1997   Lexical access in aphasic and nonaphasic speakers. *Psychological Review* 104: 801-838.
Donders, Franciscus C.
  1849   De bewegingen der hersenen en de veranderingen der vaatvulling van de Pia Mater, ook bij gesloten onuitzetbaren schedel regtstreeks onderzocht [The movements of the brain and the changes of the content of the Pia Mater, also directly investigated with a closed skull]. *Nederlandsch Lancet. Tijdschrift voor de Geneeskundigen Wetenschappen in Haren Geheelen Omvang* 5: 521-553.
Donders, Franciscus C.
  1868   Over de snelheid van psychische processen. *Onderzoekingen gedaan in het Physiologisch Laboratorium der Utrechtsche Hoogeschool, 1868-1869, Tweede reeks* II: 92-120. Reprinted as Donders, Franciscus C. (1969). On the speed of mental processes. *Acta Psychologica* 30: 412-431.

Donders, Franciscus C.
1870   *De physiologie der spraakklanken, in het bijzonder van die der Neder-landsche taal* [The physiology of speech sounds, in particular those of the Dutch language]. Utrecht: Van der Post.
Eimas, Peter D., Suzan B. Marcovitz Hornstein and Paula Patton
1990   Attention and the role of dual codes in phoneme monitoring. *Journal of Memory and Language* 29: 160-180.
Foss, Donald J.
1969   Decision processes during sentence comprehension: Effects of lexical item difficulty and position upon decision times. *Journal of Verbal Learning and Verbal Behavior* 8: 457-462.
Frauenfelder, Uli H. and Guus Peeters
1998   Simulating the time-course of spoken word recognition: An analysis of lexical competition in TRACE. In: Jonathan Grainger and Arthur M. Jacobs (eds.), *Localist connectionist approaches to human cognition.* Hillsdale, NJ: Erlbaum.
Frauenfelder, Uli H. and Juan Segui
1989   Phoneme monitoring and lexical processing: Evidence for associative context effects. *Memory & Cognition* 17: 134-140.
Fromkin, Victoria
1971   The non-anomalous nature of anomalous utterances. *Language* 47: 27-52.
Garrett, Merrill F.
1975   The analysis of sentence production. In: Gordon II. Bower (ed.), *The psychology of learning and motivation*, 133-177. New York: Academic Press.
Glaser, Wilhelm R. and Franz-Josef Düngelhoff
1984   The time course of picture-word interference. *Journal of Experimental Psychology: Human Perception and Performance* 10: 640-654.
Griffin, Zenzi M. and Kathryn Bock
2000   What the eyes say about speaking. *Psychological Science* 11: 274-279.
Grosjean, François
1980   Spoken word recognition processes and the gating paradigm. *Perception & Psychophysics* 28: 267-283.
Harley, Trevor A.
1993   Phonological activation of semantic competitors during lexical access in speech production. *Language and Cognitive Processes* 8: 291-309.
Hickok, Gregory and David Poeppel
2000   Towards a functional neuroanatomy of speech perception. *Trends in Cognitive Sciences* 4: 131-138.

Indefrey, Peter and Willem J. M. Levelt
  2000   The neural correlates of language production. In: Michael Gazzaniga
          (ed.), *The new cognitive neurosciences*, 845-865. Cambridge, MA:
          MIT Press.
Jescheniak, Jörg and Willem J. M. Levelt
  1994   Word frequency effects in speech production: Retrieval of syntactic in-
          formation and phonological form. *Journal of Experimental Psychol-
          ogy: Learning, Memory, and Cognition* 20: 824-843.
Lahiri, Aditi and William D. Marslen-Wilson
  1991   The mental representation of lexical form: A phonological approach to
          the recognition lexicon. *Cognition* 38: 243-294.
Levelt, Willem J. M.
  1989   *Speaking: From intention to articulation.* Cambridge, MA: MIT Press.
Levelt, Willem J. M.
  1999   Models of word production. *Trends in Cognitive Sciences* 3: 223-232.
Levelt, Willem J. M., Ardi Roelofs and Antje S. Meyer
  1999a   A theory of lexical access in speech production. *Behavioral and Brain
          Sciences* 22: 1-38.
Levelt, Willem J. M., Ardi Roelofs and Antje S. Meyer
  1999b   Multiple perspectives on word production. *Behavioral and Brain Sci-
          ences* 22: 61-75.
Levelt, Willem J. M., Herbert Schriefers, Dirk Vorberg, Antje S. Meyer, Thomas
          Pechmann and Jaap Havinga
  1991a   The time course of lexical access in speech production: A study of pic-
          ture naming. *Psychological Review* 98: 122-142.
Levelt, Willem J. M., Herbert Schriefers, Dirk Vorberg, Antje S. Meyer, Thomas
          Pechmann and Jaap Havinga
  1991b   Normal and deviant lexical processing: A reply to Dell and O'Seagh-
          dha. *Psychological Review* 98: 615-618.
Liberman, Alvin M., Franklin S. Cooper, Donald P. Shankweiler and Michael
          Studdert-Kennedy
  1967   Perception of the speech code. *Psychological Review* 74: 431-461.
Lupker, Stephen J.
  1979   The semantic nature of response competition in the picture-word inter-
          ference task. *Memory & Cognition* 7: 485-495.
MacKay, Donald G.
  1987   *The organization of perception and action: A theory for language and
          other cognitive skills.* New York: Springer-Verlag.
MacLeod, Colin M.
  1991   Half a century of research on the Stroop effect: An integrative review.
          Psychological Bulletin 109: 163-203.

Marslen-Wilson, William
  1973   Linguistic structure and speech shadowing at very short latencies. *Nature* 244: 522-523.
Marslen-Wilson, William D., Helen E. Moss and Stef van Halen
  1996   Perceptual distance and competition in lexical access. *Journal of Experimental Psychology: Human Perception and Performance* 22: 1376-1392.
Marslen-Wilson, William D. and Paul Warren
  1994   Levels of perceptual representation and process in lexical access: Words, phonemes, and features. *Psychological Review* 101: 653-675.
Marslen-Wilson, William D. and Alan Welsh
  1978   Processing interactions and lexical access during word recognition in continuous speech. *Cognitive Psychology* 10: 29-63.
Marslen-Wilson, William D. and Pienie Zwitserlood
  1989   Accessing spoken words: The importance of word onsets. *Journal of Experimental Psychology: Human Perception and Performance* 15: 576-585.
Martin, Nadine, Deborah A. Gagnon, Myrna F. Schwartz, Gary S. Dell and Eleanor M. Saffran
  1996   Phonological facilitation of semantic errors in normal and aphasic speakers. *Language and Cognitive Processes* 11: 257-282.
McClelland, James L. and Jeffrey L. Elman
  1986   The TRACE model of speech perception. *Cognitive Psychology* 18: 1-86.
McGuire, Philip K., David A. Silbersweig and Chris D. Frith
  1996   Functional neuroanatomy of verbal self-monitoring. *Brain* 119: 907-917.
McCusker, Leo X., Michael L. Hillinger and Randolph G. Bias
  1981   Phonological recoding and reading. *Psychological Bulletin* 89: 217-245.
McQueen, James M., Dennis Norris and Anne Cutler
  1999   Lexical influences in phonetic decision-making: Evidence from subcategorical mismatches. *Journal of Experimental Psychology: Human Perception and Performance* 25: 1363-1389.
Meyer, Antje S. and Herbert Schriefers
  1991   Phonological facilitation in picture-word interference experiments: Effects of stimulus onset asynchrony and types of interfering stimuli. *Journal of Experimental Psychology: Learning, Memory, and Cognition* 17: 1146-1160.
Meyer, Antje S., Astrid M. Sleiderink and Willem J. M. Levelt
  1998   Viewing and naming objects: Eye movements during noun phrase production. *Cognition* 66: B25-B33.

Meyer, Antje S. and Femke F. van der Meulen
   2000   Phonological priming effects on speech onset latencies and viewing times in object naming. *Psychonomic Bulletin & Review* 7: 314-319.

Monsell, Stephen
   1987   On the relation between lexical input and output pathways for speech. In: Alan Allport, Donald G. MacKay, Wolfgang Prinz and Eckart Scheerer (eds.), *Language perception and production: Relationships between listening, speaking, reading, and writing*, 273-311. London: Academic Press.

Morton, John
   1969   Interaction of information in word recognition. *Psychological Review* 76: 165-178.

Moss, Helen E., Samantha F. McCormick and Lorraine K. Tyler
   1997   The time course of activation of semantic information during spoken word recognition. *Language and Cognitive Processes* 12: 695-731.

Nickels, Lyndsey and David Howard
   1995   Phonological errors in aphasic naming: Comprehension, monitoring, and lexicality. *Cortex* 31: 209-237.

Norris, Dennis
   1994   Shortlist: A connectionist model of continuous speech recognition. *Cognition* 52: 189-234.

Norris, Dennis, James M. McQueen and Anne Cutler
   2000a   Merging information in speech recognition: Feedback is never necessary. *Behavioral and Brain Sciences* 23: 299-325.

Norris, Dennis, James M. McQueen and Anne Cutler
   2000b   Feedback on feedback on feedback: It's feedforward. *Behavioral and Brain Sciences* 23: 352-370.

Paus, Tomas, David W. Perry, Robert J. Zatorre, Keith J. Worsley and Alan C. Evans
   1996   Modulation of cerebral blood flow in the human auditory cortex during speech: Role of motor-to-sensory discharges. *European Journal of Neuroscience* 8: 2236-2246.

Price, Cathy, Peter Indefrey and Miranda van Turennout
   1999   The neural architecture underlying the processing of written and spoken word forms. In: Colin M. Brown and Peter Hagoort (eds.), *The neurocognition of language*, 212-240. Oxford: Oxford University Press.

Roelofs, Ardi
   1992   A spreading-activation theory of lemma retrieval in speaking. *Cognition* 42: 107-142.

Roelofs, Ardi
1996   Serial order in planning the production of successive morphemes of a word. *Journal of Memory and Language* 35: 854-876.
Roelofs, Ardi
1997a   The WEAVER model of word-form encoding in speech production. *Cognition* 64: 249-284.
Roelofs, Ardi
1997b   Syllabification in speech production: Evaluation of WEAVER. *Language and Cognitive Processes* 12: 657-693.
Roelofs, Ardi
1998   Rightward incrementality in encoding simple phrasal forms in speech production: Verb-particle combinations. *Journal of Experimental Psychology: Learning, Memory, and Cognition* 24: 904-921.
Roelofs, Ardi
1999   Phonological segments and features as planning units in speech production. *Language and Cognitive Processes* 14: 173-200.
Roelofs, Ardi
2002   Spoken language planning and the initiation of articulation. *Quarterly Journal of Experimental Psychology, Section A: Human Experimental Psychology* 55: 465-483.
Roelofs, Ardi
2003   Goal-referenced selection of verbal action: Modeling attentional control in the Stroop task. *Psychological Review* 110: 88-125.
Roelofs, Ardi
in press Error biases in spoken word planning and monitoring by aphasic and nonaphasic speakers: Comment on Rapp and Goldrick (2000). *Psychological Review.*
Roelofs, Ardi and Peter Hagoort
2002   Control of language use: Cognitive modeling of the hemodynamics of Stroop task performance. *Cognitive Brain Research* 15: 85-97.
Roelofs, Ardi and Antje S. Meyer
1998   Metrical structure in planning the production of spoken words. *Journal of Experimental Psychology: Learning, Memory, and Cognition* 24: 922-939.
Roelofs, Ardi, Antje S. Meyer and Willem J. M. Levelt
1996   Interaction between semantic and orthographic factors in conceptually driven naming: Comment on Starreveld and La Heij (1995). *Journal of Experimental Psychology: Learning, Memory, and Cognition* 22: 246-251.
Roelofs, Ardi, Antje S. Meyer and Willem J. M. Levelt
1998   A case for the lemma-lexeme distinction in models of speaking: Comment on Caramazza and Miozzo (1997). *Cognition* 69: 219-230.

Schriefers, Herbert, Antje S. Meyer and Willem J. M. Levelt
    1990   Exploring the time-course of lexical access in language production:
            Picture-word interference studies. *Journal of Memory and Language*,
            29: 86-102.
Shattuck-Hufnagel, Stefanie
    1979   Speech errors as evidence for a serial-order mechanism in sentence
            production. In: William E. Cooper and Edward C. T. Walker (eds.),
            *Sentence processing: Psycholinguistic studies presented to Merrill
            Garrett*, 295-342. Hillsdale, NJ: Erlbaum.
Simon, J. Richard
    1967   Choice reaction time as a function of auditory S-R correspondence,
            age and sex. *Ergonomics* 10: 659-664.
Starreveld, Peter A. and Wido La Heij
    1996   Time-course analysis of semantic and orthographic context effects in
            picture naming. *Journal of Experimental Psychology: Learning, Mem-
            ory, and Cognition* 22: 896-918.
Stemberger, Joseph P.
    1985   An interactive activation model of language production. In: Andrew
            W. Ellis (ed.), *Progress in the psychology of language*, 143-186. Lon-
            don: LEA.
Stroop, J. Ridley
    1935   Studies of interference in serial verbal reactions. *Journal of Experi-
            mental Psychology* 18: 643-662.
Swinney, David, William Onifer, Penny Prather and Max Hirshkowitz
    1979   Semantic facilitation across modalities in the processing of individual
            words and sentences. *Memory & Cognition* 7: 159-165.
Tanenhaus, Michael K., Michael J. Spivey-Knowlton, Kathleen M. Eberhard and
            Julie C. Sedivy
    1995   Integration of visual and linguistic information during spoken language
            comprehension. *Science* 268: 1632-1634.
Warren, Robert E.
    1972   Stimulus encoding and memory. *Journal of Experimental Psychology*
            94: 90-100.
Wernicke, Carl
    1874   *Der aphasische Symptomenkomplex*. Breslau: Cohn & Weigert.
Wise, Richard J.S., Sophie K. Scott, S. Catrin Blank, Cath J. Mummery, Kevin
            Murphy and Elizabeth A. Warburton
    2001   Separate neural subsystems within 'Wernicke's area'. *Brain* 124: 83-95.
Zwitserlood, Pienie
    1989   The locus of the effects of sentential-semantic context in spoken-word
            processing. *Cognition* 32: 25-64.

Articulatory Phonology: A phonology for public language use

Louis Goldstein and Carol A. Fowler[1]

1. Introduction

The goals of the theoretical work that we describe here are twofold. We intend first to develop a realistic understanding of language forms as language users know them, produce them and perceive them. Second we aim to understand how the forms might have emerged in the evolutionary history of humans and how they arise developmentally, as a child interacts with speakers in the environment.

A seminal idea is that language forms (that is, those entities of various grain sizes that theories of phonology characterize) are the means that languages provide to make between-person linguistic communication possible, and, as such, they are kinds of public action, not the exclusively mental categories of most theories of phonology, production and perception. A theory of phonology, then, should be a theory about the properties of those public actions, a theory of speech production should be about how those actions are achieved, and a theory of speech perception should be about how the actions are perceived.

A theory of the emergence of phonological structure in language, from this perspective, is about how particulate language forms emerged in the course of communicative exchanges between people. Therefore, it predicts that the forms will have properties that adapt them for public language use: for speaking and for being perceived largely from acoustic speech signals.

Articulatory Phonology provides the foundation on which we build these theoretical ideas.

2. Articulatory Phonology

2.1. Phonology as a combinatoric system

The most fundamental property of speech communication is its phonological structure: it allows a small (usually <100) inventory of primitive units to combine in different ways to form the vast array of words that constitute the vocabularies of human languages. It shares this combinatoric property with just a few other natural systems, such as chemical compounding and genetic recombination. The theoretical underpinnings of this class of natural systems have recently come under scrutiny (Abler 1989; Fontana and Buss 1996). In all such *self-diversifying* systems (Abler 1989; Studdert-Kennedy 1998), the atomic units are discretely distinct from one another, and they retain their discreteness when they combine to form new *objects*. This appears to be a necessary property of such systems. If, instead, the combination operation were to involve blending of units defined as points along some scale, the diversity of the combinations would tend to decrease as more and more atoms join – all combinations would tend toward the mean value of the scalar units. Other properties of these natural systems such as *recurring substructures* and *hierarchy* also have been shown to depend on the fact that combination involves creation of new objects in which atoms retain their discrete identities (Fontana and Buss 1996).

The combinatoric structure of speech appears to be at odds with measurements of speech that we can make in the laboratory. Early attempts to find discrete, re-combinable units in the acoustic record (Cooper et al. 1952; Harris 1953) yielded surprising failure, and such failures have been replicated ever since, and extended to the articulatory, electromyographic, aerodynamic, and auditory domains (but cf. Stevens' [1989, 1999] quantal theory which attempts to isolate some invariant acoustic properties). Continuous, context-dependent motion of a large number of degrees of freedom is what we find in physical records. As a response to this failure, phonological units (segments) have been removed from the domain of publicly observable phenomena, and have been hypothesized to be fundamentally mental units that are destroyed or distorted in the act of production, only to be reconstructed in the mind of the perceiver (e.g., Hockett 1955; Ohala 1981).

Articulatory Phonology (Browman and Goldstein 1992a, 1995a) has proposed, following Fowler (1980), that the failure to find phonological units in the public record was due to looking at too shallow a description of the act of speech production, and that it is, in fact, possible to decompose *vocal tract action* during speech production into discrete, re-combinable units. The central idea is that while the articulatory and acoustic *products* of speech production actions are continuous and context-dependent, the actions themselves that engage the vocal tract and regulate the motions of its articulators are discrete and context-independent. In other words, phonological units are abstract with respect to the articulatory and acoustic variables that are typically measured, but not so abstract as to leave the realm of the vocal tract and recede into the mind. They are abstract in being coarse-grained (low dimensional) with respect to the specific motions of the articulators and to the acoustic structure that may specify the motions.

2.2. Units of combination (atoms) are constriction actions of vocal organs

Articulatory Phonology makes three key hypotheses about the nature of phonological units that allow these units to serve their dual roles as units of action and units of combination (and contrast). These are: that vocal tract activity can be analyzed into constriction actions of distinct vocal organs, that actions are organized into temporally overlapping structures, and that constriction formation is appropriately modeled by dynamical systems.

2.2.1. Constriction actions and the organs that produce them

It is possible to decompose the behavior of the vocal tract during speech into the formation and release of constrictions by six distinct constricting devices or *organs*: lips, tongue tip, tongue body, tongue root, velum, and larynx. Although these constricting organs share mechanical degrees of freedom (articulators and muscles) with one another (for example, the jaw is part of the lips, tongue tip, and tongue body devices), they are intrinsically distinct and independent. They are distinct in the sense that the parts of the vocal anatomy that approach one another to form the constrictions are different, and they are independent in the sense that a constriction can be formed by one of these devices without necessarily producing a constriction in one of the others (a point made by Halle 1983, who referred to organs as *articulators*). Thus, constricting actions of distinct organs, actions known as *gestures*, can be taken as atoms of a combinatoric system – they satisfy the property of discrete differences (Browman and Goldstein 1989; Studdert-Kennedy 1998). Two combinations of gestures can be defined as potentially *contrasting* with one another if, for example, they include at least one distinct constriction gesture. The words *pack* and *tack* contrast with one another in that the former includes a lips gesture and the latter a tongue tip gesture.

The words *hill*, *sill*, and *pill* contrast with one another in the combination of constricting organs engaged at the onset of the word. *Hill* begins with a gesture of the larynx (glottal abduction); *sill* adds a gesture of the tongue tip organ to the laryngeal one and *pill* adds a lip gesture. These three gestures (larynx, tongue tip, and lips) all combine to create the contrasting molecule *spill*. The analysis of the onset of *spill* as composed of three gestures differs from an analysis of this form as composed of a sequence of two feature bundles (/s/ and /p/), in which each of those bundles has some specification for the larynx and a supralaryngeal gesture. Evidence in favor of the three-gesture specification has been discussed in Browman and Goldstein (1986).

Of course, not all phonological contrasts involve gestures of distinct organs. For example, *pin* and *fin* differ in the nature of the lip gestures at the beginning of the words. The discrete differentiation of the gestures involved in such contrasts critically depends on the public properties of a phonological system, and is discussed in the last section of this paper. However, it can also be argued that between-organ contrasts are the primary ones within phonological systems. For example, while all languages contrast constriction gestures of the lips, tongue tip, and tongue body, within-organ contrasts (such as [p-f], or [t-T]) are not universal.

2.2.2. Coordination of gestures and overlap

While traditional theories of phonology hypothesize that the primitive units combine by forming linear sequences, Articulatory Phonology hypothesizes that gestures are coordinated into more elaborated "molecular" structures in which gestures can overlap in time. Such *coproduction* of gestures can account for much of the superficial context-dependence that is observed in speech. The reason for this can be found in the nature of the distinct constricting organs, which share articulators and muscles. When two gestures overlap, the activities of the individual mechanical degrees of freedom will depend on both (competing) gestures. For example, consider the coproduction of a tongue tip constriction gesture with the tongue body gesture for different vowels (as in /di/ and /du/). The same (context-independent) tongue tip gesture is hypothesized to be produced in both cases, but the contribution of the various articulatory degrees of freedom (tongue tip, tongue body) will differ, due to the differing demands of the vowel gestures. The theory of task dynamics (Saltzman 1986, 1995, as discussed below) provides a formal model of such context-dependent variability.

Gestures are hypothesized to combine into larger molecules by means of coordinating (bonding) individual gestures to one another. This coordination can be accomplished by specifying a phase relation between the pair of coupled dynamical systems that control the production of the gestures within a task dynamic model (Browman and Goldstein 1990; Saltzman and Byrd 2000). Figure 1 shows how the gestures composing the utterance "team," are arranged in time, using a display called a *gestural score*. The arrows connect individual gestures that are coordinated with respect to one another. Recent work within Articulatory Phonology (Browman and

Goldstein 2000; Byrd 1996) has shown that the pairs of coordinated of gestures vary in how tightly they are bonded. *Bonding strength* is represented in the figure by the thickness of the arrows. Note that while there is no explicit decomposition of this molecule into traditional segmental units, the gestures that constitute segments (tongue tip and larynx gesture for /t/, lip and velum gesture for /m/) are connected by the thicker lines. High bonding strength is also found for gestures that compose a syllable onset, even when they do not constitute a single segment (e.g., tongue tip and lip gestures in the onset cluster /sp/), and it is not known at present whether their bonding differs from the intrasegmental bonds. In principle, bonding strength can be used to used to define a hierarchy of unit types, including segments, onset and rimes, syllables, feet, and words. The more tightly bonded units are those that we would expect to cohere in speech production and planning, and therefore, in errors.

Bonding strength can also be seen to correlate with combinatoric structure of gestures and may, in fact, emerge from that combinatoric structure developmentally. Syllable onsets are tightly bonded, and the number and nature of consonant combinations that can occur as syllable onsets (in English and in languages generally) is highly restricted (usually in accordance with the sonority hierarchy). The coordination of the onset gestures with the vowel is much looser, and there are virtually no constraints on combinations of onsets with vowels in languages – it is here that systems typically exhibit free substitutability. Thus, each onset recurs frequently with different vowels, a distribution that could allow the coordination of the onsets to be highly stabilized (through frequency of experience), but would not afford such stabilization for particular onset-vowel combinations

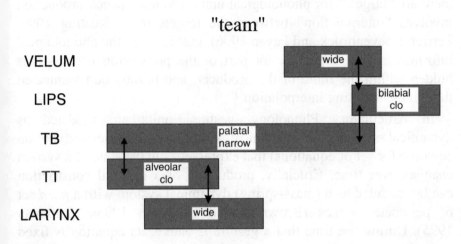

Figure 1. Gestural score for the utterance "team" as generated automatically by the model of Browman and Goldstein (1992a). The rows correspond to distinct organs (TB = "Tongue Body", TT = "Tongue Tip"). The labels in the boxes stand for gesture's goal specification for that organ. For example, "alveolar" stands for a *tongue tip constriction location* 56 degrees up from the horizontal and "clo" stands for a *tongue tip constriction degree* of −3.5mm (the tongue tip compresses against the palate). The arrows connect gestures that are critically coordinated, or phased, with respect to one another. The thicker arrows represent tighter *bonding strengths* between coordinated gestures.

not afford such stabilization for particular onset-vowel combinations (since they occur relatively infrequently). Thus, onsets (and in the limiting case, segments) can be considered *ions* of a combinatoric system: internally cohesive structures of atoms that recombine readily with other such structures.

2.2.3. Dynamical specification

One aspect of the physical description of speech seems particularly at odds with a description of discrete units: the fact that articulators move continuously over time. This continuous motion is modeled in most theories of phonology or speech production by assuming that there are "targets" for phonological units, and that speech production involves "interpolation" between the targets (e.g., Keating 1990; Perrier, Loevenbruck and Payan 1996). In this view, the phonological information (the target) is not part of the production itself – it is hidden within the mind of the producer, and is only communicated though the resulting interpolation.

In Articulatory Phonology, gestural units are modeled as dynamical systems. A dynamical system is characterized by an equation (or set of equations) that expresses how the state of a system changes over time. Crucially, production of a gestural constriction can be modeled as a (mass-spring) dynamical system with a *fixed* set of parameter values (Browman and Goldstein 1995a; Saltzman 1995). During the time that a gesture is active, its equation is fixed and time-invariant, even though the articulators are moving continuously. Moreover, the *way* in which the articulators move over time is specific to the particular dynamical system involved, and therefore, the gestural unit is specified directly in the motion itself.

2.3. Evidence for gestures as units of speech production

How can we test the hypothesis that the act of speech production can be decomposed into gestures – actions that form local constrictions? There is little direct evidence in the products of speech production (acoustics or articulator movements) for discrete units, as has been long observed. One kind of indirect evidence involves analysis-by-synthesis. It is possible to examine articulator motions and to infer from them a plausible gestural structure (such as that in Figure 1). The resulting structure can then be used as input to a gestural production model in order to test whether motions matching those of the original data are generated. This strategy has, in limited contexts at least, been used successfully to support particular hypotheses about gestural decomposition (Browman 1994; Browman and Goldstein 1992b; Saltzman and Munhall 1989).

Recently, some more direct evidence for decomposing speech production and/or planning into gestural structures has been obtained from speech production errors. Errors have long been used as evidence for linguistic units of various types (e.g., Fromkin 1973). The underlying assumption is that errors can result from systematic "misplacement" of linguistic units within a larger structure that is active during speech planning. For example, errors have been used to support the reality of abstract segments (internal, non-public units) as units of phonological encoding in speech production (e.g., Shattuck-Hufnagel 1983; Shattuck-Hufnagel and Klatt 1979). Transcriptions of errors suggest that segments are the most common units involved in errors (exhibiting changes in position, such as anticipations, perseverations, and exchanges). Evidence that the segments involved in errors are abstract (and not phonetic) is found in the fact that segments appear to be phonetically accommodated to the new contexts created for them by the errors. For example in the error *slumber party* → *lumber sparty* (Fromkin 1973), the /p/ is aspirated in *party* but unaspirated in *sparty*. In addition, errors involving segments have also been claimed to be (almost always) phonotactically well-formed strings of the language. These facts have been modeled (Shattuck-Hufnagel 1983) as arising during phonological planning by the insertion of a segmental unit into an incorrect *slot* in the phonological *frame*. Though incorrect, the slot is of the appropriate type for the segment in question, which accounts for the observed phonotactic well-formedness. Thus, utterances with errors are thought to be generally well-formed, both phonetically and phonotactically.

That this view of speech errors is complete was called into question by Mowrey and McKay (1990) who collected EMG data during the production of tongue twisters and found anomalous patterns of muscle activity that were not consistent with the notion that utterances with errors are phonetically and phonotactically well formed. Experiments in our laboratory have generated kinematic data that confirm and extend their results (Goldstein et al. submitted; Pouplier and Goldstein submitted;). These experiments involve repetition of simple two-word phrases such as *cop top*, in which the syllables are identical except for their initial consonants. Speakers who produce these phrases consistently produce errors of *gestural intrusion*, in which a "copy" of the oral constriction gesture associated with one of the initial consonants is produced during the other initial consonant. For example, in *cop top* a copy of the tongue dorsum gesture for the initial /k/ in *cop* can be observed during the /t/ in top (and conversely, a copy of the tongue tip gesture for /t/ can be observed during the /k/). These intrusions are usually reduced in magnitude compared to an intended gesture (and therefore such errors are often not perceived), but they can become as large as intended gestures, in which case a speech error is perceived.

These gestural intrusion errors cannot result from moving an abstract segment to the wrong position within a phonotactically well-formed frame. First, an intruded gesture is typically partial in magnitude. If an abstract segment were to move to an incorrect position, there is no reason why it should result in a reduced gesture. Second, intruded gestures are produced concurrently with the gesture(s) of the intended consonant, which may not exhibit reduction (For example, when the tongue dorsum gesture of /k/ intrudes on the /t/ of *top*, the tongue tip gesture for /t/ is still produced). Every speaker exhibits more errors of gestural intrusion than reduction. Thus, the speaker appears to be producing the gestures of the two words at the same time, which is not a phonotactically well-formed structure. In contrast, gestural intrusion errors can be readily accounted for if the structures involved in speech production and/or planning are gestural. The intrusion errors can be viewed as spontaneous transitions to a more intrinsically stable mode of coordination in which all gestures are produced in a 1:1 frequency-locking mode (which is known to be the most stable coordinative state in motor activities generally, e.g., Haken et al. 1996). For example, in the correct production of *cop top*, the tongue dorsum gesture for /k/ is coordinated in a 1:2 pattern with the gestures for the rime /ɒp/ (*op*), as is the tongue tip gesture for /t/. In productions with gestural intrusion, the relation with the rime gestures becomes 1:1, and, if both initial consonants exhibit intrusion errors (which does occur), then all gestures are produced in a 1:1 pattern.

It is important to note that gestural structures remain discrete in space and time in gestural intrusion errors, even when they are partial. Spatially, the articulatory record shows the simultaneous production of two distinct gestures, not a blended intermediate articulation. Temporally, the erroneous gesture is synchronized with the other initial consonant gesture, and does not slide continuously between its "home" and its intrusion site.

In some cases, a reduction of an intended gesture is observed when a gestural intrusion occurs. Such errors can be modeled as resulting from the competition between the intrinsically stable 1:1 mode and the learned gestural coordination patterns (molecules) of the language. These learned coordination patterns (for English) do not allow for both gestures (e.g., tongue tip for /t/ and tongue dorsum for /k/) to occur together.

How does this approach to speech errors account for cases like *slumber party* → *lumber sparty* that have been used to argue for the role of abstract mental units in speech production? The oral constriction gesture for /s/ (and possibly its laryngeal gesture) could be assumed to intrude at the beginning of the word *party*, and to reduce at the beginning of the word *slumber*. Alternatively, the gestural ion for /s/ may be mis-coordinated or mis-selected in the production of the phrase (the possible existence of such errors has not been ruled out). Under either interpretation, the resulting pattern of coordination of the oral and laryngeal gestures for /s/ and /p/ could combine to produce an organization that would be identified as an unaspirated [p], though articulatory data would be required to determine exactly how this comes about (see Browman and Goldstein 1986; Munhall and Löfqvist 1992; Saltzman and Munhall 1989).

2.4. *Phonological knowledge as (abstract) constraints on gestural coordination*

The goal of a phonological grammar is to account for native speakers' (implicit) knowledge of phonological structure and regularities in a particular language, including an inventory of lexically contrastive units, constraints on phonological forms, and systematic alternations to lexical forms that result from morphological combination and embedding in a particular prosodic context. If phonological forms are structures of coordinated gestures, as hypothesized in Articulatory Phonology, then gestural analysis should reveal generalizations (part of speakers' knowledge) that are obscured when phonological form is analyzed in some other way (in terms of features, for example). The property that most saliently differentiates gestural analyses from featural analyses is that gestural primitives are intrinsically temporal and thus can be explicitly coordinated in time. We therefore expect to find phonological generalizations that refer to patterns or modes of coordination, abstracting away from the particular actions that are being coordinated. Several examples of abstract coordination constraints have, in fact, been uncovered.

The coordination relation specified between two closure gestures will determine the resulting aerodynamic and acoustic consequences – whether there is an audible release of trapped pressure between the closures or not. So in principle one could characterize a sequence of closures either in terms of their abstract coordination pattern or their superficial release characteristics. Which characterization do speakers employ in their phonological knowledge? Gafos (2002) has shown that a crucial test case can be found when the same abstract coordination pattern can give rise to different consequences depending on whether the closures employ the same or distinct organs. In such cases, he finds languages in which the generalization must be stated in terms of coordination pattern not in terms of the superficial release properties. In Sierra Popoluca (Clements 1985; Elson 1947), releases are found between sequences of heterorganic consonants, but lack of release is found for homorganic sequences. A generalization can be stated in terms of an abstract coordination pattern (the onset of movement for the second closure beginning just before the release of the first closure), but not in terms of release. Note that an abstract decomposition of the articulatory record into gestures is required here. In the case of a homorganic sequence, it is not possible to observe the onset of movement of the second closure in the articulatory record – a single closure is observed. But the temporal properties of this closure fall out of a gestural analysis, under the assumption that there are two gestural actions in the homorganic case, coordinated just as they are in the heterorganic case (where they can be observed). In Sierra Popoluca, the generalization is a relatively superficial phonetic one (characterizing the form of the consonant sequence) that does not have consequences for the deeper (morpho)-phonology of the language. But Gafos then shows that in Moroccan Arabic, a similar coordination constraint interacts with other constraints (such as a gestural version of the obligatory contour principle) in determining the optimal set of (stem) consonants to fill a morphological template. In this case, constraints on the coordination of gestures contribute to an account of morphophonological alternations.

Another example of abstract coordination modes in phonology involves syllable structure. Browman and Goldstein (1995b) have proposed that there are distinct modes of gestural coordination for consonant gestures in an onset versus those in a coda, and that these modes are the public manifestations of syllable structure. In an onset, a synchronous mode of coordination dominates – consonant gestures tend to be synchronous with one another (to the extent allowed by an overall constraint that the gestures must be recoverable by listeners), while in a coda, a sequential mode dominates. Synchronous production is most compatible with recoverability when a narrow constriction is coproduced with a wider one (Mattingly 1981), and therefore is most clearly satisfied in the gestures constituting single segments, which typically involve combinations of a narrow constriction of the lips, tongue tip, or tongue body with a wider laryngeal or velic gesture (e.g., voiceless or nasal stops) or a wider supralaryngeal gesture (e.g., "secondary" palatalization, velarization, or rounding). Indeed the compatibility of synchronous production with recoverability may be what leads to the emergence of such segmental ions in phonology. But there is evidence that even multi-segment gestural structures (e.g., /sp/) exhibit some consequences of a tendency to synchronize onsets (Browman and Goldstein 2000).

Browman and Goldstein show that there are several featurally distinct types of syllable position-induced allophony that can be modeled as lawful consequences of these different coordination styles of onsets and codas. For example, vowels in English are nasalized before coda nasal consonants (but not before onset nasals). Krakow (1993) has shown that this can be explained by the fact that the oral constriction and velum-lowering gestures are synchronous in onsets, but sequential in codas, with the velum gesture preceding. The lowered velum superimposed on an open vocal tract is what is identified as a nasalized vowel. A very similar pattern of intergestural coordination can account for the syllable position differences in [l] – "lighter" in onsets and represented featurally as [-back], "darker" in codas and represented as [+back] (Browman and Goldstein 1995b; Krakow 1999; Sproat and Fujimura 1993). In this case the two coordinated gestures are the tongue tip closure and tongue dorsum retraction. Thus, two processes that are quite distinct in terms of features are lawful consequences of a single generalization about gestural coordination – the distinct styles of coordination that characterize onsets and codas. Compatible differences in coordination have been found for [w] (Gick in press) and for [r] (Gick and Goldstein 2002).

3. Parity in public language use

Articulatory Phonology provides a foundation on which compatible theories of speech production and perception may be built. Because these compatible theories are about between-person communication, a core idea that they share is that there must be a common phonological currency among knowers of language forms, producers of the forms and perceivers of them. That is, the language forms that language users know, produce and perceive must be the same.[2]

3.1. The need for a common currency in perceptually guided action, including speech

The common currency theme emerges from research and theories spanning domains that, in nature, are closely interleaved, but that may be traditionally studied independently. In speech, the need for a common currency so that transmitted and received messages may be the same is known as the parity requirement (e.g., Liberman and Whalen 2000).

The various domains in which the need for a common currency has been noted are those involving perception and action. An example is the study of imitation by infants. Meltzoff and Moore (1977, 1983, 1997, 1999) have found that newborns (the youngest 42 minutes after birth) are disposed to imitate the facial gestures of an adult. In the presence of an adult protruding his tongue, infants attempt tongue protrusion gestures; in the presence of an adult opening his mouth, infants attempt a mouth opening gesture.

It is instructive to ask how they can know what to do. As Meltzoff and Moore (e.g., 1997, 1999) point out, infants can see the adult's facial gesture, say, tongue protrusion, but they cannot see their own tongue or what it is doing. They can feel their tongue proprioceptively, but they cannot feel the adult's tongue. Meltzoff and Moore (1997, 1999) suggest that infants employ a "supramodal representation," that is, a representation that transcends any particular sensory system. To enable the infant to identify his or her facial or vocal tract "organs" with those of the model, the representation has to reflect what is common between the visually perceived action of the adult model and the proprioceptively perceived tongue and its action by the infant. The commonality is captured if the supramodal representation is of "distal" objects and events (tongues, protrusion gestures), not of the perceptual-system-specific proximal properties (reflected light patterns, proprioceptive feels) of the stimulation.

We will use the term "common currency" in place of "supramodal representation" to refer, not to properties of a representation necessarily, but merely to what is shared in information acquired cross-modally, and as we will see next, to what is shared in perceptual and action domains. To be shared, the information acquired cross-modally and shared between perception and action plans has to be distal; that is, it has to be about the perceived and acted-upon world. It cannot be about the proximal stimulation.

Imitation is perceptually guided action, and Meltzoff and Moore might have noted that a similar idea of a common currency is needed to explain how what infants perceive can have an impact on what they do. Hommel et al. (2001) remark that if perceptual information were coded in some sensory way, and action plans were coded in some motoric way, perceptual information could not guide action, because there is no common currency. They propose a "common coding" in which features of the perceived and acted upon world are coded both perceptually and in action plans. Here, as for Meltzoff and Moore, common currency is achieved by coding distal, not proximal properties in perception, and, in Hommel et al.'s account, by coding distal action goals, not, say, commands to muscles, in action plans.

In speech, two sets of ideas lead to a conclusion that speech production and perception require a common currency.

First, infants imitate speech (vowels) beginning as young as 12 weeks of age (Kuhl and Meltzoff 1996), and they integrate speech information cross-modally. That is, they look longer at a film of a person mouthing the vowel they are hearing than at a film of a model mouthing some other vowel (Kuhl and Meltzoff 1982). Both findings raise issues that suggest the need for a common currency, first between perceived infant and perceived adult speech, and second between speech perceived by eye and by ear.

Although imitation of vowels may involve information obtained intra- rather than cross-modally (as in tongue protrusion), how infants recognize a successful imitation remains a challenging puzzle. The infant has a tiny vocal tract, whereas the adult model has a large one. Infants cannot rely on acoustic similarity between their vowels and the model's to verify that they are imitating successfully. They need some way to compare their vowels with the adult's. Likewise, they need a way to compare visible with acoustically specified vowels. How can the infant know what facial gesture goes with what acoustic signal? The problem is the same one confronted by infants attempting to imitate facial gestures.

A solution analogous to that proposed by Meltzoff and Moore (1997, 1999) is to propose that listeners extract distal properties and events from information that they acquire optically and acoustically.[3] In this case, the distal events are gestural. Infants can identify their vowel productions with those of the adult model, because they perceive actions of the vocal tract (for example, tongue raising and backing and lip protrusion). In the gestural domain, these actions are the same whether they are achieved by a small or a large vocal tract. (This is not to deny that a nonlinear warping may be required to map an infant's vocal tract onto an adult's. It is to say that infants have lips, alveolar ridges on their palates, soft palates, velums, etc. They can detect the correspondence between the organs of their vocal tract and regions of their vocal tract with those of an adult. They can detect the correspondence of their actions using their organs in those regions with the actions of an adult.) The actions are also the same whether they are perceived optically or acoustically.

A second route to a conclusion that speaking and listening require a common currency is different from the first, but not unrelated to it. It concerns the fact that language serves a between-person communicative function. Liberman and colleagues (e.g., Liberman and Whalen 2000) use the term "parity" to refer to three requirements of language if it is to serve its communicative function. The first two relate to between-person communication. (The third is that, within a language user, specializations for speaking and listening must have co-evolved, because neither specialization would be useful without the other.) The first is that what counts for the speaker as a language form also has to count for the listener. As Liberman and Whalen put it, /ba/ counts, a sniff does not. If speakers and listeners did not share recognition of possible language forms, listeners would not know which of the noises produced by a speaker should be analyzed for its linguistic content. The second requirement is more local. It is that, for language to serve as a communication system, characteristically, listeners have to perceive accurately the language forms that talkers produce. There has to be "parity" or sufficient equivalence between phonological messages sent and received.

Articulatory Phonology provides a hypothesis about a common currency for speaking and listening. Like the other common currencies that we have considered, this one is distal.

3.2. Articulatory Phonology provides the common currency for speech

To communicate, language users have to engage in public, perceivable activity that counts as doing something linguistic for members of the language community. Listeners have to perceive that activity as linguistic and to perceive it accurately for communication to have a chance of taking place.

Language forms are the means that languages provide for making linguistic messages public. If language is well adapted to its public communicative function, then we should expect the forms to be (or to be isomorphic with) the public actions that count as talking. In particular, we should expect the forms to be such that they can be made immediately available to a listener – available, that is, without mediation by something other than the language forms. This is their nature in Articulatory Phonology.

However, in most phonologies, as we noted earlier (section 2.1), this is not their nature. In phonologies other than Articulatory Phonology, atomic language forms are mental categories. Moreover, in accounts of speech production and perception, the activities of the vocal tract that count as speaking are not isomorphic with those language forms, due in part, to the ostensibly destructive or distorting effects of coarticulation. This means that elements of phonological competence are only hinted at by vocal tract actions. Further, because vocal tract actions cause the acoustic signals that constitute the listener's major source of information about what was said, the acoustic signals likewise do not provide information that directly specifies the elements of phonological competence. Perception has to be reconstructive. In this system, talkers' phonological messages remain private. If communication succeeds, listeners represent the speaker's message in their head. However, transmission of the message is quite indirect. Language forms go out of existence as the message is transformed into public action and come back into existence only in the mind of the listener. This is not a parity-fostering system.

In contrast, Articulatory Phonology coupled with compatible theories of speech production and perception represents a parity-fostering system. Elements of the phonological system are the public actions of the vocal tract that count as speaking. What language users may have in their heads is knowledge about those phonological elements, not the elements themselves. If phonological atoms are public actions, then they directly cause the structure in acoustic speech signals, which, then, provides information directly about the phonological atoms. In this theoretical approach, language forms are preserved throughout a successful communicative exchange; they are not lost in the vocal tract and reconstituted by the perceiver.

Note that this hypothesis is not incompatible with the possibility that there are certain types of phonological processes that depend on the coarser topology of the gestural structures involved (e.g., syllable count, syllabification, foot structure and other prosodic domains) and not on the detailed specification of the actions involved. The hypothesis would claim that these coarser properties are ultimately derivable from the more global organization of public actions and do not represent purely mental categories that exist independently of any actions at all.

3.3. An integrative theory of phonological knowing, acting and perceiving

The gestures of Articulatory Phonology are dynamical systems that, as phonological entities, are units of contrast; as physical entities, they are systems that create and release constrictions in the vocal tract. A compatible theory of speech production is one that spells out how those systems generate constrictions and releases and how the gestures that form larger language forms are sequenced. To maintain the claim that atomic language forms are preserved from language planning to language perception, the account has to explain how coarticulated and coarticulating gestures nonetheless maintain their essential properties.

One such account is provided by task dynamics theory.

3.3.1. Task dynamics

Speech production is coordinated action. Like other coordinated actions, it has some properties for which any theory of speech production needs to provide an account. One property is equifinality. This occurs in systems in which actions are goal-directed and in which the goal is abstract in relation to the movements that achieve it. In Articulatory Phonology, the gesture for /b/ is lip closure. A gesture counts as a lip closure whether it is achieved by a lot of jaw closing and a little lip closing or by jaw opening accompanied by enough lip closing to get the lips closed.

Talkers exhibit equifinality in experiments in which an articulator is perturbed on line (e.g., Gracco and Abbs 1982; Kelso et al. 1984; Shaiman 1989). They also exhibit it in their coarticulatory behavior. In the perturbation research of Kelso et al., for example, a speaker repeatedly produced /baeb/ or /baez/ in a carrier sentence. On a low proportion of trials, unpredictably, the jaw was mechanically pulled down during closing for the final consonant in the test syllable. If the consonant was /b/, extra downward movement of the upper lip achieved lip closure on perturbed as compared to unperturbed trials.

If the consonant was /z/, extra activity of a muscle of the tongue allowed the tongue to compensate for the low position of the jaw. Equifinality suggests that gestures are achieved by systems of articulators that are coordinated to achieve the gestures' goals. These systems are known as synergies or coordinative structures. The synergy that achieves bilabial closure includes the jaw and the two lips, appropriately coordinated.

It is the equifinality property of the synergies that achieve phonetic gestures that prevents coarticulation from destroying or distorting essential properties of gestures. An open vowel coarticulating with /b/ may pull the jaw down more-or-less as the mechanical jaw puller did in the research of Kelso et al. However, lip closure, the essential property of the labial stop gesture is nonetheless achieved.[4]

The task dynamics model (e.g., Saltzman 1991, 1995; Saltzman and Kelso 1987; Saltzman and Munhall 1989) exhibits equifinality and therefore the nondestructive consequences of coarticulation needed to ensure that gestures are achieved in public language performance.

In the task dynamics model, the synergies that achieve gestures are modeled as dynamical systems. The systems are characterized by attractors to the goal state of a phonetic gesture. These goal states are specified in terms of "tract variables." Because, in Articulatory Phonology, gestures create and release constrictions, tract variables define the constriction space: they are specific to the organs of the vocal tract that can achieve constrictions, and they specify a particular constriction degree and location for that constricting organ. For example, /d/ is produced with a constriction of the tongue tip organ; the relevant tract variables are "TTCL" and "TTCD" (tongue tip constriction location and constriction degree). They are parameterized for /d/ so that the constriction location is at the alveolar ridge of the palate and constriction degree is a complete closure. In task dynamics, gestural dynamics are those of a damped mass-spring, and the dynamics are such that gesture-specific tract variable values emerge as point attractors. The dynamical systems exhibit the equifinality property required to understand how coarticulation can perturb production of a gesture without preventing achievement of its essential properties.

In one version of task dynamics, gestures are sequenced by the gestural scores generated by Articulatory Phonology from a specification of coordination (phase) relation among the gestures. Each gesture is associated with an activation wave that determines the temporal interval over which the gesture exerts an influence on the dynamics of the vocal tract. Due to coarticulation, activation waves overlap.

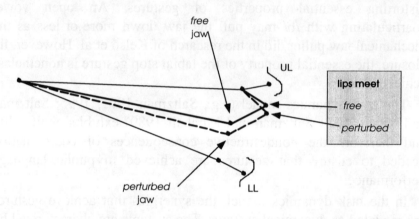

Figure 2. Simulation of lip and jaw behavior under task dynamic control. The dashed line shows the position of the jaw and lips when the jaw is *perturbed* (by being mechanically restrained in a low position), and the solid line shows the positions when the jaw is *free* to move. The lips close in both cases, but increased movement of both upper and lower lips contributes to the closure goal in the *perturbed* condition (after Saltzman 1986).

Figure 2 shows a model vocal tract (lips and jaw only) under task dynamic control achieving lip closure under perturbed and unperturbed (free) conditions. When the jaw is prevented from closing (the dashed line in Figure 2), the lips compensate by moving farther than on unperturbed productions (the solid line). Figure 3 shows equifinal production of /d/ during coarticulation with different vowels. The top of the figure shows the shape of the front part of the tongue during the /d/ closure in the utterances /idi/, /ada/, /udu/ (as measured by x-ray microbeam data). The bottom of the figure shows the front part of the tongue during closure for /idi/, /ada/, /udu/ as generated by the computational gestural model (Browman and Goldstein 1992a), incorporating the task-dynamics model. The constriction of the tip of the tongue against the palate is the same (in location and degree) across vowel contexts, even though the overall shape of the tongue varies considerably as a function of vowel.

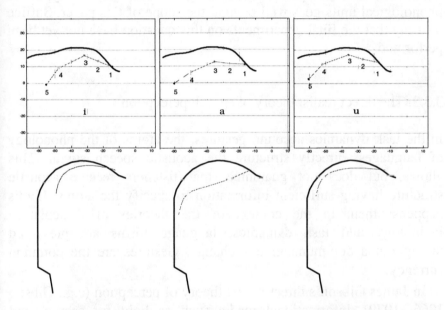

Figure 3. Equifinality of tongue tip closure: data and simulation. **Top**: Spatial positions of X-ray pellets during medial consonants of /pi'tip/, /pa'tap/, and /pu'tup/. Pellets on the surface of the tongue are connected by line segments are numbered from 1 (anterior) to 5 (posterior). Curve is an estimate of the position of speaker's palate. Units are millimeters. **Bottom**: Simulation of /idi/, /ada/, /udu/ using computational gestural model (Browman and Goldstein 1992a), incorporating task dynamics. Front part of tongue during /d/ is shown superimposed on overall outline of vocal tract. (Simulation was not an attempt to model the specific data shown, but employed general principles of gestural score constriction for English.)

Equifinality (or motor equivalence) in the task space is also a key property of other models of speech production, for example that developed by Guenther and his colleagues (e.g., Guenther 1995; this volume). A salient difference between Guenther's model and Saltzman's task dynamics model is that Guenther's model employs acoustic states in addition to orosensory states (which include constriction parameters) to specify speech goals, while the task dynamics model is completely constriction based. Summarizing the arguments for or against acoustic goals for various types of phonological units goes well beyond the scope of this paper. Suffice it to say that the final experiments on this question have not yet been performed.

3.3.2. The direct realist theory of speech perception

In the task dynamics account, gestures, the atoms of the phonology of languages, directly structure the acoustic speech signal. This allows, but does not guarantee, that listeners receive acoustic structure having sufficient information to specify the atoms. If this happens, then, in the context of the theories of Articulatory Phonology and task dynamics, language forms are preserved throughout a communicative exchange. Gestures are the common currency.

In James Gibson's direct realist theory of perception (e.g., Gibson 1966, 1979), informational media such as light for seeing, and acoustic energy for hearing do specify their distal sources. This is because there is a causal relation between properties of distal objects and events and structure in those media, and because distinctive properties of objects and events tend to structure the media distinctively. In this way, structure in media imparted to sensory systems serves as information for its distal source. In the account, whereas perceivers detect patterned energy distributions that stimulate their sense organs (the "proximal stimulus"), they perceive the properties and events in the world ("distal" events) that the energy distributions provide information about.

In the direct realist theory of speech perception (Best 1995; Fowler 1986, 1996), the gestures (distal events) that causally structure acoustic speech signals (proximal stimulation) are, in turn, specified by them. When the same gestures causally structure reflected light, they may also be specified by reflected light structure. This gives rise to the common currency that allows infants as well as adults to integrate speech information cross-modally.

Readers unfamiliar with direct realism sometimes ask how infants learn to connect the patterns of stimulation at their sense organs with the properties that stimulation specifies in the world. This question, however, has to be ill-posed. The only way that perceivers can know the world is via the information in stimulation. Therefore, the infant cannot be supposed to have two things that need to be connected: properties in the world and stimulation at sense organs. They can only have stimulation at the sense organs that, from the start, gives them properties in the world. This is not to deny that perceptual learning occurs (e.g., E. Gibson and Pick 2000; Reed 1996). It is only to remark that learning to link properties of the world with stimulation at the sense organs is impossible if infants begin life with no such link enabled.

The claim that listeners to speech perceive gestures has not been accepted in the speech community, but there is evidence for it. Summaries of this evidence are available elsewhere. Here we provide just a few examples.

3.3.2.1. Perception tracks articulation, I: Findings that led to Liberman's motor theory

Two findings were pivotal in Liberman's development of his motor theory of speech perception (e.g., Liberman 1957, 1996; Liberman et al. 1967). Both findings reflect how listeners perceive stop consonants. Liberman and colleagues had found that identifiable stop consonants in consonant-vowel syllables could be synthesized by preserving either of two salient cues for it, the second formant transition into the vowel or the stop burst.

In a study in which consonants were specified by their second formant transitions, Liberman and colleagues (Liberman et al. 1954) found that the transitions for the /d/ in /dV/ syllables were quite different depending on the vowel. /di/ and /du/ provided a striking comparison in this respect. The second formant transition of /di/ is high and rising in frequency to the level of the high second formant (F2) for /i/. The transition of /du/ is low and falling in frequency down to the level of the low F2 for /u/. Isolated from the rest of the syllable, the transitions sound different from one another in just the ways that their acoustic properties suggest; that is, they sound like high and low pitch glides. In context, however, they sound alike. Liberman (1957) recognized that the property that the /d/s in /di/ and /du/ share is articulatory. They are produced as constriction gestures of the tongue tip against the alveolar ridge of the palate. Because of coarticulation with the vowel, the transitions, which are generated after the constriction is released, are determined not only by the consonantal gesture, but by the vowel gesture or gestures as well.

Liberman and colleagues (Liberman, Delattre, and Cooper 1952) reported a complementary finding. /di/ and /du/ provide instances in which very different acoustic cues lead to identical perceptions of consonants that were produced in the same way. The complementary finding was that identical acoustic cues can signal very different percepts in different vocalic contexts. In this study, voiceless stops were signaled by the bursts that are produced just as stop constriction gestures are released. Liberman et al. found that the same stop burst, centered at 1440 Hz was identified as /p/ before vowels identified as /i/ and /u/, but as /k/ before /a/. Because of coarticulation with the following vowel, a stop burst at 1440 Hz had to be produced with different constriction gestures in the context of /i/ and /u/ versus /a/. These two findings led Liberman (1957) to conclude that when articulation and acoustics "go their separate ways," perception tracks articulation.

3.3.2.2. Perception tracks articulation, II: Parsing

That perception tracks articulation has been shown in a different way. Coarticulation results in an acoustic signal in which the information for a given consonant or vowel is distributed often over a substantial interval, and in that interval, production of other gestures also shapes the acoustic signal. Listeners parse the signal along gestural lines, extracting information for more than one gesture from intervals in which the acoustic signal was shaped by more than one gesture. Perception of fundamental frequency (F0) provides a striking example. The fundamental frequency of a speech signal is the result of converging effects of many gestures. Most notably, the fundamental frequency contour marks an intonational phrase. In addition, however, it can be raised or lowered locally by production of high or low vowels, which have, respectively, high and low intrinsic F0s (e.g., Whalen and Levitt 1995; Whalen et al. 1995). (That is, when talkers produce /i/ and /a/, attempting to match them in pitch, /i/ has a higher F0 than /a/.) The F0 contour may also be raised on a vowel that follows a voiceless obstruent (e.g., Silverman 1986, 1987). Remarkably, listeners do not perceive the F0 contour as the intonation contour; they perceive it as the intonation contour after parsing from F0 the effects of intrinsic F0 of vowels and of consonant devoicing. That is, two equal F0 peaks (marking pitch accents in the intonation contour) are heard as different in pitch height if one is produced on an /i/ and one on an /a/ vowel (Silverman 1987) or if one occurs on a vowel following an unvoiced and one a voiced obstruent (Pardo and Fowler 1997). The parsed F0 information is not discarded by perceivers. Parsed information about vowel intrinsic F0 is used by listeners as information for vowel height (Reinholt Peterson 1986); parsed information about consonant voicing is used as such (Pardo and Fowler 1997).

Nor are findings of gestural parsing restricted to perception of information provided by F0. Listeners use coarticulatory information for a forthcoming vowel as such (e.g., Fowler and Smith 1986; Martin and Bunnell 1981, 1982), and that coarticulatory information does not contribute to the perceived quality of the vowel with which it overlaps temporally (e.g., Fowler 1981; Fowler and Smith 1986). That is, information in schwa for a forthcoming /i/ in an /´bi/ disyllable does not make the schwa vowel sound high; rather, it sounds just like the schwa vowel in /´ba/, despite substantial acoustic differences between the schwas. It sounds quite different from itself cross-spliced into a /ba/ context, where parsing will pull the wrong acoustic information from it.

3.3.2.3. The common currency underlying audiovisual speech perception

In the McGurk effect (McGurk and MacDonald 1976), an appropriately selected acoustic syllable or word is dubbed onto a face mouthing something else. For example, acoustic /ma/ may be dubbed onto video /da/. With eyes open, looking at the face, listeners report hearing /na/; with eyes closed, they report hearing /ma/. That is, visible information about consonantal place of articulation is integrated with acoustic information about voicing and manner. How can the information integrate?

Two possibilities have been proposed. One invokes associations between the sights and sounds of speech in memory (e.g., Diehl and Kluender 1989; Massaro 1998). The other invokes common currency. Visual perceivers are well-understood to perceive distal events (e.g., lips closing or not during speech). If, as we propose, auditory perceivers do too, then integration is understandable in the same way that, for example, Meltzoff and Moore (1997) propose that cross-person imitation of facial gestures is possible. There is common currency between events seen and heard.

As for the association account, it is disconfirmed by findings that replacing a video of a speaker with a spelled syllable can eliminate any cross-modal integration, whereas replacing the video with the haptic feel of a gesture retains the effect (Fowler and Dekle 1991). There are associations in memory between spellings and pronunciations (e.g., Stone, Vanhoy, and Van Orden 1997; Tanenhaus, Flanigan, and Seidenberg 1980). Any associations between the manual feel of a speech gesture and the acoustic consequence should be considerably weaker than those between spelling and pronunciation. However, the magnitudes of cross-modal integration worked the other way.

Returning to the claim of the previous sections that listeners track articulations very closely, we note that they do so cross-modally as well. Listeners' parsing of coarticulated speech leads to "compensation for coarticulation" (e.g., Mann 1980). For example, in the context of a preceding /l/, ambiguous members of a /da/ to /ga/ continuum are identified as /ga/ more often than in the context of /r/. This may occur, because listeners parse the fronting coarticulatory effects of /l/ on the stop consonant, ascribing the fronting to /l/, not to the stop. Likewise, they may parse the backing effects of /r/ on the stop (but see Lotto and Kluender 1998, for a different account). Fowler, Brown and Mann (2000) found qualitatively the same result when the only information distinguishing /r/ from /l/ was optical (because an ambiguous acoustic syllable was dubbed onto a face mouthing /r/ or /l/), and the only information distinguishing /da/ from /ga/ was acoustic. Listeners track articulation cross-modally as well as unimodally.

3.3.2.4. Infants perceive gestures audiovisually

We have already cited findings by Kuhl and Meltzoff (1982) showing that four to five month old infants exhibit cross-modal matching. Given two films of a speaker mouthing a vowel, infants look longer at the film in which the speaker is mouthing the vowel they hear emanating from a loud speaker situated between the film screens. Converging with this evidence from cross-modal matching that infants extract supramodal, that is, distal world properties both when they see and hear speech is evidence that five month olds exhibit a McGurk effect (Rosenblum, Schmuckler, and Johnson 1997). Thus, infants extract gestural information from speech events before they can appreciate the linguistic significance of the gestures.

Development of that appreciation will accompany acquisition of a lexicon (e.g., Beckman and Edwards 2000).

3.3.3. A short detour: Mirror neurons

Our chapter is about the character of public language use. However, by request, we turn from that topic to consider a mechanism that, by some accounts, might plausibly underlie maintenance of a common currency between production and perception of speech. That is the mirror neuron uncovered in the research of Rizzolatti and colleagues (e.g., Gallese et al. 1996; Rizzolatti et al. 1996).

Mirror neurons, found in area F5 of the monkey cortex, fire both when the monkey observes an action, for example, a particular kind of reaching and grasping action, and when the monkey performs the same action. This is, indeed, a part of a mechanism that connects action to corresponding perceptions, and so part of a mechanism that arguably might underlie speech perception and production if those skills have the character that we propose. Indeed, it is notable that mirror neurons are found in the monkey homologue of Broca's area in the human brain, an area that is active when language is used.

However, we hasten to point out that mirror neurons in no way *explain* how production and perception can be linked or can be recognized to correspond. Indeed, mirror neurons pose essentially the same theoretical problem that we are addressing in this chapter, but now at the level of neurons rather than of whole organisms. How can a neuron "recognize" the correspondences that mirror neurons do? They fire in the brain of a monkey when a *human* (or other monkey) performs an appropriate action or when the same action is performed by the monkey itself. But how can the same action be recognized as such? Presumably the theory of mirror neuron performance will have to include some concept of common currency of the sort we have proposed for human speaker/listeners. In short, mirror neurons must constitute the culmination of the operations of a very smart neural mechanism the workings of which we understand no better than we understand the achievements of perceiver/actors.

3.3.4. Articulatory Phonology, task dynamics and direct realism

Articulatory Phonology, task dynamics and direct realism together constitute a mutually consistent account of public communication of language forms. Articulatory Phonology provides gestures that are public actions as well as being phonological forms. Task dynamics shows how these forms can be implemented nondestructively despite coarticulation. Direct realism suggests that gestures are perceptual objects.

Together, these accounts of phonological competence, speech production and speech perception constitute a perspective on language performance as parity-fostering.

4. Public language and the emergence of phonological structure

We have argued that the most basic phonological units must be discrete and re-combinable, and also that phonological units should provide a currency common to speech production and perception. Putting these two desiderata together means that we should find the same categorical units common to both speech perception and production that can serve as phonological primitives. In this section, we review some preliminary work that investigates the basis for decomposing production and perception into discrete units. This leads, in turn, to some predictions about the emergence of phonological categories in the course of phonological development and these appear to be borne out.

4.1. Distinct organs

We argued that one basis for discrete units in speech production could be found in the constricting organs of the vocal tract (lips, tongue tip, tongue body, tongue root, velum, larynx). They are anatomically distinct from one another and capable of performing constricting actions independently of one another. Note, too, that there is generally no continuum on which the organs lie, so that the notion of a constriction intermediate between two organs is not defined, e.g., between a velic constriction and a laryngeal constriction. (Although one could argue that the boundaries between the tongue organs are less sharp in this particular sense, they still exhibit distinctness and independence.) Studdert-Kennedy has proposed that this "particulation" of the vocal tract into organs could have provided the starting point for the evolution of (arbitrary) discrete categories in language (Studdert-Kennedy 1998; Studdert-Kennedy and Goldstein in press).

But what of discrete organs in speech perception? Evidence for perception of discrete organs can be found in the experiments on facial mimicry in infants described above (Meltzoff and Moore 1997). The imitations by infants are specific to the organ used by the adult model, even though they are not always correct in detail (for example, an adult gesture of protruding the tongue to the side might be mimicked by tongue protrusion without the lateral movement). Meltzoff and Moore report that when a facial display is presented to infants, all of their facial organs stop moving, except the one involved in the adult gesture.

So infants are able to distinguish facial organs (lips, tongue, eyes) as distinct objects, capable of performing distinct classes of actions. The set of organs involved in speech intersects with those on the face (lips and tongue common to both, though the tongue is further decomposed into tongue tip and tongue body), and also includes the glottis and the velum. As gestures of the speech organs are usually specified by structure in the acoustic medium (in addition to, or instead of) the optic medium, we would predict that acoustic medium could also be used to trigger some kind of imitative response on the part of infants to gestures of the speech-related organs (not necessarily speech gestures). So, for example, we would expect that infants would move their lips if presented with an auditory lip smack, or with [ba] syllables. Such experiments are being pursued in our laboratory.[5] Prima facie evidence that infants can, in fact, use acoustic structure in this way can be found in their categorical response to speech sounds produced with distinct organs, e.g., "place" distinctions – oral gestures of lips vs. tongue tip vs. tongue body – in newborns (Bertoncini et al. 1987). While it had been claimed (Jusczyk 1997) that young infants exhibit adult-like perception of *all* phonological contrasts tested (not just between-organ contrasts) some recent reports suggest that certain contrasts may not be so well perceived by young infants, or may show decreased discriminability at ages 10-12 months, even when they are present in the ambient language. These more poorly discriminated contrasts are all within-organ contrasts. For example, Polka, Colantonio, and Sundara (2001) found that English-learning infants aged 6-8 months showed poor discrimination of a /d – D/ contrast, a within-organ distinction that is contrastive in English. Best and McRoberts (in press) report decreased discriminability for a variety of within-organ contrasts at ages 10-12 months, *regardless* of whether they are contrastive in the language environment in which the child is being raised, but good discrimination of between-organ contrasts, even when the segments in question are not contrastive in the learning environment (e.g. labial vs. coronal ejective stops for English-learning infants).

The remarkable ability of infants to distinguish organs leads naturally to a view that distinct organs should play a key role in the emergence of phonology in the child. Recent analyses of early child phonology provide preliminary support for such a view. Ferguson and Farwell (1975), for example, showed that narrow phonetic transcriptions of a child's earliest words (first 50) are quite variable. The initial consonant of a given word (or set of words) was transcribed as different phonetic units on different occasions, and Ferguson and Farwell (1975) argue that the variability is too extreme for the child to have a coherent phonemic system, with allophones neatly grouped into phonemes, and that the basic unit of the child's production must therefore be the whole word, not the segment. However, if the child's word productions are re-analyzed in terms of the organs involved, it turns out that children are remarkably consistent in the organ they move at the beginning of a given word (Studdert-Kennedy 2000, in press; Studdert-Kennedy and Goldstein, in press), particularly the oral constriction organ (lips, tongue tip, tongue body). Thus, children appear to be acquiring a relation between actions of distinct organs and lexical units very early in the process of developing language. Organ identity is common to production and perception and very early on is used for lexical contrast.

4.2. Mutual attunement and the emergence of within-organ contrasts

As discussed earlier, distinct actions of a given organ can also function as contrastive gestures. Such contrastive gestures typically differ in the attractor states of the tract variables that control the particular organ. For example, *bet*, *vet*, and *wet* all begin with gestures of the lips organ, but the gestures contrast in the state (value) of the Lip Aperture (LA) tract variable (degree of lip constriction). Lips are most constricted for "bet," less so for *vet*, and least constricted for *wet*. Tongue tip gestures at the beginning of the words *thick* and *sick* differ the value of the Tongue Tip Constriction Location (TTCL) tract variable (position of the tongue tip along upper teeth and/or palate). The contrasting attractor values along LA or TTCL are in principle points along a continuum. How are these continua partitioned into contrasting states?

One hypothesis is that the categories emerge as a consequence of satisfying the requirement that phonological actions be shared by members of a speech community. In order to satisfy that requirement, members must attune their actions to one another. Such attunement can be seen in the spread of certain types of sound changes in progress (e.g. Labov 1994), in the *gestural drift* found when a speaker changes speech communities (Sancier and Fowler 1997), and in the babbling behavior of infants as young as 6 months old (de Boysson-Bardies et al. 1992; Whalen, Levitt, and Wang 1991). Mutual attunement must be accomplished primarily through the acoustic medium. Because the relation between constriction parameters and their acoustic properties is nonlinear (Stevens 1989), certain regions of a tract variable continuum will afford attunement, while others will not. Thus, the categories we observe could represent just those values (or regions) of the tract variable parameters that afford attunement. They are an example of self-organization through the public interaction of multiple speakers.

It is possible to test this hypothesis through computational simulation of a population of agents that acts randomly under a set of constraints or conditions. (For examples of self-organizing simulations in phonology, see Browman and Goldstein 2000; de Boer 2000; Zuraw 2000). In a preliminary simulation designed to investigate the partitioning of a tract variable constriction continuum into discrete regions, agents interacted randomly under the following three conditions: (a) Agents attempt to attune their actions to one another. (b) Agents recover the constriction parameters used by their partners from the acoustic signal, and that recovery is assumed to be noisy. (c) The relation between constriction and acoustics is nonlinear.

The simulation investigated an idealized constriction degree (CD) continuum and how it is partitioned into three categories (corresponding to stops, fricatives, and glides). Figure 4 shows the function used to map constriction degree to a hypothetical acoustical property, which could represent something like the overall amplitude of acoustic energy that emerges from the vocal tract during the constriction. The crucial point is that the form of the nonlinear function follows that hypothesized by Stevens (1989) for constriction degree and several other articulatory-acoustic mappings. Regions of relative stability (associated with stops, fricatives, and glides) are separated by regions of rapid change. The constriction degree continuum was divided into 80 equal intervals.

Two agents were employed. Each agent produced one of the 80 intervals at random, with some *a priori* probability associated with each interval. At the outset, all probabilities were set to be equal. The simulation then proceeded as follows. On each trial, the two agents produced one of the 80 intervals at random. Each agent then recovered the CD produced by its partner from its acoustic property, and compared that CD value to the one it produced itself. If they matched, within some criterion, the agent incremented the probability of producing that value of CD again. The recovery process works like this. The function in Figure 4 is a true function, so an acoustic value can be mapped uniquely onto the CD value. However, since we assume the acoustics to be noisy in the real world, a range of CD values is actually recovered, within +/- 3 acoustic units of that actually produced.

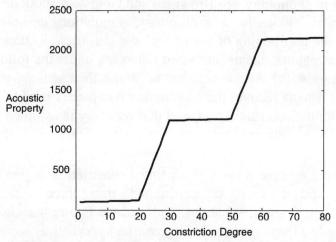

Figure 4. Mapping between Constriction Degree and a hypothetical Acoustic Property used in agent-based computational experiment. Shape of function after Stevens (1989).

Typical results of such a simulation (60,000 trials) are shown in Figure 5. For both agents (T1 and T2), the CD productions are now partitioned into 3 modes corresponding to the stable states of Figure 4. These values of CD in these regions are relatively frequently matched because of their acoustic similarity: Several values of CD fall into the +/-3 acoustic unit noise range in these regions, while only a few fall within the +/- 3 range in the unstable regions. Thus, mutual attunement, a concept available only in public language use, gives rise to discrete modes of constriction degree, under the influence of a nonlinear articulatory-acoustic map.

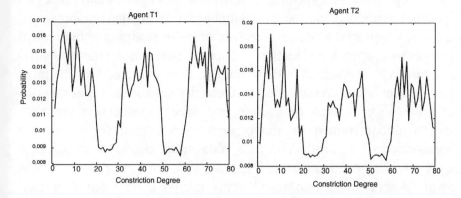

Figure 5. Results of agent-based experiment. Probability distributions of the two agents (T1 and T2) emitting particular values of constriction degree (60,000 iterations).

The role of attunement in partitioning within-organ contrasts is further supported by the developmental data described above. While children's early words are consistent in the oral constriction organ employed, and match the adult models in this regard, they are quite variable in within-organ properties, such as constriction degree (or constriction location). The simulations suggest that within-organ categories emerge only from attunement, which presumably takes some time. This conclusion is further bolstered by the recent perceptual findings with infants 10-12 months of age (Best and McRoberts in press), showing reduced discrimination for within-organ contrasts, even when the contrasts can be found in the language the child is about to acquire. At this age, infants have only begun to attune their vocal behavior to the language environment (de Boyssson-Bardies et al. 1992), and therefore partitioning of within-organ categories is expected to be incomplete.

5. Conclusions

In the fields of linguistics and psycholinguistics, there is an almost exclusive focus on the individual speaker/hearer and on the covert knowledge (linguistics) or the covert mental categories and processes (psycholinguistics) that support language use. In these approaches, there has appeared to be no scientific harm in studying phonological competence, speech production and speech perception independently, and that is how research in these domains has proceeded for the most part. Independent investigation of these domains means that theories of phonology, speech production and speech perception are each largely unconstrained by the others. Phonological forms are not constrained to be producible in a vocal tract, descriptions of vocal tract activities need not be, and are not, descriptions of phonological forms, and neither phonological forms, nor vocal tract activities need to be perceivable.

There *is* scientific harm in this approach, however, because language use is almost entirely a between-person activity, and it matters whether or not listeners perceive the language forms that speakers intend to convey. In our view, the prevalent views that language forms are mental categories, that coarticulation ensures that vocal tract activity is not isomorphic with the forms, and that listeners perceive acoustic cues are the erroneous consequences of the exclusive focus on the individual language user.

We start from the premise that languages evolved to be spoken and heard and, therefore, that language forms – the means that languages provide for making language use public – are likely to be public events. We have shown that a phonological system can be composed of public vocal events – that is, gestures. The gestures, not acoustic cues, can be supposed to be perceived. And public language forms can be shown to emerge, with the properties of ready produceability and perceivability that language forms do have, from imitative communicative exchanges between people. This, we argue, is real language.

Notes

1. Preparation of the manuscript was supported by NICHD Grant HD-01994, and NIDCD grants DC-03782 and DC-02717 to Haskins Laboratories.

2. Obviously, this sameness has to be within some tolerance. For example, not everyone who speaks the same language speaks the same dialect.

3. This is not the solution adopted by Meltzoff and Kuhl (1994) to explain audiovisual integration of speech. They propose that, during cooing and babbling, as infants produce speech-like acoustic signals, they learn a mapping from articulations to acoustic signals. Articulations, like other facial or vocal tract actions, can be perceived supramodally. Accordingly, the articulation-acoustic mapping can underlie audiovisual integration of speech.

4. It is, of course, possible that the essential properties of a gesture may fail to be completely achieved in some prosodic, stylistic, or informational contexts. For example, a closure gesture may be reduced and fail to result in complete closure. In such cases, the reduction can serve as information about the context. If the case of coarticulation, however, the essential properties of a gesture would be *systematically* obscured (and never achieved), if it were not for equifinality.

5. MacNeilage (1998) has argued that speech emerges from oscillatory movements of the jaw without specific controls for lips, tongue tip, and tongue body. It is possible that infants' early production of utterances with the global rhythmical properties of speech have the properties he proposes. However, infants may have some control of individual movements of the separate organs. It is just their integration into a more global structure that occurs only after that global structure is established through mandibular oscillation.

References

Abler, William
    1989   On the particulate principle of self-diversifying systems. *Journal of Social and Biological Structures* 12: 1-13.

Beckman, Mary and Jan Edwards
    2000   The ontogeny of phonological categories and the primacy of lexical learning in linguistic development. *Child Development* 71: 240-249.

198   *Louis Goldstein and Carol A. Fowler*

Bertoncini, Josiane, Ranka Bijeljac-Babic, Sheila E. Blumstein and Jacques Mehler
    1987   Discrimination in neonates of very short CV's. *Journal of the
                  Acoustical Society of America* 82: 31-37.
Best, Catherine T.
    1995   A direct realist perspective on cross-language speech perception.
                  In: Winifred Strange and James J. Jenkins (eds.), *Cross-
                  Language Speech Perception*, 171-204. Timonium, MD: York
                  Press.
Best, Catherine T. and Gerald W. McRoberts
    In press   Infant perception of nonnative contrasts that adults assimilate in
                  different ways. *Language and Speech.*
de Boer, Bart
    2000   Self-organization in vowel systems. *Journal of Phonetics* 28:
                  441-465.
de   Boysson-Bardies,   Benedicte,   Marilyn   Vihman,   Liselotte   Roug-
                  Hellichius,Catherine Durand, Ingrid Landberg and Fumiko Arao
    1992   Material evidence of infant selection from the target language: a
                  cross-linguistic study. In: Charles Ferguson, Lise Menn, and
                  Carol Stoel-Gammon (eds.), *Phonological Development: Models,
                  Resesarch, Implications*, 369-391. Timonium, MD: York Press.
Browman, Catherine P.
    1994   Lip aperture and consonant releases. In: Patricia Keating (ed.),
                  *Phonological Structure and Phonetic Form: Papers in
                  Laboratory Phonology III*, 331-353. Cambridge: Cambridge
                  University Press.
Browman, Catherine P. and Louis Goldstein
    1986   Towards an articulatory phonology. *Phonology Yearbook* 3: 219-
                  252.
Browman, Catherine P. and Louis Goldstein
    1989   Articulatory gestures as phonological units. *Phonology* 6: 151-
                  206.
Browman, Catherine P. and Louis Goldstein
    1990   Gestural specification using dynamically-defined articulatory
                  structures. *Journal of Phonetics* 18: 299-320.
Browman, Catherine P. and Louis Goldstein
    1992a   Articulatory phonology: An overview. *Phonetica* 49: 155-180.
Browman, Catherine P. and Louis Goldstein
    1992b   Targetless schwa: An articulatory analysis. In: Gerard J.
                  Docherty and D. Robert Ladd (eds.), *Papers in Laboratory
                  Phonology II: Gesture, Segment, Prosody*, 26-56. Cambridge:
                  Cambridge University Press.

Browman, Catherine P. and Louis Goldstein
1995a   Dynamics and articulatory phonology. In: Robert Port and
             Timothy van Gelder (eds.), *Mind as Motion: Explorations in the
             Dynamics of Cognition,* 175-193. Cambridge, MA: MIT Press.
Browman, Catherine P. and Louis Goldstein
1995b   Gestural syllable position effects in American English. In:
             Fredericka Bell-Berti and Lawrence Raphael (eds.), *Producing
             Speech: Contemporary Issues,* 19-33. New York: American
             Institute of Physics.
Browman, Catherine P. and Louis Goldstein
2000   Competing constraints on intergestural coordination and self-
             organization of phonological structures. *Bulletin de la
             Communication Parlée* 5: 25-34.
Byrd, Dani
1996   Influences on articulatory timing in consonant sequences.
             Journal of Phonetics 24: 209-244.
Clements, G. N.
1985   The geometry of phonological features. *Phonology Yearbook* 2:
             225-252.
Cooper, Franklin S., Pierre C. Delattre, Alvin M. Liberman, John M. Borst and
             Louis J. Gerstman
1952   Some experiments on the perception of synthetic speech sounds.
             Journal of the Acoustical Society of America 24: 597-606.
Diehl, Randy L. and Keith R. Kluender
1989   On the objects of speech perception. *Ecological Psychology* 1:
             121-144.
Elson, Ben
1947   Sierra Popoluca syllable structure. *International Journal of
             American Linguistics* 13: 13-17.
Ferguson, Charles A. and Carol B. Farwell
1975   Words and sounds in early language acquisition. *Language* 51:
             419-439.
Fontana, Walter and Leo Buss
1996   The barrier of objects: From dynamical systems to bounded
             organizations. In: John Casti and Anders Karlquist (eds.),
             Boundaries and Barriers, 56-116. Addison-Wesley, Reading,
             MA.
Fowler, Carol A.
1980   Coarticulation and theories of extrinsic timing. *Journal of
             Phonetics* 8: 113-133.

Fowler, Carol A.
1981   Production and perception of coarticulation among stressed and
              unstressed vowels. *Journal of Speech and Hearing Research* 46:
              127-139.
Fowler, Carol A.
1986   An event approach to the study of speech perception from a
              direct-realist perspective. *Journal of Phonetics* 14: 3-28.
Fowler, Carol A.
1996   Listeners do hear sounds, not tongues. *Journal of the Acoustical
              Society of America* 99: 1730-1741.
Fowler, Carol A., Julie Brown and Virginia Mann
2000   Contrast effects do not underlie effects of preceding liquid
              consonants on stop identification in humans. *Journal of
              Experimental Psychology: Human Perception and Performance*
              26: 877-888.
Fowler, Carol A. and Dawn J. Dekle
1991   Listening with eye and hand: Crossmodal contributions to speech
              perception. *Journal of Experimental Psychology: Human
              Perception and Performance* 17: 816-828.
Fowler, Carol A. and Mary Smith
1986   Speech perception as "vector analysis": An approach to the
              problems of invariance and segmentation. In: Joseph S. Perkell
              and Dennis H. Klatt (eds.), *Invariance and Variability in Speech
              Processes*, 123-136. Hillsdale, NJ: Lawrence Erlbaum
              Associates.
Fromkin, Victoria
1973   *Speech Errors as Linguistic Evidence.* The Hague: Mouton.
Gafos, Adamantios
2002   A grammar of gestural coordination. *Natural Language and
              Linguistic Theory* 20: 269-337.
Gallese, Vittorio, Luciano Fadiga, Leonardo Fogassi and Giacomo Rizzolatti
1996   Action recognition in the premotor cortex. *Brain* 119: 593-609.
Gibson, Eleanor and Anne Pick
2000   *An Ecological Approach to Perceptual Learning and
              Development.* Oxford: Oxford University Press.
Gibson, James J.
1966   *The Senses Considered as Perceptual Systems.* Boston, MA:
              Houghton-Mifflin.
Gibson, James J.
1979   *The Ecological Approach to Visual Perception.* Boston, MA:
              Houghton Mifflin.

Gick, Bryan
In press   Articulatory correlates of ambisyllabicity in English glides and
            liquids. In: John Local, Richard Ogden and Rosalind Temple
            (eds.), *Laboratory Phonology VI: Constraints on Phonetic
            Interpretation.* Cambridge: Cambridge University Press.
Gick, Bryan and Louis Goldstein
2002   Relative timing of the gestures of North American English /r/.
            Journal of the Acoustical Society of America 111: 2481.
Goldstein, Louis, Marianne Pouplier, Larissa Chen and Dani Byrd
Submitted   Dynamic action units slip in speech production errors. *Nature.*
Gracco, Vincent L. and James H. Abbs
1982   Compensatory response capabilities of the labial system to
            variation in onset of unanticipated loads. *Journal of the
            Acoustical Society of America* 71: S34.
Guenther, Frank
1995   Speech sound acquisition, coarticulation, and rate effects in a
            neural network model of speech production. *Psychological
            Review* 102, 594-621.
Haken, Hermann, Lieke Peper, Peter J. Beek and Andreas Dafferthofer
1996   A model for phase transitions. *Physica D* 90: 179-196.
Halle, Morris
1983   On distinctive features and their articulatory implementation.
            Natural Language and Linguistic Theory 1: 91-105.
Harris, Cyril M.
1953   A study of the building blocks in speech. *Journal of the
            Acoustical Society of America* 25: 962-969.
Hockett, Charles
1955   *A Manual of Phonetics.* Bloomington, Indiana: Indiana
            University Press.
Hommel, Bernhard, Jochen Müsseler, Gisa Aschersleben and Wolfgang Prinz
2001   The theory of event coding (TEC): A framework for perception
            and action planning. *Behavioral and Brain Sciences* 24: 849-937.
Jusczyk, Peter
1997   *The Discovery of Spoken Language.* Cambridge, MA: MIT Press.
Keating, Patricia A.
1990   The window model of coarticulation: Articulatory evidence. In:
            John Kingston and Mary E. Beckman (eds.), *Papers in
            Laboratory Phonology I: Between the Grammar and Physics of
            Speech*, 451-470. Cambridge: Cambridge University Press.

Kelso, J. A. Scott, Betty Tuller, Eric Vatikiotis-Bateson and Carol A. Fowler
1984   Functionally specific articulatory cooperation following jaw perturbations during speech: Evidence for coordinative structures. *Journal of Experimental Psychology: Human Perception and Performance* 10: 812-832.

Krakow, Rena
1993   Nonsegmental influences on velum movement patterns: Syllables, segments, stress and speaking rate. In: Marie Huffman and Rena Krakow (eds.), *Phonetics and Phonology, 5: Nasals, Nasalization and the Velum,* 87-116. New York: Academic Press.

Krakow, Rena
1999   Physiological organization of syllables: a review. *Journal of Phonetics* 27: 23-54.

Kuhl, Patricia and Andrew Meltzoff
1982   The bimodal perception of speech in infancy. *Science* 218: 1138-1141.

Kuhl, Patricia and Andrew Meltzoff
1996   Infant vocalizations in response to speech: Vocal imitation and developmental change. *Journal of the Acoustical Society of America* 100: 2425-2438.

Labov, William
1994   *Principles of Linguistic Change. Volume 1: Internal Factors.* Oxford: Basil Blackwell.

Liberman, Alvin M.
1957   Some results of research on speech perception. *Journal of the Acoustical Society of America* 29: 117-123.

Liberman, Alvin M.
1996   *Speech: A Special Code.* Cambridge, MA: Bradford Books.

Liberman, Alvin, Franklin S. Cooper, Donald Shankweiler and Michael Studdert-Kennedy
1967   Perception of the speech code. *Psychological Review* 74: 431-461.

Liberman, Alvin, Pierre Delattre and Franklin S. Cooper
1952   The role of selected stimulus variables in the perception of the unvoiced-stop consonants. *American Journal of Psychology* 65: 497-516.

Liberman, Alvin M., Pierre Delattre, Franklin S. Cooper and Louis Gerstman
1954   The role of consonant-vowel transitions in the perception of the stop and nasal consonants. *Psychological Monographs: General and Applied* 68: 1-13.

Liberman, Alvin M. and Douglas H. Whalen
　　2000　　　On the relation of speech to language. *Trends in Cognitive Sciences* 4: 187-196.
Lotto, Andrew and Keith Kluender
　　1998　　　General contrast effects in speech perception: Effect of preceding liquid on stop consonant identification. *Perception & Psychophysics* 60: 602-619.
MacNeilage, Peter F.
　　1998　　　The frame/content theory of evolution of speech production. *Behavioral and Brain Sciences* 21: 499-511.
Mann, Virginia
　　1980　　　Influence of preceding liquid on stop-consonant perception. *Perception & Psychophysics* 28: 407-412.
Martin, James G. and Timothy Bunnell
　　1981　　　Perception of anticipatory coarticulation effects in /stri, stru/ sequences. *Journal of the Acoustical Society of America* 69: S92.
Martin, James G. and Timothy Bunnell
　　1982　　　Perception of anticipatory coarticulation effects in vowel-stop consonant-vowel syllables. *Journal of Experimental Psychology: Human Perception and Performance* 8: 473-488.
Massaro, Dominic
　　1998　　　*Perceiving Talking Faces*. Cambridge, MA: MIT Press.
Mattingly, Ignatius
　　1981　　　Phonetic representation and speech synthesis by rule. In: Terry Myers, John Laver and John Anderson (eds.), *The Cognitive Representation of Speech*, 415-420. Amsterdam: North Holland Publishing Company.
McGurk, Harry and John MacDonald
　　1976　　　Hearing lips and seeing voices. *Nature* 264: 746-748.
Meltzoff, Andrew N. and Patricia Kuhl
　　1994　　　Faces and speech: Intermodal processing of biologically relevant signals in infants and adults. In: David Lewkowicz and Robert Likliter (eds.), *The Development of Intersensory Perception: Comparative Perspectives*, 335-369. Hillsdale, NJ: Lawrence Erlbaum.
Meltzoff, Andrew N. and M. Keith Moore
　　1977　　　Imitation of facial and manual gestures by human infants. *Science* 198: 75-78.
Meltzoff, Andrew N. and M. Keith Moore
　　1983　　　Newborn infants imitate adults' facial gestures. *Child Development* 54: 702-709.

204   *Louis Goldstein and Carol A. Fowler*

Meltzoff, Andrew N. and M. Keith Moore
    1997   Explaining facial imitation: a theoretical model. *Early Development and Parenting* 6: 179-192.
Meltzoff, Andrew N. and M. Keith Moore
    1999   Persons and representation: Why infant imitation is important for theories of human development. In: Jacqueline Nadel and George Butterworth (eds.), *Imitation in Infancy*, 9-35. Cambridge: Cambridge University Press.
Mowrey, Richard and Ian MacKay
    1990   Phonological primitives: Electromyographic speech error evidence. *Journal of the Acoustical Society of America* 88: 1299-1312.
Munhall, Kevin G. and Anders Löfqvist
    1992   Gestural aggregation in speech: Laryngeal gestures. *Journal of Phonetics* 20: 111-126.
Ohala, John
    1981   The listener as a source of sound change. In: Carrie Masek, Roberta Hendrick and Mary Frances Miller (eds.), *Papers from the Parasession on Language and Behavior,* 178-203. Chicago: Chicago Linguistics Society.
Pardo, Jennifer and Carol A. Fowler
    1997   Perceiving the causes of coarticulatory acoustic variation: Consonant voicing and vowel pitch. *Perception & Psychophysics* 59: 1141-1152.
Perrier, Pascal, Hélène Loevenbruck and Yohan Payan
    1996   Control of tongue movements in speech: the Equilibrium Point Hypothesis perspective. *Journal of Phonetics* 24: 53-75.
Polka, Linda, Connie Colantonio and Megha Sundara
    2001   A cross-language comparison of d-/ð/ perception: Evidence for a new developmental pattern. *Journal of the Acoustical Society of America* 109: 2190-2201.
Pouplier, Marianne and Louis Goldstein
    Submitted   Asymmetries in speech errors: Production, perception and the question of underspecification. *Journal of Phonetics*.
Reed, Edward
    1996   *Encountering the World: Toward an Ecological Psychology.* Oxford: Oxford University Press.
Reinholt Peterson, Niels
    1986   Perceptual compensation for segmentally-conditioned fundamental-frequency perturbations. *Phonetica* 43: 31-42.

Rizzolatti, Giacomo, Luciano Fadiga, Vittorio Gallese and Leonardo Fogassi
1996   Premotor cortex and the recognition of motor actions. *Cognitive Brain Research 3*: 131-141.
Rosenblum, Lawrence, Mark Schmuckler and Jennifer Johnson
1997   The McGurk effect in infants. *Perception & Psychophysics* 59: 347-357.
Saltzman, Elliot L.
1986   Task dynamic coordination of the speech articulators: A preliminary model. Generation and modulation of action patterns. In: Herbert Heuer and Christoph Fromm (eds.), *Experimental Brain Research, Series 15*, 129-144. New York: Springer-Verlag.
Saltzman, Elliot L.
1991   The task dynamic model in speech production. In: Herman F. M. Peters, Wouter Hulstijn and C. Woodruff Starkweather (eds.), *Speech Motor Control and Stuttering*, 37-52. Amsterdam: Elsevier Science Publishers.
Saltzman, Elliot L.
1995   Dynamics and coordinate systems in skilled sensorimotor activity. In: Robert Port and Timothy van Gelder (eds.), *Mind as Motion: Explorations in the Dynamics of Cognition*, 150-173. Cambridge, MA: MIT Press.
Saltzman, Elliot L. and Dani Byrd
2000   Task-dynamics of gestural timing: Phase windows and multi-frequency rhythms. *Human Movement Science* 19: 499-526.
Saltzman, Elliot L. and J. A. Scott Kelso
1987   Skilled action: A task-dynamic approach. *Psychological Review* 94: 84-106.
Saltzman, Elliot L. and Kevin G. Munhall
1989   A dynamical approach to gestural patterning in speech production. *Ecological Psychology* 1: 333-382.
Sancier, Michele and Carol A. Fowler
1997   Gestural drift in a bilingual speaker of Brazilian Portuguese. *Journal of Phonetics* 25: 421-436.
Shaiman, Susan
1989   Kinematic and electromyographic responses to perturbation of the jaw. *Journal of the Acoustical Society of America* 86: 78-88.
Shattuck-Hufnagel, Stefanie
1983   Sublexical units and suprasegmental structure in speech production. In: Peter MacNeilage (ed.), *The Production of Speech*, 109-136. New York: Springer-Verlag.

Shattuck-Hufnagel, Stefanie and Dennis Klatt
1979   Minimal uses of features and markedness in speech production: Evidence from speech errors. *Journal of Verbal Learning and Verbal Behavior* 18: 41-55.

Silverman, Kim
1986 F_0 cues depend on intonation: The case of the rise after voiced stops. *Phonetica* 43: 76-92.

Silverman, Kim
1987   *The Structure and Processing of Fundamental Frequency Contours.* PhD Dissertation, Department of Psychology, Cambridge University.

Sproat, Richard and Osamu Fujimura
1993   Allophonic variation in English /l/ and its implications for phonetic implementation. *Journal of Phonetics* 21: 291-311.

Stevens, Kenneth N.
1989   On the quantal nature of speech. *Journal of Phonetics* 17: 3-45.

Stevens, Kenneth N.
1999   *Acoustic Phonetics.* Cambridge, MA: MIT Press.

Stone, Gregory, Mickie Vanhoy and Guy Van Orden
1997   Perception is a two-way street: Feedforward and feedback in visual word recognition. *Journal of Memory and Language* 36: 337-359.

Studdert-Kennedy, Michael
1998   The particulate origins of language generativity. In: James Hurford, Michael Studdert-Kennedy and Christopher Knight (eds.), *Approaches to the Evolution of Language*, 202-221. Cambridge: Cambridge University Press.

Studdert-Kennedy, Michael
2000   Imitation and the emergence of segments. *Phonetica* 57: 275-283.

Studdert-Kennedy, Michael
In press   Mirror neurons, vocal imitation, and the evolution of particulate speech. In: Vittorio Gallese and Maxim Stamenov (eds.), *Mirror Neurons and the Evolution of the Brain and Language.* Amsterdam: John Benjamins.

Studdert-Kennedy, Michael and Louis Goldstein
In press   Launching language: The gestural origin of discrete infinity. In: Morten Christiansen and Simon Kirby (eds.), *Language Evolution: The States of the Art.* Oxford: Oxford University Press.

Tanenhaus, Michael, Helen Flanigan and Mark Seidenberg
 1980   Orthographic and phonological activation in auditory and visual word recognition. *Memory & Cognition* 8: 513-520.

Whalen, Douglas H., Andrea G. Levitt and Qi Wang
 1991   Intonational differences between the reduplicative babbling of French- and English-learning infants. *Journal of Child Language* 18: 501-516.

Whalen, Douglas H. and Andrea G. Levitt
 1995   The universality of intrinsic F0 of vowels. *Journal of Phonetics* 23: 349-366.

Whalen, Douglas H., Andrea G. Levitt, Pai Ling Hsaio and Iris Smorodinsky
 1995   Intrinsic F0 of vowels in the babbling of 6-, 9-, and 12-month old French- and English-learning infants. *Journal of the Acoustical Society of America* 97: 2533-2539.

Zuraw, Kie
 2000   *Patterned Exceptions in Phonology.* PhD Dissertation, Department of Linguistics, University of California, Los Angeles.

Neural control of speech movements

Frank H. Guenther

1. Introduction

Controlling speech movements for producing the syllables that make up a spoken utterance requires a complex integration of many different types of information by the brain, including auditory, tactile, proprioceptive, and muscle command representations. This chapter addresses these representations and their interactions with reference to a model of the neural processes involved in the production of speech sounds such as phonemes and syllables. The model has been developed to account for a wide variety of experimental data concerning articulator movements in adults and the development of speaking skills in children. Neural correlates of the model's components have been identified, thus allowing the model to serve as a framework for interpreting and organizing the accumulating mass of data from functional imaging studies of the human brain.

Before proceeding, it will be useful to define some reference frames that are believed to be involved in the planning of speech movements. For the present purposes, a "reference frame" can be thought of as a coordinate frame that best captures the form of information represented in a particular part of the nervous system. For example, motoneurons that project to the articulatory musculature encode information in a *muscle length reference frame*. Interactions between brain regions can be thought of as transformations of information between the corresponding reference frames. The following paragraphs define several reference frames that are important for speech production.

1.1. Muscle length reference frame

This frame describes the lengths and shortening velocities of the muscles that move the speech articulators. At the level of the facial nuclei in the brain stem, which project to the articulatory musculature, muscle lengths or contractile states must be coded in order to position the speech articulators. However, this does not imply that the speech motor system utilizes an invariant muscle length target for each speech sound, and in fact much experimental data speak against this kind of target. For example, insertion of a bite block between the teeth forces a completely different set of muscle lengths to produce the same vowel sound, yet people are capable of compensating for bite blocks even before the first glottal pulse (Lindblom, Lubker, and Gay 1979), illustrating the human motor system's capacity to use different muscle length configurations to produce the same phoneme under different conditions. Sensory signals from muscle spindles in the articulatory muscles also represent information about muscle lengths and shortening velocities. These signals project to the cranial nuclei and upward to primary somatosensory cortex via the ventral posterior medial nucleus (VPMN) of the thalamus.

1.2. Articulator reference frame

The *articulator reference frame*, or articulator space, refers to a reference frame whose coordinates roughly correspond to the primary movement degrees of freedom of the speech articulators (e.g., Mermelstein 1973; Rubin, Baer, and Mermelstein 1981; Maeda 1990). Although it is clear that the primary movement degrees of freedom are closely related to the musculature, the articulator reference frame is often assumed to be of lower dimensionality than the muscle reference frame. For example, several muscles may move together in a synergy that effectively controls a single movement degree of freedom. Such a representation may be utilized, for example, at the level of primary motor cortex and primary somatosensory cortex. Within this view, the corticobulbar tract projections from motor cortex to facial nuclei in the brain stem perform an articulatory-to-muscular transformation, and projections from the muscle spindles to the primary somatosensory cortex via the cranial nerve nuclei and thalamus perform a muscular-to-articulatory transformation.

For the purposes of this article, the distinction between an articulator reference frame and a muscle length reference frame is relatively unimportant, and we will therefore typically equate the two. The distinction becomes more important, however, for lower-level modeling of the kinematics and dynamics of the speech articulators (e.g., Laboissière, Ostry, and Perrier 1995; Ostry, Gribble, and Gracco 1996; Stone 1991; Wilhelms-Tricarico 1995, 1996).

1.3. Tactile reference frame

This reference frame describes the states of pressure receptors (mechanoreceptors) on the surfaces of the speech articulators, as well as the cells in primary somatosensory cortex that receive projections from pressure receptors via the cranial nerve nuclei and thalamus. For example, pressure produced when the tongue tip is pressed against the hard palate is registered by neural mechanoreceptors in the tongue and palatal surfaces. Mechanoreceptors provide important information about articulator positions when contact between articulators is made, but provide little or no information when contact is absent. Here we will use the term *orosensory* to refer to a combination of tactile and muscle length information that represents the articulator configuration accurately throughout the range of articulations used in speech.

1.4. Constriction reference frame

Several researchers have proposed reference frames for speech production whose coordinates describe the locations and degrees of key constrictions in the vocal tract (e.g., Browman and Goldstein 1990; Coker 1976; Guenther 1994, 1995a; Saltzman and Munhall 1989). Typical constrictions include a tongue body constriction, tongue tip constriction, and lip constriction. It is important to note that the relationship between the constriction frame and the articulator frame is one-to-many; that is, a given set of constriction locations and degrees can be reached by an infinite number of different articulator configurations. In the case of a vowel, for example, the same target tongue body constriction could be reached with the mandible high and the tongue body low relative to the mandible under normal conditions, or with the mandible lower and the tongue body higher if a bite block is present. This one-to-many relationship makes it possible for a movement controller that uses invariant constriction targets and an appropriate mapping between the constriction and articulator frames to overcome constraints on the articulators (such as a bite block) by utilizing different articulator configurations to produce the same constrictions (e.g., Saltzman and Munhall 1989; Guenther 1992, 1994, 1995a). This ability to use different movements to reach the same goal under different conditions, called *motor equivalence*, is a ubiquitous property of biological motor systems and is addressed further in Section 4. In this chapter, we will assume that constriction information is part of the orosensory representation of the vocal tract.

1.5. Acoustic reference frame

The acoustic reference frame describes important properties of the acoustic signal produced by the vocal tract (e.g., formant frequencies, amplitudes, and bandwidths).

1.6. Auditory perceptual reference frame

The central nervous system has access to acoustic signals only after transduction by the auditory system. In the current chapter, the term "auditory perceptual" will be used to refer to the transduced version of the acoustic signal (cf. Miller 1989; Savariaux, Perrier, and Schwartz 1995) as represented in auditory cortical areas. Although the important aspects of the auditory representation for speech are still not fully understood, several researchers have attempted to characterize them. In the implementation of the DIVA model described below, we utilize the auditory perceptual frame proposed by Miller (1989), although we acknowledge the incompleteness of this auditory representation for capturing all of the perceptually important aspects of speech sounds. This auditory perceptual space is made up of three dimensions:

$$x_1 = \log(F1/SF0)$$

$$x_2 = \log(F2/F1)$$

$$x_3 = \log(F3/F2)$$

where $F1$, $F2$, and $F3$ are the first three formants of the acoustic signal, and $SF0 = 168(F0/168)^{1/3}$, where $F0$ is the fundamental frequency of the speech waveform. This space was chosen by Miller (1989) in part because these coordinates remain relatively constant for the same vowel when spoken by men, women, and children, unlike formant frequencies.

2. The DIVA model of speech production

Our laboratory has developed a neural network model of speech motor skill acquisition and speech production called the DIVA model (for Directions Into Velocities of Articulators). The model addresses the neural representations underlying speech production, as well as the nature of the interactions (or *mappings*) between these representations. The model describes speech production processes from the syllable level "on down"; i.e., it addresses the transformation of syllable- or phoneme-sized speech targets into the muscle commands that carry out the desired speech sound. For an account of the higher-level processes involved in transforming sentences into syllables for production, see Levelt (1989; Levelt, Roelofs, and Meyer 1999), and for a different perspective on syllable production, see Fujimura (2000).

A simplified block diagram of the DIVA model is provided in Figure 1. Each block in the diagram corresponds to a set of neurons that together constitute a neural representation, and arrows and filled semicircles correspond to mappings between the neural representations. Three of the mappings in the model, indicated by filled semicircles in the figure, are tuned during a "babbling stage" in which random movements of the speech articulators provide tactile, proprioceptive, and auditory feedback signals. This information is used to tune parameters that correspond to synaptic weights. These synaptic weights constitute the learned neural mappings, which effectively encode speaker-specific information about the relationships between articulator movements and their tactile, proprioceptive, and auditory consequences. After learning, these mappings are used for phoneme production. Because the model is a self-organizing neural network whose parameters are tuned during an action-perception cycle, it requires no explicit knowledge about the physical geometry of the vocal tract being controlled.

The synaptic weights of the first mapping, labeled "convex region targets" in the figure, encode targets for each phoneme the model encounters during babbling. These targets are defined in a planning space made up of auditory and orosensory dimensions. For example, the target for vowel sounds specifies a range of acceptable values of formant ratios (see Section 1). To account for the human ability to learn phoneme-specific and language-specific limits on acceptable articulatory and acoustic variability, the learned speech sound targets take the form of multidimensional regions, rather than points, in the planning space. This notion of phonemic targets as multidimensional regions provides a simple and unified explanation for many long-studied speech phenomena (see Guenther 1995a for details). This topic is addressed in Section 3.

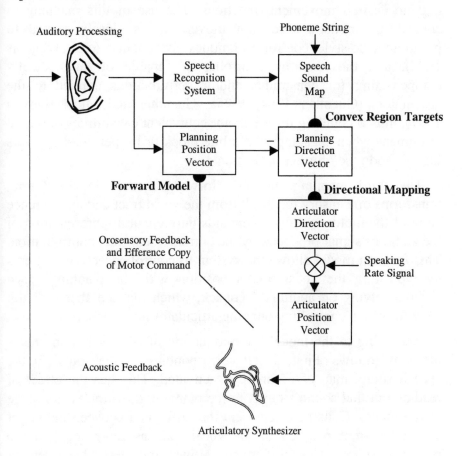

Figure 1. Overview of the DIVA model. Filled semicircles represent learned neural mappings. See text for details.

The second neural mapping, labeled "directional mapping" in the figure, transforms desired movement directions in planning space into movement directions in an articulator space closely related to the vocal tract musculature. This mapping embodies a solution to the inverse kinematic problem for control of a redundant manipulator (in this case, the vocal tract). The model posits that, during babbling, the brain learns a transformation from desired movement directions in auditory and orosensory spaces into articulator velocities that carry out the desired movement directions. The use of this mapping to control the model's articulator movements is closely related to pseudoinverse-style control techniques in robotics (e.g., Liégeois 1977), and the resulting controller is capable of automatically compensating for constraints and/or perturbations applied to the articulators (Guenther 1994, 1995a; Guenther and Micci Barreca 1997), thus accounting for the motor equivalent capabilities observed in humans when speaking with a bite block or lip perturbation. This topic is addressed further in Section 4.

The third mapping, labeled "forward model" in the figure, transforms orosensory feedback from the vocal tract and an efference copy of the motor outflow commands into a neural representation of the auditory signal produced by the current vocal tract configuration. This forward model allows the system to control speech movements by indicating the vocal tract's position with the planning space without relying on auditory feedback, which may be absent or too slow for use in controlling ongoing articulator movements.

According to the model, the production of a speech sound takes place as follows. First, a cell corresponding to the sound in the speech sound map of Figure 1 is activated. This has the effect of reading out that sound's target to the planning direction vector stage of the model. Cells here represent the difference between the target and the current position of the vocal tract as represented in the planning space. This difference defines the desired movement direction in the planning space, which consists of auditory and orosensory dimensions. The desired movement direction in planning space is transformed into a commanded movement direction in articulator space via the directional mapping projecting from the planning direction vector to the articulator direction vector stages. These directional commands are translated into positional commands at the articulator position vector stage. As the vocal tract moves to the target, the planning position vector is continuously updated via orosensory feedback and an efference copy of the motor command;

this information is mapped into the planning space via the forward model.

Computer simulations have been used to verify that the model provides a unified explanation for a wide range of data on articulator kinematics and motor skill development (Guenther 1994, 1995a,b; Guenther, Hampson, and Johnson 1998; Callan et al. 2000) that were previously addressed individually rather than in a single model. The model's explanations for several speech production phenomena are discussed in the next two sections, which deal with two important issues addressed by the model: the nature of the brain's "targets" for speech motor control, and the manner in which the nervous system achieves motor equivalence in speech.

3. The nature of speech sound targets

Most accounts of speech production involve some sort of "target" that the motor system hopes to achieve in order to produce a particular speech sound. For example, phoneme targets in the task-dynamic model (Saltzman and Munhall 1989) take the form of locations and degrees of key constrictions of the vocal tract. Targets in the DIVA model take the form of regions in a planning space consisting of auditory and orosensory dimensions (e.g. formant ratios and vocal tract constrictions). Each cell in the model's speech sound map (see Figure 1) represents a different sound (phoneme or syllable). The synaptic weights on the pathways projecting from a speech sound map cell to cells in the planning direction vector represent a target for the corresponding speech sound in planning space. When the changing vocal tract configuration is identified by the speech recognition system as producing a speech sound during babbling, the appropriate speech sound map cell's activity is set to 1. This in turn causes learning to occur in the synaptic weights of the pathways projecting from that cell, thereby allowing the model to modify the target for the speech sound based on the current configuration of the vocal tract.

To explain how infants learn phoneme-specific and language-specific limits on acceptable articulatory variability, the targets take the form of convex regions in planning space. This "convex region theory" is a generalization of Keating's (1990) "window model" of coarticulation to a multi-dimensional movement planning space consisting of auditory and constriction dimensions in addition to articulatory dimensions (see Guenther 1995 for further discussion of this topic).

Figure 2 schematizes the learning sequence for the vowel /i/ along two dimensions of planning space, corresponding to lip aperture and tongue body height. The first time the phoneme is produced during babbling, synaptic weights that project from the speech sound map cell for /i/ are adjusted to encode the position in planning space that led to proper production of the phoneme on this trial. In other words, the model has learned a target for /i/ that consists of a single point in the planning space, as schematized in Figure 2a. The next time the phoneme is babbled, the speech sound map cell expands its learned target to be a convex region that encompasses the previous point and the new point in planning space, as shown in Figure 2b; this can occur via a simple and biologically plausible learning law (Guenther 1995a). In this way, the model is constantly expanding its convex region target for /i/ to encompass all of the various vocal tract configurations that can be used to produce /i/.

An important aspect of this work concerns how the nervous system extracts the appropriate forms of auditory and orosensory information that define the different speech sounds. For example, how is it that the nervous system ''knows'' that it is lip aperture, and not lower lip height or upper lip height, that is the important articulatory variable for stop consonant production? How does the nervous system know that whereas lip aperture must be strictly controlled for bilabial stops, it can be allowed to vary over a large range for many other speech sounds, including not only vowels but also velar, alveolar, and dental stops? How does the nervous system of a Japanese speaker know that tongue tip location during production of /r/ can often vary widely, while the nervous system of an English speaker knows to control tongue tip location more strictly when producing /r/ so that /l/ is not produced instead?

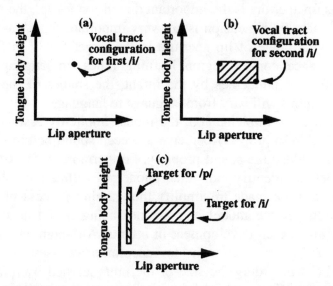

Figure 2.   Learning of the convex region target for the vowel /ı/ along planning dimensions corresponding to lip aperture and tongue body height. (a) The first time /i/ is produced during babbling, the learned target is simply the configuration of the vocal tract when the sound was produced. (b) The second time /i/ is babbled, the convex region target is expanded to encompass both vocal tract configurations used to produce the sound. (c) Schematized convex regions for /i/ and /p/ after many productions of each sound during babbling. Whereas the target for /i/ allows large variation along the dimension of lip aperture, the target for the bilabial stop /p/ requires strict control of this dimension, indicating that the model has learned that lip aperture is an important aspect of /p/ but not /i/.

The manner in which targets are learned in the DIVA model provides a unified answer to these questions. Consider the convex regions that result after many instances of producing the vowel /i/ and the bilabial stop /p/ (Figure 2c). The convex region for /p/ does not vary over the dimension of lip aperture but varies largely over the dimension of tongue body height; this is because all bilabial stops that the model has produced have the same lip aperture (corresponding to full closure of the lips), but tongue body height has varied. In other words, the model has learned that lip aperture is the important dimension for producing the bilabial stop /p/. Furthermore, whereas lip aperture is the important dimension for /p/, the model has learned that this dimension is not very important for /i/, as indicated by the wide range of lip aperture in the target for /i/ in Figure 2c. Finally, since convex region learning relies on language-specific recognition of phonemes by the infant, the shapes of the resulting convex regions will vary from language to language.

As currently implemented, the model implicitly assumes that an infant is able to properly perceive a speech sound before he/she can learn to produce the sound properly. Furthermore, it is assumed that the infant can identify individual phonemes within a syllable. These assumptions are made to simplify the learning process in computer simulations of the model and are not being posed as hypotheses concerning speech development in infants. Although we believe the model is general enough to accommodate several different possibilities regarding the size of the units learned by infants (e.g., syllables vs. phonemes) and the relationship between perceptual and production learning, these complex issues are currently beyond the scope of the model's explanatory capabilities.

An interesting property of the model's learning process is that the model can learn to "ignore" totally unimportant orosensory or auditory dimensions by allowing variability throughout the entire range of such dimensions. For example, no harm is done by including dimensions that are important only for some languages but not for others, since speakers of languages that do not use a dimension can simply learn to ignore it. The babbling process causes the system to learn small target ranges for acoustically important planning dimensions (i.e., those that must be carefully controlled to successfully produce the desired sound, such as formant ratios for a vowel), and large ranges for relatively unimportant dimensions. When moving to a learned target, the model moves to the point on the convex region target that is closest to the current configuration of the vocal tract. If the vocal tract configuration is already within the range for a particular target dimension, no further movement is planned along this dimension. The effect of these properties on articulator movements is a general tendency not to move an articulator unless it needs to be moved, thus allowing the model to make very efficient movements (see Guenther 1995a; Guenther and Micci Barreca 1997; Guenther, Hampson, and Johnson 1998; Perkell et al. 2000).

The convex region theory of the targets of speech provides a unified explanation for a number of long-studied speech production phenomena. A brief summary of some of these data explanations is provided below; see Guenther (1995a) for further detail.

Convex region targets provide a natural framework for interpreting data on motor variability in speech: the motor system is careful to control movements along dimensions that are important for a sound (i.e., dimensions with small target ranges), but not movements along dimensions that are not important (those with large target ranges). The model accordingly shows more variability for acoustically unimportant dimensions as compared to acoustically important dimensions, as seen in the experimental results of Perkell and Nelson (1985).

The theory's explanation for carryover coarticulation is simple and straightforward: when producing a phoneme from different initial configurations of the vocal tract, different positions on the convex region target will be reached, as schematized in Figure 3, since the model moves to the closest point on the target region. The end effect of this is that the configuration used to produce a sound will depend on which sound precedes it, with the model choosing a configuration that is as close as possible to the preceding configuration. In contrast to the view of carryover coarticulation as the result of mechano-inertial effects, carryover coarticulation in the DIVA model is "planned" in the sense that it results from explicit movement commands. This planning does not require advance knowledge of later segments, but instead arises from the interaction between the configuration of the vocal tract at the start of a segment and the convex region target for the segment. As pointed out by Daniloff and Hammarberg (1973), the mechano-inertial explanation is inadequate since large carryover effects are seen at low speeds and may spread over two or three segments, indicating a deliberate process for producing these effects. Based on a study requiring subjects to begin an utterance before knowing its end, Whalen (1990) also hypothesized that carryover effects are probably largely planned, but to a lesser degree than anticipatory effects.

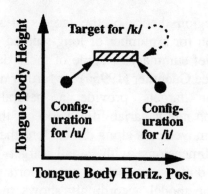

Figure 3.   Convex region theory account of carryover coarticulation in /k/ production. Approaching the target for /k/ from the configuration corresponding to the back vowel /u/ in "luke" leads to a final tongue body configuration that is further back than when approaching from the configuration corresponding to the front vowel /i/ in "leak".

The convex region theory's explanation of anticipatory coarticulation posits that the target region for a speech sound is reduced in size based on context in order to provide a more efficient sequence of articulator movements. Because the amount of anticipatory coarticulation is limited by the size of the convex region targets in the model, it accounts for experimental results showing decreased coarticulation in cases where smaller targets are necessitated, including speech in languages with more crowded vowel spaces (Manuel 1990), speech hyperarticulated for clarity (Picheney, Durlach, and Braida 1985, 1986; Lindblom and MacNeilage 1986) or stress (De Jong, Beckman, and Edwards 1993), and speech of small children who may have not yet learned the full range of variation allowed for some phonemes (Thompson and Hixon 1979; Kent 1983; Sereno and Lieberman 1987).

The model also provides an explanation for data regarding the effects of speaking rate on articulator movements (Guenther 1995a).

Shrinking of target regions for better accuracy during slower speech, as suggested by the well-known speed-accuracy trade-off known as Fitts' Law (e.g., Woodworth 1899; Fitts 1954), leads to differential effects for vowels and consonants: the speed of consonant movements decreases as one would expect, but the speed of vowel movements remains approximately constant or even increases. This is in concert with experimental data on speaking rate effects (e.g., Gay, Ushijima, Hirose, and Cooper 1974). The model shows how a single control process can produce these differential effects due to inherent differences in the shapes of the target convex regions for vowels and consonants. Despite the differential effects on movement velocities, the ratio of maximum velocity to movement distance increases by about the same amount for the two sound types, again as seen in human speaking data. Furthermore, cross-speaker differences in strategies for increasing speaking rate are captured by variation of a single parameter in the model.

4. Motor equivalence and directional mappings

Motor equivalence is the ability to carry out the same task using different motor means. For example, people are capable of producing written letters with very similar shapes using their wrist and fingers or shoulder and elbow (Merton 1972), their dominant or non-dominant arms (Raibert 1977; Wright 1990), and even using pens attached to their feet or held in their teeth (Raibert 1977). Motor equivalence is seen in a wide variety of human behaviors, including handwriting, reaching (e.g., Cruse, Brüwer, and Dean 1993), and speaking (e.g., Abbs and Gracco 1984; Lindblom, Lubker, and Gay 1979; Savariaux, Perrier, and Orliaguet 1995), and in a wide variety of species, including turtles (Stein, Mortin, and Robertson 1986) and frogs (Berkinblit, Gelfand, and Feldman 1986). The ubiquity of motor equivalence is no doubt the evolutionary result of its utility: animals capable of using different motor means to carry out a task under different environmental conditions have a tremendous advantage over those that cannot.

An enlightening example of motor equivalent behavior is the ability to use redundant degrees of freedom to compensate for temporary constraints on the effectors while producing movement trajectories to targets. For example, people normally use jaw movements during speech, but they can also successfully produce phonemes with a bite block clenched in their teeth by increasing lip and tongue movements to compensate for the fixed jaw. Compensation occurs immediately and automatically; i.e., without requiring practice with the bite block (Lindblom, Lubker, and Gay 1979), though a smaller additional increment in performance can be gained with some practice (Baum, McFarland, and Diab 1996; McFarland and Baum 1995).

The DIVA model has been formulated to deal with the problem of motor equivalence. The model stresses *automatic* compensation, i.e.:

- it successfully compensates for constraints on the effectors even if the constraints have never before been experienced,
- it does not require new learning or practice under the constraining conditions, and
- it does not invoke special control strategies to deal with constraints, instead utilizing the same control scheme used during unconstrained movements.

Automatic compensation can greatly reduce the computational requirements of movement planning, potentially freeing up cognitive resources for more important or more difficult tasks.

In order to understand the motor equivalent capabilities of the model, it is useful to consider a simplified view of the movement control process wherein movement trajectories are planned within some reference frame (the planning frame), and these trajectories are mapped into a second reference frame that relates closely to the effector or articulator system that carries out the movements. For example, one can consider speech production as the process of formulating a trajectory within a planning frame to pass through a sequence of targets, each corresponding to a different phoneme in the string being produced. The dimensions of this planning frame might correspond to acoustic quantities or locations and degrees of key constrictions in the vocal tract. The planned trajectory can then be mapped into a set of articulator movements that realize the trajectory. The articulator movements are defined within an articulator reference frame that relates closely to the musculature or primary movement degrees of freedom of the speech articulators. The process of mapping from the planning frame to the articulator frame need not wait until the entire trajectory has been planned, but instead may be carried out in concurrence with trajectory planning.

Based on a number of theoretical analyses and numerical simulation results, we have posited that maximal automatic compensation is possible if trajectory planning is carried out in a reference frame that relates closely to the task space for the movement (e.g., 3D space for reaching or an acoustic-like space for speaking), rather than a frame that relates more closely to the effector or articulator system (Bullock, Grossberg, and Guenther 1993; Guenther 1992, 1994, 1995a,b; Guenther, Hampson, and Johnson 1998; Guenther and Micci Barreca 1997). The use of auditory and orosensory dimensions that relate closely to the acoustic signal in the model's planning space is motivated by these findings.

Trajectories planned in task space must still be carried out by articulator or effector movements. One possibility is to use a position-to-position mapping from task space to articulator space; e.g., each point in acoustic space could be mapped to an articulator configuration that would achieve that acoustic result. Another possibility is to use a directional mapping from desired movement directions in task space into movement directions in articulator space. The DIVA model uses the latter form of mapping because it provides the automatic compensation for externally imposed constraints on effector motion (Guenther 1992, 1994, 1995a,b; Guenther, Hampson, and Johnson 1998). The use of a directional mapping for movement control is closely related to robotic controllers that utilize a generalized inverse, or pseudoinverse, of the Jacobian matrix relating task and effector spaces (e.g., Baillieul, Hollerbach, and Brockett 1984; Hollerbach and Suh 1985; Klein and Huang 1983; Liégeois 1977; Mussa-Ivaldi and Hogan 1991; Whitney 1969).

The ability to reach targets in pseudoinverse-style controllers such as the DIVA model is very robust to error in the directional mapping. This can been seen in the following example. Imagine an intended straight-line movement to a target in task space (e.g., auditory space for a speech sound), as schematized in Figure 4. Assume that a 30° error in the directional mapping causes the actual trajectory to veer upward from the desired straight-line trajectory. The planning direction vector (indicated by dashed arrows in the figure) always points from the current position to the target. As the actual trajectory moves further away from the desired trajectory, the planning direction vector points more and more downward to counteract the error. The system thus "steers in" toward the target. As long as the directional mapping is off by less than 90°, the target will be successfully reached, although for large directional errors the trajectory will deviate significantly from a straight line.

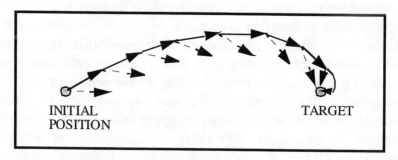

INITIAL   TARGET
POSITION

Figure 4.   Robustness to error in the directional mapping for targeted movements. Here a 30° error in the mapping causes the actual trajectory to veer from the desired straight-line trajectory. Dashed arrows indicate the desired task space movement direction at each point along the trajectory. As the actual trajectory moves further away from the desired trajectory, the task space direction vector points more and more downward to counteract this error in movement direction, allowing the system to "steer in" toward the target. As long as the directional mapping is off by less than 90°, the target will be successfully reached.

This automatic error-correction property has important implications for biological movement control. First, it suggests how a person can easily overcome constraints on the effectors (such as a cast limiting arm movement during reaching or a bite block limiting jaw movement during speaking) that effectively introduce error in the directional mapping, and thus provides an explanation for one form of motor equivalence. Simulations verifying the abilities of the DIVA model to overcome errors in the directional mapping due to blockage of one or more speech articulators are provided elsewhere (Guenther 1992, 1994, 1995a,b; Guenther, Hampson, and Johnson 1998). Second, it implies that even coarsely learned directional mappings, such as those possessed by an infant in the early months of life, can be used to reach objects or produce speech sounds, although with imperfect movement trajectories. Finally, it shows how error correction capabilities can automatically arise from the same mechanism used to control normal movements, unlike a controller that aims for postural targets and must somehow choose a new postural target if the normal target is inaccurate or unreachable due to external constraints.

5. Hypothesized neural correlates of the DIVA model

One advantage of the neural network approach is that it allows one to analyze the brain regions involved in speech in terms of a well-defined theoretical framework, thus allowing a deeper understanding of the brain mechanisms underlying speech. Figure 5 illustrates hypothesized neural correlates for several central components of the DIVA model. These hypotheses are based on a number of neuroanatomical and neurophysiological studies, including lesion/aphasia studies, brain imaging studies involving magnetoencephalography (MEG), positron emission tomography (PET), and functional magnetic resonance imaging (fMRI), and single-cell recordings from cortical and subcortical areas in animals. (For a related review of neuroimaging data on speech, see Indefrey and Levelt 2000.)

The pathway labeled 'a' in the figure corresponds to projections from premotor cortex to primary cortex, hypothesized to underlie feedforward control of the speech articulators. Pathway b represents hypothesized projections from premotor cortex (lateral BA 6) to higher-order auditory cortical areas in the superior temporal gyrus (BA 22) and orosensory association areas in the supramarginal gyrus (BA 40). These projections are hypothesized to carry target sensations associated with motor plans in premotor cortex. For example, premotor cortex cells representing the syllable /bi/ project to higher-order auditory cortex cells; these projections represent an expected sound pattern (i.e., the auditory representation of the speaker's own voice while producing /bi/). Similarly, projections from premotor cortex to orosensory areas in the supramarginal gyrus represent the expected pattern of somatosensory stimulation during /bi/ production. Pathway b is hypothesized to encode the convex region targets for speech sounds in the DIVA model, corresponding to the pathway between the speech sound map and planning direction vector in Figure 1.

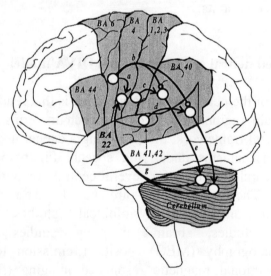

Figure 5. Hypothesized neural correlates of several central components of the DIVA model. BA = Brodmann's Area. See text for details.

One interesting aspect of the model in Figure 5 is the role of auditory cortical areas in speech production as well as speech perception. According to the model, auditory "targets" project from premotor cortical areas to the posterior superior temporal gyrus (pathway b), where they are compared to incoming auditory information from primary auditory cortex (pathway d). The difference between the target and the actual auditory signal represents an "error" signal that is mapped through the cerebellum (pathway f), which transforms the auditory error into a motor velocity signal that can act to zero this error (pathway g). This projection through the cerebellum to motor cortex forms a component of the Directions Into Velocities of Articulators mapping that gives the DIVA model its name.

Evidence that auditory cortical areas in the superior temporal gyrus and temporal plane are involved in speech production comes from a number of neuroimaging studies. For example, Hickok et al. (2000) report activation in left posterior superior temporal gyrus areas (planum temporale, superior temporal sulcus) during a PET visual object naming task in which the subject's auditory feedback of his/her own productions was masked with noise. Bookheimer et al. (1995) report activations near primary auditory cortex in a similar task. Paus et al. (1996) also reported activation in the area of the left planum temporale during a PET object-naming task. These authors attributed this activation to "motor-to-sensory discharges", compatible with pathway b in Figure 5. This interpretation receives support from an MEG study by Levelt et al. (1998), who showed that the auditory cortical activations during speech production slightly preceded the initiation of articulatory processes. All of these results provide support for the notion of auditory perceptual targets for speech production, in keeping with a central aspect of the DIVA model (e.g., Guenther 1995b; Guenther et al. 1998; see also Perkell et al. 1995; Bailly et al. 1991).

The model also proposes a novel role for the supramarginal gyrus (BA 40) in speech production. This brain region has been implicated in phonological processing for speech perception (e.g., Caplan, Gow, and Makris 1995; Celsis et al. 1999), as well speech production

(Geschwind 1965; Damasio and Damasio 1980). The current model proposes that, among other things, the supramarginal gyrus represents the difference between target oral sensations (projecting from premotor cortex via pathway b in Figure 5) and the current state of the vocal tract (projecting from somatosensory cortex via pathway c). This difference represents the desired movement direction in orosensory coordinates and is hypothesized to map through the cerebellum to motor cortex, thus constituting a second component of the Direction Into Velocities of Articulators mapping.

Not shown in Figure 5, for the sake of clarity, is the insular cortex (BA 43), buried within the Sylvian fissure. The anterior insula has been shown to play an important role in speech articulation (e.g., Dronkers 1996). This region is contiguous with the frontal operculum, which includes portions of the premotor and motor cortices related to oral movements. We adopt the view that the anterior insula has similar functional properties to the premotor and motor cortices. This view receives support from fMRI studies showing activation of anterior insula during non-speech tongue movements (Corfield et al. 1999), PET results showing concurrent primary motor cortex and anterior insula activations during articulation (Fox et al. 2001), and PET results showing concurrent lateral premotor cortex and anterior insula activations during articulation (Wise et al. 1999).

An important purpose of the model outlined in Figure 5 is to generate predictions that serve as the basis for focused functional imaging studies of brain function during speech. For example, the model of Figure 5 predicts that perturbation of a speech articulator such as the lip during speech should cause an increase in activation in the supramarginal gyrus, since the perturbation will cause a larger mismatch between orosensory expectations and the actual orosensory feedback signal. The model further predicts that extra activation will be seen in the cerebellum and motor cortex under the perturbed condition, since pathway e in Figure 5 would transmit the extra supramarginal gyrus activation to the cerebellum and on to motor cortex (pathways e, g). We are currently testing these and other predictions of the model using fMRI and MEG.

6. Summary

This chapter has described a model of the neural processes underlying speech production. This model has been designed to provide a simple and unified account for a wide range of experimental data, including functional brain imaging, psychophysical, physiological, anatomical and acoustic data. The model has also been used to study the effects of auditory feedback on speech in normally hearing individuals, hearing impaired individuals, and cochlear implant recipients (Perkell et al. 2000). According to the model, the goals of speech movements are regions in a planning space whose dimensions relate closely to the acoustic signal. It is hypothesized that projections from premotor cortex to higher-order auditory and somatosensory cortical areas encode these sound targets. Planned trajectories are mapped into articulator movements via a directional mapping between the planning and articulator spaces. This mapping is hypothesized to involve a pathway from higher-order auditory and somatosensory cortical areas through the cerebellum to the motor cortex.

Acknowledgements

This research was supported by the National Institute on Deafness and other Communication Disorders (NIH grants R01 DC02852, F. Guenther PI; R01 DC01925, R01 DC03007, J. Perkell, PI).

References

Collins, Allan M. and Elizabeth F. Loftus
    1975   A spreading-activation theory of semantic processing. *Psychological Review* 82: 407-428.
Abbs, James H. and Vincent L. Gracco
    1984   Control of complex motor gestures: Orofacial muscle responses to load perturbations of lip during speech. *Journal of Neurophysiology* 51: 705-723.
Baillieul, John, John Hollerbach and Roger W. Brockett
    1984   Programming and control of kinematically redundant manipulators. *Proceedings of the 23rd IEEE Conference on Decision and Control*, 768-774. New York: IEEE.
Bailly, Gerard, Rafael Laboissière and Jean-Luc Schwartz
    1991   Formant trajectories as audible gestures: An alternative for speech synthesis. *Journal of Phonetics* 19: 9-23.
Baum Shari R., David H. McFarland and Mai Diab
    1996   Compensation to articulatory perturbation: perceptual data. *Journal of the Acoustical Society of America* 99: 3791-3794.
Berkinblit, Misha B., Israil M. Gelfand and Anatol G. Feldman
    1986   A model of the aiming phase of the wiping reflex. In: S. Grillner, P. S. G. Stein, D. G. Stuart, H. Forssberg and R. M. Herman (eds.), *Neurobiology of vertebrate locomotion*, 217-227. London: Macmillan.
Bookheimer, Susan Y., Thomas A. Zeffiro, Teresa Blaxton, William Gaillard and William Theodore
    1995   Regional cerebral blood flow during object naming and word reading. *Human Brain Mapping* 3: 93-106.
Browman, Catherine and Louis Goldstein
    1990   Gestural specification using dynamically-defined articulatory structures. *Journal of Phonetics* 18: 299-320.
Bullock, Daniel, Stephen Grossberg and Frank H. Guenther
    1993   A self-organizing neural network model for redundant sensory-motor control, motor equivalence, and tool use. *Journal of Cognitive Neuroscience* 5: 408-435.
Callan, Daniel, Raymond Kent, Frank H. Guenther and Houri K. Vorperian
    2000   An auditory-feedback-based neural network model of speech production that is robust to developmental changes in the size and shape of the articulatory system. *Journal of Speech, Language and Hearing Research* 43: 721-736.

Caplan, David, David Gow and Nikos Makris
    1995   Analysis of lesions by MRI in stroke patients with acoustic-phonetic processing deficits. *Neurology* 45: 293-298.
Celsis, Pierre, Kader Boulanouar, J. P. Ranjeva, Isabelle Berry, Jean-Luc Nespoulous and F. Chollet
    1999   Differential fMRI responses in the left posterior superior temporal gyrus and left supramarginal gyrus to habituation and change detection in syllables and tones. *NeuroImage* 9: 135-144.
Coker, Cecil H.
    1976   A model of articulatory dynamics and control. *Proceedings of the IEEE* 64: 452-460.
Corfield, Douglas R., Kevin Murphy, O. Josephs, Gereon R. Fink, Richard S. J. Frackowiak, Abraham Guz, Lewis Adams and R. Turner
    1999   Cortical and subcortical control of tongue movement in humans: A functional neuroimaging study using fMRI. *Journal of Applied Physiology* 86: 1468-1477.
Cruse, Holk, M. Brüwer and Jeffrey Dean
    1993   Control of three- and four-joint arm movement: Strategies for a manipulator with redundant degrees of freedom. *Journal of Motor Behavior* 25: 131-139.
Damasio, Hanna and Antonio R. Damasio
    1980   The anatomical basis of conduction aphasia. *Brain* 103: 337-350.
Daniloff, Raymond and R. E. Hammarberg
    1973   On defining coarticulation. *Journal of Phonetics* 1: 239-248.
De Jong, Kenneth, Mary E. Beckman and Jan Edwards
    1993   The interplay between prosodic structure and coarticulation. *Language and Speech* 36: 197-212.
Dronkers, Nina F.
    1996   A new brain region for coordinating speech articulation. *Nature* 384: 159-161.
Fitts, Paul M.
    1954   The information capacity of the human motor system in controlling the amplitude of movement. *Journal of Experimental Psychology* 47: 381-391.
Fox, Peter T., Aileen Huang, Lawrence M. Parsons, Jin-Hu Xiong, Frank Zamarippa, Lacy Rainey and Jack L. Lancaster
    2001   Location-probability profiles for the mouth region of human primary motor-sensory cortex: Model and validation. *NeuroImage* 13: 196-209.

Fujimura, Osamu
    2000   The C/D model and prosodic control of articulatory behavior. *Phonetica* 57: 128-138.

Gay, Thomas, T. Ushijima, H. Hirose and Franklin S. Cooper
    1974   Effects of speaking rate on labial consonant-vowel articulation. *Journal of Phonetics* 2: 47-63.

Geschwind, Norman
    1965   Disconnexion syndromes in animals and man. I. *Brain* 88: 237-294.

Guenther, Frank H.
    1992   *Neural models of adaptive sensory-motor control for flexible reaching and speaking.* Doctoral dissertation, Boston University, Boston.

Guenther, Frank H.
    1994   A neural network model of speech acquisition and motor equivalent speech production. *Biological Cybernetics* 72: 43-53.

Guenther, Frank H.
    1995a   Speech sound acquisition, coarticulation, and rate effects in a neural network model of speech production. *Psychological Review* 102: 594-621.

Guenther, Frank H.
    1995b   A modeling framework for speech motor development and kinematic articulator control. *Proceedings of the XIIIth International Conference of Phonetic Sciences* Vol. 2, 92-99. Stockholm, Sweden: KTH and Stockholm University.

Guenther, Frank H., Carol Y. Espy-Wilson, Suzanne E. Boyce, Melanie L. Matthies, Majid Zandipour and Joseph S. Perkell
    1999   Articulatory tradeoffs reduce acoustic variability during American English /r/ production. *Journal of the Acoustical Society of America* 105: 2854-2865.

Guenther, Frank H., Michelle Hampson and David Johnson
    1998   A theoretical investigation of reference frames for the planning of speech movements. *Psychological Review* 105: 611-633.

Guenther, Frank H. and Daniele Micci Barreca
    1997   Neural models for flexible control of redundant systems. In: P. Morasso and V. Sanguineti (eds.), *Self-organization, Computational Maps, and Motor Control*, 383-421. Amsterdam: Elsevier-North Holland.

Hickok, Gregory, Peter Erhard, Jan Kassubek, A. Kate Helms-Tillery, Susan Naeve-Velguth, John P. Strupp, Peter L. Strick and Kamil Ugurbil
 2000 A functional magnetic resonance imaging study of the role of left posterior superior temporal gyrus in speech production: Implications for the explanation of conduction aphasia. *Neuroscience Letters* 287: 156-160.

Hollerbach, John M. and Ki C. Suh
 1985 Redundancy resolution of manipulators through torque optimization. *Proceedings of the IEEE International Conference on Robotics and Automation*, 1016-1021. New York: IEEE.

Indefrey, Peter and Willem J. M. Levelt
 2000 The neural correlates of language production. In M. Gazzaniga (ed.), *The new cognitive neurosciences*, 2nd Edition, 845-865. Cambridge, MA: MIT Press.

Keating, Patricia A.
 1990 The window model of coarticulation: Articulatory evidence. In: J. Kingston and M. E. Beckman (eds.), *Papers in laboratory phonology I: Between the grammar and physics of speech*, 451-470. Cambridge, UK: Cambridge University Press.

Kent, Raymond D.
 1983 The segmental organization of speech. In: P. Г. MacNeilage (ed.), *The production of speech*, 57-89. New York: Springer-Verlag.

Klein, Charles A. and Ching-Hsiang Huang
 1983 Review of pseudoinverse control for use with kinematically redundant manipulators. *IEEE Transactions on Systems, Man, and Cybernetics* SMC-13: 245-250.

Laboissière, Rafael, David J. Ostry and Pascal Perrier
 1995 A model of human jaw and hyoid motion and its implications for speech production. *Proceedings of the XIIIth International Conference of Phonetic Sciences* Vol. 2, 60-67. Stockholm, Sweden: KTH and Stockholm University.

Levelt, Willem J. M.
 1989 *Speaking: From intention to articulation.* Cambridge, MA: MIT Press.

Levelt, Willem J. M., Peter Praamstra, Antje S. Meyer, P. Helenius and R. Salmelin
 1998 An MEG study of picture naming. *Journal of Cognitive Neuroscience* 10: 553-567.

Levelt, Willem J. M., Ardi Roelofs, Antje S. Meyer
    1999   A theory of lexical access in speech production. *Behavioral and Brain Sciences* 22: 1-75.
Liégeois, Alain
    1977   Automatic supervisory control of the configuration and behavior of multibody mechanisms. *IEEE Transactions on Systems, Man, and Cybernetics,* SMC-7: 869-871.
Lindblom, Bjorn, James Lubker and Thomas Gay
    1979   Formant frequencies of some fixed-mandible vowels and a model of speech motor programming by predictive simulation. *Journal of Phonetics* 7: 147-161.
Lindblom, Bjorn and Peter F. MacNeilage
    1986   Action theory: Problems and alternative approaches. *Journal of Phonetics* 14: 117-132.
McFarland, David H. and Shari R. Baum
    1995   Incomplete compensation to articulatory perturbation. *Journal of the Acoustical Society of America* 97: 1865-73.
Maeda, Shinji
    1990   Compensatory articulation during speech: Evidence from the analysis and synthesis of vocal tract shapes using an articulatory model. In: William J. Hardcastle and Alain Marchal (eds.), *Speech production and speech modelling,* 131-149. Boston: Kluwer Academic Publishers.
Manuel, Sharon Y.
    1990   The role of contrast in limiting vowel-to-vowel coarticulation in different languages. *Journal of the Acoustical Society of America* 88: 1286-1298.
Mermelstein, Paul
    1973   Articulatory model for the study of speech production. *Journal of the Acoustical Society of America* 53: 1070-1082.
Merton, P. A.
    1972   How we control the contraction of our muscles. *Scientific American* 226: 30-37.
Miller, James D.
    1989   Auditory-perceptual interpretation of the vowel. *Journal of the Acoustical Society of America* 85: 2114-2134.
Mussa-Ivaldi, A. Ferdinando and Neville Hogan
    1991   Integrable solutions of kinematic redundancy via impedance control. *International Journal of Robotics Research* 10: 481-491.

Ostry, David J., Paul L. Gribble and Vincent L. Gracco
    1996   Coarticulation of jaw movements in speech production: Is context sensitivity in speech kinematics centrally planned? *Journal of Neuroscience* 16: 1570-1579.
Paus, Tomas, David W. Perry, Robert J. Zatorre, Keith J. Worsley and Alan C. Evans
    1996   Modulation of cerebral blood flow in the human auditory cortex during speech: Role of motor-to-sensory discharges. *European Journal of Neuroscience* 8: 2236-2246.
Perkell, Joseph, Frank H. Guenther, Harlan Lane, Melanie Matthies, Pascal Perrier, Jennell Vick, Reiner Wilhelms-Tricarico and Majid Zandipour
    2000   A theory of speech motor control and supporting data from speakers with normal hearing and with profound hearing loss. *Journal of Phonetics* 28: 233-272.
Perkell, Joseph S., Melanie L. Matthies, Mario A. Svirsky and Michael I. Jordan
    1995   Goal-based speech motor control: A theoretical framework and some preliminary data. *Journal of Phonetics* 23: 23-35.
Perkell, Joseph S. and Nelson, W. L.
    1985   Variability in production of the vowels /i/ and /a/. *Journal of the Acoustical Society of America* 77: 1889-1895.
Picheny, Michael A., Nathaniel I. Durlach and Louis D. Braida
    1985   Speaking clearly for the hard of hearing I: Intelligibility differences between clear and conversational speech. *Journal of Speech and Hearing Research* 28: 96-103.
Picheny, Michael A., Nathaniel I. Durlach and Louis D. Braida
    1986   Speaking clearly for the hard of hearing II: Acoustic characteristics of clear and conversational speech. *Journal of Speech and Hearing Research* 29: 434-446.
Raibert, Marc H.
    1977   Motor control and learning by the state space model. Technical Report AI-M-351, Massachusetts Institute of Technology.
Rubin, Philip, Thomas Baer and Paul Mermelstein
    1981   An articulatory synthesizer for perceptual research. *Journal of the Acoustical Society of America* 70: 321-328.
Saltzman, Elliot L. and Kevin G. Munhall
    1989   A dynamical approach to gestural patterning in speech production. *Ecological Psychology* 1: 333-382.
Savariaux, Christophe, Pascal Perrier and Jean P. Orliaguet
    1995   Compensation strategies for the perturbation of the rounded vowel [u] using a lip tube: A study of the control space in speech production. *Journal of the Acoustical Society of America* 98: 2428-2442.

Savariaux, Christophe, Pascal Perrier and Jean-Luc Schwartz
    1995   Perceptual analysis of compensatory strategies in the production
            of the French rounded vowel [u] perturbed by a lip tube.
            *Proceedings of the XIIIth International Congress of Phonetic
            Sciences* Vol. 3, 584-587. Stockholm, Sweden: KTH and
            Stockholm University.
Sereno, Joan A. and Philip Lieberman
    1987   Developmental aspects of lingual coarticulation. *Journal of
            Phonetics* 15: 247-257.
Stein, Paul S. G., L. I. Mortin and G. A. Robertson
    1986   The forms of a task and their blends. In: S. Grillner, P. S. G.
            Stein, D. G. Stuart, H. Forssberg and R. M. Herman (eds.),
            Neurobiology of Vertebrate Locomotion, 201-216. London:
            Macmillan.
Stone, Maureen
    1991   Toward a model of three-dimensional tongue movement. *Journal
            of Phonetics* 19: 309-320.
Thompson, A. E. and T. J. Hixon
    1979   Nasal air flow during normal speech production. *Cleft Palate
            Journal* 16: 412-420.
Whalen, Douglas H.
    1990   Coarticulation is largely planned. *Journal of Phonetics* 18: 3-35.
Whitney, D. E.
    1969   Resolved motion rate control of manipulators and human
            prostheses. *IEEE Transactions on Man-Machine Systems*, MMS-
            10: 47-53.
Wilhelms-Tricarico, Reiner
    1995   Physiological modeling of speech production: Methods for
            modeling soft-tissue articulators. *Journal of the Acoustical
            Society of America* 97: 3085-3098.
Wilhelms-Tricarico, Reiner
    1996   A biomechanical and physiologically-based vocal tract model
            and its control. *Journal of Phonetics* 24: 23-38.
Wise, Richard J., J. Greene, Christian Büchel and Sophie K. Scott
    1999   Brain regions involved in articulation. *Lancet* 353: 1057-1061.
Woodworth, Robert S.
    1899   The accuracy of voluntary movement. *Psychological Review* 3:
            1-114.

Wright, Charles E.
    1990   Generalized motor programs: Reexamining claims of effector independence in writing. In: Marc Jeannerod (ed.), *Attention and performance XIII: Motor representation and control*, 294-320. Hillsdale, NJ: Erlbaum.

When words come to mind: Electrophysiological insights on the time course of speaking and understanding words

Miranda van Turennout, Bernadette Schmitt, and Peter Hagoort

1. Introduction

Speaking involves the translation of an idea into a linear sequence of sounds. Whereas an idea, or thought, is verbally unspecified, speech consists of strings of words with a clear temporal order. A listener needs to extract the meaning of the sequence of spoken sounds by mapping the acoustic signal onto the appropriate words in the mental lexicon. A few decades of psycholinguistic research has provided detailed information about the different processing levels underlying speaking and listening. An issue that is still under debate, however, concerns the orchestration in real time of the retrieval of the distinct types of knowledge required to produce and understand fluent speech. In recent years electrophysiological methods have provided data that enable a fine-grained temporal analysis of production and comprehension processes. In this chapter, we will review recent studies that have used event-related brain potentials (ERPs) to track the time course of semantic, syntactic and phonological processing stages in the production and comprehension of single words and noun phrases. These studies have provided estimates of the time that is needed for the retrieval of distinct types of lexical information. We will use these time course data to evaluate predictions from computational models of language processing. Specifically, we will compare the empirical data with the time course estimates derived from the WEAVER++ model of speech production (Levelt, Roelofs, and Meyer 1999). Obviously, the data could also be used to evaluate alternative models of speech production (e.g., Caramazza 1997; Dell 1986) and comprehension (e.g., Norris 1994; Perfetti 1999). Although an interesting enterprise, it is beyond the scope of this chapter to critically review all current models of speech production and comprehension in the light of the available ERP data. Instead, we will focus on testing one specific model (WEAVER++) to demonstrate the value of electrophysiological data for language production and comprehension research. Before discussing the ERP studies, we will briefly sketch the main characteristics of WEAVER++, and describe the ERP method that was used to examine temporal parameters of language processing.

2. A model of speech production: WEAVER++

In describing the processing mechanisms underlying the transformation of a thought into speech, theories of speech production usually distinguish between semantic, grammatical, and phonological processing levels (e.g., Bock 1982; Butterworth 1989; Dell 1986; Garrett 1975, 1980; Kempen and Huijbers 1983; Levelt 1989). At the semantic level an input structure is prepared for the speech formulator. This input structure is often called the message (e.g., Garrett 1975; Levelt 1989), and selects from the many aspects of an idea the ones to be uttered. The message represents the speaker's intention, and specifies the content of the utterance. During grammatical processing, the semantic structure is translated into a syntactic representation. The semantic structure drives the activation and selection of the appropriate word representations in the mental lexicon. These representations are often called *lemmas* (Kempen and Huijbers 1983), and can be thought of as entries in the mental lexicon specifying a word's syntactic properties. Lemma activation makes available the syntactic characteristics of a lexical item that are needed for grammatical encoding (such as word-class and grammatical gender; see Kempen and Huijbers 1983; Levelt 1989; Roelofs 1992). Grammatical procedures are initiated to assign syntactic relations between the lexical items, and to determine their serial order in the utterance (Levelt 1989). During phonological processing, the sound form of the utterance is created. This involves the retrieval from the mental lexicon of the phonological properties of the words (e.g., the phonological segments of a word, its stress pattern, and its number of

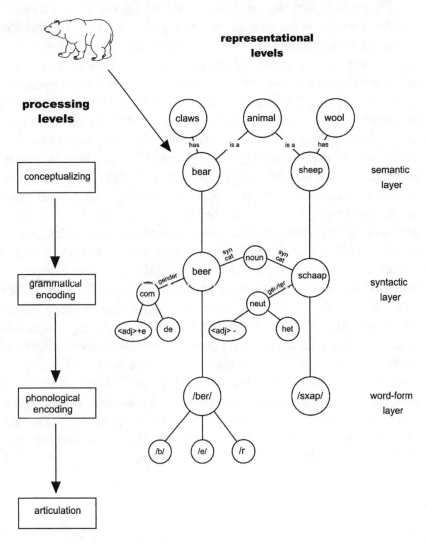

Figure 1. Illustration of the WEAVER++ model of speech production

syllables), and the construction of larger phonological units (e.g., phonological words and phrases). The end product of phonological encoding is a phonetic plan of the utterance to be executed by the articulators (for details see, for example, Dell 1986; Levelt 1989; Meyer 1992).

Figure 1 depicts the structure of WEAVER++. In this model, the mental lexicon is conceived of as a network, and information is retrieved from the network by means of spreading activation. The lexical network consists of three layers of nodes. First, at the semantic layer there are concept nodes and labeled links between the nodes. Following Collins and Loftus (1975), each node represents a single concept, and the meaning of the concepts is stored via labeled links between the nodes. For example, the 'is-a' link between the concept *bear* and the concept *animal* specifies that bear is a subtype of animal. Each lexical concept (that is, a concept for which a word exists) is represented by an independent node. The lexical concept nodes are linked to nodes at the second layer of the network: the syntactic layer. The syntactic layer contains lemma nodes, syntactic property nodes, and labeled links between them. At this stratum, the syntax of words is specified. For example the 'syntactic category' link between the lemma node *bear* and the syntax node *noun* indicates that the word "bear" is a noun. Lemmas also contain morpho-syntactic slots for parameters to be filled in during grammatical encoding, such as tense (e.g., present or past), number (single or plural), and person (first, second or third). The next layer is the word-form layer. In this layer, word-form nodes are linked to lemma nodes and they represent roots and affixes. Word-form nodes point to segment nodes, and to the metrical structure of a word. The actual syllables of a word are constructed on line, and depend on the phonological context in which a word occurs.

3. Temporal characteristics of speech production in WEAVER++

An important characteristic of the WEAVER++ model of lexical access is that it explicitly incorporates time information (Levelt, Roelofs, and Meyer 1999). Lemmas are retrieved by means of forward spreading of activation in the network. As a result of semantic encoding, activation spreads through the conceptual network down to the syntactic stratum. Due to the spreading of activation at the semantic layer a set of lemma nodes will be activated. The activational level of a lemma can be computed for each particular point in time. A lemma's activational level is determined by its activation at point t, and the rate with which this activation decays, plus the activational level of the connected nodes and the weights on the links between the nodes. The probability that a lemma indeed becomes selected at a particular point in time is given by the ratio of its own activational level and the activational level of other lemma nodes at that point in time (the Luce ratio). The expected lemma retrieval time can be computed given this ratio (see Roelofs 1992 for details). Once a lemma has been selected, activation spreads to the word-form stratum. The important assumption at this point in the theory is that *only* selected lemmas will activate their word form. For the time course of word retrieval this assumption implies that lemma selection will always *precede* activation of the word form. In the word-form stratum, activation spreads forward from word-form nodes to segment and syllable nodes. Nodes are selected according to similar rules as described for lemma selection. When a word-form node has been activated by its lemma, it immediately activates all of its segments, and its metrical frame. To achieve syllabification, the segments are associated with the syllable nodes within the metrical frame. The association proceeds from left to right: from the segment whose link is labeled first to the one whose link is labeled second and so forth. This implies that a word form is built up in a serial order, from its beginning to its end.

4. Using event-related brain potentials to track the time course of speaking

To examine the temporal dynamics of retrieving distinct types of lexical information at the millisecond-level, an on-line measure is required that taps into these processes as they proceed in time. Although reaction time research has provided insights into the coarse temporal organization of the processes involved in speaking (see, for example, Levelt et al. 1991), reaction times do not provide a continuous measure of the ongoing process. Recently, event-related brain potentials (ERPs) have been introduced into the field of speech production research. One of the attractive characteristics of ERPs is that they provide a continuous measure of the brain's electrical activity as it occurs in real-time. However, because of the artifacts that are evidently caused by the physical realization of speech, the investigation of brain potentials preceding and during speaking has been controversial (but see Eulitz, Hauk, and Cohen 2000 for a study on EEG correlates of phonological encoding during picture naming). In recent studies, however, these problems have been overcome by the use of an experimental paradigm that taps into separate processing stages of speech production before articulation has started. The experimental paradigm involves the measurement of the lateralized readiness potential (LRP), and the N200 component in connection to a task that combines a response decision with a go/nogo judgment.

4.1. The Lateralized Readiness Potential (LRP)

The lateralized readiness potential (LRP) is derived from the readiness potential (RP), a negative-going, motor-related brain potential that starts to develop 800 to 1000 ms prior to the onset of voluntary (hand) movements (Kornhuber and Deecke 1965). Later portions of the RP develop asymmetrically over the left and right motor cortex, being more negative over the scalp site contralateral to the moving hand. Kutas and Donchin (1980) showed that the lateralization of the readiness potentials was directly affected by the extent to which individuals were informed about the response hand. This finding led them to suggest that the asymmetric part of the readiness potential can be used as an index of motor preparation. Consistent with this idea, single cell recordings from monkey cortex showed that the lateralized part of the readiness potential is generated, at least in part, in the motor cortex (e.g., Arezzo and Vaughan 1980; Miller, Riehle, and Requin 1992; Requin 1985; Riehle and Requin 1989). Moreover, scalp recorded ERPs from humans showed that the amount of lateralization of the readiness potential appears to be directly related to the onset of overt motor behavior. That is, an overt response is initiated at the moment at which the lateralized readiness potential has reached a particular threshold value (Gratton et al. 1988). In addition, it has been shown that the readiness potential can start to lateralize even when a response has not yet been completely specified, suggesting that the onset of the LRP is related to motor preparation, and not execution (for an overview see Coles 1989; Coles et al. 1995). Together these findings support the idea that the lateralized part of the RP provides a real-time measure of selective response preparation.

To isolate the lateralized part of the RP from all other lateralized potentials, the LRP is computed with respect to the correct response hand (cf. Coles 1989; De Jong et al. 1988). First, on each trial the amount of lateralized activity is obtained by subtracting the potentials recorded from above the left (C3') and right (C4') motor cortices. These difference waveforms are averaged separately for trials in which the left versus the right hand was cued (Figure 2A). Second, to cancel out lateralized potentials that are not specifically related to response preparation, the average lateralization obtained for the left-hand trials is subtracted from the average lateralization obtained for the right-hand trials (Figure 2B). The resulting LRP reflects the average amount of lateralization occurring as a result of central motor preparation.

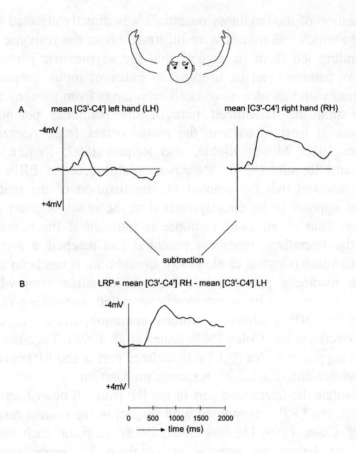

Figure 2.   Derivation of the Lateralized Readiness Potential (LRP).

   A First, on each trial, for each sample point, the difference is obtained
   between potentials recorded from electrode sites C3' and C4', located
   above the left and right motor cortices. These difference waveforms are
   averaged separately for trials in which the left versus the right hand is
   cued.

   B Second, to cancel out lateralized potentials that are not specifically
   related to response preparation, the waveform obtained for the left-hand
   trials is subtracted from the waveform obtained for the right-hand trials.
   The resulting LRP reflects the average amount of lateralization
   occurring as a result of the motor preparation of response hands.

4.2. The LRP and partial information transmission

The LRP has been used in a variety of studies to assess the interaction between information processing and motor control (see Coles et al. 1995, for an overview). In particular, the LRP has been used to detect transmission of partial information between perceptual and motor processes (e.g., Coles 1989; De Jong et al. 1988; Miller and Hackley 1992; Osman et al. 1992; Smid et al. 1992). Some of the most compelling evidence that response preparation can start on the basis of partial stimulus information comes from studies in which the LRP technique is combined with a two-choice reaction go/nogo paradigm (e.g., Miller and Hackley 1992; Osman et al. 1992; Smid et al. 1992). In this paradigm, one attribute of a stimulus indicates a left- or right-hand response, while another attribute of the same stimulus indicates whether or not the response has to be given. The distinction between response hands is usually determined by an easily identifiable stimulus attribute while the go/nogo distinction is determined by a more difficult to discriminate stimulus attribute. For example, Miller and Hackley (1992) presented individuals with large and small Ss and Ts, and assigned these stimuli to left and right hand responses, or nogo reactions. Letter shape determined left versus right response hand, and letter size indicated whether the response should be given or withheld. The idea behind the paradigm is that if response preparation begins as soon as stimulus information is extracted, the stimulus attribute that becomes available early during the perceptual analysis (i.e., shape) could be used to prepare a response hand before the slower attribute (i.e., size) becomes available to distinguish between go/nogo. The critical predictions in the Miller and Hackley study concerned the presence of an LRP on nogo trials. If shape information is used to differentially activate response hands before the stimulus size is fully analyzed, one expects to observe an LRP on both go and nogo trials. The results show that, indeed, an LRP initially develops on nogo trials at about the same latency as on go-trials, but after some time returned to baseline in the absence of an overt response. This indicates that partial stimulus information activated the correct response hand before complete stimulus information became available to determine whether go or nogo was the correct reaction. Similar results were obtained independently by Osman et al. (1992), and by Smid et al. (1992), who used the same experimental paradigm but different stimulus sets. An important finding in the Osman et al. (1992) study was that they could separately manipulate the moment at which an LRP started to develop, and the moment at which the go and nogo LRP started to diverge. This clearly indicates that the LRP is differentially sensitive to the time course of the processes that lead to response hand selection and to the time course of the processes that lead to the go/nogo distinction.

Taken together, these studies provide strong evidence that the LRP is a real-time measure of the selection and preparation of motor responses. Moreover, they show that preliminary stimulus information is transmitted to the motor system, and used for response selection before complete stimulus information is available. This implies that, when combined with the two-choice go/nogo paradigm, the LRP provides an index of the relative moments in time at which different aspects of a stimulus become available for response selection.

4.3. The N200

A second ERP component that has recently been used to examine the time course of language-related processes is the N200. The N200 is a negative going potential, mainly distributed over fronto-central electrode sites, which develops around 200 ms after stimulus onset in experimental situations where a response needs to be withheld. Although the functional significance of the N200 is not as clear-cut as is the case for the LRP, a number of reports have linked the N200 to response inhibition processes. Electrophysiological recordings from prefrontal cortex in monkeys have demonstrated that during the performance of a go/nogo task, a N200 response occurs on nogo relative to go trials (Sasaki, Gemba, and Tsujimoto 1989). Moreover, Sasaki, Gemba, and Tsujimoto (1989) demonstrated that response inhibition could be induced on go trials by stimulating the prefrontal cortex of the monkey at the latency where an N200 response occurred on nogo trials. These results suggest that the N200 reflects, at least in part, response inhibition processes in prefrontal cortex. Thorpe and colleagues (1996) applied this characteristic of the N200 to examine the time course of visual processing. In their study, participants viewed pictures of complex visual scenes and were asked to respond only in cases where an animal was present in the scene. When comparing ERPs elicited on go and nogo trials, an enhanced negativity occurred on nogo relative to go trials, this negativity peaking at around 150 ms after picture onset. The authors interpreted this potential as an N200, and argued that in the context of a go/nogo paradigm, the peak latency of the N200 can be used to indicate the moment at which sufficient information is available to inhibit a response. On the basis of this interpretation, they concluded that at around 150 ms after stimulus onset, sufficient visual information was available to know whether or not an animal was present in the scene.

5. Electrophysiological evidence on the time course of speaking

5.1. *Semantic retrieval as the initial processing stage*

Applying the LRP logic to the study of spoken word production, Van Turennout, Hagoort, and Brown (1997) examined the relative moments at which semantic and phonological information is retrieved during word production. An illustration of their experimental paradigm is presented in Figure 3. The main experimental task was picture naming. In addition, on half of the trials subjects performed a semantic-phonological classification task before producing the word. The classification task consisted of the conjunction of a go/nogo decision and a left- or right-hand response. In this example, response hand was determined by the semantic classification, and the phonological classification determined whether or not a push-button response should be given. The logic behind the procedure is as follows. First, it is assumed that the semantic and phonological properties of the word that are required to perform the classification tasks become available automatically via the speech production system. If, during picture naming, semantic re-

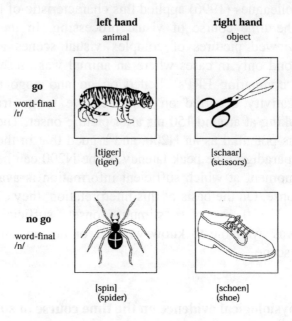

Figure 3. Example of the choice-reaction go/nogo paradigm using a semantic/phonological categorization task. In the figure, the picture names are shown in Dutch and English below the pictures. The four pictures depicted here represent separate trials for the four experimental conditions. An animal cues a left-hand response, and an object cues a right-hand response. The response has to be executed if the picture name ends with an /r/ (go trials), but is withheld if it ends with an /n/ (no-go trials). After Van Turennout et al. (1997).

trieval precedes the retrieval of phonological form, the results of the semantic classification will be transmitted to the response system earlier than the results of the word-initial phoneme classification. In this case, preparation of the response hand can start on the basis of semantic information before phonological information informs the subject whether to respond. As a consequence, an LRP should develop not only for go-trials, but initially also for nogo trials, without an overt response. The early availability of semantic information enables response preparation, but when information about the word's phonological form becomes available, this then overrules further response preparation on the nogo trials. This is exactly the pattern of results that was observed (see Figure 4A). In parallel with the development of an LRP on go trials, an LRP developed on nogo trials for a short period of time, suggesting a temporal advantage of semantic information over phonological information. The early available semantic information served as partial information, and therefore response preparation could start before sufficient phonological information was available to complete the go/nogo analysis.

A possible concern could be that both types of information are retrieved at the same moment during word production, but that because of the task configuration, the response hand is always selected before the go/nogo decision is made. Therefore, to validate the logic behind the paradigm, the task assignment was reversed in another condition. In this task configuration the response hand was determined by phonology and go/nogo was determined by semantics, testing the early use of phonological information. Earlier LRP studies had shown that in a choice reaction go/nogo task subjects assign priority to the extraction of stimulus information that can be used to select a response hand (Coles et al. 1995), which in this case is the phonological information. Nevertheless, if semantics is indeed retrieved before phonology, then an LRP should develop only on go-trials, and not on nogo trials. Indeed, the data showed that whereas an LRP was present on go trials, no significant LRP was observed on nogo trials (see Figure 4B). The absence of an LRP on nogo trials indicates that, on these trials, phonological information did not affect response preparation. Phonological information started to activate response hands only after the semantically based go/nogo distinction had been made. One of the important aspects of this experiment is that subjects were focused on the early use of

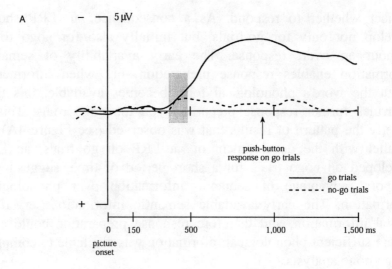

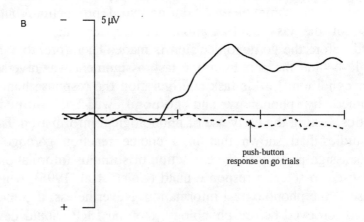

Figure 4. **A** Grand averaged LRPs on go and nogo trials. The semantic decision determined response hand; the word-final phoneme decision determined go/nogo. The shaded area shows the time interval in which the go and nogo LRPs were significantly different from baseline but not from each other.

B Grand averaged LRPs on go and nogo trials for the experiment in which the semantic decision determined go/nogo and the word-final phoneme decision determined the response hand. No significant lateralization of the readiness potential was obtained on nogo trials. After Van Turennout et al. (1997).

phonological information for the rapid selection of response hand. Given the task configuration, there was every reason for the subjects to assign priority to retrieving the phonological information of the noun to select a response hand, before retrieving the semantic information. However, the data demonstrated that phonological information was not available to be used as partial information to activate response hand. Apparently, even if subjects are encouraged to use phonological information earlier than semantic information, they do not. These findings indicate that semantic information influences response preparation at an earlier moment in time than phonological information, and rule out the possibility that the early response preparation observed on nogo trials was due to strategic control over the use of partial information.

Using a similar experimental paradigm, but with German stimulus materials and subjects, Schmitt, Münte, and Kutas (2000) replicated the LRP findings on semantic and phonological processing reported by Van Turennout et al. (1997). Interestingly, in addition to effects on response preparation as measured by the LRP, Schmitt and colleagues reported differential effects of response inhibition as measured by the N200 on nogo trials. They found that when the go/nogo decision was contingent on semantic information the N200 peaked about 90 ms earlier than when the go/nogo decision was contingent on phonological information. This suggests that semantic information was retrieved, and available to the response system about 90 ms earlier than phonological information. These results nicely parallel the LRP data, and again demonstrated that during speech production semantic processing precedes phonological encoding.

Following the same logic, Schmitt et al. (2001a) examined the temporal relation between semantic and syntactic processing. According to WEAVER++, semantic information is not only available prior to phonological information, but also prior to syntactic information. Alternatively, semantic and syntactic information might become available simultaneously. Schmitt et al. (2001a) aimed to disassociate between these two accounts using the following procedure. Subjects were involved in a picture-naming task and in addition, they made go/nogo decisions based on an object's semantic specifications (is the depicted object heavier or lighter than 500 gram) and on a syntactic feature of the depicted noun (is the noun's grammatical gender male or female). The results showed that when semantics determined response hand, a nogo LRP was present between 452 and 540 ms after picture onset. This suggests that the response was prepared on the basis of semantic information, while syntactic information was not yet available to make the go/nogo decision. Importantly, when syntax determined response hand, an LRP was observed only on go trials, and not on nogo trials. The N200 data showed a similar pattern of results: When the go/nogo decision was contingent on semantic information, the average peak latency of the N200 effect was 73 ms earlier than when it was based on syntactic information. Thus, consistent with time course predictions derived from WEAVER++, these results suggest that semantically driven processes onset earlier than syntactically based processing.

Although the results described above are consistent with the view that semantic processing precedes syntactic and phonological encoding, they do not necessarily imply strict seriality of processing stages. It could very well be that, although lemma and word-form retrieval are triggered by semantic activation, these retrieval operations do not wait until a full semantic analysis of an object has been completed. To address this issue, Abdel Rahman, Van Turennout, and Levelt (submitted) examined whether phonological encoding in picture naming is mediated by basic semantic feature retrieval, or proceeds independently. According to decompositional views of semantics (e.g., Bierwisch and Schreuder 1992; Dell et al. 1997) object naming is mediated by sets of basic semantic features, which in combination constitute the meaning of a word. In contrast, in WEAVER++ lexical meanings are represented in a non-decompositional fashion, that is, as entities without internal structure. This means that retrieval of distinct semantic features is not essential for naming, and can, in principle, proceed in parallel to word form encoding, as long as the relevant lexical concept has been retrieved.

To distinguish between serial and parallel processing with the LRP in a two-choice go/nogo paradigm, Abdel Rahman and colleagues manipulated the retrieval latency of the basic semantic feature animacy, and examined whether this manipulation affected the time course of phonological encoding. In a manual two-choice go/nogo task, pictures of objects were classified according to both semantic and phonological information. The manual choice response (i.e., left or right response hand) was based on an animacy classification whereas the go/nogo decision was based on an initial phoneme classification. To selectively manipulate the duration of animacy retrieval a task mixing procedure was introduced. The manual response was based on either the animacy classification throughout the entire block of trials, or was randomly alternated by an additional semantic classification (i.e., does the object occur in or outside the water). In the alternating case a color cue indicated whether the decision had to be based on animacy or on inside/outside the water. The logic behind this manipulation is as follows. If phonological encoding is mediated by semantic feature retrieval, then its onset should vary as a function of the speed with which a semantic feature is retrieved. In contrast, if the two processes can proceed in parallel, the phonological code retrieval should not be affected by the speed of semantic processing. The results showed that a nogo LRP was present in the blocked classification mode. This replicated earlier findings showing that semantic features are typically retrieved faster than phonological information. However, no sign of early response preparation was found in the mixed classification mode, indicating that phonological encoding can proceed while semantic feature retrieval is not yet completed. These results suggest that a basic semantic feature like animacy, although usually retrieved prior to name phonology, is not essential for the initiation of phonological encoding. This means that lemma retrieval and word form encoding do not necessarily depend on the retrieval of pre-defined semantic attributes. Simultaneous activation of semantic and phonological features is in clear contrast with a strictly serial account, and consistent with a parallel account of semantic and phonological processing. In WEAVER++, the selection of a concept always precedes phonological encoding. Therefore, the data seem to be at odds with predictions from WEAVER++. However, in WEAVER++ concepts are represented in a non-decompositional way. That is, lexical concepts are represented as undivided wholes, and distinct semantic features of the concept are retrieved through labeled links to other concepts (for example, DOG 'is an' ANIMAL). This means that, after a lexical concept has been selected, related semantic features can be retrieved in parallel with lemma retrieval and phonological encoding. Therefore, in principal, WEAVER++ allows for word form encoding to start without having a core semantic feature such as animacy available yet.

5.2. *Lemma retrieval precedes phonological encoding*

In another series of experiments, Van Turennout, Hagoort, and Brown (1998) investigated the time course of lemma retrieval and phonological encoding. According to WEAVER++ lemma retrieval is strictly separated from phonological encoding in time. Using the LRP go/nogo paradigm in combination with noun-phrase production, Van Turennout et al. (1998) demonstrated that if a word's syntactic gender, which is represented at the lemma level, is mapped onto response hand while the go/nogo decision is determined by a word's initial phoneme, an LRP developed on both go and nogo trials. When task assignments were reversed, an LRP developed on go trials only. Consistent with the WEAVER++ model, these results clearly demonstrate that speakers retrieve lemma and phonological information in a fixed temporal order: a word's syntactic properties are retrieved before its phonological properties, but the reverse is not possible: speakers do not activate a word's phonology without having previously retrieved its syntax.

The length of time interval during which syntactic but no phonological information was available could be estimated by comparing go and nogo LRPs (see Figure 5). Two time points are of interest here. First, the go and nogo LRPs started to develop at about 370 ms after picture onset. Thus, at that moment syntactic gender was available to select the correct response hand. Second, at about 410 ms after picture onset the go and nogo LRPs diverged sharply.

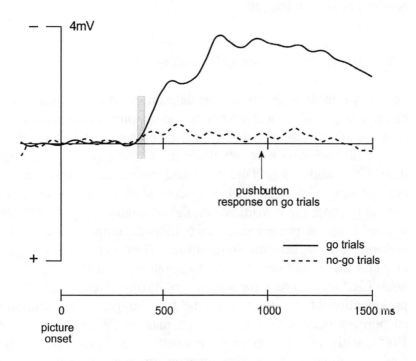

Figure 5. Grand averaged LRPs on go trials and nogo trials. The syntactic gender decision determined response hand; the word-initial phoneme decision determined go/nogo. Significant lateralization of the readiness potential was obtained both on go and on nogo trials from 370 ms after picture onset. The shaded area shows the time interval in which the go and the nogo LRPs were significantly different from the baseline, but not from each other. The right border of the shaded area marks the moment (410 ms) at which phonological information leads to the termination of the syntactic response preparation on nogo trials. After Van Turennout et al. (1998).

While the go LRP continued to develop, the nogo LRP gradually returned to the baseline. This indicates that there was already enough phonological information available 40 ms after LRP onset to make the go nogo distinction. Thus, in noun phrase production it takes only about 40 ms to retrieve a word's initial phoneme once its syntactic gender has been retrieved.

5.3. Seriality in phonological encoding

So far, we have been discussing data on the relative time course of distinct stages of lexical access in speech production. However, the LRP paradigm has also been used to obtain evidence on the time course of information retrieval within a single processing stage. In their 1997 study, Van Turennout and colleagues demonstrated that the duration of a nogo LRP was dependent on the position of the critical phoneme in a word. When the go/nogo decision was based on a word's initial phoneme, a nogo LRP developed on the basis of semantic information for about 40 ms. However, when the go/nogo decision was based on a word's final phoneme, a semantically based nogo LRP was present for a period of 120 ms (see Figure 4A). This prolongation of the duration of the LRP suggests that phonological encoding proceeds in a left-to-right manner (Wheeldon and Levelt 1995), with information about a word's initial phoneme becoming available about 80 ms earlier than information about a word's final phoneme. This result was obtained for words with an average length of 1.5 syllables. Most likely, the retrieval time of the non-initial segments will vary with word length.

5.4. Time estimates

Taken together, the electrophysiological data provide strong support for the WEAVER++ model of speech production. In addition, the combined LRP and N200 data provide detailed time estimates of the duration of the distinct processing stages. In sum, when subjects are involved in picture naming, the selection of a lexical concept takes place around 150-225 ms after picture onset, syntactic encoding (i.e. lemma retrieval) in the time window of 225 and 275 ms, and phonological encoding between 275 and 400 ms (see also Hagoort and Van Turennout 1997; Levelt 2001). Depending on task context, however, additional semantic (and perhaps also additional syntactic) processing continues after phonological retrieval, arguing against a strictly sequential architecture, and in favor of a more cascaded architecture of the speech production system (Abdel Rahman, Van Turennout, and Levelt submitted).

6. The time course of information access in single word comprehension

In essence, language comprehension is about mapping sounds or orthographies onto meaning. Blueprints of the listener and the reader assume that word form processing triggers the retrieval of syntactic and semantic word information which gets integrated into the utterance context (see Cutler and Clifton 1999 for listening; see Perfetti 1999 for reading). The final result is a message-level representation of the overall meaning of the utterance.

Although most of psycholinguistic research has focused on language comprehension rather than language production, strangely enough the time course of lemma and semantic retrieval in single word comprehension is a largely uncharted area. Models of word recognition implicitly assume that upon word form retrieval, syntactic and semantic information associated with a particular word form are immediately available. Although most models of language comprehension include assumptions about temporal properties of information between phonetic, phonological and lexical processing levels, none of these models contain time course predictions for the retrieval of the different levels of lexical and semantic information. The only model that makes such predictions is WEAVER++, which was originally designed as a model for speech production.

In WEAVER++ it is assumed that language production and comprehension share common levels of semantic and lemma representations, but have distinct levels of form representations.

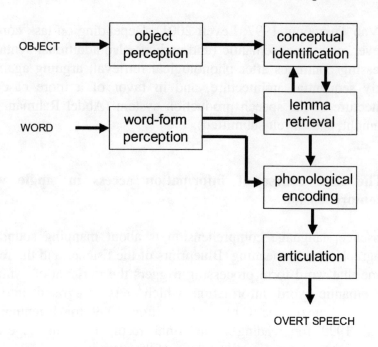

WEAVER++: after Roelofs (in press, *Psychological Review*)

Figure 6. Illustration of the interaction between word production and comprehension in WEAVER++.

In WEAVER++, incoming word form information enters a form level for comprehension. Activation of a representation at this form level spreads to the lemma level, which gives access to syntactic information. From the lemma level, information spreads to the conceptual level to allow the retrieval of word meaning. The flow of information between levels proceeds over time (see Levelt, Roelofs, and Meyer 1999). Under the assumption that the comprehension system relies on the same lemma and conceptual levels, the time course of information flow between levels for comprehension should be the reverse as the one for production (see Figure 6). For example, phonological analysis should be accomplished first, followed by lemma retrieval, followed by the retrieval of the lexical concept.

These time-course issues in comprehension have been addressed in a series of recent ERP studies, using LRP and N200 measures as introduced above.

6.1. Phonological versus semantic encoding during listening

Rodriguez-Fornells and colleagues (2002) investigated whether phonological information is available prior to semantic information, as predicted by WEAVER++. Behavioral studies have indicated that lexical candidates can be activated on the basis of word-initial phonological information (e.g., McQueen, Norris, and Cutler 1994; Zwitserlood 1989), suggesting that word meaning might already be activated after only the beginning of a word has been heard. Rodriquez-Fornells et al. focused on the N200 component as a measure for the availability of phonological and semantic information during spoken word comprehension. Subjects listened to sequences of nouns and had to carry out a left hand/right hand response together with a go/nogo decision. As in a typical two choice go/nogo paradigm, in one condition (go/nogo=semantics) participants were asked to respond (go trials) or to refrain from responding (nogo trials) depending on the semantic category of the stimulus (e.g., go=animal, nogo=object). In this condition the response-hand assignment was defined by the phonological properties of the stimulus (one hand if the initial phoneme was a consonant, the other hand if it was a vowel). In the other condition (go/nogo=phonology) the response contingencies were reversed, i.e. response preparation was based on semantics and the go/nogo decision was based on phonological information.

Figure 7 displays the topographic scalp distribution of the N200 effects. The left column depicts an early time window (480-520 ms after word onset). It shows that over frontal scalp sites the N200-effect is clearly visible for phonology but not for semantics. The right column shows a later time window (570-610 ms after word onset). In this window the phonological N200-effect has disappeared and the semantic N200-effect is fully visible. That is, the moment in

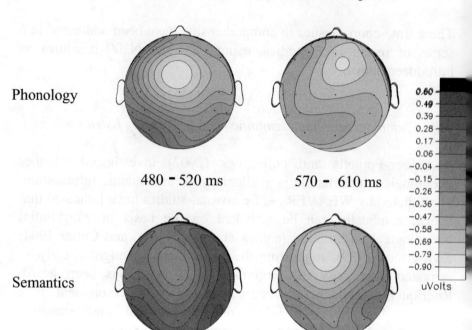

Figure 7. Scalp distribution of the N200 during listening to words. Shown are
topographic mean voltage maps for two time windows. Left: 480-520 ms
after word onset (time window for the phonological N200 effect). Right:
570-610 ms after word onset (time window for the semantic N200 effect).

time at which the nogo and go waveforms maximally deviate is 90
ms earlier when the phonological information determines go/nogo
than when semantic information determines go/nogo. From these
results it can be inferred that during spoken word processing
phonological information becomes available about 90 ms prior to
semantic information. These results are in line with findings from
lexical decision ERP studies in reading (Bentin et al. 1999).
Importantly, for the retrieval of semantic and phonological
information the temporal relation of N200 peak latencies was
reversed compared to N200 results in single word production. As we
discussed above, several ERP studies on object naming have
demonstrated that semantic retrieval precedes phonology by 40-160

ms. The ERP comprehension data together with the production data provide support for the WEAVER++ model.

6.2. Syntactic versus semantic encoding during listening

In addition to the relative time course of semantic and phonological retrieval during single word processing, Schmitt et al. (2001b) investigated the time course of the information flow between syntactic and semantic processing levels in listening. Models like WEAVER++ would seem to predict that syntactic information is available prior to semantic information (but see later). Again, the N200 component was used to compare semantic and syntactic information access. Subjects listened to sequences of nouns and had to carry out a two choice go/nogo decision. In one condition (go/nogo=semantics) participants were asked to respond or to refrain from responding depending on the semantic category of the stimulus (e.g., go=animal, nogo=object). In this condition the response-hand assignment was defined by the syntactic properties of the stimulus. In the other condition (go/nogo=syntax) the response contingencies were reversed, i.e. response preparation was based on semantics and the go/nogo decision was based on syntactic gender information. Figure 8 shows the nogo-go difference waves for both conditions. The observed negativity in the difference waves is the N200 effect. The N200 effect peaked earlier in the go/nogo=semantics condition than in the go/nogo=syntax condition by a significant 69 ms. This finding clearly shows that semantic information became available prior to syntactic information. The observed time shift of peak latencies is comparable with the earlier described shift of syntactic and semantic N200 effects during object naming (80 ms, Schmitt et al. 2001a, b).

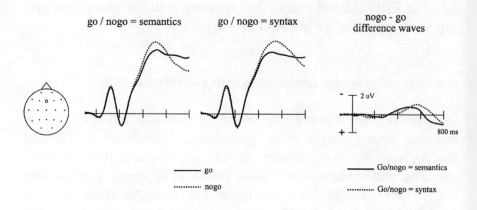

Figure 8. Grand average ERPs from the syntactic vs. semantic listening experiment on go and nogo trials in the go/nogo=semantics condition (left column), and the go/nogo=syntax condition (middle column). The ERPs were time-locked to speech onset. Both conditions are associated with a frontal negativity that is larger for nogo than for go trials. In the right column, the 'nogo minus go' difference waves for the two conditions are shown superimposed. Displayed are data from the frontal electrode site Fz.

6.3. Syntactic versus semantic encoding during reading

Müller and Hagoort (2001) investigated the time course of syntactic and semantic decoding during reading. These authors analyzed both LRP and N200 effects in relation to the retrieval of lemma and semantic information. As is the case for listening, WEAVER++ would seem to predict that, in reading, lemma information precedes semantic information (see Figure 6). In this experiment, participants read single Dutch nouns presented on a computer screen and performed a two choice go/nogo task. For one group of participants the syntactic gender of the word indicated the response hand (left/right) and the semantic category of the word determined whether the response had to be executed or not (go/nogo). Another group of participants received reversed instructions, so that semantic category indicated response hand and syntactic gender determined response execution. LRPs were derived for the go- and nogo-conditions of both instruction groups. Under the assumption that syntax precedes semantics in comprehension, the following LRP pattern was expected: (i) When response preparation is contingent on syntactic information and the go/nogo decision is contingent on semantic information, a nogo LRP should evolve due to early availability of syntactic information. (ii) When response preparation is based on semantic information, the nogo LRP should be absent. The reason for this is that response preparation starts after syntactic information has been able to instruct the go/nogo decision. However, the LRP results that were obtained showed exactly the opposite pattern. When semantics specified response hand and gender determined response execution, a significant deviation from baseline was found for nogo-trials, starting at 484 ms after stimulus onset. It ran parallel to the standard LRP effect on go-trials until 524 ms and then returned to baseline without causing an overt response. This indicates that preparation of the response hand (based on semantics) occurred before gender information was able to instruct the system not to respond. A nogo-LRP was not observed when gender specified response hand and semantics determined response execution. The data indicated that for comprehension in reading, as for comprehension in listening and for picture naming, semantics is available earlier than syntactic information. This finding was further supported by the N200 effects in the same study.

In sum, whereas the finding for phonology versus semantics supports the model of Levelt and colleagues (1999) and the underlying WEAVER++ assumptions, the findings that semantics precedes syntax in both listening and reading seems to be at odds with the model. However, a simulation of the Müller and Hagoort (2001) LRP data in the WEAVER++ model (Roelofs personal communication) showed exactly the pattern of results that was obtained. According to Roelofs, this seemingly contradictory outcome can be explained by the fact that, in WEAVER++ lexical concept nodes connect to a much larger network than lemma nodes. This means that, given the information flow in the model, activation is built up faster for semantic feature nodes than for syntactic feature nodes. As a consequence, even when lemma selection precedes lexical concept selection, a semantic feature can be activated and retrieved earlier than a syntactic feature. This is compatible with the LRP and N200 findings that lemma-related information is activated later in time than concept-related information. The difficulty in testing time course predictions from models like WEAVER++ lies in the fact that in network models are empty nodes. This means that, for example, lemma and concept nodes can only be probed indirectly through its related gender or semantic category nodes. This provides a challenge for future experiments testing the temporal dynamics of WEAVER++.

7. Concluding remarks

In this chapter we presented electrophysiological data on the time course of the information flow during single word processing in both speaking and listening/reading. In both cases at least three completely different types of information are at stake, and have to be retrieved with high speed and accuracy. These information types concern the sound pattern (or their orthographic correlates) of words, their syntactic specifications (lemma) and word meanings.

Before turning to conclusions we need to address two concerns related to the use of the two-choice go/nogo paradigm in language research. A first concern when using picture classification tasks to probe speech-related processes is that critical features could be retrieved from different linguistic representations than the ones used in speech production. However, picture naming is one of most commonly used tasks in the study of speech production because it is assumed to engage the same processes as the ones that occur naturally in speaking (see Glaser 1992 for an overview). Thus, the same linguistic representations are accessed when naming pictures or speaking naturally. Since in all of the experiments described above pictures were named either implicitly or explicitly, it seems very unlikely that the picture classification tasks activated different linguistic representations than the ones used for picture naming, and thus, natural speech. For a detailed account of this issue see Schmitt, Münte, and Kutas (2000). A second concern when using classification tasks is that they involve information retrieval as well as choice-response selection. As a consequence, the LRP and N200 data provide time estimates of retrieval time *plus* additional processes associated with response selection. This means that, when using complicated decision tasks, one needs to take care that response selection processes do not differ between conditions. This can be accomplished in pilot studies (see for example Abdel Rahman, Van Turennout, and Levelt submitted) or through consistency in results across different task configurations. For example, validation for the assumption that the LRP reflects temporal estimates of information retrieval comes from a comparison between LRP results of a study in which word-initial phoneme decision was combined with semantic decision (Van Turennout, Hagoort, and Brown 1997), and LRP results from a study in which word-initial phoneme decision was combined with syntactic decision (Van Turennout, Hagoort, and Brown 1998). The LRP data showed that in the semantic configuration, word-initial phonological information became available for response preparation at 400 ms after picture onset. In the syntactic configuration, the moment that the go and nogo waveforms started to diverge due to the availability of the noun's initial phoneme was at 410 ms. Even though different subjects participated in the two studies, and the pictures were also different, the moment at which phonological information became available is strikingly similar. This suggests that indeed the derived LRPs are probing automatic information retrieval during language processing.

In language production models (e.g., Dell 1986; Caramazza 1997; Levelt 1989; Levelt, Roelofs, and Meyer 1999) it is generally assumed that the information flow is from concept to lemma to sound. This claim is strongly supported by the electrophysiological data on speaking that have been obtained in recent years and were discussed above. The LRP and N200 data even allow for a fairly fine-grained estimation of the relative timing of the retrieval/selection of the three different information types in speaking. However, the data also showed that the time course of information retrieval at these levels is not fixed. Instead, the exact temporal profile of information retrieval is flexible and open to influences from task or input context. Thus, it remains to be seen whether the temporal profile for single word production in a picture-naming paradigm can be generalized to the more common situation of producing words in the context of a larger utterance/message.

For single word comprehension the situation is less clear. First, in language comprehension research the division of labor has been between researchers studying word recognition and researchers investigating sentence processing. Models of word recognition are not explicit about the temporal profile of the retrieval processes beyond accessing word form information. Sentence processing researchers start with the availability of semantic and syntactic information. In-between is the gap that connects word form access to syntactic and semantic integration of lexical information into the context. What is lacking is information about the temporal profile of lemma and concept-related retrieval processes once word form information is accessed. Surprisingly enough, the only model with a time course prediction for word comprehension originates from the domain of language production (i.e. WEAVER++). This model predicts the reversed information flow for comprehension, compared to speaking. That is, in comprehension the information flows from word form to lemma to concept. The LRP and the N200 data that we discussed above showed a more complicated pattern. Although word form was always preceding semantic information, semantic information was retrieved before syntactic information. This is compatible with a number of architectures. One possible architecture is that word forms activate lemmas and lexical concepts in parallel, with differential retrieval times for both. Alternatively, the data are consistent with the assumption that a concept has to be selected before a lemma can be retrieved. This assumption, however, does not seem to be compatible with the finding that we can retrieve lemma information for Jabberwocky sentences for which no lexical concepts are available (e.g., Münte, Matzke, and Johannes 1997). Finally, as WEAVER++ simulations show, despite their seeming counter-evidential nature, the data are even compatible with a model that requires lemma selection before concept retrieval. Clearly, additional studies are required to determine which of the possible architectures for single word comprehension is the most likely one.

In the meantime, the time course data that were obtained are not without significance for our views on language comprehension. For instance, in a recent model of comprehension based on ERP data, Friederici (2002) has claimed that in sentence processing there is a first phase from 100-300 ms in which the initial syntactic structure is formed on the basis of lemma information (i.e. word category). Only in a later phase (300-500 ms) lexical-semantic processes take place. These claims are based on the latencies of the ERP effects for violations of word category and lexical-semantics, respectively, in a sentence context. However, the consistent finding that in single word comprehension semantic information is earlier available than lemma information is in clear disagreement with the claims put forward by the sentence comprehension model by Friederici (2002). To account for this inconsistency between data and theory, one could make the additional assumption that, although semantic information is available earlier than lemma information, it is integrated later. However, for all we know about the incremental nature of language processing, this seems a highly implausible assumption. This illustrates that information on the temporal profile of single word comprehension is not without consequences for higher order models of sentence comprehension.

In conclusion, when words come to mind either through an idea or through sound, time plays a crucial role in connecting sounds and meanings. This was first realized by Donders (1868), who measured the duration of mental processes with the help of the 'noematachograph' and other mechanical instruments. Today we can directly record the brain signals related to mental events of interest. As we showed, this results in an even more fine-grained temporal profile than was possible with the precision instruments in Donders' times.

References

Abdel Rahman, Rasha, Miranda van Turennout and Willem J. M. Levelt

submitted　Phonological encoding is not contingent on semantic feature retrieval: An electrophysiological study on object naming.

Arrezo, Joseph and Herbert G. Vaughan, Jr.

1980　Cortical sources and topography of the motor potential and the somatosensory evoked potential in the monkey. In: H. H. Kornhuber and L. Deecke (eds.), *Motivation, motor, and sensory processes of the brain: Progress in brain research* (Vol. 54), 77-83. Amsterdam: Elsevier.

Bentin, Schlomo, Y. Mouchetant-Rostaing, Marie-Helene Giard, J. F. Echallier and J. Pernier

1999　ERP manifestations of processing printed words at different psycholinguistic levels: Time course and scalp distribution. *Journal of Cognitive Neuroscience* 11: 235-260.

Bierwisch, Manfred and Rob Schreuder

1992　From lexical concepts to lexical items. *Cognition* 42: 23-60.

Bock, J. Kathryn

1982　Toward a cognitive psychology of syntax: Information processing contributions to sentence formulation. *Psychological Review* 89: 1-47.

Butterworth, Brian

1989　Lexical access in speech production. In: William Marslen-Wilson (ed.), *Lexical representation and process*, 108-135. Cambridge, MA: MIT Press.

Caramazza, Alfonso

1997　How many processing levels are there in lexical access? *Cognitive Neuropsychology* 14: 177-208.

Coles, Michael G. H.

1989　Modern mind-brain reading: Psychophysiology, physiology, and cognition. *Psychophysiology* 26: 251-269.

Coles, Michael G. H., Hendrikus G. O. M. Smid, Martin K. Scheffers and Leun J. Otten

1995　Mental chronometry and the study of human information processing. In: Michael D. Rugg and Michael G. H. Coles (eds.), *Electrophysiology of mind: event-related brain potentials and cognition*, 86-113. New York: Oxford University Press.

Collins, Allan M. and Elizabeth F. Loftus
1975   A spreading-activation theory of semantic processing. *Psychological Review* 82: 407-428.

Cutler, Anne and Charles Clifton
1999   Comprehending spoken language: a blueprint of the listener. In: Colin M. Brown and Peter Hagoort (eds.), *The neurocognition of language*, 132-166. Oxford: Oxford University Press.

De Jong, Ritske, Martinus Wierda, Gijsbertus Mulder and Lambertus J. M. Mulder
1988   Use of partial stimulus information in response processing. *Journal of Experimental Psychology: Human Perception and Performance* 14: 682-692.

Dell, Gary S.
1986   A spreading-activation theory of retrieval in sentence production. *Psychological Review* 93: 283-321.

Dell, Gary S., Myrna F. Schwartz, Nadine Martin, Eleanor M. Saffran and David Gagnon
1997   Lexical access in aphasic and nonaphasic speakers. *Psychological Review* 104: 801-838.

Donders, Fransiscus C.
1868   Over de snelheid van psychische processen [On the speed of psychological processes]. *Onderzoekingen gedaan in het Physiologisch Laboratorium der Utrechtse Hoogeschool [Research in the Physiological Laboratory at Utrecht Academy]*, 2: 92-120.

Eulitz, Carsten, Olaf Hauk and Rudolf Cohen
2000   Electroencephalographic activity over temporal brain areas during phonological encoding in picture naming. *Clinical Neurophysiology* 111: 2088-2097.

Friederici, Angela D.
2002   Towards a neural basis of auditory sentence processing. *Trends in Cognitive Sciences* 6: 78-84.

Garrett, Merrill F.
1975   The analysis of sentence production. In: G. H. Bower (ed.), *The psychology of learning and motivation: Advances in research and theory* (Vol. 9), 133-177. New York: Academic Press.

Garrett, Merrill F.
1980   Levels of processing in sentence production. In: Brian Butterworth (ed.), *Language production* (Vol. 1), 177-220. London: Academic Press.

Glaser, Wilhelm R.
1992   Picture naming. *Cognition* 42: 61-105.
Gratton, Gabriel, Michael G. H. Coles, Erik Sirevaag, C. W. Eriksen and Emanuel Donchin
1988   Pre- and poststimulus activation of response channels: A psychophysiological analysis. *Journal of Experimental Psychology: Human Perception and Performance* 14: 331-344.
Hagoort, Peter and Miranda van Turennout
1997   The electrophysiology of speaking: Possibilities of event-related potential research for speech production. In: Wouter Hulstijn, H. Peters, and Pascal van Lieshout (eds.), *Speech motor production and fluency disorders: Brain research in speech production*, 351-361. Amsterdam: Elsevier.
Kempen, Gerard and Pieter Huijbers
1983   The lexicalization process in sentence production and naming: Indirect election of words. *Cognition* 14: 185-209.
Kornhuber, H. H. and L. Deecke
1965   Hirnpotentialänderungen bei Willkürbewegungen und passiven Bewegungen des Menschen: Bereitschaftspotential und reafferente Potentiale [Brain potential changes associated with voluntary and passive movements in humans: Readiness potential and reafferent potentials]. *Pflüger's Archive* 284: 1-17.
Kutas, Marta and Emanuel Donchin
1980   Preparation to respond as manifested by movement-related brain potentials. *Brain Research* 202: 95-115.
Levelt, Willem J. M.
1989   *Speaking. From intention to articulation*. Cambridge, MA: MIT Press.
Levelt, Willem J. M.
2001   Spoken word production: a theory of lexical access. *Proceedings of the National Academy of Sciences of the United States of America* 98: 13464-13471.
Levelt, Willem J. M., Ardi Roelofs and Antje S. Meyer
1999   A theory of lexical access in speech production. *Behavioral and Brain Sciences* 22: 1-75.
Levelt, Willem J. M., Herbert Schriefers, Dirk Vorberg, Antje S. Meyer, Thomas Pechmann and Jaap Havinga
1991   The time course of lexical access in speech production: A study of picture naming. *Psychological Review* 98: 122-142.

McQueen, James M., Dennis G. Norris and Anne Cutler
    1994   Competition in spoken word recognition: Spotting words in other
                words. *Journal of Experimental Psychology: Learning, Memory,
                and Cognition* 20: 621-638.
Meyer, Antje S.
    1992   Investigation of phonological encoding through speech error
                analyses: Achievements, limitations, and alternatives. *Cognition*
                42: 181-211.
Miller, Jeff and Steven A. Hackley
    1992   Electrophysiological evidence for temporal overlap among
                contingent mental processes. *Journal of Experimental
                Psychology: General* 121: 195-209.
Miller, Jeff, Alexa Riehle and Jean Requin
    1992   Effects of preliminary perceptual output on neuronal activity of
                the primary motor cortex. *Journal of Experimental Psychology:
                Human Perception and Performance* 18: 1121-1138.
Müller, Oliver and Peter Hagoort
    2001   Access to lexical information in comprehension – semantics
                before syntax. Poster presented at the 8th Wintercongress of the
                Dutch Society for Psychonomicsm, 14-15 December. Egmond
                aan Zee, The Netherlands.
Münte, Thomas F., M. Matzke, and S. Johannes
    1997   Brain activity associated with syntactic incongruencies in words
                and pseudowords. *Journal of Cognitive Neuroscience* 9: 300-
                311.
Norris, Dennis
    1994   Shortlist: A connectionist model of continuous speech
                recognition. *Cognition* 52: 189-234.
Osman, Allen M., T. R. Bashore, Michael G. H. Coles, Emanuel Donchin and
        David E. Meyer
    1992   On the transmission of partial information: Inferences from
                movement-related brain potentials. *Journal of Experimental
                Psychology: Human Perception and Performance* 18: 217-232.
Perfetti, Charles A.
    1999   Comprehending written language: a blueprint of the reader. In:
                Colin M. Brown and Peter Hagoort (eds.), *The neurocognition of
                language*, 167-208. Oxford: Oxford University Press.

Requin, Jean
  1985   Looking forward to moving soon: Ante factum selective processes in motor control. In: Michael I. Posner and O. Marin (eds.), *Attention and Performance XI*, 147-167. Hillsdale, NJ: Erlbaum.

Riehle, Alexa and Jean Requin
  1989   Monkey primary motor and pre-motor cortex: Single-cell activity related to prior information about direction and extent of an intended movement. *Journal of Neurophysiology* 61: 534-549.

Roelofs, Ardi
  1992   A spreading-activation theory of lemma retrieval in speaking. *Cognition* 42: 107-142.

Roelofs, Ardi
  in press   Goal-referenced selection of verbal action: Modeling attentional control in the Stroop task. *Psychological Review*.

Rodriguez-Fornells, Antoni, Bernadette M. Schmitt, Marta Kutas and Thomas F. Münte
  2002   Electrophysiological estimates of the time course of semantic and phonological encoding during listening and naming. *Neuropsychologia* 40: 778-787.

Sasaki, K., Gemba H. and Tsujimoto T.
  1989   Suppression of visually initiated hand movement by stimulation of the prefrontal cortex in the monkey. *Brain Research* 495: 100-107.

Schmitt, Bernadette M., Thomas F. Münte and Marta Kutas
  2000   Electrophysiological estimates of the time course of semantic and phonological encoding during implicit picture naming. *Psychophysiology* 37: 473-484.

Schmitt, Bernadette M., Kolja Schiltz, Wanda Zaake, Marta Kutas and Thomas F. Münte
  2001a   An electrophysiological analysis of the time course of conceptual and syntactic encoding during tacit picture naming. *Journal of Cognitive Neuroscience* 13: 510-522.

Schmitt, Bernadette M., Antoni Rodriguez-Fornells, Marta Kutas and Thomas F. Münte
  2001b   Electrophysiological estimates of semantic and syntactic information access during tacit picture naming and listening to words. *Neuroscience Research* 41: 293-298.

Smid, Hendrikus G. O. M., Gijsbertus Mulder, Lambertus J. M. Mulder and Gerrit J. Brands

1992   A psychophysiological study of the use of partial information in stimulus-response translation. *Journal of Experimental Psychology: Human Perception and Performance* 18: 1101-1119.

Thorpe, Simon, D. Fize and C. Marlot

1996   Speed of processing in the human visual system. *Nature* 381: 520-522.

Van Turennout, Miranda, Peter Hagoort and Colin M. Brown

1997   Electrophysiological evidence on the time course of semantic and phonological processes in speech production. *Journal of Experimental Psychology: Learning, Memory, and Cognition* 23: 787-806.

Van Turennout, Miranda, Peter Hagoort and Colin M. Brown

1998   Brain activity during speaking: From syntax to phonology in 40 milliseconds. *Science* 280: 572-574.

Wheeldon, Linda R. and Willem J. M. Levelt

1995   Monitoring the time course of phonological encoding. *Journal of Memory and Language* 34: 311-334.

Zwitserlood, Pienie

1989   The locus of the effects of sentential-semantic context in spoken-word processing. *Cognition* 32: 25-64.

Phonology in bilingual language processing: Acquisition, perception, and production

Núria Sebastián-Gallés and Judith F. Kroll

1. Introduction

Who are bilinguals? Until recently, bilinguals were considered a special population, of interest in their own right, for how they managed to negotiate life with two languages, but not for the contribution they might make to the study of the central questions in psycholinguistics of acquisition, comprehension, and production. More recently, that perception has changed so that bilinguals are now viewed as being, if anything, more representative of language users than their monolingual counterparts and providing a unique opportunity for psycholinguists to identify constraints in language learning, representation and processing.

In this chapter we examine the perception and production of phonological information by individuals who are exposed to two languages early in life, by adult second language learners attempting to gain skill in a nonnative language and by proficient bilingual adults who use their two languages at a high level of skill. Although the study of these groups in the past has been associated with different disciplinary approaches (e.g., developmental psychology, child language research, second language acquisition, bilingualism), we view the mechanisms that support the acquisition process and proficient use of two languages among skilled bilinguals as having a common cognitive basis. It is this basis that is the focus of the research we review.

Before we begin, it is important to be clear about who we consider to be the bilinguals who are the subjects of our study and to say a few words about the structural relations across languages that may or may not be critical for comparing different bilingual groups. We take bilinguals to be any individuals who use more than one language on a regular basis. The broad manner in which we will operationalize bilingualism does not restrict us to adults who are balanced in their two languages following initial exposure early in life. To the contrary, we believe that few bilinguals are truly balanced but that a related set of important questions about language processing can be asked about individuals who acquire a second language (L2) early in childhood or later in adulthood, about very young infants exposed to two languages and about individuals who are in the process of acquiring a second language but would by no means be considered proficient bilinguals. This in no way minimizes the potential importance of age of acquisition (e.g., Johnson and Newport 1989; Kim et al. 1997; Weber-Fox and Neville 1996) but identifies it as one variable among many rather than the defining property of who counts as a bilingual. In the studies we review, we attempt to be clear about the nature of the participant groups, but accept a wide range of experience with two languages as being equally informative about different aspects of the way in which phonology functions in language perception and production.

A special feature of research on bilingualism is that it is possible to exploit particular characteristics of the bilingual's two languages as a tool to investigate the implications of structural differences across languages. Because the psycholinguistics of bilingualism is still a relatively new field, there are many specific language comparisons that have not yet been studied. Within these constraints, we consider language differences wherever there is sufficient evidence for interesting, if preliminary, conclusions.

The chapter is organized around three central issues on which there has been research with bilingual individuals. First we consider how infants in bilingual learning environments, exposed to more than one language from birth, develop the means to distinguish and acquire the sound systems to which they are exposed. Second, we examine the representation and processing of the speech perception system by adult bilinguals. Finally, we ask whether bilinguals activate the phonological properties of words in both languages when they are reading, hearing, or speaking words in one of their languages alone.

2. The bilingual infant: Acquiring two languages from birth

If a pre-requisite for learning language is the ability to distinguish it from other sounds, we assume that a pre-requisite for becoming bilingual is to be able to realize the existence of more than one language in the environment. How long does it take a bilingual infant (or child) to discriminate his/her two languages? The answer to this question relates to one of the central issues of bilingual language development: When do children exposed to two languages separate both systems? Some researchers propose that language differentiation in bilinguals does not take place before the third year of life, once functional categories have emerged (Genesee 1989; Redlinger and Park 1980; Vihman 1985; Volterra and Taeschner 1978), but more recent studies (De Houwer 1990; Genesee, Nicoladis, and Paradis 1995) offer evidence for an earlier differentiation. A characteristic common to all of these studies is that they base their conclusions on production data. But important developments in language perception must precede language production. Thus, it may be the case that past research has underestimated the actual linguistic knowledge of bilingual infants and toddlers during the initial stages of language development.

Research during the past decade on early language acquisition in monolingual babies has shown that during the first months of life a great deal of "attuning" to the maternal language takes place (Jusczyk 1997; Mehler and Christophe 1994; Werker and Tees 1999). In this context, it is reasonable to explore the development of linguistic perceptual capacities of bilinguals and to compare them with those of monolingual infants.

2.1. Early language discrimination capacities

Young infants, including newborns, are able to discriminate some languages, but not others. For instance, newborn infants are able to discriminate between French and Russian or English and Italian, but they cannot discriminate English and Dutch or Spanish and Italian (Bahrick and Pickens 1988; Christophe and Morton 1998; Mehler et al. 1988; Moon, Cooper, and Fifer 1993). Recently, Ramus, Nespor, and Mehler (1999) proposed that these early language discrimination capacities can be understood in terms of the ability of infants to perceive the vowel/consonant ratio and variability in the speech signal. In fact, this proposal can be considered to be a quantification of the classification of languages according to their rhythmic properties already put forward by a number of linguists (Abercrombie 1967; Pike 1945) and used by psycholinguists to account for some cross-linguistic speech segmentation phenomena in stress, syllable and mora-timed languages (Cutler et al. 1983; Mehler et al. 1981; Otake et al. 1993; Sebastián-Gallés et al. 1992). According to this classification, languages like English, Dutch or Russian are all stress-timed, whereas Spanish, Italian, French, and Catalan are syllable-timed and Japanese is mora-timed. The ability of newborns to discriminate between languages appears to depend on the capacity to distinguish between languages belonging to these different rhythmic groups. It will not be until four to six months that (monolingual) infants will be able to start making some within-group distinctions (Bosch and Sebastián-Gallés 2000; Nazzi, Jusczyk, and Johnson 2000).

If newborn infants can distinguish between languages belonging to different rhythmic groups, infants raised in bilingual environments where languages like English and French or Japanese and Italian are spoken should be able to discriminate the two languages from the very beginning. Unfortunately, these particular cases have not yet been examined. Infants raised in bilingual environments where languages of the same rhythmic group are spoken face a very different situation. If these languages cannot be discriminated at birth, it may well be the case that infants exposed to them simultaneously may consider the two languages as one for a relatively long period of time. Bosch and Sebastián-Gallés (2001a) studied the language discrimination capacities of infants exposed to Spanish and Catalan from birth and observed that at four and a half months of age they were able to discriminate the two languages and their performance was comparable to that of monolingual Spanish or Catalan infants. Thus, the conclusion based on perception rather than production is that bilingual infants, even under the most challenging perceptual circumstances, are able to discriminate languages that share many phonological properties.

Although these data suggest that monolingual and bilingual infants share the same precocious language discrimination capacities, other data indicate that these capacities may not be fully equivalent. In general, infants are faster to orient to familiar than to unfamiliar stimuli. In particular, it has been shown that monolingual infants orient more rapidly to a familiar (maternal) language than to an unfamiliar (unknown) one (Bosch and Sebastián-Gallés 1997; Dehaene-Lambertz and Houston 1998). Bosch and Sebastián-Gallés (1997) studied how monolingual and bilingual four and a half month-old infants oriented to a familiar (maternal) language and to an unknown (English) language. While monolingual Spanish and monolingual Catalan infants oriented more rapidly to the maternal language than to English, bilingual Spanish-Catalan infants showed just the opposite pattern of results, with faster orientation to English than to the maternal language (Spanish or Catalan). Interestingly, monolingual and bilingual infants did not differ in their absolute times for the unknown language (English) but bilingual infants were slower than monolingual infants to orient to the maternal language. The pattern of bilingual results was replicated with Italian as the unknown language suggesting that the result generalizes even when the unknown language is rhythmically similar to the maternal one. Bosch and Sebastián-Gallés (2001b) showed that this differential pattern of results between monolingual and bilingual infants is still observed at six months of age. Although the reason for longer orientation times to the maternal language in bilingual infants is still unclear, the results suggest important differences between monolingual and bilingual infants at this very early stage of language development. Moreover, bilingual infants seem able to discriminate some within-class rhythmic contrasts that monolingual infants fail to exhibit (Bosch and Sebastián-Gallés 2000). As mentioned previously, between four to six months, monolingual infants start to be able to make some, but not all, within-class discriminations. For instance, Nazzi et al. (2000) showed that monolingual American five-month olds could discriminate between British-English and Dutch and also between American-English and British-English, but that they were unable to differentiate German and Dutch (also two stress-timed languages). Similarly, Bosch and Sebastián-Gallés (2000) observed that monolingual Spanish and Catalan infants could not discriminate between Italian and Spanish, whereas they could discriminate Catalan from both Spanish and Italian. However, unlike monolingual infants, the bilingual infants in the same study were able to discriminate Italian from Spanish as well as Italian from Catalan. These data may indicate more refined language discrimination capacities for bilingual infants, at least for those exposed to rhythmically similar languages.

2.2. The development of phonotactic knowledge

Being able to differentiate the sounds of different languages may be a prerequisite for language acquisition but it does not necessarily imply that infants raised in bilingual environments use that information to construct separate representations for each language nor that they use their discrimination capacity to filter out one of the languages to "focus" on the building of the other. Thus, it might well be the case that bilingual infants, in spite of their discrimination abilities, mix both languages for an extended period of time.

While there is ample literature and debate about early language acquisition in young children in the production domain (see Bhatia and Ritchie 1999 for a review), very little infant research has addressed the perception domain. In fact, there are only two studies that have addressed, more or less directly, whether bilingual infants build both languages separately or not (Sebastián-Gallés and Bosch 2002; Werker, Burns, and Fennell 2001).

One of the major achievements of language development during the first year of life is the development of the capacity to segment lexical units from the continuous speech stream. In order to be able to do this, infants must learn different properties about the phonology of their language, for example, what constitutes a proper word beginning or word ending, what is the most common stress pattern and so on. Most of these properties refer to the phonotactics of the language and they are acquired by computing the frequency of occurrence of particular sequences of segments. Learning these particular properties of the maternal language occurs mostly during the second half of the first year of life (for a review see Jusczyk 1997). One way to analyze how the bilingual infant builds the knowledge of his/her two languages is to examine the acquisition of phonotactic knowledge. One possibility is that bilingual infants concentrate on just one of their two languages, filtering out or ignoring the other language until a later point. By this account, bilingual infants would be quite similar in their dominant language to monolingual infants. Alternatively, bilingual infants may develop phonotactic knowledge of both languages at the same time. If so, then no dominance might emerge. Of course, both predictions require that we take into consideration the fact that the acquisition of phonotactic knowledge is highly sensitive to the frequency of occurrence of patterns: Infants show sensitivity to frequent patterns only. If we assume that bilingual infants have less exposure to each language independently than monolingual infants, then they might be expected to show a delay for uncommon patterns.

Sebastián-Gallés and Bosch (2002) tested these predictions in a series of studies in which ten-month-old monolingual and bilingual Catalan-Spanish infants were examined on their knowledge of some phonotactic patterns that exist in Catalan, but not in Spanish. Unlike Catalan, Spanish does not allow final word complex consonant clusters. Therefore, a sequence of phonemes ending with two or more consonants cannot be a proper word in Spanish. Catalan accepts some final word complex consonant clusters, although not all consonant clusters are possible. For instance, "pirn" could be a possible word in Catalan, but "pikf" could not be. Neither of these examples could be a word in Spanish. Research with monolingual infants has shown that nine-month-olds (Jusczyk, Luce, and Charles Luce 1994) prefer to listen to lists of stimuli that conform to the phonotactics of their maternal language compared to lists of stimuli that do not. Accordingly, when presented with lists containing stimuli with final word consonant clusters that exist or do not exist in Catalan, monolingual Catalan infants should show a preference for those that are allowed in Catalan. In contrast, Spanish monolingual infants should show no preference because both types of stimuli are not possible in their maternal language. This is indeed what was found; when bilingual infants were tested, the results showed that only bilingual infants exposed primarily to Catalan showed a pattern of orientation similar to that of monolingual Catalan infants. Bilingual infants exposed primarily to Spanish showed an intermediate pattern: They did not differ from the Catalan dominant bilinguals, but like Spanish monolingual infants, they did not show any preference for any type of stimuli. Although this is a complex pattern of data, the results appear to be more consistent with the hypothesis that bilingual infants show very early language dominance, at least, as far as phonotactic knowledge is concerned (for a more detailed explanation see Sebastián-Gallés and Bosch 2002).

To summarize, research with bilingual infants has shown that when perceptual capacities are analyzed, these infants show very precocious language discrimination capacities, challenging proposals suggesting a relatively long period of language confusion. Available results also suggest that by four to six months of age, under some circumstances, bilingual infants may have more refined language discrimination abilities than monolingual infants. Finally, the results of research on early stages of vocabulary development (i.e., learning of phonotactics) are consistent with the notion that bilingual infants prioritize one language over the other such that very early language dominance can be observed.

3. Representation and processing of different sound systems

One of the most difficult tests for any bilingual is the perfect mastery of the pronunciation of the second language. In this section we review the consequences of bilingualism for different aspects of phonological knowledge, focusing on the perceptual system (see Flege, this volume, for a discussion of the relationship between perception and production).

As in other language domains, a central research issue is to what extent bilinguals possess one or two phonological systems (and also whether one or the other "dominates"). Furthermore, and perhaps in contrast with other domains, a crucial question is the existence and nature of the interactions between the phonological systems of the bilingual's two languages. That is, we can ask whether the acquisition of the phonological system of the L2 takes place through that of the L1 and also whether the acquisition of the L2 can modify the properties of L1 phonology. As we will see below, these questions have been addressed in the context of models of segment processing.

Bilinguals do not appear to have difficulty in acquiring and processing many L2 phonemes, but others are particularly problematic. Different models have been advanced to account for these differences, in particular, the Perceptual Assimilation Model (Best 1995) and the Speech Learning Model (Flege 1995, this volume). Although the models take different theoretical perspectives and make different assumptions about the underlying mechanisms responsible for speech perception, they generate similar predictions about experimental outcomes. One of the main characteristics of these models is the way they explain the processing of different phonemes by bilinguals. In doing so, they take into account the relative distribution of the phonemes of both languages. For instance, both models assume that when the very same phoneme exists in both languages, the bilingual should not have any problem in processing it; the same would occur if a particular phoneme only exists in one language and it is very different from those existing in the other language (e.g., the well known illustration of American English speakers perceiving different Zulu clicks, Best, McRoberts, and Sithole 1988). However, bilinguals should experience important learning and processing difficulties when a particular phoneme in one of the languages shares only some similarities with the phoneme of the other language. In this case the relative perceptual similarity may or may not allow for the existence of two phonemes (one for each language) or the creation of a new intermediate category, the result of blending the properties of each phoneme. One consequence of this latter case is the particular difficulties that many bilinguals experience in perceiving contrasts in their L2, non-existing in their L1 when the L2 contrast implies two phonemes more or less equidistant to the single L1 phoneme. This is the case of the difficulties experienced by Japanese speakers learning the /ɹ/-/l/ contrast in English: Japanese only has a single phoneme falling roughly in between English /ɹ/-/l/. It has been suggested that general mechanisms of the speech processing system, such as categorical perception, may be responsible for these patterns of data.

While there is general agreement about the conditions that give rise to relative ease or difficulty in learning foreign sounds, there is intense disagreement about the limits of plasticity of the phoneme learning system. As mentioned above, it is during the first months of life that the perceptual system becomes attuned to the phonetic inventory of the maternal language. In fact, this processing has been characterized as a perceptual "loss": Older infants are worse at perceiving some phonemic contrasts non-existing in the maternal language than younger infants. Different authors (Flege 1995; Lively et al. 1994) in more or less specific ways propose that provided an early and/or intensive exposure, it should be possible to perfectly acquire foreign contrasts. The question is whether the perceptual "loss" produced during the first years of life can be reversed in highly competent bilinguals (i.e., individuals who have not acquired both languages simultaneously). Most proposals about the acquisition of phonemic categories argue that the perceptual system does not lose the capacity to perceive the relevant acoustic information (Mann 1986; Miyawaki et al. 1975; Werker and Tees 1984). Different researchers have proposed that the native speaker will focus on a more abstract linguistic level of processing, freeing attentional resources to process language in a more efficient way (Jusczyk 1993; Lively et al. 1994; Mayberry and Eichen 1991). Given the capacities of the auditory system, it should be theoretically possible to attain native-like speech perception with the appropriate input.

In fact, recent neuropsychological data confirm the high degree of plasticity of the auditory perceptual system. Bilingual studies are scarce and most research has focused on native versus non-native comparisons and on the neurological changes that are induced as a consequence of training programs. Although these studies do not directly address bilingualism, they are still relevant to the issues reported here and will be reviewed briefly.

Little is known about whether underlying neural-sensory representations of speech are actually altered by an individual's linguistic experiences. Most of the evidence has been obtained analyzing ERP responses, in particular analyzing the differences in the Mismatch Negativity (MMN). The MMN is a characteristic

Negativity (MMN). The MMN is a characteristic electrophysiological response component produced when a series of identical sounds (the standard) is interrupted by a different stimulus (the deviant); interestingly, the MMN can be elicited when the stimuli are not behaviorally discriminated. One particularly relevant property of the MMN to the present issues is that its amplitude is smaller for non-native contrasts than for native ones. An important problem with much of the behavioral evidence is that measures are in many cases based only on "yes-no" perceptions. In categorical perception tasks, for instance, participants are asked to report whether a particular sound is perceived as a specific phoneme or not. By depending on direct and conscious measures, the results of many of the behavioral studies may have underestimated the actual representation and processing status of bilinguals' phonological competence level.

Näätänen et al. (1997) studied the perception of Finnish vowels by Estonian and Finnish listeners. The Estonian and Finnish languages have very similar vowel structures, for example, the vowels /e/, /o/ and /ø/, which differ only in the second formant (F2) frequency, exist in both languages. However, only Estonian has the vowel /ɯ/, whose formant values fall approximately between /ø/ and /o/. The results of this study showed larger MMN responses for across language phonemic category differences than for within language category. That is, in an odd-ball paradigm, when the phoneme /e/ was the standard, Finnish participants showed a larger MMN response when the deviant stimulus was /ø/ than for /ɯ/, while Estonian participants showed a similar response for /ø/ than for /ɯ/. The explanation Näätänen and coworkers provided for the differences between the groups was that Finnish participants did not have a phonetic category for the vowel /ɯ/, while Estonian participants did. Research using the MMN to explore how native and non-native phonetic categories are processed converges on the conclusion that the MMN reflects a relatively abstract level of processing in which language specific categories play a role. For example, Winkler et al. (1999) came to a similar conclusion in a study analyzing the perception of Hungarian and Finnish vowel contrasts in speakers of these two languages as did Phillips et al. (1995) studying the /ɹ-/l/ contrast with Japanese (see also Sharma and Dorman 2000, comparing Hindi English listeners with the [ba]-[pa] Hindi-but not English- contrast and Rivera-Gaxiola et al. 2000 exploring the perception of the labial /ba/-Hindi dental/retroflex [da] contrast for English speaking participants). However, Dehaene-Lambertz, Dupoux, and Gout (2000) did not observe this pattern of results with native French participants listening the Hindi dental/retroflex alveolar plosive [d] contrast.

The other relevant group of studies concerns the neuronal changes produced as a result of training programs. Tremblay et al. (1997) observed an increase in the MMN response, largest in the left hemisphere, for individuals trained in a bilabial (unfamiliar) VOT contrast. The increase also generalized to an untrained alveolar contrast. The changes also occurred very rapidly (the "first day of significant change" occurred after the first training session). In fact Tremblay, Kraus, and McGee (1998) also observed that for many participants changes in the MMN were obtained before any significant behavioral change was displayed. Taken together, these results suggest that the perceptual system does not lose its capacity to perceive the acoustic properties of the speech sounds, and that the changes induced by exposure to new phonemes occur very rapidly. These findings can thus account for the fact that there is a great deal of evidence showing that even relatively late bilinguals can improve their non-native speech perception abilities. In fact, it seems that final performance levels depend on the quantity and quality of the second language input (see, for instance, Flege this volume; MacKay et al. 2001).

Despite the evidence for a high degree of plasticity, the general observation is that when highly skilled bilinguals who have learned both languages in naturalistic circumstances are compared in their L1 and L2, there is some perceptual processing advantage for the L1 (Bosch, Costa, and Sebastián-Gallés 2000; Mack 1989; Pallier, Bosch, and Sebastián-Gallés 1997; Sebastián-Gallés and Soto-Faraco 1999). Moreover, individuals who have learned to differentiate difficult non-native contrasts seem to do so by using different acoustic parameters than those used by native listeners. For instance, Underbakke et al. (1988) observed that while spectral differences between F2 and F3 are the primary cues to distinguish [ɹ] and [l] for native American English speakers, Japanese listeners used temporal differences to distinguish them. If we assume that native speakers use the most adaptive and efficient mechanisms to process their language, then it could be the case that at least for their second language, bilinguals use less efficient procedures.

Sebastián-Gallés and Soto-Faraco (1999) reported results that are consistent with these conclusions. They used the gating task to compare Spanish dominant with Catalan dominant Spanish-Catalan bilinguals in their ability to distinguish stimuli only differing in Catalan-specific contrasts. All participants in this experiment had been raised as monolinguals for the first six years of life, but from that age on they experienced intensive exposure to both languages and in their present life they used both languages in an equivalent way. In this experiment, participants performed a variation of the classic forward gating task. In the classical gating task, participants are presented with successively longer portions of a stimulus (starting from the beginning) and they are asked to identify which stimulus the portion corresponds to; each presentation is called "a gate". The modification used in this experiment was such that at each gate, participants were given two alternatives and they were forced to choose one of them. The focus in this experiment was on Spanish-dominant bilinguals who, on the last gate (when the whole stimulus was presented), were indistinguishable from the Catalan-dominant bilinguals; that is, they were able to perceive the contrast. These Spanish-dominant bilinguals, in spite of their mastery of Catalan, performed more poorly than Catalan-dominant bilinguals in the intermediate gates: They needed (slightly, but significantly) more information to identify the stimuli.

The results of these experiments are in clear contrast with the results of the training studies reviewed above. In spite the rapid changes observed in the MMN as a result of short exposures to new sounds, bilinguals in the "real world" seem to experience difficulty in acquiring some sounds in their L2. We will return to this issue below.

Related to the issues of plasticity there is the question that early (and continued) exposure to the second language is a crucial factor in determining native-like performance in phonological processing in bilinguals. Again, there are few studies that have explored the phonological systems of bilinguals who have acquired their second language very early in life. Mack (1989) analyzed English-French bilinguals who learned L2 before the age of eight. She compared both monolinguals and bilinguals in perception (identification and discrimination) and production tasks in two different English contrasts /d-tʰ/ and /ɪ-i/. The performance of bilinguals who had English as their maternal language did not differ from the performance of monolingual English participants, suggesting that first language categories are not modified by early exposure to another language. Consistent with these findings are the results of Pallier, Bosch, and Sebastián-Gallés (1997) who observed that Spanish dominant Catalan-Spanish bilinguals (i.e., individuals who first learned Spanish at home and before the age of four/six learned Catalan) had difficulties in acquiring the Catalan phonemic contrast /e/-/ɛ/ (in Spanish there is only one /e/ category falling roughly in between both Catalan ones, a crucial characteristic for making a contrast particularly difficult to be learned). These results demonstrate that in naturalistic circumstances (without highly specialized training), the speech perception system does not seem to be prone to modify initial phonetic categories.

Most of the studies in this domain have examined performance for simple syllables or nonsense strings of phonemes. This seems to be a reasonable approach, since the interest is centered on how phonemes are processed and lexical or other higher-level influences are in principle undesired. However, one may wonder about the lexical consequences of the acoustic information registered by the perceptual system (as the psychophysiological studies reviewed above show). Recently, Pallier, Colomé, and Sebastián-Gallés (2001) addressed this issue by comparing repetition priming effects to pairs of words differing minimally in contrasts existing in both languages of bilinguals or in just one of their languages. It is well known that lexical decision times are faster on a repeated word trial than on the first presentation. In this experiment, Pallier et al. observed that Spanish-dominant speakers (whose maternal language was Spanish and who were likely not to perceive some Catalan-specific contrasts) considered the occurrence of the second member of a minimal pair equivalent to the exact repetition of the same item; that is, the reaction times (RTs) to words when preceded by themselves in the list (RTs to the second occurrence of /netə/ in a list) were equivalent to the RTs observed when words hewere preceded by the other member of the minimal pair (in this case /netə/ preceded by /nɛtə/ in the same list). However, Catalan-dominant bilinguals whose maternal language was Catalan and who can perceive these contrasts, did not show the repetition effect for these pairs (none of the bilinguals showed repetition savings for minimal pairs of words containing phonemes shared in both languages: /pɔt-bɔt/). In short, Spanish-dominant bilinguals, but not Catalan-dominant bilinguals treated Catalan-specific minimal pairs as homophones. These results indicate that in spite of detailed recording of acoustic information by the auditory/speech perceptual system, this information is not integrated in the language processing system.

The experiments reviewed in this section illustrate the challenge that the use of new methodologies (in this case, electrophysiological ones) imply for speech processing. ERP studies have confirmed the very rapid changes that occur in the brain as a consequence of exposure to new sound systems, already suggested by some researchers. However, it remains to be understood why this plasticity is not easily translated into real world processing. Additional research will be required to understand why bilinguals experience such great difficulty in perceiving and producing sounds of their L2 in the context of larger language units, in particular words.

4. The representation and processing of phonology in the bilingual lexicon

4.1. General issues

Experimental studies of word recognition within the monolingual domain make it abundantly clear that phonology is active regardless of whether it is obligatory, regardless of whether the input is a written or spoken word and in the case of reading, regardless of whether the language of input makes the availability of the sound code easy or hard to derive (e.g., Berent and Perfetti 1995; Lukatela and Turvey

1994; Tan and Perfetti 1999; Van Orden 1987). In word production tasks, in which an overt spoken response is required, there is evidence not only for activation of the phonology of the intended utterance, but also for the phonology of lexical alternatives (e.g., Jescheniak and Schriefers 1998; Peterson and Savoy 1998). The suggestion then is that phonology is available quite automatically during perception tasks and that competition among phonological competitors potentially extends quite far into the process of selecting a single word for production. Each of these observations carries an important set of implications for bilinguals for whom phonological representations across the two languages may be simultaneously activated and competing in both perception and production tasks. We consider the evidence first for perception and then for production.

4.2. Perception

When a proficient bilingual is faced with the task of recognizing a printed word, information about words in both languages appears to be active and to contribute to the speed and accuracy of performance. Although early work on the bilingual lexicon suggested an independent status for each language lexicon (e.g., Gerard and Scarborough 1989; Smith 1997), more recent studies provide overwhelming evidence in favor of the view that access to words in the bilingual's two languages is nonselective (e.g., Brysbaert 1998; Dijkstra, Van Jaarsveld, and Ten Brinke 1998) and that at least in some cases the lexicon might be integrated (e.g., Van Heuven, Dijkstra, and Grainger 1998). The evidence for this view is based primarily on studies, which exploit the cross-language properties of words. For example, in languages such as Dutch and English, many words share similar or identical spelling. In the case of interlingual homographs, or false friends, those similar words do not map onto the same meaning in each language (e.g., the English word "room" means cream in Dutch). In the case of cognates, they do correspond to the same meaning (e.g., the word "bed" is the same in English and Dutch). In general, the finding is that even when bilinguals are reading words in one language alone, there is evidence that both language alternatives are active. Van Hell and Dijkstra (in press) showed that Dutch-English bilinguals were faster to recognize cognates than noncognates in a lexical decision task even when the task was performed in the native language, Dutch, and when the participants had no instruction to use any other language. Finding that cognates are faster than noncognates for a task performed in L2 might not seem terribly surprising since L2 tends to be processed more slowly than L1. However, finding the same effects in L1 provides compelling evidence for the nonselective nature of lexical access across the bilingual's languages.

The facilitation observed for cognates in visual lexical decision experiments could be attributable to the overlap in orthography or to the similarity of phonology. Although orthography may be identical for words in different languages, phonology is rarely the same. The results of a number of studies that have examined the manner in which phonology is activated across languages in word recognition tasks suggest that despite the presence of phonological differences across most bilinguals' two languages, there is activation of the phonology as well as the orthography. In an early study on this topic, Nas (1983) asked Dutch-English bilinguals to perform lexical decision in English, their L2. In one condition of the experiment, orthographically valid nonwords in English were pseudohomophones with real words in Dutch (e.g., the nonword "deanst" which sounds like the Dutch word "dienst"). The results showed that the time to reject the pseudohomophones as not being English words was longer than the time to reject nonhomophonic nonwords, suggesting that the Dutch phonology was available and intruding when bilinguals made lexical decisions in English alone (see also Altenberg and Cairns 1983).

More recent experiments have replicated and extended these findings. Dijkstra, Grainger, and Van Heuven (1999) examined the performance of proficient Dutch-English bilinguals recognizing English words that were interlingual cognates or homographs but that differed in the degree to which the orthography and phonology were similar in Dutch and English. To illustrate, a cognate such as "sofa" has the identical orthography and similar phonology in both languages. In contrast, a cognate such as "wild" has the same orthography in Dutch and English but is pronounced differently in each language. Likewise, a cognate such as "news" in English and "nieuws" in Dutch has different orthography but very similar pronunciation. By manipulating the similarity of the orthography and phonology across languages for words with shared semantics (i.e., cognates) or without (i.e., homographs), it was possible to tease apart the relative contribution of the nontarget orthography and phonology during word recognition. Dijkstra et al. analyzed the performance on these items in a progressive demasking task and in visual lexical decision. In each case the task required the recognition of words in English, the L2 for these Dutch-English bilinguals. In the progressive demasking task, the target word alternates with a mask and over presentations, the duration of the target gradually increases while the duration of the mask gradually decreases. The dependent measure is the time that participants require until they are able to accurately identify the target. In lexical decision, participants are presented with a string of letters and must simply decide whether they are a real word in the specified language. The results of both tasks showed that shared orthography and semantics facilitated recognition performance. In contrast, shared phonology produced inhibition. There are a number of reasons why the orthography and phonology may have functioned differently under these circumstances, but the important feature of the results for the present discussion is that the phonology of the nontarget language, in this case Dutch, influenced performance even when the tasks were performed in English alone.

One might ask whether the findings we have reviewed are somehow particular to Dutch-English bilinguals. Dutch and English are similar languages in many respects and Dutch university students, who are the participants in most of these studies, are potentially an unusual sample of bilinguals in that they are required to use both Dutch and English quite actively in academic settings. A number of other recent studies show clearly that the evidence based on Dutch-English bilinguals generalizes to other bilingual groups. Brysbaert, Van Dyck, and Van de Poel (1999) reported a study using a masked priming paradigm, in which a prime word was preceded by a visual mask to make it difficult or impossible for participants to identify it consciously. The goal of the study was to determine whether the performance of Dutch-French bilinguals would be facilitated when a Dutch (L1) prime word was phonologically related to a French (L2) target word, even under these conditions in which they could not report seeing the prime. For example, the Dutch word "wie" might be the related prime for the French word "oui" and the bilinguals simply had to type the target word they saw. Despite the fact that the masking of the prime prevented participants from having conscious access to the information it contained, Brysbaert et al. showed that the magnitude of the cross-language homophone priming was similar to the magnitude of within language homophone priming for French monolinguals, again suggesting that access to the bilingual lexicon is nonselective, with information about both the orthography and phonology of lexical competitors activated in parallel.

What about the case in which the bilingual's two languages do not share orthography? It is interesting to observe that the absence of cross-language orthography appears to enhance the salience of cross-language phonology. Gollan, Forster, and Frost (1997) found masked translation priming for both cognates and noncognates from L1 to L2 when the two languages were Hebrew and English, however the magnitude of priming was greater for cognates which, for these languages, only share the phonological aspect of their lexical form. Bowers, Mimouni, and Arguin (2000) reported repetition priming between Arabic and French, again languages, which do not share orthography.

In all the studies reviewed thus far, performance was assessed in tasks that involved visual presentation of words for responses that do not require spoken production. Demonstrating that the phonology associated with words in both languages is active during visual recognition is important, but does not tell us how this information is involved in the computation of spelling-to-sound correspondences in reading aloud.

To investigate the role of cross-language phonology in reading, Jared and Kroll (2001) asked English-French bilinguals to read aloud a set of words in English without any prior knowledge that their French would be used in the experiment. The participants first read a list of English words, were then later interrupted with a list of French words to name and then finally read aloud a second list of English words. Three types of English words comprised the critical materials in the experiment. The words differed in whether or not they possessed enemies in English or French. An enemy is a word, which shares a similar spelling pattern with the target word but is pronounced differently. For example, the word "pint" in English is an enemy of the word "hint" because although they share the same "int" word body, it maps differently to phonology in each case. Some English words had no enemies in either English or French. Others had French enemies only (e.g., "pier") or English enemies only (e.g., "dough"). Jared and Kroll found that before the presentation of the French naming task, native English speakers were slower to name English words with English enemies, but that naming latencies for words with French enemies were no different than controls. Following the interpolated task, English speakers who were relatively proficient in French were sensitive to both the presence of English and French enemies. The results demonstrate that when the nontarget language is required to be active, as it presumably was following the French naming task and when bilinguals are sufficiently proficient, the phonology of both languages is engaged during word naming. The results support the general conclusion of the recent research on word recognition in favoring a nonselective model of lexical access, but also extend these results to suggest that the phonology of the nontarget language influences the computation of spelling-to-sound correspondences when words must be spoken.

One of the methodological problems in many of the cross-language word recognition studies is that the words that share orthographic and phonological properties in both of the bilingual's two languages are often not equally representative within each language alone. For example, Spanish words with English word bodies (e.g., "cine") tend to be less representative of Spanish than control words (Schwartz 2000). Finding that they take longer to name could therefore be a reflection of the intrusion of the other language or simply a property of the word itself. Schwartz, Kroll, and Diaz (2001) attempted to address this concern in a word naming study in which the critical items were cognates, similar to those used by Dijkstra, Grainger, and Van Heuven (1999). Schwartz et al. compared word-naming performance for English-Spanish bilinguals on cognates which had been rated on the similarity of their orthography and phonology. To illustrate, in Spanish and English, the cognate "piano" has the same spelling and a very similar pronunciation in both languages, whereas the cognate "real" has the same spelling but very different pronunciations in the two languages. Bilinguals named cognates and noncognate controls in lists of words that were blocked by language. The results showed that the time to name cognates was a function of the match between the orthography and phonology. Naming latencies were fastest for cognates for which both the orthography and phonology were similar or both were dissimilar. When one code was similar and the other not, there was a cost to naming time. The magnitude of this effect was larger when naming in the L2 than L1, but as in the study by Jared and Kroll (2001), also significant for L1. A control group of monolingual English speakers revealed no differences across these conditions, suggesting that the effect is a reflection of the activation of orthography and phonology in both languages when words must be read aloud.

The evidence for the visual recognition of words shows that when bilinguals process words in one language, the phonology of their other language is also activated and influences performance. In some respects, these findings might be considered surprising, because the visual nature of these tasks, particularly when overt speech is not required, would not seem to demand that the phonology be engaged. However, the ambiguity associated with visual input, particularly when languages share the same alphabet, often means that there are few cues to language selection that might potentially function to minimize cross-language influences (see Thomas and Allport 2000, for a discussion of language-specific orthography). In this respect, one might expect a very different pattern of cross-language interaction for spoken word recognition because the input tends to be less ambiguous.

A number of studies have examined the processing of spoken guest words from the nontarget language in the course of sentence context (e.g., Li 1996; Soares and Grosjean 1984). Like the visual cross-language word recognition studies, the results of these experiments tend to support the notion that the nontarget language is active but that its influence is constrained by a range of factors that affect its relative activation. On one hand, some of the results of these studies suggest that listeners can utilize cues that might help to identify and select the language more quickly. However, the presence of phonological ambiguity across languages has also been shown to delay recognition (e.g., Grosjean 1988).

A new approach to the question of whether spoken words activate cross-language relatives has been reported by Spivey and Marian (1999) who tracked eye movements of Russian-English bilinguals as a way of determining whether the names of objects with similar sounding names across bilingual's two languages were more likely to be fixated than objects whose names were unrelated to the translation of the target object. In this paradigm, a bilingual participant is seated in front of a grid-like display containing a central fixation point and four objects placed in the corners of a square. The task is to move a named object to another location in the square. The Russian name of the target object (e.g., a stamp which is "marku" in Russian) sounded like the English name of another object in the array (e.g., in this case the word "marker"). The remaining objects in the array had names, which bore no phonological similarity to the spoken word. The critical result was that bilinguals were more likely to fixate on the distractor object whose name in the other language sounded like the target, relative to controls. Like the results of other spoken word recognition studies in sentence context, these findings are particularly striking because the context, in this case the semantic properties of the objects in the display, did not induce a language selective strategy.

4.3. Production

Models of lexical access in spoken production attempt to capture the sequence of events that enable an individual to speak an individual word (Levelt 1989). A key feature of these models is to hypothesize about the nature of the information that is active at any given moment in time during the sequence leading up to the spoken response. Early models supported a strictly serial view in which a single candidate was selected from among activated lexical alternatives or lemmas and then phonologically specified (e.g., Levelt et al. 1991). Recent studies of language production in monolinguals are more consistent with a cascade model in which alternative candidates are activated in parallel but, unlike fully interactive models, activation from the set of phonological competitors is hypothesized not to provide feedback to the level of an abstract lexical representation or lemma. Using a modification of the picture-word Stroop paradigm (see below), Peterson and Savoy (1998) showed that at short stimulus onset asynchronies (SOAs), phonology was active for both the primary and secondary names of objects with close synonym names (e.g., sofa vs. couch). At longer SOAs, the phonological effect for secondary names diminished, suggesting that the process of lemma selection was complete (and see Cutting and Ferreira 1999; Damian and Martin 1999; Jescheniak and Schriefers 1998). An implication of these results is that the locus of selection depends on the presence of close competitors at the lemma level (but see Levelt, Roelofs, and Meyer 1999 for an alternative account). Close competitors may include close synonyms but not simply words that are semantically related. For monolinguals, the case of close synonyms may be unusual and therefore not hold serious consequences for sorting out the words to speak (e.g., Levelt et al. 1999). However, for proficient bilinguals, for whom virtually every concept has at least two lexical alternatives, translation equivalents may normally function as close competitors.

The question of interest then is whether bilinguals have the phonology of nontarget words on the tips of their tongues. Recent experiments have provided mixed answers to this question. In most of this research, the picture-word interference paradigm has been adapted to the cross-language case. Briefly, in the within-language version of the task, a picture is presented and preceded or followed by a visually presented or spoken distractor word. The time from the onset of the picture presentation to the onset of the distractor is the stimulus onset asynchony (SOA). When the distractor precedes the picture, the SOA is negative. When the distractor follows the picture, the SOA is positive. The task is simply to name the picture and ignore the distractor. The logic of the task is to manipulate the relation of the distractor to the name of the picture as a way of determining whether semantics, phonology, or both are active. By manipulating the SOA, it is possible to identify the locus of this activity. The typical pattern of results in many past experiments is that distractors semantically related to the name of the picture produce interference in picture naming whereas distractors related to the phonology of the picture's name produce facilitation (e.g., Lupker 1979, 1982; Rosinski 1977; Starreveld and La Heij 1995). In general, semantic effects tend to be observed early in the planning of a spoken utterance (i.e., at short SOAs) and phonological effects tend to be observed closer in time to the actual articulation of the word (i.e., at late SOAs), although there is disagreement about the precise timing and interpretation of these effects (e.g., Levelt et al. 1991; Schriefers, Meyer, and Levelt 1990; Starreveld 2000).

In bilingual picture-word interference experiments, the effects of distractor words on picture naming are compared across conditions in which the distractors appear in the same language in which the picture is named or in the bilingual's other language. A series of bilingual picture-word interference studies have examined the influence of cross-language distractors on picture naming as a way of identifying the locus of language selection in production (Costa and Caramazza 1999; Costa, Miozzo, and Caramazza 1999; Hermans 2000; Hermans et al. 1998). A number of critical results have been observed for the cross-language conditions. Semantic distractors produce interference in picture naming regardless of whether the language of the distractor is the same or different than the word to be spoken. This suggests that there is nonselective lexical access, with activation of candidates in both languages, at least to the level of abstract lexical representations or lemmas.

But does selection occur at the lemma level or does the process continue such that phonological alternatives are also active for each language alternative? Costa, Miozzo, and Caramazza (1999) and Hermans et al. (1998) investigated this issue by including some distractors that were phonologically related to the translation of the picture's name. In the Hermans et al. experiments, a "phono-Dutch" condition was included in which the distractors, in either English or in Dutch, sounded like the name of the picture in Dutch. To illustrate, if the picture was to be named as "mountain" in English, the Dutch word "berm" which sounds like "berg" (mountain in Dutch) might be presented. Because participants were required to name the picture in English, their L2, these phono-Dutch distractors should only produce an effect if the translation equivalent they resemble is also active. Hermans et al. found interference for the phono-Dutch distractors with the time course following the pattern of interference observed for the semantic distractors. That is, the interference induced by the phono-Dutch distractors occurred relatively early in the planning of the utterance, like semantic distractors, but unlike phonological distractors. The latter produced facilitation at the long but not short SOAs relative to the onset of the target picture. They concluded that lexical candidates in the nontarget language were active briefly but not specified phonologically. If the translation of the picture's name had been encoded to the point of having the phonological representation available, then the results should have been similar to the monolingual results reported by Peterson and Savoy (1998) and Jescheniak and Schriefers (1998). That they were not suggests that translation equivalents do not function as within-language synonyms. Rather, the language of the alternative appears to provide a cue to selection unavailable in the monolingual case (see Costa et al. 1999 for a language-selective account of these results and Miller and Kroll in press for an illustration of how language cues may enable early selection).

A number of other results in the bilingual picture-word interference studies raise the issue of whether the task itself is likely to constrain the nature of the conclusions. Perhaps the most curious is the finding of translation facilitation, reported both by Costa, Miozzo, and Caramazza (1999) and Hermans (2000). In the picture-word task, picture naming is typically facilitated when the distractor word is the actual word that names the picture. This identity facilitation has been observed in many different studies and was replicated by both Costa et al. and Hermans. However, what happens when the distractor is the translation of the picture's name? If lexical access is language nonselective, such that alternative lexical candidates are available in both languages, then the translation equivalent should be the most problematic distractor in that it is itself the closest competitor. Surprisingly, each of these studies reported facilitation for the translation-identity condition. Bilinguals were faster to name pictures when the distractor they actually saw or heard was the correct name in the wrong language than when the distractor was an unrelated control. The magnitude of facilitation for the translation condition was of course smaller than that for the identity condition and only significant at short SOAs. The result was interpreted as an effect of the conceptual priming initiated by the bottom-up processing of the distractor. However, if the distractor itself is inducing processing that interacts with the planning of the picture's name, how can we identify those aspects of the data that tell us something about production from those that tell us more about the processing encouraged by the demands of the task? The picture-word interference task has provided a remarkably stable basis on which both monolingual and bilingual language production has been modeled. However, it is possible that the particular nature of the dual-task also contributes to the observed conclusions regarding lexical and language selection.

To answer the question of whether the phonology of both language alternatives is available, it would seem useful to have converging evidence from other tasks. Three recent studies have taken this approach, using simple picture naming, cued picture naming, or phoneme monitoring. In none of these tasks is a distractor presented. (See also Poulisse 1997, 1999, for research on speech errors in bilinguals and second language learners and Gollan and Silverberg 2001, for evidence on tip-of-the tongue states in bilinguals.)

Costa, Caramazza, and Sebastián-Gallés (2000) performed a simple picture-naming task in which the names of some of the pictures were cognates in the bilingual's two languages. They found faster naming times for cognates relative to noncognate controls in both languages, suggesting that the other language alternative was available. It would seem most plausible to interpret the result as arising from facilitation due to shared phonology because even highly similar cognates are unlikely to share the same lexical representation (e.g., the cognate may be marked differently for grammatical gender in each language).

Kroll et al. (2000) also examined the cognate facilitation effect but within a cued pictured naming paradigm, which allows the time course of these effects to be observed. In the cued task, a picture is presented and followed by a tone cue following a variable SOA. The cue can be either a high or a low tone. The participant is instructed to name the picture in one language following a high tone and in the other language following the low tone. In control conditions, the language is specified in advanced. The participants name the picture in that language following one of the tone cues and simply say "no" following the other cue. Kroll et al. performed these experiments with two different groups of bilinguals, one Dutch-English and the other English-French. In each case, under mixed language conditions, cognate facilitation was observed for both L1 and L2 and that facilitation extended far into the time course for L1 but disappeared after short SOAs for L2. The results thus replicate Costa et al. (2000) in finding cognate facilitation. However, the inclusion of the mixed vs. blocked conditions allows a set of further comparisons. In the mixed conditions, cognate facilitation was observed for both languages. When the languages were blocked, thereby making the activation of the non-target alternative optional rather than required, there was still cognate facilitation, but only for L2. That is, the phonology of the more dominant L1 alternative appeared to be necessarily active when naming in the L2, but the reverse did not hold. The overall comparison of mixed and blocked conditions also showed that like research on language switching (e.g., Meuter and Allport 1999) the mixed language requirement induced more of a cost to L1 than to L2. The asymmetry in the effects of language mixture suggests that normally when processing in L2, L1 is active and influences performance. When processing in L1, L2 may or may not be active, but the time course of processing the more dominant language may allow selection to occur at an earlier point in time.

One further result reported by Kroll et al. (2000) deserves mention. In that study an additional comparison was included in which some pictures to be named in L2 had names that were interlingual homophones with words in L1. For example, if the picture to be named was a picture of a leaf to be called "leaf" in English, the Dutch translation equivalent was "blad" but there is also a word in Dutch "lief" which is not semantically related to the meaning of leaf. Kroll et al. found inhibition for L2 homophones, which can only be understood as feedback from the activation of the phonology to the semantics.

Finally, Colomé (2001) reported the results of a phoneme monitoring study in which Catalan-Spanish bilinguals had to determine whether a specified letter was included in the name of a picture. The task was performed in Catalan only and the phonemes could belong to the picture's name in Catalan, to its translation equivalent in Spanish, or to neither. For example, if the target picture was a table, then the phoneme /t/ was used to probe "taula", the word for table in Catalan, /m/ for "mesa" the word for table in Spanish and /f/ as a control which was included in neither critical word. Participants had to respond "yes" if the phoneme was present in the name and "no" otherwise. The comparison of interest was the time to respond "no" to the phoneme associated with the translation equivalent relative to the time to respond "no" to the control. Over a series of experiments using this paradigm, Colomé observed persistent effects of the nontarget phonology, suggesting that both lexical alternatives were active and phonologically specified.

The results of production studies therefore converge closely with the results of perception studies in showing that lexical access appears to be language nonselective and that phonological codes are activated not only for target words but also for nontarget alternatives. One interesting aspect of the comparison between perception and production is that in the perception studies, it is the phonology of lexical form relatives that is engaged. That is, words that sound like the target word are activated regardless of the language from which they are drawn. In the production studies, it is the phonology of the translation equivalent that is active in addition to phonological neighbors of the utterance itself.

A further implication of the production results concerns the issue of language selection: How is it that bilinguals eventually manage to speak the correct language, not making many errors and not mixing language randomly outside of intentional code switching, if the system is so fundamentally nonselective? It must be the case that a range of cues to selection are available to bilinguals, from the constraints induced by the presence of sentence and discourse context, from aspects of the linguistic input that might be used to allow early rather than late language selection and perhaps from nonlinguistic information in the environment itself. But what is clear from our review on lexical access is that the lexical system is quite permeable across languages on many dimensions, including the phonology.

5. Final remarks

Considering bilingualism not an exotic case within cognitive science, but an important and well-defined domain is something less and less disputed. The interaction of different disciplines is helping not only in better understanding bilingualism by itself, but also in putting it in a more central position within cognitive science. In the briefly reviewed studies, we hope to have been able to sketch a picture of the field and also highlighted how the study of bilingualism can enable a better understanding of general cognitive mechanisms.

One important contribution of bilingualism to cognitive science is that of providing new insights about brain plasticity. It is well known that not all aspects of learning a second language are equally difficult, for instance, learning new words is something relatively easy, but mastering some aspects of phonology and syntax can be quite difficult (perhaps impossible!). Why is this? What are the limits of our brain to acquire and process two languages?

Another relevant question in studying language processing is the understanding of the relationships between different language subsystems. Bilingualism seems to be a particularly attractive situation to analyze how acquiring information at one level can modify other linguistic domains. First language acquisition follows quite similar sequences in all human beings and without denying its relevance, across individual variation is quite small. But when bilinguals are considered important differences emerge between individuals. What is the origin of this variability? There are many different potential answers, one of them is that because of the particular interactions between both language systems, language differences and similarities may have important contributions in this variation.

Finally, bilingualism can be also useful in addressing general questions about cognitive representations and processes. The studies reviewed in the last section on production illustrate the way in which bilingual research can provide constraints on the architecture of language processing models that would otherwise be unavailable from research on speakers of a single language only. Bilingualism thus provides an effective tool for psycholinguistic research in addition to being of interest on its own. We anticipate that the approach we have described will contribute to our increasing knowledge of basic language mechanisms in monolinguals and bilinguals alike.

Acknowledgements

The writing of this chapter was supported in part by a grant from the U.S. National Science Foundation, BCS-0111734, to Judith F. Kroll and by a grant from the MacDonnell Foundation to Núria Sebastián-Gallés.

Refereneces

Abercrombie, David
    1967   *Elements of General Phonetics.* Edinburgh: Edinburgh University Press.
Altenberg, Evelyn P. and Helen S. Cairns
    1983   The effects of phonotactic constraints on lexical processing in bilingual and monolingual subjects. *Journal of Verbal Learning and Verbal Behavior* 22: 174-188.
Bahrick, Lorraine E. and Jeffrey N. Pickens
    1988   Classification of bimodal English and Spanish language passages by infants. *Infant Behavior and Development* 11: 277-296.
Berent, Iris and Charles A. Perfetti
    1995   A rose is a REEZ: The two-cycles model of phonology assembly in reading English. *Psychological Review* 102: 146-184.
Best, Catherine T., Gerald W. McRoberts and Nomathemba N. Sithole
    1988   The phonological basis of perceptual loss for non-native contrasts: maintenance of discrimination among Zulu clicks by English-speaking adults and infants. *Journal of Experimental Psychology: Human Perception and Performance* 14: 345-360.
Best, Catherine T.
    1995   A direct realist view of cross-language speech perception. In Winifred Strange (ed.), *Speech Perception and Linguistic Experience,* 171-206. Baltimore, MD: York Press.

Bhatia, Tej K. and William C. Ritchie
    1999   The bilingual child: Some issues and perspectives. In William C.
                Ritchie and Tej K. Bhatia (eds.), *Handbook of Child Language
                Acquisition*, 569-643. San Diego: Academic Press.
Bosch, Laura, Albert Costa and Núria Sebastián-Gallés
    2000   First and second language vowel perception in early bilinguals.
                European Journal of Cognitive Psychology 12: 189-222.
Bosch, Laura and Núria Sebastián-Gallés
    1997   Native-language recognition abilities in four-month-old infants
                from monolingual and bilingual environments. *Cognition* 65: 33-
                69.
Bosch, Laura and Núria Sebastián-Gallés
    2000   *Exploring four-month-old infants' abilities to discriminate lan-
                guages from the same rhythmic class*. Paper presented at the Inter-
                national Conference on Infant Studies, 16-19 July 2000, Brighton,
                UK.
Bosch, Laura and Núria Sebastián-Gallés
    2001a   Evidence of early language discrimination abilities in infants from
                bilingual environments. *Infancy* 2: 29-49.
Bosch, Laura and Núria Sebastián-Gallés
    2001b   Early language differentiation in bilingual infants. In Jasone Cenoz
                and Fred Genesee (eds.), *Trends in Bilingual Acquisition*, 71-93.
                Amsterdam, NL: John Benjamins Publ. Co.
Bowers, Jeffrey S., Zohra Mimouni and Martin Arguin
    2000   Orthography plays a critical role in cognate priming: Evidence
                from French/English and Arabic/French cognates. *Memory &
                Cognition* 28: 1289-1296.
Brysbaert, Marc
    1998   Word recognition in bilinguals: Evidence against the existence of
                two separate lexicons. *Psychologica Belgica* 38: 163-175.
Brysbaert, Marc, Goedele van Dyck and Marijke van de Poel
    1999   Visual word recognition in bilinguals: Evidence from masked
                phonological priming. *Journal of Experimental Psychology: Hu-
                man Perception and Performance* 25: 137-148.
Christophe, Anne and John Morton
    1998   Is Dutch native English? Linguistic analysis by two-month-olds.
                Developmental Science 1: 215-219.
Colomé, Àngels
    2001   Lexical activation in bilinguals' speech production: language-
                specific or language independent? *Journal of Memory and Lan-
                guage* 45: 721-736.

Costa, Albert and Alfonso Caramazza
  1999   Is lexical selection language specific? Further evidence from Span-
              ish-English bilinguals. *Bilingualism: Language and Cognition* 2:
              231-244.
Costa, Albert, Alfonso Caramazza and Núria Sebastián-Gallés
  2000   The cognate facilitation effect: Implications for models of lexical
              access. *Journal of Experimental Psychology: Learning, Memory
              and Cognition* 26: 1283-1296.
Costa, Albert, Michele Miozzo and Alfonso Caramazza
  1999   Lexical selection in bilinguals: Do words in the bilingual's two
              lexicons compete for selection? *Journal of Memory and Language*
              41: 365-397.
Cutler, Anne, Jacques Mehler, Dennis Norris and Juan Seguí
  1983   A language-specific comprehension strategy. *Nature* 304: 159-
              160.
Cutting, James C. and Victor S. Ferreira
  1999   Semantic and phonological information flow in the production
              lexicon. *Journal of Experimental Psychology: Learning, Memory
              and Cognition* 25: 318-344.
Damian, Markus F. and Randi C. Martin
  1999   Semantic and phonological codes interact in single word produc-
              tion. *Journal of Experimental Psychology: Learning, Memory and
              Cognition* 25: 345-361.
De Houwer, Annick
  1990   *The acquisition of two languages from birth: A case study.* Cam-
              bridge: Cambridge University Press.
Dehaene-Lambertz, Ghislaine, Emmanuel Dupoux and Ariel Gout
  2000   Electrophysiological correlates of phonological processing: A
              cross-linguistic study. *Journal of Cognitive Neuroscience* 12: 635-
              647.
Dehaene-Lambertz, Ghislaine and Derek Houston
  1998   Faster orientation latencies toward native language in two-month
              old infants. *Language and Speech* 41: 21-43.
Dijkstra, Ton, Jonathan Grainger and Walter J. B. van Heuven
  1999   Recognizing cognates and interlingual homographs: The neglected
              role of phonology. *Journal of Memory and Language* 41: 496-518.
Dijkstra, Ton, Henk van Jaarsveld and Sjoerd Ten Brinke
  1998   Interlingual homograph recognition: Effects of task demands and
              language intermixing. *Bilingualism: Language and Cognition* 1:
              51-66.
Flege, James E.
  1995   Second language speech learning: Theory, findings and problems.
              In Winifred Strange (ed.), *Speech Perception and Linguistic Ex-
              perience*, 233-272. Baltimore, MD: York Press.

Genesee, Fred
1989   Early bilingual development: one language or two? *Journal of Child Language* 16: 161-179.
Genesee, Fred, Elena Nicoladis and Johanna Paradis
1995   Language differentiation in early bilingual development. *Journal of Child Language* 22: 611-631.
Gerard, Linda D. and Don L. Scarborough
1989   Language-specific access of homographs by bilinguals. *Journal of Experimental Psychology: Learning, Memory and Cognition* 15: 305-315.
Gollan, Tamar, Kenneth I. Forster and Ram Frost
1997   Translation priming with different scripts: Masked priming with cognates and noncognates in Hebrew-English bilinguals. *Journal of Experimental Psychology: Learning, Memory and Cognition* 23: 1122-1139.
Gollan, Tamar and Nina Silverberg
2001   Tip-of-the-tongue states in Hebrew-English bilinguals. *Bilingualism: Language and Cognition* 4: 63-83.
Grosjean, François
1988   Exploring the recognition of guest words in bilingual speech. *Language and Cognitive Processes* 3: 233-274.
Hermans, Daan
2000   *Word production in a foreign language.* Unpublished doctoral dissertation, University of Nijmegen, Nijmegen, The Netherlands.
Hermans, Daan, Theo Bongaerts, Kees de Bot and Rob Schreuder
1998   Producing words in a foreign language: Can speakers prevent interference from their first language? *Bilingualism: Language and Cognition* 1: 213-229.
Jared, Debra and Judith F. Kroll
2001   Do bilinguals activate phonological representations in one or both of their languages when naming words? *Journal of Memory and Language* 44: 2-31.
Jescheniak, Joerg D. and Herbert Schriefers
1998   Discrete serial versus cascading processing in lexical access in speech production: Further evidence from the coactivation of near-synonyms. *Journal of Experimental Psychology: Learning, Memory and Cognition* 24: 1256-1274.
Johnson, Jacqueline S. and Elissa L. Newport
1989   Critical period effects in second language learning: The influence of maturational state on the acquisition of English as a second language. *Cognitive Psychology* 21: 60-99.
Jusczyk, Peter W.
1993   From general to language-specific capacities: the WRAPSA Model of how speech perception develops. *Journal of Phonetics* 21: 3-28.

Jusczyk, Peter W.
1997   *The discovery of spoken language.* Cambridge, MA: MIT Press.
Jusczyk, Peter W., Paul A. Luce and Jan Charles Luce
1994   Infants' sensitivity to phonotactic patterns in the native language. *Journal of Memory and Language* 33: 630-645.
Kim, Karl H. S., Norman R. Relkin, Kyoung-Min Lee and Joy Hirsch
1997   Distinct cortical areas associated with native and second languages. *Nature* 388: 171-174.
Kroll, Judith F., Ton Dijkstra, Niels Janssen and Herbert Schriefers
2000   Selecting the language in which to speak: Experiments on lexical access in bilingual production. *Abstracts of the Psychonomic Society* 5: 109.
Levelt, Willem J. M.
1989   *Speaking: From Intention to Articulation.* Cambridge, MA: The MIT Press.
Levelt, Willem J. M., Ardi Roelofs and Antje S. Meyer
1999   A theory of lexical access in speech production. *Behavioral and Brain Sciences* 22: 1-75.
Levelt, Willem J. M., Herbert Schriefers, Dirk Vorberg, Antje S. Meyer, Thomas Pechmann and Jaap Havinga
1991   The time course of lexical access in speech production: A study of picture naming. *Psychological Review* 98: 122-142.
Li, Ping
1996   Spoken word recognition of code-switched words by Chinese-English bilinguals. *Journal of Memory and Language* 35: 757-774.
Lively, Scott E., David B. Pisoni, Reiko A. Yamada, Yoh'-ichi Tohkura and Toru Yamada
1994   Training Japanese listeners to identify English /r/ and /l/ III. Long-term retention of new phonetic categories. *Journal of the Acoustical Society of America* 96: 2076-2087.
Lukatela, George and Michael T. Turvey
1994   Visual lexical access is initially phonological: 1. Evidence from associative priming by words, homophones and pseudohomophones. *Journal of Experimental Psychology: General* 123: 107-128.
Lupker, Stephen J.
1979   The semantic nature of response competition in the picture-word interference task. *Memory & Cognition* 7: 485-495.
Lupker, Stephen J.
1982   The role of phonetic and orthographic similarity in picture-word interference. *Canadian Journal of Psychology* 36: 349-367.

Mack, Molly
1989   Consonant and vowel perception and production: Early English-French bilinguals and English monolinguals. *Perception & Psychophysics* 46: 189-200.
MacKay, Ian R. A., James E. Flege, Thorsten Piske and Carlo Schirru
2001   Category restructuring during second-language speech acquisition. *Journal of the Acoustical Society of America* 110: 516-528.
Mann, Virginia A.
1986   Distinguishing universal and language-dependent levels of speech perception: Evidence from Japanese listeners' perception of English [l] and [r]. *Cognition* 24: 169-196.
Mayberry, Rachel and Ellen Eichen
1991   The long-lasting advantage of learning sign language in childhood: Another look at the critical period for language acquisition. *Journal of Memory and Language* 30: 486-512.
Mehler, Jacques and Anne Christophe
1994   Language in the infant's mind. *Philosophical Transactions of the Royal Society of London* B346: 13-20.
Mehler, Jacques, Jean-Yves Dommergues, Uli Frauenfelder and Juan Seguí
1981   The syllable' s role in speech segmentation. *Journal of Verbal Learning and Verbal Behavior* 20: 298-305.
Mehler, Jacques, Peter W. Jusczyk, Ghislaine Lambertz, Nilofar Halsted, Josiane Bertoncini, and Claudine Amiel-Tison
1988   A precursor of language acquisition in young infants. *Cognition* 29. 143-178.
Meuter, Renate F. I. and Alan Allport
1999   Bilingual language switching in naming: asymmetrical costs of language selection. *Journal of Memory and Language* 40: 25-40.
Miller, Natasha A. and Judith F. Kroll
in press   Stroop effects in bilingual translation. *Memory & Cognition.*
Miyawaki, Karen, Winifred Strange, Robert R. Verbrugge, Alvin M. Liberman, James J. Jenkins, and Osamu Fujimura
1975   An effect of linguistic experience: The discrimination of [r] and [l] by native speakers of Japanese and English. *Perception & Psychophysics* 18: 331-340.
Moon, Chang, Robert Cooper and William Fifer
1993   Two-day-olds prefer their native language. *Infant Behavior and Development* 16: 495-500.
Näätänen, Risto, Anne Lehtokoski, Mietta Lennes, Marie Cheour, Minna Huotilainen, Aantti Iivonen, Martti Vainio, Paavo Alku, Risto J. Ilmoniemi, Aavo Luuk, Jueri Allik, Jane Sinkkonen and Kimmo Alho
1997   Language-specific phoneme representations revealed by electric and magnetic brain responses. *Nature* 385: 432-434.

Nas, Gerard
    1983   Visual word recognition in bilinguals: Evidence for a cooperation
                between visual and sound based codes during access to a common
                lexical store. *Journal of Verbal Learning and Verbal Behavior* 22:
                526-534.
Nazzi, Thierry, Peter W. Jusczyk and Elizabeth K. Johnson
    2000   Language Discrimination by English-Learning 5-Month-Olds: Ef-
                fects of Rhythm and Familiarity. *Journal of Memory and Lan-
                guage* 43: 1-19.
Otake, Takashi, Giyoo Hatano, Anne Cutler and Jacques Mehler
    1993   Mora or syllable? Speech segmentation in Japanese. *Journal of
                Memory and Language* 32: 258-278.
Pallier, Christophe, Laura Bosch and Nuria Sebastián-Gallés
    1997   A limit on behavioral plasticity in vowel acquisition. *Cognition* 64:
                B9-B17.
Pallier, Christophe, Àngels Colomé and Núria Sebastián-Gallés
    2001   The influence of native-language phonology on lexical access: Ex-
                emplar-based vs. abstract lexical entries. *Psychological Science*
                12: 445-449.
Peterson, Robert R. and Pamela Savoy
    1998   Lexical selection and phonological encoding during language pro-
                duction: Evidence for cascaded processing. *Journal of Experimen-
                tal Psychology: Learning, Memory, and Cognition* 24: 539-557.
Phillips, Colin, Alec Marantz, Marilyn McGinnis, David Pesetsky, Kenneth Wex-
                ler, Alan Yellin, David Poeppel, Tim Roberts and Howard Rowley
    1995   Brain Mechanisms of speech perception: a preliminary report. *MIT
                Working Papers in Linguistics* 26: 125-163.
Pike, Kenneth L.
    1945   *The Intonation of American English.* Ann Arbor, MI: Univ. of
                Michigan Press.
Poulisse, Nanda
    1997   Language production in bilinguals. In Annette M. B. de Groot and
                Judith F. Kroll (eds.), *Tutorials in Bilingualism: Psycholinguistic
                Perspectives,* 201-224. Mahwah, NJ: Lawrence Erlbaum Publish-
                ers.
Poulisse, Nanda
    1999   *Slips of the Tongue. Speech Errors in First and Second Language
                Acquisition.* Amsterdam/Philadelphia, PA: John Benjamins.
Ramus, Franck, Marina Nespor and Jacques Mehler
    1999   Correlates of linguistic rhythm in the speech signal. *Cognition* 73:
                265-292.
Redlinger, Wendy and Tschang Z. Park
    1980   Language mixing in young bilingual children. *Journal of Child
                Language* 7: 337-352.

Rivera-Gaxiola, Martiza, Gergely Csibra, Mark Johnson and Annette Karmiloff-Smith
2000   Electrophysiological correlates of cross-linguistic speech perception in native English speakers. *Behavioral Brain Research* 111: 13-23.
Rosinski, Richard R.
1977   Picture-word interference is semantically based. *Child Development* 48: 643-647.
Sebastián-Gallés, Núria, and Laura Bosch
2002   The building of phonotactic knowledge in bilinguals: The role of early exposure. *Journal of Experimental Psychology: Human Perception and Performance* 28: 974-989.
Sebastián-Gallés, Nuria, Emmanuel Dupoux, Juan Seguí, and Jacques Mehler
1992   Contrasting syllabic effects in Catalan and Spanish. *Journal of Memory and Language* 31: 18-32.
Sebastián-Gallés, Nuria and Salvador Soto-Faraco
1999   On-line processing of native and non-native phonemic contrasts in early bilinguals. *Cognition* 72: 112-123.
Schriefers, Herbert, Antje S. Meyer, and Willem J. M. Levelt
1990   Exploring the time-course of lexical access in production: Picture-word interference studies. *Journal of Memory and Language* 29: 86-102.
Schwartz, Ana
2000   *Reading Spanish words with English word-bodies: Activation of spelling to sound correspondences across languages.* Unpublished Master's Thesis, Pennsylvania State University, University Park, PA.
Schwartz, Ana, Judith F. Kroll, and Michele Diaz
2001   *Mapping orthography to phonology: More evidence for nonselective cross-language activation.* Poster presented at the 42nd Annual Meeting of the Psychonomic Society, Orlando, FL.
Sharma, Anu and Michael F. Dorman
2000   Neurophysiologic correlates of cross-language phonetic perception. *Journal of the Acoustical Society of America* 107: 2697-2703.
Smith, Marilyn C.
1997   How do bilinguals access lexical information? In Annette M. B. de Groot and Judith F. Kroll (eds.), *Tutorials in Bilingualism: Psycholinguistic Perspectives,* 145-168. Mahwah, NJ: Lawrence Erlbaum Publishers.
Soares, Carlos and Francois Grosjean
1984   Bilinguals in a monolingual and a bilingual speech mode: The effect on lexical access. *Memory & Cognition* 12: 380-386.

Spivey, Michael J. and Viorica Marian
  1999   Cross talk between native and second languages: Partial activation
             of an irrelevant lexicon. *Psychological Science* 10: 281-284.
Starreveld, Peter A.
  2000   On the interpretation of onsets of auditory context effects in word
             production. *Journal of Memory and Language* 42: 497-525.
Starreveld, Peter A. and Wido La Heij
  1995   Semantic interference, orthographic facilitation and their interac-
             tion in naming tasks. *Journal of Experimental Psychology: Learn-
             ing, Memory and Cognition* 21: 686-698.
Tan, Li Hai and Charles A. Perfetti
  1999   Phonological and associative inhibition in the early stages of Eng-
             lish word identification: Evidence from backward masking. *Jour-
             nal of Experimental Psychology: Human Perception and Perform-
             ance* 25: 59-69.
Thomas, Michael S. C. and Alan Allport
  2000   Language switching costs in bilingual visual word recognition.
             Journal of Memory and Language 43: 44-66.
Tremblay, Kelly, Nina Kraus, Thomas D. Carrell and Therese McGee
  1997   Central auditory system plasticity: Generalization to novel stimuli
             following listening training. *Journal of The Acoustical Society of
             America* 102: 3762-3773.
Tremblay, Kelly, Nina Kraus and Therese McGee
  1998   The time course of auditory perceptual learning: neurophysiologi-
             cal changes during speech-sound training. *Neuroreport* 9: 3557-
             3560.
Underbakke, Melva, Linda Polka, Terry L. Gottfried and Winifred Strange
  1988   Trading relations in the perception of /r/-/l/ by Japanese learners of
             English. *Journal of the Acoustical Society of America* 84: 90-100.
Van Hell, Janet G. and Ton Dijkstra
  in press   Foreign language knowledge can influence native language per-
             formance in exclusively native contexts. *Psychonomic Bulletin and
             Review*.
Van Heuven, Walter J. B., Ton Dijkstra and Jonathan Grainger
  1998   Orthographic neighborhood effects in bilingual word recognition.
             Journal of Memory and Language 39: 458-483.
Van Orden, Guy C.
  1987   A ROWS is a ROWS: Spelling, sound, and reading. *Memory &
             Cognition* 15: 181-198.
Vihman, Marilyn M.
  1985   Language differentiation by the bilingual infant. *Journal of Child
             Language* 12: 297-324.

Volterra, Virginia and Traute Taeschner
  1978   The acquisition and development of language by bilingual chil-
              dren. *Journal of Child Language* 5: 311-326.
Weber-Fox, Christine M. and Helen J. Neville
  1996   Maturational constraints on functional specializations for language
              processing: ERP evidence in bilingual speakers. *Journal of Cogni-
              tive Neuroscience* 8: 231-256.
Werker, Janet, Tracey Burns and Chris Fennell
  2001   *Speech perception and word learning in infants growing up bilin-
              gual.* Paper presented at the Bilingualism and Brain Plasticity
              Workshop, Trieste (Italy).
Werker, Janet F. and Richard C. Tees
  1984   Phonemic and phonetic factors in adult cross-language speech per-
              ception. *Journal of the Acoustical Society of America* 75: 1866-
              1878.
Werker, Janet F. and Richard C. Tees
  1999   Influences on infant speech processing: Toward a new synthesis.
              Annual Review of Psychology 50: 509-535.
Winkler, Istvan, Anne Lehtoksoki, Paavo Alku, Martti Vainio, Istvan Czigler, Vel-
              eria Csepe, Olli Aaltonen, Ilkka Raimo, Kimmo Alho, Heikki
              Lang, Aantti Iivonen and Risto Nätäänen
  1999   Pre-attentive detection of vowel contrasts utilizes both phonetic
              and auditory memory representations. *Cognitive Brain Research* 7:
              357-369.

Assessing constraints on second-language segmental production and perception

James Emil Flege

1. Introduction

A great deal of research has examined the production and perception of phonetic segments in a second language (L2). The impetus for much of this work has been the desire to understand why individuals who learn an L2 – especially those who began learning the L2 in late adolescence or adulthood – differ from monolingual native speakers of the target L2. A variety of proposals have been offered as to whether L2 speech learning is "constrained" in comparison to L1 speech learning, what is the basis for such constraints (should they exist), whether constraints differ for production and perception, and whether L2 learners must inevitably differ from L2 native speakers.

The purpose of this chapter is to review theory and evidence relating to the production and perception of L2 phonetic segments. Section 2 reviews theoretical issues, considering segmental production and perception separately. Section 3 summarizes the results of empirical research examining L2 vowel production and perception in light of the theoretical issues. The relation between segmental production and perception is considered in Section 4. Finally, Section 5 briefly sets goals for future research.

2. Theory

2.1. Production

Studies of L2 production have focused on the production of individual L2 vowels and consonants, consonant clusters, words, and whole sentences (see Leather and James 1996, for review). It is common to observe divergences from L2 phonetic norms in the speech of L2 learners. Controversy exists as to whether individuals who began learning the L2 in childhood ("early" learners) will differ from L2 native speakers. However, there is agreement that the magnitude of native versus non-native differences is generally greater for individuals who began learning the L2 in adolescence and adulthood ("late" learners) than for early learners (see Long 1990 for review). This has led to the proposal that L2 speech learning is constrained by a critical period arising from the loss of neural "plasticity" (McLaughlin 1977; Patkowski 1989).

Adherents of the critical period hypothesis suggest that the capacity for successful speech and language learning declines beyond the critical period. For example, DeKeyser (2000: 518-519) suggested that

> Somewhere between the ages of 6-7 and 16-17, everybody loses the mental equipment required for the abstract patterns underlying a human language, and the critical period really deserves its name … It may be that the severe decline of the ability to induce abstract patterns implicitly is an inevitable consequence of fairly general aspects of neurological maturation and that it simply shows up most clearly in language acquisition.

Production and perception are not usually differentiated in discussions of the critical period hypothesis. However, Scovel (1988: 62) observed that:

> Pronunciation is the only part of language which is directly "physical" and which demands neuromuscular programming. Only pronunciation requires an incredible talent for sensory feedback of where the articulators are and what they are doing. And only pronunciation forces us to time and sequence motor movements. All other aspects of language are entirely "cognitive" or "perceptual" in that they have no physical reality.

This suggests the possibility that if L2 acquisition is constrained by a critical period, it may affect segmental production and perception differently.

Bever (1981: 196) hypothesized that segmental production and perception are aligned via a "psychogrammar" that is used in L1 acquisition to develop "conjoint" representations of perception and production. Bever hypothesized that the psychogrammar decays as L1 phonology acquisition reaches completion, which marks the end of a critical period for speech learning. Following the critical period, speech production and perception develop independently in such a way that individuals "often learn to discriminate sounds ... they cannot distinctively produce."

Other accounts of the relation between segmental production and perception have appeared in the literature. Pisoni (1995: 22-23) observed that the relation between production and perception is "complex" but that it nonetheless reflects the properties of a "unitary articulatory event." He concluded that talkers produce "precisely the same acoustic differences that are distinctive in perceptual analysis," and that the relation between speech production and perception is "unique" among category systems. However, a close relation between perception and action may be a general characteristic of brain functioning. Churchland (1986: 473) observed that "evolution [has] solved the problem of sensory processing and motor control simultaneously," so that "theories [must] mimic evolution and aim for simultaneous solutions as well." According to Edelman's theory of neuronal group selection (1989: 54-56), a "dynamic loop ... continually matches gestures and posture to several kinds of sensory signals," so that perception "depends upon and leads to action" and motor activity is seen as an "essential part of perceptual categorization."

Kuhl and Meltzoff (1996: 2425; see also Kuhl 2000: 11854) concluded that the information specifying auditory-articulatory relations must be "exquisitely detailed," and that even adults may have an "internalized auditory-articulatory 'map' that specifies the relations between mouth movements and sound." These authors noted, however, that an asymmetry exists in early stage of L1 speech learning. Specifically, the "formation of memory representations ... derives initially from perception of the ambient input and then acts as guides for motor output."

This last observation has been extended to L2 speech learning. Rochet (1995) examined the perception of a synthetic French /i/-/y/-/u/ continuum by speakers of Portuguese and English. The native Portuguese participants tended to misidentify /y/-quality vowels as /i/ whereas native English participants tended to misidentify the same vowels as /u/. In a repetition task, the native Portuguese subjects realized /y/-quality vowels as /i/ whereas the native English participants tended to realize them as /u/. From this, Rochet concluded (1995: 404) that some L2 production errors are "the consequence of the target phones having been assigned to an L1 category." Flege (1995) suggested that L2 production accuracy is limited by perceptual accuracy. More specifically, he hypothesized that the production of an L2 phonetic segment will typically be no more native-like than its perceptual representation and might, in early stages of learning, be less native-like.

2.2. *Perception*

Several hypotheses regarding constraints on L2 perception have appeared in the literature, all of which assume that the perception of L2 phonetic segments is influenced by the L1 phonological system. Trubetzkoy (1939/1958) compared the L1 phonological system to a "sieve" through which L2 vowels and consonants must pass. Michaels (1974) noted that Russians tend to substitute /t/ for English /θ/ whereas Japanese learners substitute /s/ even though both Russian and Japanese have /t/ and /s/ (which are classified as non-strident and continuant sounds, respectively). Michaels hypothesized that Russians' perception of "non-stridency" in English /θ/ leads them to substitute the closest non-strident Russian sound, /t/, whereas Japanese speakers' perception of "continuancy" in English /θ/ leads them to substitute the closest continuant sound in Japanese, /s/. An implication of Michaels' (1974) hypothesis is that the relative importance of distinctive features may differ across languages, and that this influences L2 segmental perception.

The filtering hypothesis might be extended to continuously vary-ing phonetic features or properties. Saudi Arabian Arabic has voiced stops (/b d g/) as well as voiceless stops (/t k/) in its inventory. If distinctive features were freely commutable, Saudi adults should have no difficulty producing English /p/. However, Flege and Port (1981) found that Saudi adults who had lived in the United States for several years did have difficulty. They tended to produce English /p/ with the temporal properties of a bilabial stop, but with the closure voicing appropriate for /b/. These participants may have had diffi-culty integrating the glottal and supraglottal gestures needed for /p/. Alternatively, they may not have perceived the properties of English /p/ accurately. Sebastián-Gallés and Soto-Faraco (1999: 112) ob-served that children learn to weight acoustic features of speech in a way that is optimal for their L1 and that, later in life, L2 speech input will be "sieved" through L1-tuned feature weights. The extent to which the feature weights are "realigned" for the processing of L2 speech sounds may depend on the age of exposure to the L2.

The Perceptual Assimilation Model (PAM) developed by Cath-erine Best and colleagues (e.g., Best 1995; Best et al. 2001) proposes that the accuracy with which L2 speech sounds are discriminated will depend on how, or if, they are perceptually "assimilated" by L1 speech sounds. Instances of distinct L2 categories that are not perceptually assimilated by any L1 category will be discriminated well, even in the absence of prior experience. However, it appears that most L2 speech sounds are perceptually assimilated by an L1 category, at least initially. That being the case, L2 speech sounds will be discriminated more accurately if they are assimilated by two distinct L1 speech sounds than if they are assimilated by a single L1 speech sound category. The PAM predicts that discrimination accuracy may also be influenced by the degree of phonetic-articulatory similarity of L2 speech sounds to L1 speech sounds. Specifically, the PAM predicts that a pair of L2 speech sounds differing in perceived degree of goodness of fit to a single L1 category will be discriminated better than a pair of L2 speech sounds judged to have an equal goodness of fit to a single L1 category.

The primary aim of the Native Language Magnet (NLM) model developed by Patricia Kuhl and colleagues (e.g., Kuhl 2000) is to account for the transition from auditory to language-specific perceptual processing. The NLM proposes that perception of the acoustic properties of speech sounds is defined by early experience. Infants perceptually sort segment-sized units into categories based on the recurrence of features they have detected in speech input. This results in a language-specific "mapping" between the categories developed for L1 speech sounds and the phonetic input that drives this crucial aspect of language acquisition. For example, Kuhl et al. (1992) compared the perception of synthetic high front vowels by 6-month-old infants being raised in English- and Swedish-speaking environments in the United States and Sweden, respectively. The English-learning infants were found to generalize their conditioned response to a good instance of English /i/ to neighboring English /i/ tokens, but did not show the same kind of response generalization (i.e., failure to discriminate) when exposed to a similar array of Swedish /y/ vowels. Swedish-learning infants, on the other hand, showed response generalization to a good Swedish /y/ token but not to a good English /i/ token.

The NLM (Kuhl 2000: 11854) proposes that infants' perceptual mapping of ambient language speech sounds creates a "complex network, or filter, through which language is perceived." Perceptual attunement to L1 categories may later shape the perception of L2 speech sounds. Interference effects may arise because of the difficulty inherent in functionally separating L1 and L2 mappings (i.e., categories), and because a neural "commitment" to L1 category mappings will later influence the processing of L2 speech sounds (see also Flege 1992). Importantly, the NLM proposes that constraints on the perception of L2 speech sounds arise from prior experience, not from a loss of plasticity that arises from normal neural maturation.

Support for the NLM account of the basis for native versus non-native perceptual differences was obtained in a study examining English /ɹ/ and /l/. Iverson et al. (2001) had native English adults and native Japanese adults living in Tokyo rate the acoustic similarity of the members of a grid of /ɹa/ and /la/ stimuli. The stimuli differed in terms of the frequencies of F2 and F3 transitions into the vowel. Multidimensional scaling analyses suggested that the perception of acoustic-phonetic dimensions was shaped by attunement to the L1 phonetic system in a way that might be conceptualized as a "warping" of the phonetic space. Specifically, the native English adults showed an augmented sensitivity to F3 differences between stimuli perceivable as English /ɹ/ and /l/, and a reduced sensitivity to F3 differences between stimuli identifiable as instances of either the /ɹ/ or the /l/ category. Unlike the native English participants, the native Japanese participants did not show a heightened discrimination of stimuli straddling the English /ɹ/-/l/ boundary. Moreover, they did not show evidence of either a stretching or a shrinking of the F3 dimension. In fact, the native Japanese participants were more sensitive to variation in the F2 than the F3 dimension.

The Iverson et al. (2001) results suggested that native speakers of Japanese develop perceptual maps that, although well suited for Japanese, may impede acquisition of the English /ɹ/-/l/ contrast (see also Flege 1988). The authors suggested that as a result of L1 interference effects, Japanese adults who do manage to establish new categories for English liquids might develop "erroneous" long-term memory representations in which variation in F2 frequency is given too much prominence and F3 frequency is given too little prominence.

Iverson et al. (2001) suggested that L1 interference effects might become progressively stronger as the L1 develops. Influence of the L1 may be "self-reinforcing" for Japanese adults if, as the result of a warping of the phonetic space, they fail to experience the same "auditory distribution" of F3 differences in English /ɹ/ and /l/ tokens as do children who are learning English as an L1 (2001: 114-115). However, according to the NLM, perceptual learning by adults is not impossible. Kuhl suggested (2000: 11855) that the influence of prior experience may be minimal for children who learn two languages simultaneously in early childhood, at least if "two different mappings" are acquired for L1 and L2 speech sounds. The best way for adult learners of an L2 to circumvent L1 interference effects may be to recapitulate infants' experience of L1 speech, that is, to receive "exaggerated acoustic cues, multiple instances by many talkers, and massed listening experience."

To summarize so far, two broad proposals have been offered in the literature to account for why the speech of L2 learners is often foreign-accented. The ability to learn to produce speech accurately may be constrained by a critical period. Alternatively, the accuracy with which L2 speech sounds are produced may be limited by the extent to which the perceptual representations developed for L2 phonetic segments resemble those of native speakers of the target L2. Several proposals have, in turn, been offered to account for inaccurate perception of L2 phonetic segments. These proposals converge on the notion that the features or properties needed to develop accurate perceptual representations may, in some instances, be inaccessible to L2 learners.

A question of central importance is whether the limitations described in the literature affect L2 perceptual learning permanently, regardless of the learner's age, the kind or amount of L2 input received, or the contexts in which the L2 has been learned or used. For example, Best and Strange (1992: 327) hypothesized that experience with an L2 may lead to the "reorganization of perceptual assimilation patterns" which may, in turn, affect discriminability. However, Best and Strange did not specify the conditions under which perceptual assimilation patterns might change, or whether limits exist on the extent of change that is possible.

2.3. The Speech Learning Model

The Speech Learning Model (SLM) developed by James Flege and colleagues (e.g., Flege 1988, 1992, 1995, 1999a, 2002) is the only extant theory that focuses explicitly on L2 speech acquisition. Its primary aim is to account for changes across the life span in the learning of segmental production and perception. The SLM starts with two broad assumptions. The first is that bilinguals cannot fully separate their L1 and L2 phonetic subsystems (see also Paradis

1993). The second, and more controversial of the two SLM starting assumptions is that the capacities underlying successful L1 speech acquisition remain intact across the life span. These capacities include the ability to accurately perceive featural patterns in speech input, to sort a wide range of segments possessing common properties into categories, and to relate vocal output to the properties perceived in speech sounds (see also Kuhl 2000). The second SLM assumption stands in contrast to the view that L2 speech learning is constrained by a critical period (e.g., Scovel 1988; DeKeyser 2000).

The SLM does not discount the proposals described earlier regarding the filtering or warping of L2 speech input. Indeed, it seems reasonable to suppose that L2 learners may filter out phonetic features or properties that are used to distinguish L2 but not L1 speech sounds in early stages of L2 speech learning. In support of this, Munro (1993) found that native Arabic men who had lived in the United States for an average of 6 years learned to produce a native-like spectral difference between English /i/ and /ɪ/, which differ spectrally from the closest vowels of Arabic (viz., /i/ and /i:/). However, these participants exaggerated the temporal difference between English /i/ and /ɪ/, as if they were producing phonologically long and short Arabic vowels rather than a tense and a lax English vowel.

There is nonetheless evidence that cross-language phonetic differences are detectable by naïve, inexperienced listeners in certain conditions, and that adults are perceptually sensitive to small divergences from the phonetic norms of their L1 (e.g., Flege 1984). This led to the SLM proposal that the filtering of L2 speech input will not persist as learners acquire a dense network of L2 lexical items that need to be differentiated phonetically. In support of this, McAllister, Flege, and Piske (2002) found that some native speakers of English and Spanish who were long-time residents of Stockholm learned to distinguish Swedish words differing in phonological quantity even though vowel duration is not used as the primary cue to vowel contrasts in either English or Spanish.

The results of Gottfried and Beddor (1988; see also Francis and Nusbaum 2002) suggested that L2 learning might result in a change in feature weighting. A synthetic continuum ranging from French /o/-

/ɔ/ was created through an orthogonal variation in the frequency of the first two vowel formants (F1, F2) and duration. Native English speakers responded to a greater extent to duration differences than native French speakers did owing to the greater overall prominence of duration as a cue to vowel identity in English than French. Native speakers of English who had studied French in school showed an English-like use of duration in classifying the French vowels. However, more advanced native English speakers of French showed less use of duration, thereby resembling native speakers of French.

Best and Strange (1992) suggested that new categories are more likely to be established for L2 speech sounds that are perceived to be "discrepant" instances of an L1 category than for L2 sounds perceived to be distant from the closest L1 sound. Conversely, the SLM predicts that the greater is the perceived phonetic dissimilarity of an L2 speech sound from the closest L1 sound, the more likely it is that a new category will be created for the L2 sound. For example, Flege (1987) found that adult native English learners of French were more successful in learning to produce French /y/ than /u/. This was attributed to the greater perceived phonetic distance of French /y/ from the closest English vowel than of French /u/ from the closest English vowel. (Perceptual assimilation data was not collected to verify this, however.)

Like the NLM, the SLM proposes that native versus non-native differences are more likely to arise as the result of interference from prior phonetic learning than from a loss of neural plasticity. The SLM proposes that even adults retain the capacities used by infants and children in successfully acquiring L1 speech, including the ability to establish new phonetic categories for the vowels and consonants encountered in an L2. However, the SLM proposes that phonetic category formation for L2 speech sounds becomes less likely with increasing age. According to the SLM, as L1 phonetic categories develop slowly through childhood and into early adolescence, they become more likely to perceptually assimilate L2 vowels and consonants. If instances of an L2 speech sound category persist in being identified as instances of an L1 speech sound, category formation for the L2 speech sound will be blocked. A limitation of the

SLM is that it does not provide a metric for determining when cross-language phonetic differences will be too small to support category formation, and whether the triggering threshold varies as a function of age or L1 system development.

Baker et al. (2002) evaluated the SLM hypothesis that as L1 vowel categories develop, L2 vowels are more likely to be identified as instances of those categories. These authors carried out a perceptual assimilation experiment with Korean adults and children who had lived in the United States for just 9 months. The results suggested that the perceptual assimilation of English vowels by Korean vowels was stronger for the Korean adults than children. Additional experiments examined Koreans who had arrived in the United States at average ages of 9 or 19 years (early and late learners) and had lived there for 9 years. One experiment examined the categorial discrimination of pairs of English vowels (/i/-/ɪ/, /ɛ/-/æ/, /u/-/ʊ/) that were perceptually assimilated by a single Korean vowel. The early learners discriminated the English vowels more accurately than the late learners did, and did not differ significantly from native English speakers. The same results were obtained in an experiment examining the production of English /i ɪ ɛ æ u ʊ/. The authors suggested that between-group differences in segmental production and perception might have been due to age-related differences in the strength of perceptual assimilation of English vowels by Korean vowels.

As mentioned earlier, language-specific attunement becomes evident in infancy (e.g., Kuhl et al. 1992). Children are generally credited with having acquired the phonemes of their L1 by the age of 8 years. However, the development of speech motor control and perceptual representations for L1 speech sounds appear to develop slowly through childhood and into adolescence (e.g., Hazan and Barrett 1999; Johnson 2000; Walley and Flege 2000). Unfortunately, the endpoint of L1 speech development has not yet been determined. If it coincided with the age thought to mark the end of a critical period for L2 acquisition, 12-15 years (Scovel 1988; Patkowski 1989), it would be difficult to differentiate a maturational account of age effects on L2 speech learning (the critical period hypothesis) from a developmental account (that of the SLM or the NLM).

The two accounts might be differentiated, however, by testing for effects of L2 learning on the production and perception of phonetic segments in the L1. The SLM proposes that the L1 and L2 phonetic subsystems of bilinguals necessarily interact because the phonic elements making up the L1 and L2 phonetic subsystems exist in a "common phonological space". According to the SLM, individual bilinguals strive to maintain contrasts between phonic elements in both the L1 and L2 phonetic subsystems in much the same way that languages maintain contrasts between the phonic elements making up a single system (see de Boer 2000 for discussion).

The SLM proposes that phonetic categories interact through mechanisms called "phonetic category assimilation" and "phonetic category dissimilation." (See Flege 2000 for examples of how both mechanisms influence L2 speech learning.) When a new category is established for an L2 speech sound in a portion of phonetic space occupied by an L1 sound, the new L2 category and the pre-existing L1 category may dissimilate from one another. If this happens, neither the L1 category nor the new L2 category will be identical to the categories possessed by monolinguals. The modification of an L1 category as the result of category dissimilation is not predicted by either a critical period hypothesis or a filtering/warping hypothesis.

Category assimilation is predicted to occur when a new category has not been established for an L2 speech sound that differs audibly from the closest L1 speech sound. In such cases, an experienced L2 learner is predicted to develop a "composite" category that merges the properties of the L1 and L2 categories that have been perceptually equated, in proportion to the input received (perhaps with greater weight accorded recent input). As a result, productions of the L2 sound will remain L1-like and productions of the corresponding L1 sound will eventually become L2-like.

In support of this, Flege (1987) observed that native French adults who had learned English, and native English adults who had learned French, produced L2 stop consonants with voice onset time (VOT) values differing from the VOT values produced by native English and French speakers, respectively. The native French learners managed to increase VOT in English stops, but not sufficiently to match

English monolinguals. Conversely, the native English learners decreased VOT in French stops, but not sufficiently to match French monolinguals. These native versus non-native differences might be attributed to the passing of a critical period or, indirectly, to the filtering/warping of L2 speech input. However, a critical period (or filtering/warping) hypothesis would not predict the observed changes in L1 production (viz., a lengthening of VOT in French stops produced by the native French participants, and a shortening of VOT in English stops by the native English participants).

L2 speech learning, as envisaged by the SLM, takes place slowly and requires a large amount of native-speaker input to be successful. This consideration is based on the observation that L1 speech develops over a long period of time (see above). Evidence for constraints on L2 speech learning can only be considered persuasive, therefore, if obtained for individuals who have received as much L2 input as is needed by children learning that language as an L1 to fully acquire its phonetic segments.

The importance of input is illustrated by the divergent results obtained in two studies examining the production of English /p t k/ by groups of native Spanish adults who learned English in childhood. Participants who had learned English primarily from native speakers of English in the United States produced voiceless English stops with the long-lag VOT values typical of English (Flege 1991a). However, participants who learned English primarily from native speakers of Spanish in Puerto Rico (Flege and Eefting 1987) produced English stops with VOT values that were intermediate to the VOT values typical for /p t k/ in Spanish and English. It appeared that the early learners in Puerto Rico based their representation of English stops on the foreign-accented input they had received from other native Spanish speakers.

The results of Flege and Liu (2001) also illustrated the importance of input. These authors examined the identification of word-final English consonants by native Chinese adults who had lived in the United States for averages of 2 and 7 years. The participants differed in the nature of their daily activities. Half of the participants in each group were enrolled as full-time students, whereas the remaining participants held occupations (e.g., laboratory technician) thought likely to reduce the frequency of interactions with native English speakers. The long-residence students obtained significantly higher identification scores than the short-residence students did, but there was no difference between non-students who differed in length of residence. The students and non-students did not differ in terms of self-reported percentage use of English (roughly 50% for both groups). This led to the inference that what led to a difference in speech perception between the long-residence students and non-students was not how frequently they used English, but with whom.

3. L2 vowel acquisition research

The studies reviewed in this section examined the acquisition of English vowels by native speakers of Spanish (Section 3.1), the acquisition of Catalan vowels by native speakers of Spanish (Section 3.2), and the acquisition of English vowels by native speakers of Italian (Section 3.3). All of the studies reviewed here examined individuals who were highly experienced in the L2. The results therefore bear on the issue of how, or to what extent, L2 speech learning is constrained.

3.1. English /i/ and /ɪ/

Spanish has fewer vowels than English does (5 versus 14 in most dialects). This raises the issue of whether native speakers of Spanish will establish new vowel categories when they learn English, or whether they will simply try to adapt Spanish vowels when producing and perceiving English vowels. This general question can be illustrated by considering the acquisition of English /i/ and /ɪ/. Spanish has a single vowel, /i/, in the portion of vowel space occupied by English /i/ and /ɪ/. Physiological and acoustic measurements (Flege 1989; Bradlow 1995) indicate that Spanish /i/ is somewhat lower in vowel space than English /i/, but somewhat higher than English /ɪ/.

Three studies examined native Spanish adults' perception of the relation between English /i ɪ/ and Spanish vowels. The results suggested that Spanish adults can detect differences between English /ɪ/ and Spanish /i/ whereas they can probably not reliably detect differences between English /i/ and Spanish /i/. Flege (1991b) found that native Spanish adults almost always classified English /i/ tokens as instances of Spanish /i/ and English /ɪ/ tokens as instance of either Spanish /i/ or /e/. Participants who spoke English as an L2 were more likely to identify English /ɪ/ tokens as "not a Spanish vowel" than Spanish monolinguals were. In a study by Flege, Munro, and Fox (1994), native Spanish adults judged English /ɪ/ and Spanish /i/ tokens to be significantly more dissimilar from one another than English /i/ and Spanish /i/ tokens. In Wayland, Flege, and Imai (under review), 78 native Spanish adults who had lived in the United States for less than seven years consistently classified English and Spanish /i/ tokens as Spanish /i/, and English /ɪ/ tokens as either Spanish /i/ or /e/. The participants also rated English and Spanish vowels as instances of the selected Spanish category. The ratings for Spanish and English /i/ tokens that were classified as Spanish /i/ did not differ significantly (means = 4.1 on a 5-point scale for both). However, the English /ɪ/ tokens that were classified as Spanish /i/ received significantly lower ratings (mean = 2.1) than the English /i/ tokens classified as Spanish /i/ did ($p < .01$).

Based on the results just presented, the SLM predicts that some native Spanish adults – and even more native Spanish children who learn English – will eventually establish a phonetic category for English /ɪ/, and therefore produce and perceive this vowel accurately. The results of two studies are consistent with these predictions.

Flege, Bohn, and Jang (1997) examined 20 native Spanish adults who had lived in the United States for an average of 5 years. The participants identified the members of a synthetic "beat-bit" (/i/-/ɪ/) continuum in which F1 frequency values and vowel duration values varied orthogonally. Some participants showed no sensitivity to the spectral (F1) manipulation, basing their responses on duration alone. However, five participants showed as large an effect of F1 frequency variation as native English speakers did.

The late learners' production of English vowels was elicited in a word-reading task. Only a few participants were found to differentiate /i/ from /ɪ/ adequately. Native English-speaking listeners identified /ɪ/s produced by the native Spanish adults as intended somewhat less often (mean = 56%) than their /i/s (mean = 63%). Importantly, acoustic analyses revealed that two of the five participants who had shown perceptual sensitivity to the English /i/-/ɪ/ distinction produced spectral and temporal differences between /ɪ/ and /i/ that were as large, or larger, than differences produced by native English speakers. Not surprisingly, the /ɪ/s and /i/s produced by these native Spanish late learners were identified correctly by native English listeners (see also Morrison 2002). Flege (1992) used the same procedures to evaluate vowels produced by native Spanish adults who had begun to learn English by school age. Acoustic analyses revealed that the early learners' /ɪ/s and /i/s differed in duration and showed no spectral overlap, and so were correctly identified by native English listeners.

In summary, the results just reviewed suggest that late L2 learners do not automatically filter out cross-language phonetic differences. It appears that most native Spanish early learners, and a few native Spanish late learners, manage to distinguish the English vowels /i/ and /ɪ/, which occur in a portion of vowel space occupied by a single Spanish vowel, /i/.

The results are consistent with predictions of the SLM, but are limited in several ways. Neither study reviewed here sought to determine if early learners use the same relative weighting of features as native English speakers do when perceiving /i/ and /ɪ/. Neither study tested the SLM prediction that native Spanish adults will be more likely to continue identifying English /ɪ/ tokens as instances of Spanish /i/ than native Spanish children will be. Finally, neither study linked native Spanish learners' perceptual assimilation patterns to their production and perception of English vowels. Late learners in the Flege, Bohn, and Yang (1997) study who perceived and produced a distinction between /i/-/ɪ/ may have done so for the reasons hypothesized by the SLM. (That is, they may have discerned the phonetic differences that distinguish English /i/ from /ɪ/, as well as the differences between English /ɪ/ and Spanish /i/.) However, they may have succeeded better than most other participants because they initially identified English /i/ and /ɪ/ as instances of two different Spanish categories (/i/ and /e/).

3.2. Catalan /e/ and /ɛ/

The results obtained in four studies carried out in Barcelona call into question an expectation generated by the SLM, viz. that most early bilinguals will establish phonetic categories for L2 vowels not found in the L1 inventory. This research examined native Spanish university students who had begun to learn Catalan by school age. The participants were said to be highly proficient in both Spanish and Catalan, and to use both of their languages frequently. Each study used a different technique to assess the perception of Catalan speech sounds. Pallier, Bosch, and Sebastián-Gallés (1997) examined the identification and discrimination of vowels in a synthetic continuum. Pallier, Colomé, and Sebastián-Gallés (2001) used the repetition priming paradigm. Sebastián-Gallés and Soto-Faraco (1999) used a version of the gating paradigm. Bosch, Costa, and Sebastián-Gallés (2000) employed the "perceptual magnet" paradigm used to evaluate the NLM.

All four studies examined Catalan /e/ and /ɛ/. These vowels occur in a portion of vowel space that is occupied by a single Spanish vowel, /e/.[1] Bosch et al. (2000) described Spanish /e/ as a vowel that occurs near the perceptual boundary between Catalan /e/ and /ɛ/, and has [e] and [ɛ] allophones. The four studies converged in showing differences between the native Spanish speakers of Catalan and native Catalan speakers of Spanish. Pallier et al. (1997: B14) concluded that even early and frequent exposure to an L2 may not enable the learning of "two new phonetic categories which overlap" a single L1 category. Sebastián-Gallés and Soto-Faraco (1999: 120) interpreted their findings to indicate a "lack of plasticity" in early bilinguals, and suggested that the malleability of the speech perception system may be limited "severely" by school age because exposure to the L1 exerts a "very strong constraint" on the "organization and acquisition of phonemic categories." Bosch et al. (2000) suggested that the early Spanish-Catalan bilinguals continued to represent Catalan vowels as "foreign" speech sounds for which "stable representations in long-term memory" were not established.

These conclusions are reminiscent of conclusions drawn from early studies examining the acquisition of English stops by native speakers of Romance languages. Caramazza et al. (1973) observed that the voiced-voiceless (e.g., /p/-/b/) boundaries of native French learners of English were intermediate to French and English monolinguals' boundaries. Caramazza et al. concluded that the early bilinguals they examined – young adults who began learning English as children – might show additional perceptual learning over time but would probably never match English monolinguals due to the continued influence of French stops. Similar findings were obtained for early Spanish-English bilinguals by Williams (1980), who concluded that early bilinguals may develop "compromise" categories reflecting the properties of phonetically different realizations of /p t k/ in the L1 and L2.

The Barcelona studies did not examine segmental production, nor assess the perceived relation between Spanish and Catalan vowels. The studies are nonetheless important because of their clear demonstration that even experienced early learners might differ from native speakers. As mentioned, Spanish does not possess an /e/-/ɛ/ contrast. The Barcelona results might, therefore, be taken as support for the hypothesis that L2 learners filter out features not needed to distinguish L1 speech sounds following attunement to the L1 phonological system in early childhood.

Additional research will be needed, however, to assess the generalizability of the Barcelona findings. Would different results have been obtained for early learners who did not frequently hear Spanish-accented Catalan (in which Catalan /e/ and /ɛ/ are sometimes not differentiated)? Would different results have been obtained for early learners who used Spanish infrequently, or who were dominant in

Catalan? It would also be useful to determine if the status of [e] and [ε] as allophones of Spanish /e/ impeded learning through the mechanism of acquired equivalence (Goldstone 1994).

3.3. English /ʌ/ and /ɚ/

The studies reviewed in this section examined the production and perception of English vowels by native speakers of Italian who immigrated to English-speaking communities in Canada during the 1950s and 1960s. The results presented here are re-analyses of just three of the vowels that were examined originally.[2]

3.3.1. Perception of /ʌ/

The English vowel /ʌ/ is posterior in vowel space to Italian /i e ε/, anterior to Italian /ɔ o u/, and slightly higher than Italian /ɑ/. When measured acoustically, /ʌ/ occurs in a portion of the F1-F2 space that is not occupied by a standard Italian vowel. Flege and MacKay (under review) asked Italian university students who had recently arrived in Canada to classify English vowels as instances of one of the seven vowels of Italian, and then rate each vowel for goodness as an instance of the selected Italian vowel category. Multiple natural tokens of English /ʌ/ were usually identified as being instances of Italian /a/. Similar classifications and goodness ratings were obtained for English /ɒ/ tokens, suggesting that native Italian speakers will, at least initially, have difficulty distinguishing English /ʌ/ from /ɒ/.

Two studies examined the categorial discrimination of English /ʌ/-/ɒ/. The participants examined by Flege, MacKay, and Meador (1999) and Flege and MacKay (under review) were highly experienced in English, having lived in Canada for averages of 35 and 36 years, respectively. Participants in both studies were selected on the basis of their age of arrival (AOA) in Canada. Research showing that degree of foreign accent is influenced by amount of continued L1 use (e.g., Piske, MacKay, and Flege 2001) motivated the decision to also use percentage self-reported Italian use as a selection criterion. In Flege, MacKay, and Meador (1999), participants in "early" and "late" groups (n = 18 each) had AOAs averaging 7 and 19 years, respectively. These participants reported using Italian more frequently (mean = 31%) than those in another group of early learners, "early-low" (mean = 8%). In Flege and MacKay (under review), the AOAs of early and late groups averaged 8 and 20 years, respectively. Half of both the early and late learners reported using Italian relatively seldom (mean = 8%) and half reported using Italian relatively often (mean = 48%).

A triadic test using multiple natural tokens of /ʌ/ and /ɒ/ was used to test /ʌ/-/ɒ/ discrimination. The three vowel tokens presented on each trial were always spoken by different talkers, and so differed physically. The participants' task was to choose the odd item out in change trials, and to indicate that there was no odd item out in no-change trials. The decision to include both change and no-change trials was motivated by the widely held view (e.g., Iverson et al. 2001) that phonetic category formation decreases sensitivity to within-category differences and increases sensitivity to differences between the new category and adjacent categories. The discrimination (A') scores calculated for each vowel contrast were based on the proportion of hits (correct selections of the odd item out in change trials) and false alarms (incorrect selections of an odd item out in no-change trials).

Native English speakers in Flege, MacKay, and Meador (1999) obtained significantly higher discrimination scores than did early and late learners who used Italian often ($p < .05$), but not early learners who used Italian seldom. In Flege and MacKay (under review), the native English group obtained significantly higher /ɒ/-/ʌ/ discrimination scores than did late learners who used Italian often, late learners who used Italian seldom, and early learners who used Italian often ($p < .05$). However, the native English group did not differ significantly from early learners who used Italian seldom.

Flege and MacKay (under review) also examined native Italian students who had recently arrived in Canada. None of the Italian students obtained discrimination scores for /ɒ/-/ʌ/ that fell within 2 SDs of the mean value obtained for age-matched native English students. However, many of the 72 experienced Italian-English bilinguals obtained /ɒ/-/ʌ/ score that fell within 2 SDs of the mean scores obtained for age-matched native English speakers. Significantly more early than late learners (26 vs. 7) met the 2-SD criterion (*p* < .05). Importantly, some participants in all four native Italian groups met the 2-SD criterion (early-low 17, early-high 9, late-low 4, late-high 3).

In summary, the results reviewed here suggest that native Italian adults initially have great difficulty discriminating English /ɒ/-/ʌ/ because instances of both English vowels tend to be perceptually assimilated by a single Italian vowel (usually /a/). The problem created by single-category assimilation appears to persist for some late learners over many decades of English use. However, some late learners, and even more early learners, obtained /ɒ/-/ʌ/ discrimination scores that fell within the range of scores obtained for native English speakers. These participants may have established a new category for English /ʌ/. In both studies reviewed, early learners who used Italian often, but not early learners who used Italian seldom, discriminated /ɒ/-/ʌ/ less accurately than native English speakers did.

3.3.2. Production of /ʌ/

Flege, MacKay and Meador (1999) examined the production of ten English vowels including /ʌ/. Words containing the vowels of interest were repeated following an aural model, then presented to native English-speaking listeners for classification. The native Italian participants' /ʌ/s were identified as intended in 64% of instances. When misheard, the native Italian participants' /ʌ/s were usually classified as instances of Canadian English /ɒ/, suggesting replacement by the nearest Italian vowel, /a/. Intelligibility scores were significantly higher for /ʌ/s produced by the native English group than by the late learners (*p* < .05). However, the native English group did not differ significantly from either group of early learners (early-low, early).

Piske et al. (2002) examined productions of the same ten English vowels using a different evaluation technique. The English vowels were presented in separate blocks to native English-speaking listeners, who rated each token for goodness as an instance of its intended category. An analysis of the goodness ratings yielded the same results as the analysis of intelligibility scores reported earlier.

Flege, MacKay, and Schirru (in press) examined vowels produced by the participants whose vowel discrimination was examined by Flege and MacKay (under review). Words repeated following an aural model were rated by native English-speaking listeners for goodness as instances of the intended English vowel category. The native English speakers' /ʌ/s obtained significantly higher ratings than /ʌ/s spoken by both groups of late learners (late-low, late-high; $p < .05$), but not by either group of early learners (early-low, early-high). The ratings obtained for /ʌ/s spoken by 35 of the 72 native Italian participants fell within 2 SDs of the mean rating obtained for native English speakers' vowels. Significantly more early than late learners' vowels met the 2-SD criterion ($p < .05$). Importantly, vowels spoken by some participants in all four native Italian groups met the criterion (early-low 15, early-high 11, late-low 3, late-high 6).

In summary, some highly experienced native Italian learners of English mispronounce /ʌ/, a mid English vowel that does not occur contrastively in Italian. The nature of the mispronunciations suggested that the native Italian participants may have used Italian /a/ in producing English /ʌ/. Productions of /ʌ/ by late but not early learners, differed significantly from vowels spoken by native English speakers; however, some late learners produced English /ʌ/ accurately.

3.3.3. Perception of /ɚ/

English /ɚ/ is located in the middle of the F1-F2 vowel space. It is posterior to Italian /i e ɛ/, anterior to Italian /ɔ o u/, and higher than Italian /a/. The F2 value of English /ɚ/ is similar to the F2 values of back Italian vowels, but its F3 value is considerably lower than the F3 value of any Italian vowel. In Flege and MacKay (under review), Italian university students classified English /ɚ/ tokens as being an instance of a front Italian vowel (/e/ 63%, /ɛ/ 15%, or /i/ 18%). The students gave /ɚ/ tokens much lower ratings (mean = 1.5 on a 5-point scale) than any other English vowel, indicating they detected the phonetic difference between English /ɚ/ and Italian vowels. The SLM predicts, therefore, that many late learners, and most if not all early learners will eventually produce and perceive English /ɚ/ accurately.

Flege and MacKay (under review) examined the discrimination of /ɚ/-/ʌ/ by experienced native Italian speakers of English. Early and late bilinguals, regardless of amount of L1 use, obtained high scores. The Italians participants' excellent discrimination of /ɚ/-/ʌ/ was not necessarily due to the establishment of an /ɚ/ category, however. Italian students who had lived in Canada for just 3 months also obtained high discrimination scores for /ɚ/-/ʌ/, probably because they judged the /ɚ/ tokens to be poor instances of a front Italian vowel and the /ʌ/ tokens to be moderately good instances of Italian /a/. Additional research using a different testing procedure will be needed, therefore, to assess the perception of /ɚ/ by experienced native Italian speakers of English.

3.3.4. Production of /ɚ/

Munro, Flege, and MacKay (1996) examined the production of English vowels by 240 native speakers of Italian who differed according to their AOA in Canada from Italy. The /ɚ/s spoken by most participants, even late learners, were usually heard as intended. However, AOA exerted a strong effect on the goodness ratings obtained for /ɚ/ productions. The /ɚ/s spoken by most (85%) participants with AOAs of 2-6 years obtained a rating that fell within 2 SDs of the mean rating obtained for 24 native English speakers. However, the /ɚ/s spoken by fewer participants with AOAs of 7-15 years (65%) and 15-23 years (10%) met the 2-SD criterion.

Piske et al. (2002) also obtained goodness ratings for /ɚ/s produced by experienced Italian-English bilinguals in Canada. The /ɚ/s spoken by native English speakers obtained significantly higher ratings than those spoken by early and late learners who used Italian often ($p < .05$), but not /ɚ/s spoken by early learners who used Italian seldom. In Flege, MacKay, and Schirru (in press), native English speakers' /ɚ/s obtained significantly higher ratings than /ɚ/s produced by both groups of late learners (late-low, late-high; $p < .05$), but not the /ɚ/s spoken by either group of early learners (early-low, early-high). Once again, the vowels spoken by some participants in all four native Italian groups received ratings that fell within 2 SDs of the native English groups' mean rating (early-low 17, early-high 15, late-low 12, late-high 7).

Syrdal and Gopal (1986) observed that an F3-F2 difference of less than 3 bark distinguishes the rhotic English vowel /ɚ/ from other English vowels. One would not expect native Italian learners of English to develop accurate perceptual representations for English /ɚ/ if they filtered out the rhotic property of /ɚ/, which is not used to distinguish Italian vowels. Flege and MacKay (under review) did not obtain the similarity scaling data needed to evaluate native Italian speakers' underlying perceptual space for /ɚ/ (see Iverson et al. 2001). Inferences concerning the participants' sensitivity to the rhotic property of English /ɚ/ was, therefore, drawn from acoustic analyses of their production of this vowel.

The /ɚ/s spoken by participants in Flege and MacKay (under review) were measured acoustically along with /ɚ/s spoken by Italian students (9 male, 9 female) living in Padua, Italy who did not speak English well or often. Vowels spoken by the 108 participants (6 groups x 18) were digitized at 22 kHz, and then measured using the Kay Elemetrics Multi-Speech program. The frequencies of F2 and F3 were measured at the acoustic midpoint of each vowel token using linear predictive coding analysis (covariance method, 14 coefficients). The frequency values were converted from Hertz to bark values because there were slightly unequal numbers of males and females in each group. A F3-F2 bark difference score was then computed for each /ɚ/ token to estimate its degree of rhoticity.

The values obtained for /ɚ/s produced by the Italian students living in Italy exceeded 3 bark, so their vowels would not be classified as rhotic according to the Syrdal and Gopal (1986) criterion. However, all four groups of Italian-English bilinguals in Canada produced /ɚ/ with F3-F2 bark difference scores averaging less than 3 bark. An ANOVA revealed that the rhotic scores obtained for all four native Italian groups were significantly smaller than the scores obtained for the Italian students in Italy ($p < .05$). Another analysis revealed that the native English speakers' /ɚ/s had significantly smaller (and thus more rhotic) F2-F3 bark difference scores than the /ɚ/s produced by both groups of late learners (late-low, late-high; $p < .05$) but not by either group of early learners (early-low, early-high). More /ɚ/s produced by early than late learners had rhotic scores the fell within 2 SDs of the mean value obtained for native English speakers ($p < .05$). However, /ɚ/s produced by some participants in all four groups of Italian-English bilinguals met the 2-SD criterion (early-low 17, early-high 15, late-low 9, late-high 7).

In summary, English /ɚ/ is unlike any Italian vowel, both in terms of its position in an F1-F2 space and its low F3 frequency. A proposal offered by Best and Strange (1992) leads to the expectation that a large phonetic distance between an L2 vowel and the closest L2 will impede establishment of a new phonetic category for the L2 vowel. However, the results reviewed here suggest that some native Italian learners of English establish a category for /ɚ/. The /ɚ/s spoken by most bilinguals were heard as intended. An analysis of goodness ratings revealed that /ɚ/s spoken by late but not early learner groups differed significantly from native English speakers' productions. However, some late bilinguals were found to have produced /ɚ/ accurately.

The results for /ɚ/ supported the SLM hypothesis that category formation remains possible across the life span, but will be less likely for late than early learners. Acoustic measurements of the rhotic property of English /ɚ/ were carried out to evaluate the hypothesis (Iverson et al. 2001) that Italian learners of English will develop erroneous categories for English /ɚ/. The results, although only preliminary, suggested that erroneous categories are not developed, and that L2 learners do not necessarily filter out properties of L2 speech sounds if those properties are not used to distinguish L1 speech sounds.

4. The relation between production and perception

This section will briefly review research relevant to the SLM hypothesis that L2 phonetic segments can be produced only as accurately as they are perceived. It will focus on the production and perception of English vowels by native speakers of Italian. A more thorough discussion is provided by Flege (1999b).

Flege, MacKay, and Meador (1999) tested the SLM hypothesis by examining the relation between vowel intelligibility and discrimination. Three scores were computed for each of 72 native Italian participants: the average discrimination of four pairs of English vowels, the average discrimination of four pairs of Italian vowels, and the average intelligiblity of ten English vowels. There was a significantly stronger correlation between English vowel production and English vowel discrimination than between English vowel production and the discrimination of Italian vowels ($p < .01$). This established a link between the production and perception of language-specific phonetic segments, not just a general tendency to produce and perceive accurately or poorly.

As mentioned earlier, English /ʌ/ tokens tend to be identified as instances of the Italian /a/ category. A second analysis examined the discrimination of English /ʌ/ and Italian /a/. The native Italian participants were assigned to subgroups based on how accurately they had produced English /ʌ/. The participants with a relatively good pronunciation of /ʌ/ ($n = 41$) obtained significantly higher /ʌ/-/a/ discrimination scores than those ($n = 31$) with a poorer pronunciation of /ʌ/ ($p < .01$). Crucially, the two subgroups' discrimination of other vowels did not differ significantly.

Flege and MacKay (under review) also assessed the relation of vowel production and perception. The discrimination scores obtained by Italian-English bilinguals for /ɒ/-/ʌ/, /i/-/ɪ/, and /ɛ/-/æ/ were averaged, as were the ratings accorded each participant's production of /ɒ ʌ i ɪ ɛ æ/. The average discrimination scores and ratings of vowel production were then standardized. The two sets of z-scores showed a moderate positive correlation ($r (70) = .68$, $p < .01$). Significant correlations between segmental production and perception were also obtained when the early and late learners were considered separately (r (34) = .55, and .45, p < .01).

In summary, the results presented here suggest that moderate positive correlations exist between the production and perception of L2 phonetic segments by experienced L2 learners. Bever (1981) hypothesized that a critical period for learning L2 speech arises from the loss of ability to align segmental production to segmental perception. The results do not support a strong version of this hypothesis. The finding that some L2 learners showed more accurate perception than production is consistent with the hypothesis that L2 segmental perception may "lead" (i.e., be more advanced than) segmental production. It also agrees with the results of laboratory training studies showing that gains derived from perceptual training may transfer to improved segmental production in the absence of production training (Rochet 1995; Bradlow et al. 1997, 1999).

5. Discussion

A number of hypotheses have been offered regarding possible constraints on L2 speech learning. Broadly speaking, two hypotheses have been offered regarding production. One is that the ability to learn to produce L2 phonetic segments not found in the L1 diminishes following a critical period. The other hypothesis is that L2 phonetic segments cannot be produced accurately unless they are perceived accurately.

Several proposals have been offered, in turn, for constraints on segmental perception. One is that features (properties) not needed to distinguish L1 speech sounds get filtered out, and so cannot be used in the development of new phonetic categories. Another hypothesis is that the auditory input associated with L2 speech sounds may be warped as the result of previous learning. Proponents of these perceptual hypotheses have suggested that the filtering/warping of L2 phonetic input may become stronger as the age of first exposure to an L2 increases. The SLM, on the other hand, proposes that the capacity to accurately perceive the phonetic properties of L2 speech sounds and to establish new categories based on those properties and to establish new categories based on those properties remains intact across the life span (although L2 category formation becomes less likely as L1 categories develop).

The evidence reviewed here provided support for each theoretical position. Iverson et al. (2001) showed that native Japanese adults weight acoustic properties that distinguish English /ɹ/ from /l/ differently than native English adults do. This supported the hypothesis that previous speech learning may lead to a warping of L2 speech input. The results obtained for early native Spanish learners of Catalan (e.g., Sebastián-Gallés and Soto-Faraco 1999) can be taken as support for the hypothesis that L2 learners filter out properties (or features) of L2 speech sounds that are not needed to distinguish L1 speech sounds. The results obtained for native Spanish and Italian learners of English supported SLM hypotheses. These studies revealed that although most late learners produced and perceived English vowels less accurately than early learners did, some succeeded in learning English vowels not found in their L1. Also, acoustic analyses suggested that neither early nor late Italian-English bilinguals filtered out the rhotic property of English /ɚ/ even though this property is not used to distinguish Italian vowels.

Additional research will be needed to determine whether persistent native versus non-native differences arise from neurological maturation, from the influence of previous phonetic learning, or both. An optimal study would be one that employed a longitudinal design and tested for changes over time in the perceived relation of L1 and L2 sounds, as well as changes in the production and perception of both L2 and L1 phonetic segments.

Such a study might be carried out to examine native English and Japanese adults' perception of the acoustic properties distinguishing English /ɹ/ from /l/. Iverson et al. (2001) observed difference in native and non-native participants' perception of properties in /ɹ/ and /l/. A question of theoretical and practical importance is whether such differences will persist indefinitely – and thus represents a true constraint on learning – or whether they will disappear following a certain amount of native-speaker input. Flege, Takagi, and Mann (1995, 1996) observed poor segmental production and perception of

English /ɹ/ and /l/ by native Japanese adults who were inexperienced in English, but more accurate production and perception by those who were highly experienced in English. It would be useful to determine if Japanese adults who are highly experienced in English will show native-like perception at the feature (property) level and, if so, how much native-speaker input is needed for this kind of change in early stages of perceptual processing to occur.

It will be necessary to study a wide range of L1-L2 pairs and L2 speech sounds in order to draw general conclusions regarding the nature of constraints, if any, on L2 speech learning. Previous research suggests that the magnitude of differences between L2 learners and monolingual native speakers of the target L2 will depend, at least in part, on the degree of perceived phonetic dissimilarity of L2 sounds from the closest L1 sound. The magnitude of differences might also depend on allophonic status. For example, it might be more difficult to learn the L2 phonemes /x/ and /y/ if they resemble the [x] and [y] allophones of a single L1 phoneme than if the L2 /x/ and /y/ phonemes resemble the primary allophones of two different L1 phonemes.

Grosjean (1999) noted that some published studies have provided little or no information about research participants, making cross-study comparison and replication difficult. He also suggested that the contexts in which languages are learned and used might influence performance in both the L1 and the L2. Care must be taken, therefore, in selecting participants for L2 research. For example, a number of factors relevant to L2 learning are typically confounded with age of L2 learning, at least in immigrant populations in North America. When the confounded variables are controlled, the effect of age of L2 learning may disappear for certain outcome measures (e.g., Flege, Yeni-Komshian, and Liu 1999).

It is especially important to consider L2 input and language use patterns when selecting participants for L2 research. It seems reasonable to think, for example, that learning an L2 /x/-/y/ contrast will be impeded if learners frequently hear fellow speakers of their L1 neutralize the L2 /x/-/y/ contrast. Some studies reviewed in Section 3 revealed differences between early learners and L2 native speakers.

This might be taken as evidence that L2 speech learning is irreversibly constrained by previous learning, through a filtering or warping of L2 input, through a loss of neural plasticity, or both. However, other studies reviewed in Section 3 suggested that differences between native speakers and early learners might be confined to early learners who continue to use their L1 often.

Another factor to consider when selecting research participants is language dominance. Piske, MacKay, and Flege (2001) examined overall degree of foreign accent in English sentences produced by early learners. As in previous research, both of two groups of early learners were found to have detectable foreign accents, although those who used their L1 (Italian) often had significantly stronger accents than those who used their L1 seldom. Importantly, some members of both early learner groups received ratings that fell within the range of ratings obtained for native English speakers' sentences.

Flege, MacKay, and Piske (2002) re-examined the foreign accent ratings obtained for the participants examined by Piske et al. after assigning them to subgroups based on language dominance. Sentences produced by Italian-dominant early learners, but not by English-dominant early learners, received significantly lower ratings than the native English speakers' sentences did. This suggested that individuals who become dominant in their L2 might not show measurable L1 interference effects. If so, and if this finding can be shown to generalize to L2 segmental production and perception, one might conclude that L1 interference effects are not inevitable, and thus that L2 speech learning is not irreversibly constrained.

Acknowledgments

This chapter was supported by a grant from the National Institute of Deafness and Other Communicative Disorders (DC00257). The author thanks Katsura Aoyama, Satomi Imai, and Kimiko Tsukada for comments on an earlier version, and Ian R. A. MacKay for his long-term collaboration.

Notes

1. Sebastián-Gallés and Soto-Faraco (1999) also examined Catalan /o/-/ɔ/, /s/-/z/ and /ʃ/-/ ʒ/, and Pallier et al. (2001) examined /o/-/ɔ/, /s/-/z/, and /m/-/n/.
2. All *p*-values were adjusted to account for the number of between-group comparisons that were made. A full description of the analyses presented in this section is available upon request.

References

Baker, Wendy, Pavel Trofimovich, Molly Mack and James Flege
    2002   The effect of perceived phonetic similarity on non-native sound learning by children and adults. In: Barbora Skarabela, Sarah Fish and Anna Do (eds.), *Proceedings of the 26th annual Boston University Conference on Language Development*, 36-47. Somerville, MA: Cascadilla Press.

Best, Catherine
    1995   A direct realistic perspective on cross-language speech perception. In: Winifred Strange (ed.), *Speech Perception and Linguistic Experience: Issues in Cross-language Research*, 171-206. Timonium, MD: York Press.

Best, Catherine, Gerald McRoberts and Elizabeth Goodell
    2001   Discrimination of non-native consonant contrasts varying in perceptual assimilation to the listener's native phonological system. *Journal of the Acoustical Society of America* 109: 775-794.

Best, Catherine and Winifred Strange
    1992   Effects of phonological and phonetic factors on cross-language perception of approximants. *Journal of Phonetics* 20: 305-330.

Bever, Thomas
    1981   Normal acquisition processes explain the critical period for language learning. In: Karl Diller (ed.), *Individual Differences and Universals in Language Learning Aptitude*, 176-198. Rowley, MA: Newbury House.

Bosch, Laura, Albert Costa and Núria Sebastián-Gallés
    2000   First and second language vowel perception in early bilinguals. *European Journal of Cognitive Psychology* 12: 189-221.

Bradlow, Ann
    1995   A comparative acoustic study of English and Spanish vowels. *Journal of the Acoustical Society of America* 97: 1916-1924.

Bradlow, Ann, David Pisoni, Reiko Yamada and Yoh'ichi Tohkura
1997   Training Japanese listeners to identify English /r/ and /l/: IV. Some effects of perceptual learning on speech production. *Journal of the Acoustical Society of America* 101: 2299-2310.

Bradlow, Ann, Reiko Yamada, David Pisoni and Yoh'ichi Tohkura
1999   Training Japanese listeners to identify English /r/ and /l/: Long-term retention of learning in perception and production. *Perception & Psychophysics* 61: 977-985.

Caramazza, Alfonso, Grace Yeni-Komshian, Edgar Zurif and Evelyn Carbone
1973   The acquisition of a new phonological contrast: The case of stop consonants in French-English bilinguals. *Journal of the Acoustical Society of America* 54: 421-428.

Churchland, Paul
1986   *Neurophilosophy.* Cambridge, MA: MIT Press.

de Boer, Bart
2000   Self-organization in vowel systems. *Journal of Phonetics* 28: 441-465.

DeKeyser, Robert
2000   The robustness of critical period effects in second language acquisition. *Studies in Second Language Acquisition* 22: 499-534.

Edelman, Gerald
1989   *The Remembered Present: A Biological Theory of Consciousness.* New York: Basic Books.

Flege, James
1984   The detection of French accent by American listeners. *Journal of the Acoustical Society of America* 76: 692-707.

Flege, James
1987   The production of "new" and "similar" phones in a foreign language: Evidence for the effect of equivalence classification. *Journal of Phonetics* 15: 47-65.

Flege, James
1988   The production and perception of speech sounds in a foreign language. In: Harris Winitz (ed.), *Human Communication and Its Disorders, A Review 1988,* 224-401. Norwood, NJ: Ablex.

Flege, James
1989   Differences in inventory size affect the location but not the precision of tongue positioning in vowel production. *Language and Speech* 32: 123-147.

Flege, James
1991a   Age of learning affects the authenticity of voice onset time (VOT) in stop consonants produced in a second language. *Journal of the Acoustical Society of America* 89: 395-411.

Flege, James
  1991b   Orthographic evidence for the perceptual identification of vowels
               in Spanish and English. *Quarterly Journal of Experimental Psy-
               chology* 43: 701-731.
Flege, James
  1992   Speech learning in a second language. In: Charles Ferguson, Lise
               Menn and Carol Stoel-Gammon (eds.), *Phonological Develop-
               ment: Models, Research, and Implications*, 565-604. Timonium,
               MD: York Press.
Flege, James
  1995   Second-language speech learning: Theory, findings, and prob-
               lems. In: Winifred Strange (ed.), *Speech Perception and Linguis-
               tic Experience: Issues in Cross-language Research*, 229-273.
               Timonium, MD: York Press.
Flege, James
  1999a   Age of learning and second-language speech. In: David Birdsong
               (ed.), *New Perspectives on the Critical Period Hypothesis for
               Second Language Acquisition*, 101-132. Hillsdale, NJ: Lawrence
               Erlbaum.
Flege, James
  1999b   The relation between L2 production and perception In: John
               Ohala, Yoko Hasegawa, Manjari Ohala, Daniel Granville and
               Ashlee Bailey (eds.), *Proceedings of the XIVth International
               Congress of Phonetics Sciences*, 1273-1276. Berkeley, CA: De-
               partment of Linguistics.
Flege, James
  2002   Interactions between the Native and Second-language Phonetic
               Systems. In: Petra Burmeister, Thorsten Piske and Andreas
               Rohde (eds.), *An Integrated View of Language Development:
               Papers in Honor of Henning Wode*, 217-244. Trier: Wissen-
               schaftlicher Verlag.
Flege, James, Ocke-Schwen Bohn and Sunyoung Jang
  1997   The effect of experience on nonnative subjects' production and
               perception of English vowels. *Journal of Phonetics* 25: 437-470.
Flege, James and Wieke Eefting
  1987   Production and perception of English stops by native Spanish
               speakers. *Journal of Phonetics* 15: 67-83.

Flege, James and Serena Liu
  2001   The effect of experience on adults' acquisition of a second lan-
               guage. *Studies in Second Language Acquisition* 23: 527-552.
Flege, James and Ian MacKay
  under review Perceiving vowels in a second language.

Flege, James, Ian MacKay and Diane Meador
1999   Native Italian speakers' production and perception of English vowels. *Journal of the Acoustical Society of America* 106: 2973-2987.

Flege, James, Ian MacKay and Thorsten Piske
2002   Assessing bilingual dominance. *Applied Psycholinguistics* 23: 567-598.

Flege, James, Ian MacKay and Carlo Schirru
in press   Interaction between the native and second language phonetic subsystems. *Speech Communication.*

Flege, James, Murray Munro and Robert Fox
1994   Auditory and categorical effects on cross-language vowel perception. *Journal of the Acoustical Society of America* 95: 3623-3641.

Flege, James and Robert Port
1981   Cross-language phonetic interference: Arabic to English. *Language and Speech* 24: 125-146.

Flege, James, Naoyuki Takagi and Virginia Mann
1995   Japanese adults can learn to produce English /ɹ/ and /l/ accurately. *Language and Speech* 38: 25-55.

Flege, James, Naoyuki Takagi and Virginia Mann
1996   Lexical familiarity and English-language experience affect Japanese adults' perception of /ɹ/ and /l/. *Journal of the Acoustical Society of America* 99: 1161-1173.

Flege, James, Grace Yeni-Komshian and Serena Liu
1999   Age constraints on second language learning. *Journal of Memory and Language* 41: 78-104.

Francis, Alexander and Howard Nusbaum
2002   Selective attention and the acquisition of new phonetic categories. *Journal of Experimental Psychology: Human Perception and Performance* 28: 349-366.

Goldstone, Robert
1994   Influences of categorization on perceptual discrimination. *Journal of Experimental Psychology: General* 123: 178-200.

Gottfied, Terry and Patrice Beddor
1988   Perception of temporal and spectral information in French vowels. *Language and Speech* 31: 57-75.

Grosjean, François
1999   Studying bilinguals: Methodological and conceptual issues. *Bilingualism: Language and Cognition* 1: 117-130.

Hazan, Valerie and Sarah Barrett
    1999   The development of phoneme categorisation in children aged 6
                to 12 years. In: John Ohala, Yoko Hasegawa, Manjari Ohala,
                Daniel Granville and Ashlee Bailey (eds.), *Proceedings of the
                XIVth International Congress of Phonetics Sciences*, 2493-2496.
                Berkeley, CA: Department of Linguistics.
Iverson, Paul, Patricia Kuhl, Reiko Yamada, Eugen Diesch, Yoh'ichi Tohkura,
                Andreas Ketterman and Claudia Siebert
    2001   A perceptual interference account of acquisition difficulties for
                non-native phonemes. *Speech, Hearing and Language: Work in
                Progress* 13: 106-118.
Johnson, Carole
    2000   Children's phoneme identification in reverberation and noise.
                Journal of Speech, Language, and Hearing Research 43: 129-
                143.
Kuhl, Patricia
    2000   A new view of language acquisition. *Proceedings of the National
                Academy of Science* 97: 11850-11857.
Kuhl, Patricia and Andrew Meltzoff
    1996   Infant vocalizations in response to speech: Vocal imitation and
                developmental change. *Journal of the Acoustical Society of
                America* 100: 2425-2438.
Kuhl, Patricia, Karen Williams, Francisco Lacerda, Kenneth Stevens and Bjorn
                Lindblom
    1992   Linguistic experience alters phonetic perception in infants six
                months of age. *Science* 255: 606-608.
Leather, Jonathan and Allan James
    1996   The acquisition of second language speech. In: William Ritchie
                and Tej Bhatia (eds.), *Handbook of Second Language Acquisi-
                tion*, 269-316. San Diego: Academic Press.
Long, Michael
    1990   Maturational constraints on language development. *Studies in
                Second Language Acquisition* 12: 251-285.
McAllister, Robert, James Flege and Thorsten Piske
    2002   The influence of the L1 on the acquisition of Swedish vowel
                quantity by native speakers of Spanish, English and Estonian.
                Journal of Phonetics 30: 229-258.
McLaughlin, Barry
    1977   Second-language learning in children. *Psychological Bulletin* 84:
                438-459.
Michaels, David
    1974   Some replacements and phonological systems. *Linguistics* 126:
                69-81.

Morrison, Geoffrey
    2002   *Effects of L1 duration experience on Japanese and Spanish lis-*
                teners' perception of English high front vowels. Unpublished MA
                thesis, Simon Fraser University, Vancouver, BC.
Munro, Murray
    1993   Productions of English vowels by native speakers of Arabic:
                Acoustic measurements and accentedness ratings. *Language and*
                Speech 36: 39-66.
Munro, Murray, James Flege and Ian MacKay
    1996   The effect of age of second-language learning on the production
                of English vowels. *Applied Psycholinguistics* 17: 313-334.
Pallier, Christophe, Laura Bosch and Núria Sebastián-Gallés
    1997   A limit on behavioral plasticity in speech perception. *Cognition*
                64: B9-B17.
Pallier, Christophe, Angels Colomé and Núria Sebastián-Gallés
    2001   The influence of non-native phonology on lexical access. Exem-
                plar-based versus abstract lexical entries. *Psychological Science*
                12: 445-449.
Paradis, Michel
    1993   Linguistic, psycholinguistic, and neurolinguistic aspects of the
                "interference" in bilingual speakers: The Activation Threshold
                Hypothesis. *International Journal of Psycholinguistics* 9: 133-
                145.
Patkowski, Mark
    1989   Age and accent in a second language: A reply to James Emil
                Flege. *Applied Linguistics* 11: 73-89.
Piske, Thorsten, James Flege, Ian MacKay and Diane Meador
    2002   The production of English vowels by fluent early and late Italian-
                English bilinguals. *Phonetica* 59: 49-71.
Piske, Thorsten, Ian MacKay and James Flege
    2001   Factors affecting degree of foreign accent in an L2: A review.
                Journal of Phonetics 29: 191-215.
Pisoni, David
    1995   Some thoughts on "normalization" in speech perception. *Re-*
                search on Spoken Language Processing, Progress Report 20: 3-
                30 (Department of Psychology, Indiana University).
Rochet, Bernard
    1995   Perception and production of L2 speech sounds by adults. In:
                Winifred Strange (ed.), *Speech Perception and Linguistic Ex-*
                perience: Theoretical and Methodological Issues, 379-410. Ti-
                monium, MD: York Press.

Scovel, Thomas
1988   *A Time to Speak. A Psycholinguistic Inquiry into the Critical Period for Human Speech.* Cambridge, MA: Newbury House.
Sebastián-Gallés, Núria and Salvador Soto-Faraco
1999   On-line processing of native and non-native phonemic contrasts in early bilinguals. *Cognition* 72: 111-123.
Syrdal, Ann and H. S. Gopal
1986   A perceptual model of vowel recognition based on the auditory representation of American English vowels. *Journal of the Acoustical Society of America* 79: 1086-1100.
Trubetzkoy, Nikolaj
1939/1958   Grundzüge der Phonologie. Göttingen: Vandenhoek & Ruprecht.
Walley, Amanda and James Flege
2000   Effects of lexical status on children's and adults' perception of native and non-native vowels. *Journal of Phonetics* 27: 307-332.
Wayland, Ratree, James Flege and Satomi Imai
under review The discrimination of English vowels by native speakers of Spanish.
Williams, Lee
1980   Phonetic variation as a function of second-language learning. In: Grace Yeni-Komshian, James Kavanagh and Charles Ferguson (eds.), *Child Phonology* (Volume 2 Perception), 185-216. New York: Academic Press.